Essays on Ayn Rand's
We the Living

Essays on Ayn Rand's
We the Living

Edited by
Robert Mayhew

LEXINGTON BOOKS
Lanham • Boulder • New York • Toronto • Oxford

LEXINGTON BOOKS

Published in the United States of America
by Lexington Books
An imprint of The Rowman & Littlefield Publishing Group, Inc.
4501 Forbes Boulevard, Suite 200, Lanham, Maryland 20706

PO Box 317
Oxford
OX2 9RU, UK

British Library Cataloguing in Publication Information Available

Library of Congress Cataloging-in-Publication Data

Essays on Ayn Rand's "We the living" / edited by Robert Mayhew.
    p.   cm.
    Includes bibliographical references and index.
    ISBN 0-7391-0697-X (cloth : alk. paper)—ISBN 0-7391-0698-8 (pbk. : alk.
paper)
    1. Rand, Ayn. We the living.   2. Soviet Union—History—Revolution,
1917–1921—Literature and the revolution.   I. Mayhew, Robert.
PS3535.A547W44   2004
813'.52—dc22   2003019414

Printed in the United States of America

∞ ™ The paper used in this publication meets the minimum requirements of
American National Standard for Information Sciences—Permanence of Paper
for Printed Library Materials, ANSI/NISO Z39.48–1992.

Contents

Preface

Given the literary quality and philosophical depth of Ayn Rand's fiction, the contrast between the popularity of her novels, on the one hand, and the scholarly attention they have received, on the other, is remarkable. Annual sales of Ayn Rand's books have recently reached the half million mark; in total, over 22 million copies have been sold. Her first novel, *We the Living*— the focus of this collection—has remained in print since its reissue in 1959, and sold over three million copies. But the attention her fiction has received in academia is virtually nonexistent. For example, in the case of *We the Living*, scholarly discussion has been confined, almost exclusively, to reference works, and until now, there has been no book-length study. One conviction uniting the contributors to this collection is that this is an unfortunate gap in the study of twentieth-century literature and thought. The present collection represents a first step toward filling this gap.

We the Living was written in the decade after Ayn Rand left Soviet Russia— during America's "Red Decade"—and she said it is the nearest to an autobiography that she would ever write. It is therefore no surprise that there is a great deal to say about the history of this work: its origins, its autobiographical nature, its reception, and its afterlife. Part 1 of this volume is devoted to the history of *We the Living*. The opening chapter is Shoshana Milgram's "From *Airtight* to *We the Living*: The Drafts of Ayn Rand's First Novel," which discusses the evolution of *We the Living* (originally titled *Airtight*) through an examination of the drafts of the novel.

The next four chapters show, in different ways, how the events, characters, and details of *We the Living* accurately portray and parallel the reality of Soviet Russia in the mid-1920s, the novel's setting. Scott McConnell's "Parallel Lives: Models and Inspirations for Characters in *We the Living*" describes the extent to which certain characters in the novel were based on people whom Ayn Rand knew. Dina Schein Garmong's " *We the Living* and the Rosenbaum Family Letters" examines the connection between the events and details of the novel and the description of life in the Soviet Union found in the letters Ayn Rand received from her family (in Russia) during the period she wrote *We the Living.* John Ridpath's "Russian Revolutionary Ideology and *We the Living*" describes the political philosophy that provides the ideological background to the novel, and the history that gave rise to it. Music is an important part of the background to *We the Living*—it plays a more significant role than in any of Ayn Rand's other novels. Michael Berliner's "The Music of *We the Living*" provides detailed information on this music, almost all of which was actual music Ayn Rand was exposed to while living in Russia.

The remaining chapters in part 1 examine what happened to *We the Living* once it was written. Richard Ralston's "Publishing *We the Living*" describes Ayn Rand's struggles during the 1930s—in the face of ideological opposition—to find a publisher for the novel. *We the Living* was the most widely reviewed of Ayn Rand's novels; Michael Berliner's "Reviews of *We the Living*" surveys dozens of these reviews. Jeff Britting's "Adapting *We the Living*" describes in detail its two adaptations: the Broadway play, *The Unconquered*, and the pirated pair of Italian films, *Noi Vivi* and *Addio Kira.* A revised edition of *We the Living* was published in 1959; Ayn Rand made over 3,000 revisions in preparing it. My chapter " *We the Living*: '36 and '59" surveys the changes she made, and offers a detailed discussion of those revisions that might *seem* to reveal a change in philosophical outlook.

Ayn Rand was a novelist-philosopher, and these two aspects of her life and literary works cannot easily be separated. The seven chapters that make up the second part of this collection attest to this. Part 2 begins with the chapters whose emphasis is literary, and ends with those more philosophical in focus.

The first two chapters provide an excellent transition from the history of Ayn Rand's first novel to its nature as a literary work. Victor Hugo was Ayn Rand's favorite writer; *We the Living* is her most Hugo-like novel. These facts are made clear in Shoshana Milgram's " *We the Living* and Victor Hugo: Ayn Rand's First Novel and the Novelist She Ranked First." In 1931, while working on *We the Living*, Ayn Rand wrote a movie original entitled *Red Pawn*— her only other work of fiction set in Russia. Jena Trammell's "*Red Pawn*: Ayn Rand's Other Story of Soviet Russia" describes the history of *Red Pawn* and what the writing of it tells us about the development of Ayn Rand's literary aesthetics, and compares *Red Pawn* and *We the Living.*

Besides being a novelist, Ayn Rand developed an original, systematic philosophy—Objectivism—which includes an aesthetics or philosophy of art. In her literary aesthetics, she describes the four essential attributes of a novel: theme, plot, characterization, and style. As the title of his chapter suggests,

Andrew Bernstein's "The Integration of Plot and Theme in *We the Living*" discusses the first two of these attributes, and how they are intimately connected in Ayn Rand's first novel. Many of the chapters in both sections of this collection treat characterization, at least indirectly. John Lewis's "Kira's Family" deals with it especially, focusing on a set of secondary—though important—characters: four members of Kira's family. Though no one chapter is devoted to *We the Living*'s style, elements of its style are discussed in both of Shoshana Milgram's chapters, and to some extent in my "Kira Argounova Laughed: Humor and Joy in *We the Living*." This latter chapter also deals with a unique aspect of Ayn Rand's philosophy—the Benevolent Universe Premise—and how such an outlook is consistent with the tragic nature of *We the Living*.

Ayn Rand's later writings on philosophy would include technical works on epistemology, metaphysics, and metaethics. At the time she wrote *We the Living*, however, her explicit philosophy consisted primarily of moral and political philosophy. This is the focus of the final two chapters in the collection. (Dealing as they do with philosophical issues, they also touch on the novel's theme.) Tara Smith's "Forbidding Life to Those Still Living" describes how *We the Living* portrays the devastating effects of collectivism on human life. In the foreword to the revised edition of *We the Living*, Ayn Rand writes: "In *Atlas Shrugged*, I show *why* men are motivated either by a life premise or a death premise. In *We the Living*, I show only that they are." Onkar Ghate's chapter, "The Death Premise in *We the Living* and *Atlas Shrugged*," discusses how this premise is presented in *We the Living* and what *Atlas Shrugged* reveals about its source.

The contributors to this collection see these chapters as part of an exploration and celebration of Ayn Rand's life, thought, and fiction. There is no better time for such an enterprise than the present—as we approach the one hundredth anniversary of Ayn Rand's birth (February 2, 2005), the popularity of her novels and the influence of her philosophy continue to grow—and there is no better place to begin than at the beginning; that is, with her first novel, *We the Living*.

Robert Mayhew
Seton Hall University
October 2003

Acknowledgments

I wish to thank Leonard Peikoff (Executor of the Estate of Ayn Rand) for permission to use previously unpublished material of Ayn Rand, and Jeff Britting (Archivist of the Ayn Rand Archives) for his assistance in accessing this material. Special thanks are due Shoshana Milgram, who not only contributed two lengthy chapters to this collection, but also provided useful comments on three others, and Tore Boeckmann, who read through and commented on the entire manuscript. Thanks also to the staff at Lexington Books, and especially Serena Krombach, for all of their help on, and support for, this project. Finally, I am very grateful to both the Ayn Rand Institute and the Anthem Foundation for Objectivist Scholarship for grants that supported this project.

Bibliographical Note

Unless otherwise indicated, quotes from Ayn Rand's *We the Living* will be followed by page number(s) in parentheses in the text and not by an endnote. Pagination refers to the sixtieth anniversary paperback edition (New York: Signet, 1996).

Several chapters quote from, and refer to information contained in, a series of biographical interviews that Ayn Rand gave in 1960–61, the tapes and transcripts of which are in the Ayn Rand Archives. References will appear in the endnotes as: Biographical interviews (Ayn Rand Archives).

I

THE HISTORY OF
WE THE LIVING

1

From *Airtight* to *We the Living*: The Drafts of Ayn Rand's First Novel

Shoshana Milgram

We the Living follows Kira Argounova from her arrival in Petersburg, eager for the "streets of a big city where so much is possible," to her death on Russia's border, where she smiles "to so much that had been possible." The journey in between dramatizes the contrast between Kira's passion for life and the living death of the collectivist state in which she refuses to remain. The project of this chapter is to trace another journey, that of Ayn Rand in creating her first novel. By examining the manuscripts in the light of the writer's original plan and the published versions, I want to describe her artistic choices as she attempted to be true to her own vision of what was possible to her in fiction at this time. The revisions—omissions, additions, and modifications of style and content—show the novelist in the process of developing her literary method and sharpening her conceptions of her theme and characters.

Ayn Rand had worked on her first novel from 1929 on. In a notebook, she outlined the novel's plot and sketched the essentials of the characters and background features she expected to need to develop her theme: the individual versus the masses, as seen in the country where the struggle was most dramatic and most tragic. The title of the novel was to be *Airtight: A Novel of Red Russia*. For several years, while working at odd jobs and in the RKO studio wardrobe, she was able to work on her novel only in slivers of time, sometimes accomplishing no more than a paragraph a day. But after she sold the screen treatment *Red Pawn* (in synopsis form) to Universal Studio in 1932, she was able to work more continuously. Her steady work on the novel took place primarily in two stints, each of several months. On April 18,

1933, she began rewriting the first part of the book, of which she had written several chapters; she completed this task on October 11, 1933. She began writing part II on December 28, 1933, and completed it March 9, 1934, revising the manuscript once by May 22, 1934, and at least once more by mid-November, 1935. As she explained to Gouverneur Morris, her friend and a fellow writer, she edited it in the face of her publisher's impatience.

> The book was sold during the first weeks of my play [*Night of January 16th*] and I have been terribly busy, giving it a final editing. Macmillan, who are going to publish it, did not want any changes made, no cuts or alterations of any kind. But I wanted to revise it once more and make a few minor changes which, I think, improved it.[1]

We know the dates on which she began and completed the writing of the two parts of the novel because Ayn Rand marked these dates on the first draft. We know, too, that her agent Jean Wick was submitting the first part of the manuscript to publishers—and transmitting to the author the accumulating negative feedback—during the months Rand was writing the second part, as well as after she completed the novel. And we know Ayn Rand's response to the suggestion, in October 1934, that she work with a collaborator:

> Anyone reading my book must realize that I am an individualist above everything else. As such, I shall stand or fall on my own work. . . . It is merely the feeling of a person who takes pride in her work. At the cost of being considered arrogant, I must state that I do not believe there is a single human being alive who could improve that book of mine in the matter of actual rewriting. . . . I would prefer not only never seeing it in print, but also burning every manuscript of it—rather than having William Shakespeare himself add one line to it which was not mine, or cross out one comma. I repeat, I welcome and appreciate all suggestions of changes to improve the book without destroying its theme, and I am quite willing to make them. But these changes will be made *by me*.[2]

It is no surprise to read these strong words from the future author of *The Fountainhead*. Earlier in the same letter, Ayn Rand explained what she meant about the theme: the novel is not primarily a love story, but the story of what the masses do to the individual. Hence the background—the depiction of existence in the Soviet Union—is in fact crucial to the theme, and not merely the setting for a romantic triangle. And because Ivan Ivanov, the border patrol soldier who shot Kira, epitomizes the evil of the Soviet Union, his biography is coherent with the theme, and "one of the best things in the book"—and not to be cut, whatever cuts must be made.[3]

Ayn Rand's statements about what most mattered in this book provide a context for looking at the changes she made. So does the fact that, after the publication of *Atlas Shrugged*, she revised *We the Living* one more time, while stating that the changes were minimal (xvi–xvii). In spite of the numerous revisions she performed, Ayn Rand was always writing the same book on the same theme: the conflict between the masses and the individual. She was, however, continually learning how to write it better. In the selection of episodes and descriptive details, Ayn Rand always emphasized the destructiveness, in everyday life, of the principle of collectivism; all of the changes—including the cuts—are consistent with that emphasis. In the characterization of Kira as the individualist and of the two very different men who love the individual in her, Ayn Rand always emphasized her passion for life and the way both Andrei and Leo are drawn to a woman whom the course of their respective lives would lead them to avoid. Here, too, all of the changes—including the philosophical discussions and romantic encounters—are consistent. And, as a writer still struggling with acquiring a foreign language and practicing a new craft, she did not automatically choose the best words or details on her first try—but she knew what she was trying to do, and she kept trying. In a sense, the cliché is true: *Plus ça change, plus c'est la même chose.*

In studying the changes, we have a wealth of material, but not a full or clear record of the creative work. The "Airtight Notebook" contains plot outlines, character lists, a list of questions to be considered in developing a character, descriptions of important characters, historical facts, and facts about daily life pertinent to the theme. The nearly complete first draft (which begins with the note: "rewriting started April 18, 1933") is a combination of typed and handwritten pages; some, if not most, of the typed pages appear to be from a still earlier draft. The end of the first chapter and the beginning of the second are missing; there are also some loose pages, none of them from the missing chapters, and some of them labeled as inserts (that could be placed into the draft) and others duplicating material that is present in the draft. In this draft, new pagination begins with the fourth chapter of part I and again with the start of part II; as the manuscript proceeds, the typed pages decrease (ending entirely after page 59 of part I, chapter 5), and the hand-written pages take over. The second draft, undated, is typed, continuously paginated, and relatively clean, but far from identical to the published version.[4]

The manuscripts do not speak for themselves. With the first draft, it is not clear where the rewriting began or when particular handwritten changes were made (on the handwritten pages, or the typed pages). Ayn Rand's notes about revising the first fourteen chapters appear to have been written after the appearance of those chapters in the existing first draft. (She writes: "Cut out 'no' sequences," which are still here.)[5] Nor is it clear when the second draft was produced. Possibly it is the one Ayn Rand completed by May 22, 1934, a few weeks after finishing part II. But given that Ayn Rand's agent was contacting publishers before Ayn Rand had completed part II of the novel, it seems likely that there would have been a clean, typed draft of part I; such a submission copy could be what is now the first part of the existing second draft, or it could be lost. And given that the published version is different from the second draft, there would have to have been at least one additional draft (perhaps the one Ayn Rand completed by mid-November, 1935).

But regardless of the dates on which the changes were made, we can see, from the words on the page, that Ayn Rand at one point expressed herself in one way, and then chose a different way. Therefore, even without the full history of all changes, the existing documents show Ayn Rand, the artist, at work. By looking at the changes and attempting to infer the reasons she made them, we attend to her intention and her skill. And some of the omitted passages are well worth reading on their own account.

REVISIONS IN THE DRAFTS: BACKGROUND
AND SECONDARY CHARACTERS

In the "Airtight Notebook," Ayn Rand listed among the proposed characters a professor, who was to represent the best of the old world. In part I, chapter 4, she wrote, but crossed out, a description of such a professor:

> "Beauty is the sublime individual experience," lectured a professor of Esthetics with a graying beard and childishly clear, blue eyes to a crowd of sheepskin coats and leather jackets, who blew on their frozen hands in an auditorium that had not been heated.

She followed this paragraph with two others featuring spoken remarks, both of which serve to contrast the professor's pronouncement:

> "We are the vanguard of the New Proletarian Culture," harangued an unshaven student standing on a pulpit of the experimental laboratory, before a row of students and jars of pickled intestines.
> "Only a pound-and-a-half today, comrade. But it's nice bread, it's almost white," said the student clerk in the University cooperative handing Kira a loaf of bread the color of the sawdust on the floor. . . . (first draft, part I, new pagination beginning with chapter 4, 8–9)

The professor, who explicitly connects beauty with individualism, is distinguished ("graying beard") and youthfully innocent ("childishly clear, blue eyes"). The student, who speaks for the militant masses, is unkempt ("unshaven") and vehement yet tedious ("harangued"). The clerk, who implements the rationing decreed by the representatives of the masses, is inaccurate (misrepresenting the color of the bread) and, at best, foolish (implying that the alleged quality of the bread compensates for its small quantity). One can see how the brief paragraphs would have supported the theme of the conflict between the individual and the masses. Yet, given that the theme is well-developed elsewhere, one can also see that these paragraphs did not fulfill a unique function, and could be cut without loss. Nor did the single sentence quoted from the professor do more than gesture at the nature of his teaching.

Ayn Rand made a second attempt to describe the aesthetics professor, in the first draft of chapter 6 of part I:

> "The spirit of beauty is higher than the spirit of religion. It is the triumphant hymn of man to his own sacredness. It is the sublime claim of a god-like being to transcend all gods."
> Professor Leskov had the blue eyes of a child, the blond beard of a Greek statue, the sunken chest of a consumptive and the chair of the History of Esthetics at the State University of Petrograd. His lectures were held in the largest auditorium, but he still had to turn his eyes, occasionally, down to the floor, in order not to miss any of his audience: for part of that audience had to sit on the floor in the aisles. No auditorium had ever been large enough for Professor Leskov's lectures. There were few red bandannas in his audience, and few leather jackets. Professor Leskov had never been known to explain the Venus de Milo by the state of the economic means of production in ancient Greece. He was known to speak Latin better than Russian, to talk of each masterpiece of art since the beginning of history tenderly and intimately, as if children of his mind, and to shrug in surprise when his learned colleagues in the Scientific Academies of Europe called him great. He spoke his lectures fiercely and solemnly, as if he were delivering a sermon, and the silence of his auditorium was that of a cathedral. (first draft, 92–93)

The professor expresses a view of art as a hymn to human greatness, a hymn that makes men greater than gods, as art itself is greater than religion. The description, moreover, reports that the circumstances of his lecture match his point: his lecture style has the fierceness and solemnity of a sermon, and the audience—a very large audience—responds with the respectful silence appropriate to a cathedral.

This description repeats the childish blue eyes of Ayn Rand's initial description; and adds to it. In this version, the beard suggests not only distinction, but the glory of classical Greek art ("the blond beard of a Greek statue"), which was indeed one of his subjects. We are told, too, that he was extraordinarily popular, but that the students who crowd the benches and aisles of his classroom include few Communists. For Marxist aesthetics, they would have to go elsewhere.

The professor has a clear role in relation to the novel's theme, and the scene has other functions as well. Kira attends this class, and the professor notices her.

Kira sat on the edge of a bench in the first row. Sometimes, the childish blue eyes roving over the auditorium stopped for a short second on the wide, gray ones under strange, broken eyebrows. (first draft, 91–92)

She has spiritual support: not only from works of art, but from a human being who has made the study of art his life's work.

Why did Ayn Rand, in revising, omit Leskov as a character and a lecturer? One possible factor is that the subject of the lecture had to change. After the first draft, Ayn Rand changed Kira's major subject from history to engineering; and a course on esthetics would be a less likely choice for her. And making Leskov a spiritual ally of Kira would have raised questions: What happens to him? Doesn't his existence contradict the presentation of Soviet society? If such a man is still allowed to draw crowds, how doomed can Russia be? Why does Kira not seek him out later? Had Leskov remained in the novel, as a representative of the individual, he would have had to be integrated into the plot, that is, destroyed—physically or spiritually or both—as happens to all within any society in which the masses rule. To leave him intact would have violated the novel's theme; to trace his destruction might have risked overloading the novel's structure. To introduce him would have been to start a trail the novel was not designed to travel.

Somewhat similar considerations may be relevant to the omission of a speech made at the election meeting of the Students' Council, and of the introductory material that served as background for that speech. In the second draft and in the published versions of the scene, Ayn Rand contrasts the two factions of students. "One side wore the green student caps of the old days, discarded by the new rulers, wore them proudly, defiantly, as an honorary badge and a challenge; the other side wore red kerchiefs and trim, military leather jackets" (71). In all versions, the first speaker is Pavel Syerov, who asserts that science "is the weapon of the class struggle." And in all versions, Pavel Syerov later comments to a neighbor, "So that's the kind of speeches they make here. What a task we have awaiting us!" (72).

In the first draft, Ayn Rand provided much more information about the first type of students, and about the university.

They were cheerful, reckless, and defiant. Their clothes were older than those of most pedestrians outside, and dirtier; their manners—graceful and assured as those of heirs to an old clan. They were haughty, and patronizing, and contemptuous toward the new, small [?] group that called itself "proletarian students," that wore leather jackets and red bandannas and claimed factories and villages as their former homes. The University had a Communist cell. It had spies among the students, said rumors. Those who wore the faded, green student caps of the old days, as an honorary badge and a challenge, sneered at rumors and talked of the freedom of science. [*crossed-out*: The State University of Petrograd had been the first to greet the spirit of freedom and the last to lose it.]

[*crossed-out*: If one studied history, one could study history, Kira found. There were a few obligatory subjects, enforced by the red band outside: "historical materialism," history of socialist[?] movements," "constitution of the R.S.F.S.R. [Russian Soviet Federated Socialist Republic]," a few others. The rest were free to choice [*sic*].]

There was a Students' Council elected at students' meetings. Kira attended the first election of the year. (first draft, chapter 5, 13–15, paginated in a fifteen-page sequence in between chapters 4 and 5)

In the later versions of this scene, Kira attends because she has met Comrade Sonia Presniakova, and intends to vote against whatever Sonia supports. In the initial version, she attends with her cousin, Irina Dunaeva, and together they hear the speech that follows Syerov's.

Irina stuck her pencil into the corner of her mouth and her strong hands clapped like a firecracker into Kira's ear.

"Applaud," she commanded in a whisper. "That's one of *ours.*"

A tall young man stood on the pulpit, his two hands grasping the desk as if to keep himself posed there for a second in a sweeping flight [?]. He had thrown a green student cap on the desk before him, like a glove challenging his adversaries.

"Comrades," his strong voice boomed with the distinct, cultured enunciation of a future lawyer addressing a courtroom, "my honorable predecessor said that he had been left for centuries to rot in the darkness of ignorance. I believe him."

The defiant applause seemed to be addressed directly to the leather jackets and red bandannas.

"He needs a little lesson in history. Our students have always been fiery enemies of tyranny. In the Czar's day, our green caps often turned red under the guns of street riots and white in the snows of Siberian exile. The spirit of our youth has never been enslaved by authority. That spirit is still the same. We have a good nose for tyranny, no matter what color that tyranny is wearing."

Loud applause rolled down to the round, pink-cheeked face of the speaker. His immaculate coat and snow-white collar were worn with the elegance of a gentleman of Western culture; his high boots were a concession to the times, but a concession obviously expensive and polished to a mirror-shine.

"We are here to study. We are here to fight for the freedom of science from a red harness. The spirit of freedom lost by the country has always lived within these halls. And it is yet to be remembered. When we leave this University, we'll go . . ."

". . . to jail!" came a menacing voice from somewhere in the audience.

"Order!" the president of the meeting commanded sternly.

"Yes, we might go to jail. We've heard that threat before. Funny, it was used by the Czar's gendarmes!"

Irina pointed to a slight, young man with a nose too long for his narrow,

consumptive face, at the speakers' table in a whispered conference with the
pale comrade Syerov.
"I'll draw that one," whispered Irina. "He's a good type."
Comrade Syerov was saying to the good type:
"So that's the kind of speeches they make here." (first draft, 45–47)

The initial version, like the others, concludes with Syerov's comments to
a soft-spoken, ominous neighbor, who assures Syerov that the day belongs
to the secret "internal front" of Red Culture. But only the first draft supplies
the speech on which Syerov comments, as well as a description of the
speaker. By omitting the speech and removing a character, Ayn Rand saves
space, and keeps the focus of the scene more on Kira, who is not interested
in politics. If the novel featured the speech, we would be wondering if it
would motivate Kira to fight, and, if not, why not. The speech is in keeping
with the novel's theme, but, given that it had no effect on the central story
line involving Kira, removing it did not create a hole (except for readers who
may have wondered what, specifically, was meant by "the kind of speeches
they make here").

It is possible, too, that the nameless student, whose "strong voice boomed
with the distinct, cultured enunciation of a future lawyer," has some connection with Sasha Chernov, whom we do not meet until chapter 2 of part II. In
the "Airtight Notebook," Ayn Rand listed as one of the characters "Sasha—
old fighter student." The student speaker may have originally been intended
to be this character.

In the novel, though, Sasha is given a more prominent role than the notebook would indicate. A history student expelled from the university, he
engages in covert revolutionary activities. He and Irina are in love; when
Victor betrays them to the G.P.U. to bolster his party standing, they are each
sentenced to ten years in Siberia, in separate camps.

Whether or not Ayn Rand originally thought of the student speaker as
Sasha, and then removed his speech when she gave him a more active role,
we can see that removing the speech does not diminish the novel, and that
enhancing the character's role strengthens it. The Sasha/Irina subplot, after
all, is coherent with the theme: they are among the individuals who are in
conflict with the masses, and destroyed by collectivism. The main plot—the
triangle of Kira, Leo Kovalensky, and Andrei Taganov—entails destruction of
a more philosophical nature. Only Ayn Rand could have written the story of
Kira, Leo, and Andrei as exemplifying the individual versus the masses.
Other writers—and historians—have chronicled the destruction of Sashas
and Irinas. But the fact that their story is more commonplace—tragically so—
than the one Ayn Rand invented does not make it bromidic. Ayn Rand gives
their relationship great emotional intensity, not only in Irina's speech about
her life as a sacred treasure (which Ayn Rand refers to, in the introduction to

the 1959 edition, as the "sanctity of life" speech, the statement of the novel's meaning), but in the couple's long, last farewell.

That this sort of intensity was not Ayn Rand's original plan for Irina, at any rate, is clear from the description of the character that appears in the "Airtight Notebook":

> A representation of the best in the average girlhood. Dependable, energetic, calm. Ambitious, beautiful. Serious. A certain amount of cunning and calculating. Unsettled and open to influence. Starts with hard work and high hopes. Gives up—or dull hopelessness. Marries an older man, bald-headed and divorced, marries without love, even without money, just for some sort of relieve [sic] in her hard, drab existence. (Representative of the average "working girl")

The original plan for Irina was coherent with the novel's theme: whatever was good in Irina was destroyed in Soviet Russia. It does not appear that the original plan for Sasha went beyond his role as an example of the "old" sort of student; he is not given, in the "notebook," the sort of paragraph-length descriptions Ayn Rand writes for such characters as Antonia Platoshkina and Rita Eksler. But the final plan for Irina and Sasha expressed a poignant loss, advanced the plot (by developing conflicts for such characters as Vasili Dunaev, Victor Dunaev, and Marisha Lavrova Dunaeva), and answered the question a reader might have asked (Why don't they fight back?)—all without interfering with the central line, the story of Kira and her lovers.

We see, then, that Ayn Rand's original plan—for Irina and for a revolutionary student speaker—was good, but that the ultimate result was much better.

Comparing the first draft with the later drafts, we see many cuts involving details of Soviet life. The longest passage, which can be found in the first draft of chapter 5 of part I, is paginated separately from the rest of the chapter. It has been reprinted in *The Early Ayn Rand* under the title "No," a word featured in each segment.[6] A series of vignettes—some of them quoting propaganda, others presenting bread lines or theatre posters—illustrate the drabness and deprivation of everyday life in all areas, from clothes to culture to chimney cleaning. In her notes for revising this chapter, Ayn Rand wrote: "Cut out the 'no' sequences—except house meeting."[7] In the second draft of this chapter, much of this material is gone. Leonard Peikoff observes: a few "elements of this montage were retained in the novel, in the form of brief paragraphs integrated with the development of the story. Evidently, Miss Rand judged that a separate extended treatment would be too static."[8] This statement makes sense; there is, in fact, no montage sequence of similar length in the novel.

Ayn Rand, to be sure, used montage effectively, at the end of chapter 16 of part I, in a series of vignettes each prefaced by "Because." In both chapters, the incidents show a principle exemplified in a variety of settings. It was important to Ayn Rand to show, as she put it in the "Airtight Notebook," "*all* the *mass* manifestations of humanity in general and the Russian revolution in particular." But the montage in chapter 16 is not only briefer than the one planned for chapter 5, but explicitly linked to a crisis in the life of a major character. In removing the "no" vignettes, Ayn Rand was eliminating material that, however appropriate given her theme, took up too much space in her novel as it was developing.

Not only in the montage passage, but elsewhere as well, Ayn Rand shortened or omitted incidents used to convey the ugliness of everyday life. One such incident, which appears (lightly crossed out) in the first draft of chapter 1, shows an envy-driven betrayal, as reported by a woman on the train carrying the Argounov family back to Petersburg:

> "They still have plenty to eat, sometimes, though, the damn counter-revolutionaries," the woman in the red bandanna commented, "I know it on first-hand information. I had a friend and she was working in a family. Had all the cooking to do, and the dirty underclothes to wash, and the three brats to comb with a fine comb every day, too. She got a miserable pittance of a wage. And she knew that they had the cellar stuffed full of white flour, and sugar, and millet. She was a smart girl, my friend was, and she figgered, why should she work for what she was getting. So she went and reported them. It was all confiscated, and they shot the old man for concealing food products, and my pal got one third of everything in the cellar. Wasn't that smart?" (first draft, 17)

The anecdote is pertinent to the picture of Soviet life, but the point it makes is already implicit in another incident that takes place on the train itself (the woman who hides in the lavatory to eat fish). The first draft of the chapter includes several similar passages about the train's various passengers. Ayn Rand, in her notes about revising, writes that the scene needs to feature Kira more (and, hence, the background less).

Additional cuts in background material involve omitting some explicit references to Marxist theory. In chapter 6 of part I:

> Kira sat at the table with a book on "Historical Materialism."
> ". . . and the class which holds the means of production dictates to society its own superstructures of morals, religion, philosophy. . . ." (first draft, 112)

In the later versions of the scene, Kira is shown reading an engineering text. Granted, as an engineer she would be less likely to be reading a textbook on a subject such as historical materialism, but describing the book more briefly allowed Ayn Rand to state that Kira was distracted from her reading by thoughts of Leo—without engaging in polemic on another topic.

She considered, but rejected, the idea of presenting the polemic in the context of Leo's studies. Leo, too, was—in the first draft—taking courses in Marxist theory, along with Greek philosophy and the history of the Crusades. From the first draft of chapter 11:

> Leo went to the university and listened to lectures about words twenty-two centuries old said by men in white togas on forums of white marble, and about the shape of steel armours that swayed [?] on charging stallions sparkling under Palestine's sun, and about the crosses over the armours, and about the hearts under them, and he had to listen, also, to lectures on "Historical Materialism." A very assured young professor told them that all historical processes are to be explained by the "economical development of the people and the means of production," that class struggle is the backbone of history, "all of us young historians of a new ruling class have to acquire, first of all, the proper ideology of proletarian scientists with which to approach the study of the world's history, for we—young, fresh, new, free from the sentimental prejudices of musty bourgeois professors—know that the kettle on the stove of a housewife and the needle in the hands of a shoemaker mean more to the course of history than any fancy curlicues [?] in the hands of a Napoleon who is nothing but a puppet on the great stage of class struggle." (first draft, 273)

The published version reports only: "He was studying history and philosophy at the Petrograd State University" (1936, 154). Ayn Rand ultimately decided that her novel did not need a critical account of the negative content of a Marxist education.

Ayn Rand similarly removed another explicit attack on Leo's university education, which was mentioned in contrast with a favorite writer of hers, O. Henry, whom Leo was reading—in the first and second drafts of chapter 14.

> "It's a new American author," he told her, "O. Henry. Splendid writing. The city of New York has six million inhabitants. You meet someone in a subway and you say "Hello." It must be delightful—a subway."
> He was smiling, half lazily, half ironically, a new smile that Kira had noticed lately; a smile she did not like, a sharp, uncomfortable smile.
> "I don't feel like going to the University today," he answered her question lazily. "Why be reminded of Proletarian Dictatorship when one can read something more amusing and in better taste? . . . (first draft, 372; second draft, 253)

Leo's attitude here is cynical rather than passionate in his disdain for "Proletarian Dictatorship," and there was abundant evidence elsewhere of this trend in him. Nor does his attraction to O. Henry, by itself, serve to sharpen his characterization or to do more than remind the reader that Leo prefers American and European culture to Russian culture, another fact that is well established elsewhere.

Additional cuts in background material, also related to culture, occur in remarks made at parties by Victor and Rita Eksler. In the first draft of chapter 12 of part I, Victor comments on a contemporary novel: "Remember the scene where she tells her lover that she's no virgin and has had an abortion? That's the Russian new woman for you" (first draft, 301). In later versions of the scene, he refers to the novel only vaguely. Ayn Rand originally intended for him to speak approvingly of a novel that praised a woman for being sexually experienced and for having an abortion—when, as we later learn, the woman he eventually marries believes it necessary to conceal such facts from him. The reference would have functioned both as an indication of Victor's hypocrisy and an illustration of what Ayn Rand referred to in the notebook as the "intentional vulgarity" of literature—both of which are established elsewhere. At the same party, Ayn Rand wrote, then crossed out, a remark by Rita Eksler, which appears to be delivered as if it were a cultural commonplace: "'Sexually and psychologically,' said Rita, 'there's no difference between the impulses of men and women'" (first draft, 307). Given her history, her denial of a double standard implies that the "impulses" are to be given full rein, and that both women and men should be promiscuous. And, given her history, there is no need for her to take up space in the novel making this statement.

Victor and Rita are themselves a kind of background material, as examples of decadents, empty of values, who succeed in the new Soviet world. It is not surprising that Ayn Rand considered matching them up. In a scene written for the first-draft version of chapter 15 of part II, they are having a secret affair:

> Victor got a twenty-four hour leave of absence from the Volkhovstroy. He arrived in Petrograd in the same train compartment with Rita Eksler. Rita Eksler crossed her long legs in very sheer foreign stockings and pulled a fluffy silver fox closer to her little nose white with genuine Coty powder, and asked:
> "Couldn't I, really, darling?"
> "No," said Victor imperiously, "under no circumstances, Rita. We can't be seen together. What do you want to drag yourself to that funeral, anyway? It's no fun. And then, my wife will probably be there. They all will."
> "Haven't you divorced her yet?"
> "I have. Last week. She's had her notice of divorce by (first draft, 514)[9]

Although the union in depravity of Victor and Rita fits the world of *We the Living*, the focus of that chapter is Andrei's funeral; their affair is not distinctly pertinent to that event, nor is it necessary for the novel. As is the case with other omissions in the background material, one can see why Ayn Rand wrote it in, and also why she left it out.

Looking at the changes Ayn Rand made in the novel, we see that, for the most part, she wrote more than she needed (as she was to do in later novels, especially *The Fountainhead*) and then removed what she did not need. In some cases, notably the speech by a student revolutionary, narrative events (i.e., Sasha's revolutionary activities) fulfilled the function of the statement that was omitted. She preferred showing to telling, as she was to explain in her lectures on fiction-writing,[10] and this preference accounts for many of her artistic choices, as the manuscripts show.

STYLISTIC REVISIONS

Many of the changes visible on the pages of the drafts show Ayn Rand working to improve the precision of her diction and the smoothness of her syntax. In the first draft of the second chapter, for example, when Victor suggests that Kira work in a Soviet office, his father asks: "Do you want her to become a reconciled slave?" (first draft, 62). The phrasing is awkward, and does not sound like English; it is also a more explicit challenge to Victor than is typical of Vasili at this point. In the second draft, "Victor, you don't really mean that" is enough.

She also worked to add vividness to her writing. Later in the scene, when Alexander Argounov says he will not take a Soviet job:

> "That's the spirit, Alexander!" Vassili [sic] Ivanovitch proclaimed triumphantly and shook his hand, stretching his big fist across the table, with a dark glance at Maria Petrovna. (first draft, 52)

But consider the second draft:

> Vasili Ivanovitch dropped his spoon and it clattered into his plate; silently, solemnly, he stretched his big fist across the table and shook Alexander Dimitrievitch's hand and threw a dark glance at Maria Petrovna. (second draft, 27)

For the second draft (which is the same as all later versions), she adds details of action and sound (dropping the spoon, the sound of clatter) and structures the syntax of the sentence for greater drama. Even the substitution of "threw a dark glance" for "with a dark glance" is an improvement, making the glance more active.

Compare the first and second drafts of her introduction of Irina:

> Irina, her daughter, came flying into the anteroom, tall, slender, eighteen, with huge eyes and the transparent skin of her mother's youth. [*crossed-out*: with a face that laughed, danced, and moved so much one did not have time to notice whether it was good-looking or not.] (first draft, 48)
>
> A door crashed open behind her and something came flying into the anteroom; something tall, tense, with a storm of hair and eyes like automobile headlights; and Galina Petrovna recognized Irina, her niece, a young lady of eighteen with the eyes of twenty-eight and the laughter of eight. (second draft, 23)

The revised version (which is the same as all later versions) includes not only more sound (crashing door) and a sharper description (combining sensory details and metaphoric language), but also two kinds of suspense. First, we wait to find out what the "something" is (instead of being told, as in the first draft, that the person entering is Irina). Then, instead of simply knowing her chronological age, we wonder why she is, in spirit, several other ages as well.

In some cases, Ayn Rand writes a general statement in a draft, then replaces it with specifics. In the second draft of chapter 4 of part I: "Visitors were rare. Galina Petrovna was eager to share her news and hopes, while Kira looked impatiently at the city lights in the window" (second draft, 60). The published versions of this scene replace the summary statement with Galina's actual "news and hopes."

Revisions are often made to be more concrete, but not always. From the same scene, compare the following:

> "Any time I'll enter a Union with that scum, you can have me cremated and feed the ashes to the pigs!" (first draft, 53)
> "When I have to take Soviet employment," said Vasili Ivanovitch, "you'll be a widow, Marussia." (second draft, 27–28)

The grotesque image, which is not necessary, is excluded from the second draft and from all later versions. The point is that union membership is a kind of death, or worse. Sometimes revisions involve the removal of adverbs or adjectives. Consider the following, from chapter 6 of part II. When Leo looks at Kira, dressed for the wedding of Victor and Marisha, he "took her hand reverently, as that of a lady at a Court reception, and kissed her palm lasciviously, as that of a courtesan" (first draft, 153; second draft, 442). For the first published version, Ayn Rand removed the superfluous adverbs: he "took her hand, as that of a lady at a Court reception, and kissed her palm, as that of a courtesan"(1936, 360). And for the revised edition, Ayn Rand improved the syntax and the emphasis, too: he "took her hand, as if she were a lady at a Court reception, and kissed her palm, as if she were a courtesan" (297).

The stylistic revisions visible on the pages of the manuscripts are evidence of Ayn Rand's continuing purposeful labor. One could learn from them all. I will conclude this section with multiple versions of passages from the novel's third chapter, entirely devoted to Kira.

The first draft version of the description of Kira's eyes reads as follows:

> Kira's eyes were dark gray, the gray of clouds from behind which the sun can be expected at any moment. [*Crossed-out*: There was a silent, sparkling laughter in them, and a profound joy of more than laughing gaiety.] From under her strange eyebrows that seemed broken in the middle where their straight, thin

line made a sharp angle, they looked at people quietly, directly, a little defiantly in their straightforward calm that seemed to tell men her sight was too clear, and none of their favorite binoculars were needed to help her look at life.

[*Crossed-out*: Her eyes were candid and open, radiant with the distant reflection of what they seemed to see; no mystery clouded their thought. But men looked into her eyes like into a sea whose waters stood still transparent as air to reveal a sunken treasure, but so deep that the bottom could not be seen.] (first draft, 86)

In revising this passage, Ayn Rand crossed out a reference to treasure below the sea (an early anticipation of Atlantis), as well as a general description of Kira's laughter.

The second draft reads as follows:

Kira's eyes were dark gray, the gray of storm clouds from behind which the sun can be expected at any moment. They looked at people quietly, directly, with something that people called arrogance, but which was only such perfection of deep, confident calm that it seemed to tell men her sight was too clear and none of their favorite binoculars were needed to help her look at life. (second draft, 38)

In revising the passage further, Ayn Rand specified that the clouds were storm clouds (perhaps a link with the storm of Irina's hair) and removed the "broken eyebrows," which were a feature of Kira's description in the first draft only. Perhaps Ayn Rand decided that the words did not convey the image she wanted. Ayn Rand also deals with the apparent incongruity of "defiantly" and "calm." Kira is self-possessed and self-sufficient, and does not think of others enough to "defy" them; "arrogance" is the name given to her calm by others. The best features of the description are there from the start; the revisions are mere polishing. The first published version is the same as the second draft (see 1936, 36); for the 1959 edition, Ayn Rand shortened "such perfection of deep, confident calm" to "a deep, confident calm" (44).

Consider the revision of the description of Kira's mouth. In the first draft:

Kira's lips were thin, long. Silent; they were cold, indomitable, and men thought of a walkure with lance and winged helmet in the sweep of battle. But a slight movement made a wrinkle in the corner of her lips—and men thought of an imp perched on top of a toadstool, laughing into the faces of daisies.

No one dared the thought of a kiss upon her proud, forbidding mouth of a priestess. But she smiled, [*crossed-out*: and her smile, slow, tender, delicate, was like a flower whose arrogant fragility invited a hand to crush it,] and men doubted the nature of the goddess she was serving. (first draft, 86–87)

The second draft is nearly the same. The spelling is changed (from "walkure" to 'Valkyre"), and the paragraphs are combined. For the first published version (1936, 36), though, the sentences about the priestess are removed.

The sentences about the priestess were designed to convey the contrast between two states of Kira's appearance. In the one, she appears forbidding; in the other, she is tender. But the sentences, as written, do not convey a clear meaning: in what sense did men doubt "the nature of the goddess she was serving"? (For Ayn Rand, moreover, a woman as priestess—as, for example, in the notes for *The Fountainhead*—is serving not a goddess, but a god.[11])

The earlier sentences, which also convey a contrast, were excellent in the first draft. The contrast here is like that of the storm clouds and the hint of sun, in the description of Kira's eyes. The image of the Valkyrie, which is a tie to Kira's Viking (a brief reference in the published versions, a cherished legend of Kira's in the drafts) and perhaps a reflection of the warrior-princess Kriemhilde in the Ring saga (dramatized in film in Fritz Lang's *Siegfried*, which Ayn Rand judged to be "as close to a great work of art as the films have yet come"[12]). The laughing imp is dramatically different—in scale and mood—from the Valkyrie, and can also be integrated with Irina's farewell sketch, drawn on the train, for Sasha.[13] The description is stronger when it includes the clear Valkyrie/imp contrast and excludes the less-clear priestess contrast.

The existing drafts show literally hundreds of stylistic revisions, and it is likely that the missing pages and drafts would show many more. Given that, as we've seen, Ayn Rand devoted so much attention to revising the content of her background material and the style of her prose, it is not surprising to see in the drafts evidence of significant revisions in the content of the central story line: the character of Kira, her love for Leo, and her relationship with Andrei.

REVISIONS IN THE MAIN STORY LINE:
KIRA AND HER LOVERS

The most important change in the content of the characterization of Kira is the change in her career. In the first draft, Kira announced to her family, on their first night back in Petersburg, that she would be going to the university:

> "What will you take?"
> "History."
> "Why history?"
> "Less boring than anything else." (first draft, 63)

In the second draft, she is planning to be an engineer; the reasons she states—there (33–34) and in the 1936 version (31–32)—emphasize objectivity: "It's the only profession where I don't have to learn one single lie. Steel is steel. Every other science is someone's guess, and someone's wish, and many people's lies." (In the 1959 version, "one single lie" became "any lies," and "Every other science" became "Most of the other sciences" [42].)

When Victor accuses her of being antisocial and neglecting her duty, her response, in the first draft, is simply:

> "Anyone in particular you have a duty to in society, Victor?
> "No. The whole."
> "If you write a whole line of zeroes, it's still—nothing." (first draft, 63)

In the second draft, and in the published versions, the exchange is as follows:

> "To whom is it I owe a duty? To your neighbor next door? Or to the militia-man on the corner? Or to the clerk in the co-operative? Or to the old man I saw in line, third from the door, with an old basket and a woman's hat?"
> "Society, Kira, is a stupendous whole."
> "If you write a whole line of zeroes, it's still—nothing." (second draft, 33–34; 1936, 31–32)

In revising this early scene, Ayn Rand makes Kira more thoughtful. Kira is more articulate—but not improbably so—on the subject of the theme, the individual versus the collective. Kira also has a better reason for choosing a subject: engineering is more objective. Justifying her choice by saying it is "less boring" than other subjects is the sort of explanation that might be suitable for Leo, who has begun to give up, but not for the passionate Kira.

In giving Kira the aspiration to be an engineer, rather than to study a subject selected only because it is "less boring" than others, Ayn Rand significantly improved the characterization, which—since Kira in the novel represents the individual—significantly enhanced the dramatization of the theme. The characterization, to be sure, was already strong in the first draft. Most of the revisions are omissions of paragraphs or scenes that would be entirely appropriate for the final version of Kira, and that seem to be cut primarily for space.

Chapter 3 of part I, which we have already examined for stylistic revisions in the description of Kira's appearance, includes several incidents, sooner or later cut from the novel, that illustrate Kira's independence and courage.

Ayn Rand wrote, but crossed out, a description of Kira as a toddler measuring herself against the statue of Apollo:

> Through the winter of her first years, she . . . waddled across the big rooms and measured her height with the white marble statue of Apollo on the landing of the main stairway, her ambition set on growing to be his size. (first draft, 87)

The image is appealing and symbolic: Kira wants to be the greatest and highest. But Ayn Rand wrote, in all later versions of the chapter, that Kira "climbed to the pedestals of statues in the parks to kiss the cold lips of Greek gods." Kira is ultimately presented not as *being* the marble Apollo, but as *loving* him.

Shortly after, the first draft has two versions of a scene involving Kira's climb to a height. The first version, which is crossed out, reads:

> In a niche high up in the wall of the stairway was a tall Gothic window opened over the city. The janitor could reach it only with the help of a big ladder. After a long search of the house, Kira, at the age of five, was found, one day, up at the window, gravely watching the city. She had climbed into the niche, accidentally pushed the ladder away, and was found twenty feet above the stairway landing. Galina Petrovna fainted. (first draft, 87–88, typed)

The incident shows Kira's daring and curiosity, but also a carelessness and an obliviousness regarding realistic danger. The second version, which immediately follows the other, reads:

> At the age of five, Kira found her way to the highest and murkiest of the mansion's attics, pushed aside the long step-ladder—its only means of communication with the world below, and, peering down from behind a dusty, broken trunk, delivered an ultimatum to her frantic elders: she refused to play with a little crippled relative of whom the family's compassion had made a general idol. [*crossed-out*: The step-ladder was put up in place, but Kira was never asked to play with the cripple again.] (first draft, 88—a handwritten page following the typed 88)

This time Kira has pushed away the ladder deliberately, and is using the situation as a bargaining device with her family. Her refusal to play with the crippled relative (i.e., someone who is valued for negative reasons) merely because he is weak indicates her desire for positive values.

The second draft of this incident, which corresponds with the published versions, is much shorter:

> When she refused to play with a crippled relative of whom the family's compassion had made a general idol—she was never asked to do it again. (second draft, 39–40)

There is no climb, no stepladder, no threat. The most important point is that Kira wanted to live her life for her own sake—and that she was allowed to do so. Ayn Rand originally planned a number of incidents (at age five, seven, etc.) in several paragraphs. Instead, she allotted a sentence to each childhood episode for this age span, reserving a longer treatment for the later years.

Ayn Rand devotes several paragraphs, for example, to Kira's time alone at the Argounov summer residence. All versions contain descriptions of her rafting through whirlpools on the river, and listening to sparkling musical tunes from the casinos below the hill. The first and second drafts also contain the following:

> Sometimes she got up at dawn for a swim in the river. A light cape wrapped tightly around her body, she ran to her rock that hung high over the water. Above the hills the sky was a pale pink, like the faint glow of blood through a white skin. The river ran dark and cold, a long steel blade that had slashed a hill in two. Kira threw her cape down. Her naked body, pink as the sky, cut through the cold air, through the gray of the hills into the river far below. Two furious spurts of water darted up, like two huge white wings that flapped open once after the flight and fell closed again. (first draft, 92; second draft, 41)

The scene did not appear in the published versions—perhaps cut for space, with the rafting scene being sufficient to convey Kira's sense of adventure—but readers of *The Fountainhead* will note that Ayn Rand did not abandon the idea of a nude swim, in a similar setting. The lake at Stanton "was only a thin steel ring that cut the rocks in half,"[14] as the river here was "a long steel blade that had slashed a hill in two."

The characterization of Kira, with regard to love and sex, was designed to contrast conventional sentimentality about love with Kira's indifference to the same (because Kira, without knowing it, wanted to love a hero). The drafts show that Ayn Rand originally intended more detail about this contrast. For example, here is a passage that appears only in the first draft:

> At the age when, their arms around each other, girls wander down garden lanes in the evening, whispering to each other their first, breathless confessions, Kira had no need to share, no flowers pressed in a book of verses, no fortune teller's prediction of her future husband's name. When classmates asked her in a whisper the greatest question of their young world: "Have you ever been kissed, Kira?" they were answered by the shake of a head with a lazy, indifferent smile.
>
> In the early spring of her graduation, Kira walked to school every morning past a [lovely? lonely?] house with carved white columns and grilled windows. It had been a nobleman's mansion transformed into a White Army prison. Kira noticed a prisoner [crossed-out: behind the bars of] in a basement window. He was a young Bolshevik officer of the Red Army. She watched him every morning, his two strong fists clutching the bars, hair thrown back, lips in one thin line on a pale face, grimly set against a silent despair. She liked his face. Once, she smiled at him. He answered. She passed by the white prison every day and he waited to see her pass. They waved to each other. Then, one day, he disappeared. She never bothered to find out where he had gone. (first draft, 94–95)

Kira's interest in the Bolshevik officer imprisoned in the mansion is juxta-posed with her lack of interest in conventional romance. The implication is that a man like that, strong and grimly defying despair, might attract her, but that the men she has met have not. This point, though, is made clearly enough elsewhere in the chapter, and through incidents that achieve multi-ple purposes.

We are told that Kira's mocking attitude discourages the intentions of con-ventional young men with humid eyes (who remind Kira of snails slithering up her bare legs). This description of Kira's mocking attitude also makes the point that young men are attracted to her, that her lack of concern with romance is not any sort of "sour grapes." We are told that she is fascinated by the silhouette of a soldier guarding an oil well, and by the sight, in a stage play, of a tall, young overseer cracking a whip. The description of the soldier guarding the oil well is a link with engineering. The description of the over-seer also makes the point that Lydia, by contrast, empathizes with the peas-ant victim cringing under the whip. Hence the paragraphs about Kira's indifference to the subject of kissing, and her exchange of smiles with the Bolshevik prisoner, are consistent with the characterization, but their point is dramatized elsewhere.

The same is true for the details, in the first draft only, about a book Lydia read and offered to Kira. "It told of a dashing young officer seducing a beau-tiful Duchess on the satin pillows of his bedroom. Kira yawned and threw the book under the bed" (first draft, 95). The text as it stands describes Lyd-ia's preferred reading as "books of delicate, sinful romance," which is suffi-cient to identify their nature.

The description of Lydia's book would have stood as a specific contrast to the one book Kira treasured, an English novel about a Viking, hated by both the king and priest of his own land, who "lived but for the joy and the won-der and the glory of the god that was himself" (49). The first and second drafts include a longer version of his story, which appears, condensed from several pages to a few sentences, in the published versions. The second-draft version, reprinted in *The Early Ayn Rand*, celebrates the Viking's conquest of a sacred city and offers a vivid image of his final triumph:

> Alone over the city, his clothes torn, the Viking stood on top of the tall white tower. There was a wound across his breast and red drops rolled slowly down to his feet.
>
> From the ravaged streets below, conquerors and conquered alike looked up at him. There was much wonder in their eyes, but little hatred. They raised their heads, but did not rise from their knees.
>
> On the tower stairs the slender queen-priestess of the sacred city lay at the Viking's feet. Her head bent so low that her golden hair swept the steps and he could see her breasts as, breathing tremulously, they touched the ground. Her

hands lay still and helpless on the steps, the palms turned up, hungry in silent entreaty. But it was not mercy they were begging of him.[15]

The writing here, and throughout the story, is eloquent. Ayn Rand condensed the legend, probably for reasons of space. (Readers of *The Fountainhead* will notice that she did not abandon the image of a conqueror at the top of a tall tower, worshipped by a slender, golden-haired priestess.)

Kira's Viking, throughout the composition of the novel, stands as Kira's ideal; in the drafts, she thinks of him in her dying moments. Given that the legend includes a romance, it is not surprising that the Viking became her romantic ideal, at least subconsciously. Hence the legend, when included, supported the features of Kira's characterization we have been examining: her longing for a hero, and her indifference to the ordinary.

The chapter in which Ayn Rand establishes Kira's characterization ends, in all versions, with two opposing conclusions: the omniscient narrator reports that Kira "entered [life] with the sword of a Viking pointing the way and an operetta tune for a battle march" and the Soviet official states that the goal of her life is "the brotherhood of workers and peasants." The incidents within that chapter—the ones that remain and the ones that were removed—support the incongruity of those conclusions. In the next two chapters, she meets Leo, and then Andrei. Her relationships with them bring the incongruity into focus.

Kira's relationship with Leo is crucial to his characterization. Leo's role in the novel was, as Ayn Rand wrote in the "Airtight Notebook," to be a man "too strong to compromise, but too weak to withstand the pressure, who cannot bend, but only break." He was, from the standpoint of the theme, an individualist in spirit who was broken by living in a society ruled by the spirit of the masses. The "breaking" takes the form of giving up on the best within him. But the best within him—which would properly include productive work—is represented in the novel only by Kira. By the time we meet him, he seems to have already given up on everything else. In order for the reader to recognize that Leo is a great value, Ayn Rand needs to make evident in the novel what Kira sees in Leo, what Leo is to and with Kira.

Although Leo is given a background (much briefer than Kira's or Andrei's), he exists in the novel almost entirely in relation to Kira. We rarely see him without her. When he goes to the sanatorium to be cured of tuberculosis, the narrative perspective does not go with him; nor does the novel accompany him to prison. We do not even see him at the theatre or at Antonina Platoshinka's apartment until Kira tracks him down. And except for rare, isolated instances, the novel does not enter his consciousness.

Leo's downward path is apparent not only in his willingness to accept his own physical death (in part I) and his spiritual death (in part II), but in some aspects of his treatment of Kira along the way. It is shocking to hear his rudeness to Kira or to see Rita Eksler draped over Leo at a party, or Vava Milov-skaia locked in his arms in the apartment he shares with Kira. (One cannot imagine any other Ayn Rand hero, whatever the provocation, conducting himself in this manner.) The challenge in creating the characterization of Leo was to evoke the height from which he falls, to show why his decline is a tragedy. And given that he has already fallen, to a large extent, by the time we meet him, the depiction of his relationship with Kira has to do the job of showing what he once was, what he could and should be, by making evident why Kira would have loved him, would have seen him as her hero, would have formed an image of his essential nature so strong that she would cling to it, and to him, in spite of all that followed.

If the novel does not show us why and how Kira loves Leo, we do not know who he really is. There simply is not enough of Leo in the novel apart from the relationship from which to judge his heroic qualities. Hence it was very important to convey that love, and the drafts show that Ayn Rand worked hard on it. The most heavily edited portions of the description of Leo are his first two meetings with Kira and their sexual encounters. Ayn Rand wrote, in her notes on revising the early chapters, that the meeting of Leo and Kira needed to be much better. And, although she ultimately judged her work here to be less than her best—she said that she had not been able to convey Kira's feeling for Leo as well as she had wished (biographical interviews)—we can see, from the drafts, the effort she put forth and the improvements she made in trying to show Leo through Kira's eyes. Kira's perspective was, in the novel as it developed, the only way to show the true Leo. No one else—certainly not Leo himself—saw him as a hero. But Ayn Rand did, and tried to show how Kira did.

The key aspect of the introduction of Leo is that Kira immediately recognized him as the image of her hero, and, almost simultaneously, recognized that their relationship would entail a struggle between the glory of his spirit and the depths of his despair. In the first draft, the immediate recognition is accomplished by a reference to Kira's Viking. Finding herself at night in the red-light district, she moves nervously to the corner.

> And then she stopped.
> [*crossed-out*: For coming down the street she saw a face. And it was the face of the Viking.]
> He was tall; his collar was raised; a cap was pulled over his eyes. His mouth, calm, severe, contemptuous, was that of an ancient chieftain who could order men to die, and his eyes were such as could watch it. They were the eyes of a Viking who drank at sunrise over the ruins of a sacred city. (first draft, 24)

The second draft (66) omits the crossed-out sentences, but retains the reference to the Viking's eyes.

When she realizes that he believes her to be a prostitute, she thinks again of the Viking, because buying the services of a prostitute does not comport with the nobility of her Viking. In a sentence crossed out in the first draft, she wrote: "She studied the man behind the Viking's face; the face that could not deceive her" (first draft, 26).

The 1936 version omits all specific references to the Viking; the reference to an "ancient chieftain" (56) would not, by itself, lead a reader to think of the Viking mentioned as being the hero of Kira's favorite story. But the references to the Viking were originally designed to cash in on the legend we associate with Kira. In the drafts, she loves this man at first sight because he is her longstanding image of her highest value. She is, in a sense, not seeing him for the first time—she has seen him all her life.

But Ayn Rand decided to shorten the Viking's legend, and to remove— from this scene and from Kira's death scene—the references to the Viking. Without the references, we have only the fact that Kira likes his face, and that he is calm and severe (like her other images of the hero, e.g., the overseer and the soldier guarding the oil well). But faces can be misleading. Kira, within the novel, has already been disappointed by a face she liked. On the day she returned to Petersburg, she looked straight into the eyes of a young soldier whose eyes "were austere and forbidding like caverns where a single flame burned under cold, gray vaults," but who "looked at her coldly, indifferently, astonished," noticing only that her eyes were strange and that "she wore a light suit and no brassiere, which fact he did not resent at all" (30— substantially the same in other versions). Kira "turned away, a little disappointed, although she did not know just what she had expected" (30). People do not always live up to their faces.

In omitting the Viking, Ayn Rand dispensed with one of the devices she had intended to use in dramatizing Kira's attraction to Leo. But she presents, with emphasis, the core of Kira's worship of this man. She asks him to take off his cap so that she can look at him. The next sentences in the published versions read: "Her face was a mirror for the beauty of his. Her face reflected no admiration, but an incredulous, reverent awe" (62). Her face is a mirror twice: it reflects his beauty, and it reflects her awe. His beauty—of soul as of face—allows her to experience awe, the ecstasy of hero-worship she craves; her awe allows him to experience his own beauty. This is the nature of the bond between them.

Most of the scene consists not of description, but of dialogue. The drafts show that Ayn Rand made major improvements from the first draft to the second. The first draft, for example, reads:

> "Teach me all you know. I want to go down, as far down as you can drag me."
>
> "I have a lot to teach you," she said simply, without a smile. (first draft, 31–32)

In the second draft, she replies instead (as she does in the published versions):

> "You know, you're very much afraid you can't be dragged down." (second draft, 70)

In the first draft, Kira does not question Leo's wish for self-degradation—but she does in the second.

When Leo asks Kira who led her into prostitution, she says: "A man." The first draft continues:

> "He disappointed you?"
> "No. Only for a short second."
> "He left you?"
> "No. He'll never leave me." (first draft, 33)

In the second draft, as in the published versions:

> "Was he worth that?"
> "Yes."
> "What an appetite!"
> "For what?"
> "For life."
> "If one loses that appetite, why still sit at the table?" (second draft, 70)

In both cases, she is in fact speaking of Leo. When she says, in the first draft, that he will never leave her, she does not have a reason for saying that. In the second draft, when she says he was worth it, she means that she is willing to pay the price for whatever the night will bring. Leo's follow-up in the second draft allows him to appreciate her appetite for life and allows her to ask him an important rhetorical question.

When the subject changes from Kira to Leo, the first draft reads as follows (Leo speaking first):

> "I know many people who don't like me."
> "That's good."
> "But I've never known a person who said it was good."
> "You look as though you should live on a desert island."
> "I was beginning to like you. Don't start giving me compliments. I've heard enough of them."
> "Sorry. It *was* a compliment. But very few people would think it so. What would you rather hear?"
> "I'd like to hear that I look like a Soviet clerk who sells soap and smiles at the customers."
> "No, you wouldn't like that. And you couldn't do it."
> "I couldn't. I have nothing to sell. But myself. And no one wants that."

"I might."

The scornful arc rose slowly. "Want to reverse our positions? Well, what price have you to offer?"

She raised her face to a ray of light.

"Look into my eyes," she said very seriously.

He bent close to her.

"What do you see there?" she asked.

[*written over the following lines*: "They're beautiful."

"I have no other mirror to offer you."]

"What do you see there?"

His face was so close she could feel his breath on her lips.

"My own reflection."

"That's the price I'll offer you."

His face did not come down. He moved away. Suddenly, he asked:

"*Are* you a . . . street woman?" (first draft, 34–37)

The second draft, which is substantially the same as the published versions, is much improved. Instead of apologizing for offering Leo a compliment, Kira surprises him with the true statement that he has in fact known one person who thought it was good not to be liked, and that that person is himself. The second draft also sets up more directly Leo's doubts that Kira is a prostitute. Instead of the mocking discussion of selling himself (which may have been intended as a foreshadowing of his ultimate condition, as a gigolo), instead of spoken words about Kira's function as Leo's mirror, the second draft has Leo saying that he is ordinary ("I'm just like any other man you've had in your bed—and like any you will have") and Kira stating: "You mean you would like to be like any other man. And you would like to think that there haven't been any other men—in my bed" (second draft, 72).

All versions end with Leo saying that he wants to see Kira again, but that they cannot be in touch. Instead, he says he will meet her again in a month, if he is still alive, and if he does not forget. Syntactically, the two subordinate clauses are of equal weight, in spite of the enormous difference in the nature of the implied possible obstacles. This sentence becomes a leitmotif of the relationship, in all versions. During the month of waiting (until October 28 in the first draft, and November 10 in the second draft and subsequent versions), Kira is described in all versions as thinking frequently of his statement (as she listens to the playing of the "Internationale" for the fifth anniversary of the revolution, in the first draft; as she reads her books, in the other versions).

The period of waiting is described most extensively in the first draft:

She never had any thought of him beyond the one that he existed. [*crossed-out*: and that thought was an end in itself.] She could not tell whether the torture of waiting was a delicious pain or a happiness too agonizing to bear; it was a sacred ordeal which she bore calmly, reverently; for every time her heart pounded suddenly, cruelly, without reason, she knew it was a pain tying her to him. (first draft, 68)

The second draft and the first published edition have only the first sentence: "She never had any thought of him beyond the one that he existed" (second draft, 87; 1936, 65). In the 1959 version, Ayn Rand adds the sentence: "But she found it hard to remember the existence of anything else" (67). For the second draft, Ayn Rand removed the references to Kira's heart pounding "cruelly, without reason" and to Kira's reverent relish for the torture and pain that tie her to Leo. It is possible that she removed the sentences because they are not clear. If, as stated, Kira did not know if the torture is pain or happiness, then why would she identify as pain the feeling of her heart pounding? The sentences express powerful emotion, but not in a clear way. Ayn Rand first restricted her description of Kira's thoughts about Leo to the fact that she thought of Leo only that he existed; she ultimately added the fact that Kira thought about Leo almost exclusively. Looking back on the novel, Ayn Rand stated that she had not portrayed Kira's feelings for Leo effectively. This paragraph may be an example. Nothing in Kira's feeling here pertains to Leo specifically. The final version speaks of the total absorption of love, but does not characterize either Leo or Kira.

Their second meeting, again heavily edited, leads, in all versions, to a plan for another meeting, and a modification of his signature statement to "I'll be alive—because I won't forget." The scene itself, in all versions, shows Leo's despair, his expressed wish not to see, not to aspire, and his belief that his relationship with Kira will rescue him from spiritual peril. Looking at the first draft in the light of later versions, we see how Ayn Rand tightened the dialogue (in the sentences spoken by both Leo and Kira), made Leo's despair more specific to his time and setting, included the element of Kira's career (and the hopeful ambition such a career implies), and removed explicit references to Leo's being "afraid" and in need of Kira's "help."

In the first draft, for example, Leo says to Kira:

> "How can you tell what I am? I might be many things, you know. I might be a fugitive murderer. I might be a spy of the G.P.U. I might be a hunted counter-revolutionary. I might be a bandit who'll kidnap you—and—"
> The look in his eyes stopped her breath.
> "Or," he continued with a light smile [indecipherable], "I might be worse than all that: I might be honorable and disappoint you."
> "It happens, that none of these makes any difference: I don't care who you are." (first draft, 77)

All later versions are substantially the same as the final version:

> "There are a few things you don't know about me."
> "I don't have to know." (82)

The revision is more economical, and avoids distracting or tantalizing the reader with questions about what Leo might be. The point is that Kira knows, by looking at him, what she needs to know.

In the first draft, Leo explains why he likes Kira:

"[*crossed-out*: I like you, because I like those who'd wear felt hats to a concert hall and an opera hat to plough a field. I like a street walker who can act like a decent woman and a decent woman who can act like a street walker.] I like you because you did something for a reason which no one dares, for the sole reason of wanting to do it."

"[*crossed-out*: That isn't unusual. I've always done it. What else can one do?] Haven't you always done what you wanted?"

"Just once: today."

"And before today?"

"Before today I've never wanted anything. Life isn't worth the desperate chance of a desire." (first draft, 78)

The later versions, which are very different from this, are substantially the same as the final version. In these versions, Leo tells her that he likes her, but instead of saying why, asks her what she is doing at the Technological Institute. After she tells him about the glass skyscraper and aluminum bridge she wants to build, he questions the value of effort and creation, and says that he has no desires except "One: to learn to desire something" (*We the Living*, 83).

Ayn Rand, in revising, first removed Leo's description of Kira as a mixture of different styles; such a sentence might have fit into a narrative description of Kira, but does not fit the context here. Leo has not actually seen Kira showing such a mixture of styles. Nor does it seem likely that he would explicitly identify the fact that she acted on a desire as something unique to Kira. And, although it makes sense that he might express a wish to learn to desire (as he does in the second draft and later versions), it does not make sense for him to say he has never wanted anything. The subtractions from the first draft are clearly improvements.

So are the additions. When Kira speaks of her skyscraper and bridge, he states that building might have been worthwhile in the past, and might be worthwhile again in the future. He admits the value of values, even though he despairs of the chance for values in his current world.

In the first draft, the difference between Leo and Kira is that being in Soviet Russia matters to Leo, whereas to Kira it is insignificant:

"We live in Soviet Russia, don't we, Kira? We'll get used to many things. If—we live."

"I suppose we live in Soviet Russia," said Kira, "or, perhaps, it's South Africa. I don't know. I've never bothered to find out."

He laughed softly.

"But won't it find you, child?"

"I don't know. I've never understood why people worry so much about such little things as what one eats, or what one wears, or where one lives." (first draft, 79–80)

The second draft and subsequent versions do not retain this part of the conversation. Although it is true that Kira is described, favorably, in terms of the trivial things that she does not allow herself to regard as important, in this novel the food and the clothing and the geographical location are literally and symbolically detrimental to her happiness—and indifference to them is not an entirely appropriate response.

The first draft continues:

"What's more important, Kira?"

"To sit here with you. To hear you say 'Kira.'"

He moved closer. She felt his breath on her cold cheek; and she bent her head a little—toward him.

"And will my little Kira always be as brave as that?" he asked very softly and very seriously. "Will she have enough to help someone who is very much afraid of the 'little things'?"

She whispered: "Yes, Leo."

"It's a difficult task, Kira."

She looked at him. Every line of his face was like a drink; and she felt intoxicated.

She got up. She stood between him and the light and the poster on the corner. She laughed.

"What's difficult, Leo? To stand between you and bread cards, and linseed oil, and proletarian brotherhood? I'll thank them for existing if I'm to be your shield."

He got up, too, and stood looking down at her.

"And I'd face them laughing like you do if I had the shield of a girl from a life as it is not being lived."

He heard how still she stood, as if his eyes were holding her on a leash. He smiled and released the reins.

"Just the thought of you," he said softly, "will be the shield—for a month." (first draft, 80–81)

In the later versions, there is no discussion of what is or isn't important, and, if there were, Kira would be able to speak of her work—and not only of Leo—as something important to her. In the later versions, Leo does not speak of being afraid, or of needing help. Instead, he expresses a wish for blindness, in order to avoid the suffering that sharp sight brings. "If only one could lose sight and come down, down to the level of those who never want it, never miss it" (*We the Living*, 83). When Kira tells him that he will not succeed in this quest for blindness, he says: "I don't know. It's funny. I found you because I thought you'd do it for me. Now I'm afraid you'll be the one to save me from it. But I don't know whether I'll thank you" (84). Whereas Kira's protective role in the first draft was to stand (symbolically and literally) between him and what she sees as unimportant (life in Soviet Russia), her role in the later versions is to protect him from a more serious and important threat, the quest for self-destruction.

The documentary evidence of Ayn Rand's work shows more revisions of the first two meetings of Leo and Kira than of any other episodes in the novel involving Leo. The revisions show an attempt to give him more stature and to remove less-than-successful passages conveying Kira's feelings. Although Ayn Rand judged him as morally superior to Andrei, she did not ultimately allot as much space to his characterization as she did to Andrei's (which will be discussed presently). Within the novel, he is less an individual to be examined in his own right, than a value held by Kira. From his expressed thoughts at the time of the second meeting (in either draft), the likely outcome for him is clear: for him to depend on Kira to shield him is a losing proposition. For Kira, nonetheless, the relationship is a significant value. Leo—for reasons that the novel does not fully dramatize—represents the spirit of the Viking, the spirit of life itself. Hence, as she walks through the snow to her unconquered death, she calls to him, the "Leo that should have been," and she wears her mother's wedding dress as she imagines a union with the man who should have been her mate. He fulfills this function in the novel in spite of the fact that Ayn Rand did not develop (or significantly revise) his characterization.

The revisions in his characterization, accordingly, pertain to his romantic encounters with Kira and her thoughts about him. The first draft contained more details suggesting pain. For example, the first draft depiction of their first embrace reads: "Her shoulders creaked when he bent her backwards and his kiss was a wound" (first draft, 133). The second draft removes the creaking shoulders: "His kiss felt like a wound" (second draft, 128). The first-draft depiction of another kiss, in a sentence removed for the second draft, reads: "His mouth bit into hers as if he were to suck the blood of her lips" (first draft, 188).

The account in the first draft of their first night together includes the following:

> He sat on the bed and held her across his lap. She did not know how long they sat thus, nor what they said. She remembered he repeated: "We are free . . . free . . . free. . . ." and when he did not say it, the waves repeated it lashing the creaking boards. She wondered if it really hurt when she bit his lips.
>
> His breath flowed under her collar; where it stopped her blood picked it up and carried it further. When his hand followed his breath—she was not startled.

When he tore off her blouse and the shirt strap buttoned on her shoulders, she lay back and watched his dark hair at her throat.

She hissed: "Take off your sweater."

[*crossed-out*: Her voice was harsh; her face was grim, without a smile, like his.] She heard her heart beating against his skin. His skin smelt like warm milk. She felt her breath at his nostrils and parted her lips slowly, as in a snarl. When his hand rose from the top of her black stockings, [*crossed-out*: she lay very still so that his fingers would find the way] nothing moved in her but her heart against his, even though his fingers hurt a little.

[*The intervening section, in which he removes her underwear, is similar in all versions. The scene ends.*]

She lay very still, as he had left her. [*crossed-out*: He had pushed her legs apart and she did not draw them together.]

His legs felt like a warm liquid against hers, [*crossed-out*: and she wondered whether they had taken their skin off, too. Then she stopped wondering. There is no line between pain and ecstasy.] Her hair fell over the edge of the bed, and she remembered that his name had three letters. (first draft, 202–4)

The revisions made directly on the first draft show Ayn Rand's removal of the harshness and grimness in Kira and the explicit reference to a painful ecstasy, as well as some physical details. For the second draft, Ayn Rand removed even more, e.g., Leo does not hold Kira on his lap, Kira does not order Leo to take off his sweater, his skin does not smell like warm milk.

In revising this sexual scene from the 1936 edition for the 1959, Ayn Rand continued the same editing trend: she removed additional physical details,[16] and, in the aftermath of this scene, she removed a reference to pain. In the 1936 edition: "In her body there still was a pain which held him close to her" (1936, 141). In the 1959 edition, pain is not the price of intimacy: "Her body still felt as if it were holding him close to her" (127).

A similar process of progressive editing can be seen in the description of Kira's worship of Leo later in the novel, in chapter 7 of part II. In all versions, Kira sees Leo after a shower, naked from the waist up, in "one of the rare moments when he looked what he could have been." In all versions, he approaches her with "contemptuous tenderness in his movement, and a command, and hunger; he was not a lover, but a slave owner." After this phrase, in the first and second drafts:

she could feel a whip in his fingers; and the feeling it gave her was more than human ecstasy. Under his hands, she felt as if she were less than the building would have been to her had she stood, ruling and imperious, on the scaffolding; she wanted to be crushed; she wished she were lying still under a real whip in his hands. (first draft, 223g–223h; second draft 494–95)

In the 1936 version, the reference to "more than human ecstasy" is gone, as is the less-than-clear image of her feeling "less than the building": "she could feel a whip in his fingers. She wanted to be crushed; she wished she were lying still under a real whip in his hands" (1936, 398). The 1959 edition removes the whip entirely, while retaining the point, common to all versions, that Leo is "the only motive she needed," i.e., that he represents the spirit of the Viking, a life that is a reason unto itself, and her worship of him means loyalty to her own life.

From her first thoughts about this novel, Ayn Rand had imagined its climax: Andrei coming to arrest Leo and discovering Kira's dresses in his apartment. In the arrest scene, Ayn Rand originally intended to describe both men in approximately equal detail, to stress the contrast between Leo's defiant confidence and Andrei's stunned grimness. In all versions, Leo plays the host and speaks with wit and poise; in all versions, Andrei is stern and expressionless. In the first draft:

> Leo walked leisurely to the mirror, adjusted his tie, straightened his hair, with the meticulous precision of a man of the world dressing for an important social engagement. [*crossed-out*: He pressed a few drops of eau-de-cologne into his handkerchief and folded it neatly in his breast pocket. Then he put on his hat and overcoat.]
>
> Andrei stood waiting [*crossed-out*: without a movement. His face was like that of a mummy that could no longer wear an expression and his skin looked like death]. (first draft, 432–33)

Ayn Rand, for the second draft (620) and the 1936 version (490), changed the "eau-de-cologne" to "toilet water"; for the 1959 version, she removed the scent entirely and added a sentence—"His fingers were not trembling any longer" (399)—to show his self-control at this point, as opposed to the slight perturbation he observes in himself at an earlier moment: "He noticed that his fingers were trembling" (399, and all earlier versions as well). This scene marks the last point in the novel in which we see the Leo Kira loves. After his stay in jail, his demeanor is different. When he returns home, he asks for clean underwear and telephones Tonia Platoshkina; regarding Kira, he does no more over the next two weeks than kiss her violently, with effort. After this scene, his eyes are "dead," and the pull of memory—"If you're still alive, and if you don't forget"—is the convulsive kicking of a dead insect. But in this scene, the last glimpse of Leo as hero, Ayn Rand originally intended to contrast him with Andrei. She changed her mind, and wrote more about Leo and less about Andrei. Along with improving the description, she gave Leo the center of the stage for his farewell to Kira, and, in essence, to his best self.

The contrasts between the two men, however, are an important element in the novel. As Kira's lover, Andrei represents a contrast—in her romantic response—to Leo; as Kira's interlocutor, Andrei represents—in his ideas—a contrast to Kira herself.

Regarding Andrei's romantic relationship with Kira, Ayn Rand contrasts Kira's feeling for him with her immediate, unquestioned, and unending love for Leo. Kira does not realize that Andrei is romantically interested in her until he avows his passion, and she never returns his love. A change in the introduction of Andrei shows Ayn Rand taking care, in this context, to remove the implication that Kira finds Andrei attractive.

In the first draft, Andrei accidentally walks into the room where Professor Leskov is lecturing; he sees Kira, and remains. When she sees Andrei, she observes his hand, the strength of which she finds attractive; the hands of Leskov, too, are described as evidence of a noble spirit.

> A strong hand, Kira thought, the kind of hand that a man likes to see on a gun and a woman on. . . .
> Professor Leskov's hands were pale and freckled. He waved them in a sweeping gesture as he shouted into his audience, as a challenge, of the marble glory of ancient gods. (first draft, 94)

In this scene, Kira is aware of Andrei as a man, and she likes what she sees of him. In the second draft and in later versions of this scene, Kira's response to Andrei is less personal. Seeing his hand, she observes that it seems "all bones, skin and nerves," but she does not think of where a woman would want to see that hand, and she makes no mental connection between his hand and the hands of a lecturer she admires. In editing the scene, Ayn Rand removed the suggestion that Andrei's hand made Kira think of a caress.

In the first-draft version of their evening at the theatre, Ayn Rand had Kira implicitly disavow any attraction to Andrei:

> The voices in the dark theater sang triumphantly of a life where joy and sorrow were both only beauty. Kira closed her eyes. Then she could see other eyes looking into hers and feel the kiss in her palm. She thought, once, that she was not fair to Andrei. But not once did she think she was being disloyal to the man for whom she was counting the minutes and hours by being here with Andrei. [*crossed-out*: Her loyalty to the man for whom she was counting the minutes and hours was like death: beyond question.] (first draft, 125–26)

This paragraph appears in no other versions. What it says, though, is consistent with the other versions: Kira loves Leo first and alone, and, although she recognizes Andrei's romantic interest in her, she has no such response to him. The probable reason for removing the paragraph is that, with no evidence anywhere of Kira's attraction to Andrei, there was no need to explain that point.

Kira discovers important facts about Andrei's feelings for her twice, both times in scenes of great emotional power, substantially the same in all versions. When Kira hears Andrei's confession of passion, she learns that he desires her desperately, and she realizes that becoming his lover would allow her to obtain the money she needs to save Leo's life. In the first draft, Ayn Rand wrote, then crossed out, a description of Kira's attitude at that moment: "against the wall, with the pride and defiance and last despair of facing a firing squad" (first draft, 496). The description could have been used in a contrast with Leo's poise upon his arrest, or with Andrei's attitude at the time of his suicide, and pride, defiance, and despair convey well the elements of Kira's emotional situation. But the sentence, as written, could imply that Andrei himself is the firing squad, and neither Kira nor the novel regards him that way. Andrei is making no claims, is asking for nothing. Kira initiates their sexual relationship. This scene, like the later scene in which Kira comes to Andrei's room after Leo's arrest, is sympathetic to Andrei, and links him with Kira.

When Andrei initially tells Kira he desires her, she says, in all versions, "I didn't know," and, when Kira ultimately tells Andrei she sold herself to him to save the life of the man she loves, he says, in all versions, "I didn't know." He tells her that he admires what she has done and would have done the same for the woman he loved, for her; then she—again, and like him—knows something that she didn't know, "something she had seen suddenly, clearly, fully for the first time" (*We the Living*, 405). The image of the firing squad does not fit Andrei—not, at any rate, in his relation with Kira.

In all versions, Ayn Rand shows positive qualities of Andrei in his relationship with Kira, who comes increasingly to respect him, but Kira never considers leaving Leo for Andrei. The only hint at any point in any version that Andrei constitutes any temptation to Kira occurs in the 1959 version of the novel. On the night Kira goes to the movies with Andrei, when his investigation of Leo is underway:

> Kira had made a date with Andrei. But when she left the tramway and walked through the dark streets to the palace garden, she noticed her feet slowing down of their own will, her body tense, unyielding, fighting her, as if she were walking forward against a strong wind. It was as if her body remembered that which she was trying to forget: the night before, a night such as her first one in the gray and silver room she had shared with Leo for over three years. Her body felt pure and hallowed; her feet were slowing down to retard her progress toward that which seemed a sacrilege because she did desire it and did not wish to desire it tonight. (381)

In the 1936 edition (as in the drafts), the passage includes the phrase "by the touch of hands and lips that had been eager and hungry and young again" (which is omitted in the 1959 edition) and ends early with "seemed a sacrilege" (1936, 368). In both cases, she sees her encounter with Andrei as a sacrilege, by contrast with her passionate night with Leo; the 1959 edition, however, points out that the encounter with Andrei constitutes a sacrilege not—as one might have assumed from the 1936 edition—because a loveless, purchased encounter is always a betrayal of romantic passion, but because her own desire for Andrei (a desire that is apparently not a new experience for her) seems to her—tonight, though not at other times—to desecrate her love for Leo. What this passage appears to be implying is that Kira has come not only to respect Andrei, but to desire him, even though her feeling for Leo is of a different and unquestioned order.

Although Ayn Rand's revisions in the romantic relationship of Kira and Andrei show her omitting suggestions of Kira's attraction to Andrei, she chose to include such a suggestion in the final version of the novel. The exception, however, shows the force of the rule. Kira resists the attraction, and implicitly affirms instead her love for Leo. Even when Kira is drawn to Andrei, he has no chance against Leo—and this fact is immensely significant, in the novel, as a device to characterize and emphasize the spiritual bond between Kira and Leo, the man with the Viking's face, the man who always meant to her, whatever his fears and self-betrayals, the spirit of reverence for life.

The bulk of Ayn Rand's revisions regarding Andrei, however, pertain to his philosophical discussions with Kira. These conversations, which begin as the duels of opponents and continue as mutual explorations, encompass the most explicit consideration of ideas in the novel. In the drafts, and from the first to the second edition, Ayn Rand edited them heavily, for style as well as content. Her task here was to show a conflict, but it is not a conflict between the entirely correct ideas of Kira and the entirely incorrect ideas of Andrei, particularly since the ostensible topic of conversation is often politics, a subject in which Kira disclaims interest and, moreover, one on which Ayn Rand, during the writing of the novel, had not fully developed her own ideas.

Although Andrei begins as a spokesperson for the Soviet state, Kira is not a spokesperson for Ayn Rand's complete response to it. Kira, as we shall see, opposes the Soviet state on the grounds of its collectivism (vs. individualism), but without addressing the issue of physical force. Her remarks, therefore, are sometimes philosophically incomplete, or confusing in implications. In dramatic context, however, Kira's speeches, often in direct response and contrast to Andrei's, show her attempting to identify what separates them, along with the values—courage, passion, and dedication—that draw them together. (Kira, after all, does not engage in extensive ideological debate with Victor Dunaev or with Comrade Sonia; they are not worth her time.) In editing, Ayn Rand worked to make Kira's statements clearer without making them indicative of an understanding beyond Kira's explicit grasp. In examining the drafts, I noticed not only changes from the first to the second, but additional changes, not marked on the manuscripts, between the second draft and the first published edition (which leads me to assume that some of Ayn Rand's work was done on pages now lost to us).

Although all of their conversations show Andrei learning from Kira, in some way, the value of life, I will focus here mainly on Ayn Rand's revisions of two of these discussions, and then on the editing of Andrei's speech to the Party Club, in which he quotes Kira directly and then expands upon and explains what he has learned.

The first draft of Kira's first conversation with Andrei includes the following:

> "Six years ago," said Kira, "I could have given you a ride in father's carriage."
> "Six years ago," said Comrade Taganov, "you'd have had to drive for me to the Putilovsky factory."
> "You've traveled fast and a long way."
> He shrugged lightly. "Oh, night work. Plenty of candles and very little of sleep."
> "And plenty of ambition?"
> "No. Hatred."
> "That takes courage. Any stops in your way?"
> "Yes. The Red Army. Do you object to that?"
> "No. Not as long as you haven't worked for the Cheka."
> "I have worked in the Cheka."
> Her arm did not leave his. She said only: "I won't say that that takes courage."
> She expected a speech of wrathful indignation. He answered very simply:
> "Don't you really think that it does? Anyone can sacrifice his own life for an idea. How many know the devotion that makes one capable of sacrificing other lives?"
> He expected a horrified protest. She answered calmly. "You're right. I never thought of that." (first draft, 99–100)

Kira appears to admire Andrei's dedication, and, although she initially objects to the Cheka, she admits that sacrificing other lives requires devotion, and she does not excoriate him. Note that Ayn Rand describes them as surprising each other, Andrei surprising Kira with his lack of defensiveness, Kira surprising Andrei with her understanding that killing people can be evidence of high devotion. After some discussion of their studies, there follows a two-page insert, which continues the subject of the Cheka and explains why Kira accepts Andrei's involvement. She objects to collectivism because it glorifies the weak.

She said:

> "I never mind the means. It's the end."
> "Too strong for you?"
> "No. Too weak."
> He looked at her again, calm, inquisitive. She explained: "I don't like the unfinished, the hesitant, the humble."
> "Nor the meek, nor the [*crossed-out*: lame in spirit] ailing [?]," he agreed.

"The hardest of metals is the most precious. Why not be as just to men?"
"The hardest and highest shall rule the world."
"For their own sake."
"No—for the collective."
"Of the weak and the ailing [?]."
"No. A collective raised by its leaders—and the only thing that can raise leaders."
"There's no such thing as a collective. There are only great numbers of small wrongs."
"There is a spirit in numbers."
"I don't believe in any spirits."
"I don't either—in that sense."
[*crossed-out*: They looked at each other. It seemed that the words they thrust at each other were hooks drawing them closer together.
He said:
"Religion is like a strong girdle. You put it on for support and pretty soon you discover that your muscles have become too flabby to function alone."
"I believe in strong muscles."
"And strong nerves."] (Insert to first draft, 101)

The cancelled section of the insert presents an opposition to religion (because it weakens people) as something they have in common. There follows a crossed-out section in which Andrei expresses his dedication to what he sees as a glorious mission, and Kira replies that joy is the enemy of his mission.

[*crossed-out*: She said: "There's one thing I don't like about the University: this bridge you have to cross. It's so long."
"I'll have to cross it tonight," he said cheerfully, "meeting of the Communist cell."
"Don't you ever get tired?"
"I haven't time to get tired. I'm taking two courses—history and law. Then, there's the Party work."
"What do you have for nerves?"
"Cat guts, I think. You see, we can't lose time. We're living at a period that's like a world's dawn. And the rays of the sun that's rising project, on a gigantic radius, our every second into centuries of accomplishments for the generations to come."
"Where did you read that?"
"I didn't. You may—someday."] (first draft, 101)

As they walk, they see a poster for a production of *Rigoletto*.

[*crossed-out*: "That," she pointed at the blue letters of the poster, "is your worst enemy."
"Why?"

"Music. Lights. Laughter. A butterfly against your ponderous machine-guns."

"Certainly. A world without sweat and sighs, a world of joy in every muscle and every breath. . . ."

"Isn't that the worst challenge to your grim proletarian ideas?"

"You love life, don't you? And you hate Communism because of it?"

"Yes."

"Well, I love it, too. And I serve Communism because of it—to bring life down to pavements within everyone's reach."

"You might spill it—on the way down."

"Not if one's hand is steady."] (first draft, 103–4)

We can see in this first-draft scene some key elements. Andrei is portrayed as admirable in his dedication. Ayn Rand distinguishes between the means Kira accepts (i.e., the Cheka) and the goal she cannot accept (i.e., serving the weak); she points out that Andrei expects Kira to be critical of the means, but that Kira criticizes the end instead. Both Kira and Andrei oppose religion, because it fosters weakness. Kira states that joy (as expressed in music) is the worst enemy of the Soviet state. Andrei states that they both love life, and that he will bring life to all. Kira warns him that he may threaten the spirit of life. In later versions of the scene, Ayn Rand improves her treatment of these elements. She reserves for later occasions the consideration of religion and music, and concentrates on three matters: Andrei's dedication, the unacceptable end versus the acceptable means, and the love of life.

In the second draft, Andrei's dedication is presented through quick questions-and-responses, leading up to an important issue (the contrast between duty and desire) that is only implicit in the first draft.

"Do you like to skate, comrade Taganov?"

"I never have. Never had the time."

"Do you like to ski?"

"Never had the time."

"Do you like to swim?"

"Yes. I've done that once."

"Once? In your whole life?"

"Yes. In the whole of it."

"I think it must be horrible to do nothing but what you have to do."

"Yes. It must be horrible. I've always done only what I wanted to do." (second draft, 111)

In the 1936 edition, in the course of a similar—but more relaxed— conversation, Kira leads Andrei to explain why he views his dedication as a personal matter:

"I thought that Communists never did anything except what they had to do; that they never believed in doing anything but what they had to do."

"That's strange," he smiled. "I must be a very poor Communist. I've always done only what I wanted to do."

"Your revolutionary duty?"

"There is no such thing as duty. If you know a thing is right, you want to do it. If you don't want to do it—it isn't right. If it's right and you don't want to do it—you don't know what right is—and you're not a man."

"Haven't you ever wanted a thing for no reason of right or wrong, for no reason at all, save one: that you wanted it?"[17]

"Certainly. That's always been my only reason. I've never wanted things unless they could help my cause. For, you see, it is my cause."

"And your cause is to deny yourself for the sake of millions?"

"No. To bring the millions up to where I want them—for my sake." (1936, 92)

This passage, which does not appear in either of the existing drafts, shows that Andrei's commitment is based on a cause he considers essentially personal. The discussion of doing what one wants uses language Ayn Rand had, in the drafts, given to Leo to describe what he admires about Kira (on the evening they first meet).

The next point is the issue of means and ends. In both the second draft and the first edition, this discussion begins with a question from Kira: "And when you think you're right, you do it at any price?" The second draft continues:

"I know what you're going to say. You're going to say, as so many of our enemies do, that you admire our ideals, but loathe our methods."

"I loathe your ideals. I admire your methods. I don't know, however, whether I'd include blood in my methods."

"Why not? Anyone can sacrifice his own life for an idea. How many know the devotion that makes you capable of sacrificing other lives?"

She looked at him. She said slowly, simply:

"I've never thought of that. Perhaps you're right."

"Why do you loathe our aim?"

"Because I don't know a worse injustice than justice for all. Because I loathe men."

"I'm glad. So do I."

"But then . . ." (second draft, 112)

Contrasting this version with the first draft, we see that Ayn Rand allows Kira to say a bit more about why she objects to the aim, that is, the "injustice" of "justice for all" (rather than the point that the aim is to serve the weak); as readers of later versions of this scene, we recognize that Ayn Rand has not yet given Kira the words to express what is wrong with the Soviet state. Instead, in the second draft (as in the first), Ayn Rand concentrates on Kira's acceptance—her admiring acceptance—of the methods. This time, the

Cheka appears only implicitly, and Kira expresses reservations about the "blood," leaving unexpressed what exactly she admires about the methods. The 1936 edition begins with a slightly expanded version of this passage:

> "I loathe your ideals. I admire your methods. If one believes one's right, one shouldn't wait to convince millions of fools, one might just as well force them. I don't know, however, whether I'd include blood in my methods." (1936, 92–93)

We note the new sentence: Kira approves of forcing fools to go along with what one believes to be right. What does she mean by "force"? Given that she (again in this version) expresses reservations about "blood," it appears that "force" might mean something other than physical force. But since "force" is presented as an alternative to "convince," it is hard to know what, other than physical force, it could mean. The new sentence appears to be part of Ayn Rand's continuing effort to sharpen Kira's condemnation of the end by contrasting this reaction with her enthusiasm for the means; the new sentence, however, is confusing (and was removed for the 1959 edition). The exchange continues, much as in the second draft:

> "Why not? Anyone can sacrifice his own life for an idea. How many know the devotion that makes you capable of sacrificing other lives? Horrible, isn't it?"
> "Not at all. Admirable. If you're right. But—are you right?"
> "Why do you loathe our ideals?" (1936, 93)

At this point, instead of simply saying that the aim is to serve weakness (as in the first draft) or that the worst injustice is justice for all (as in the second draft), Kira expresses herself in many powerful paragraphs that do not appear in either draft. She attacks the claim that man must live for the state. She states that "the best of us" live for our own sake, for something private and inviolable, "something in us which must not be touched by any state, by any collective, by any number of millions" (1936, 93). Eventually, too, she says that the worst injustice is justice for all, by which she appears to mean that the state attempts to "make people equal" in defiance of the reality that they are not the same. Ayn Rand later edited these paragraphs further, removing for the 1959 edition (89–90) the confusing implication that the millions should be sacrificed for the few (which, to judge from the pattern, is Kira's inversion of the expected statement, and is not offered as her considered formulation of her own position). Ayn Rand also removed the sentence about the injustice of justice for all; as she commented in response to a letter from Nathan Blumenthal (later Nathaniel Branden), it "is a bad sentence when taken out of context."[18] These eloquent paragraphs do not appear in the drafts at all—or at any rate not in the drafts we have.

I'll conclude the consideration of Ayn Rand's editing of Andrei by looking at his speech to the Party Club. He begins with a quotation from Kira's speech to him (after he learns of her relationship with Leo): "you've locked us airtight, airtight till the blood vessels of our spirits burst!" He goes on, though, to address the subject he and Kira had considered in their very first conversation, the love of life. Having confronted what he himself has done to the woman he loved, and having understood that his cause has essentially done to the spirit of life what he has done to Kira, he grasps at last that the ideal she loathed is indeed loathsome.

In the first and second drafts (the second is shorter and tighter, but they are substantially the same), Andrei considers the value of the individual, the value of life:

> We came as a solemn army to bring a new life to men. . . . We thought that everything that breathed could live. Can it? And aren't those who can live, aren't they too precious to be touched in the name of any cause? We've taken thousands of lives. In those thousands—were there three that could have lived? [*crossed-out*: There aren't many of them and so they don't count with us. But should they count? Or are the cobblestones all that should count? Is any future worth any manure?] Is any battle worth the life of one good soldier? What cause is worth those who fight for it? And aren't those who can fight, aren't they the cause itself and not the means? (first draft, 457, ellipses added)

He then states that the Soviet state has acted to destroy life, and he points out that collectivism is the enemy of life:

> Listen, you consecrated warriors of a new life! Are we sure we know what we are doing? In the name of life—what are we doing to life? We're driving men with the bleeding whip through the furthermost of all agonies to lash them into the perfection of a new humanity. But what of that new humanity? Do we want the crippled, creeping, crawling, meek, hand-licking, broken monstrosities we'll create, the new freaks breathing a new gas? Are we not castrating life in order to perpetuate it? [*crossed-out*: What is life? Does a man live when another man stands by his side? When two men stand by his side? When ten men surround him? When a million men march and his feet shuffle after theirs? Or is it something in him alone that lives, something that is his, and that cannot be shared and should not be shared? Haven't we taken something so delicate and sacred that one should handle it only with a surgeon's [glove?] and torn it out with bare fingers with dirty fingernails bitten off.] (first draft, 458)

Finally, he attacks the goal itself (as Kira had attacked it, in their first conversation).

> Anything is permitted to us if we're right. [*crossed-out*: We're right if our aim is right] But our aim? Our aim, comrades? What are we doing? Do we want to feed a starved humanity in order to let it live? Or do we want to strangle its life in order to feed it?" (first draft, 459)

These are remarkable paragraphs—and they would be impressive from the pen of any writer. They show what Andrei has learned from the full measure of his experience with Kira. But these paragraphs were not good enough for Ayn Rand. In the 1936 edition, we see (in addition to edited versions of these paragraphs) new statements, reminiscent of those in the 1936-edition version of his first conversation with Kira, about the private, reverent sacredness of the individual's life. In the first edition, Andrei says:

> No one can tell men what they must live for. No one can take that right if he doesn't want to face a monster, a horror which is not for human eyes to bear. Because, you see, there are things in men, in the best of us, which are above all states, above all collectives, things too precious, too sacred, things which no outside hand should dare to touch. . . . Every honest man lives for himself. . . . You cannot change it because that's the way man is born, alone, complete, an end in himself. You cannot change it any more than you can cause men to be born with one eye instead of two, with three legs or two hearts. No laws, no books, no G.P.U. will ever grow an extra nose on a human face. No Party will ever kill that thing in men which knows how to say 'I.' (1936, 501, ellipses added)

In the paragraphs that appear in the 1936 edition (and which do not appear in the drafts), Andrei identifies the principle of human life: man is an end in himself. In the person of Andrei, Ayn Rand expressed—defiantly, and in the face of the enemy—a perspective on the theme of individualism that was key to the novels that were immediately to follow: *Anthem* and *The Fountainhead.*

But Andrei's speech in the 1936 edition—vastly improved from the drafts—still had room for improvement. In the 1959 edition, the paragraph quoted above reads as follows:

> No one can tell men what they must live for. No one can take that right—because there are things in men, in the best of us, which are above all states, above all collectives! Do you ask: what things? Man's mind and his values. . . . No laws, no Party, no G.P.U. will ever kill that thing in man which knows how to say 'I.' You cannot enslave man's mind, you can only destroy it. (408, ellipses added)

Ayn Rand revised Andrei's speech one more time, not long after completing *Atlas Shrugged* (1957), the novel that was the ultimate answer, on the deepest level, to the enslavement of the human mind. And, as one more element of the revision, she removed the sort of statement about the ends justifying the means ("We are right if our aim is right," "Anything is permitted to us if our aim is right") that had survived the first draft, the second draft, and the 1936 edition.

Examining the progressive improvements in *We the Living* shows Ayn Rand, in her first novel, unwavering in her commitment to achieve emotional power and philosophical clarity. As Kira lived her life in the spirit of the Viking, knowing always that life was a reason unto itself, so Ayn Rand wrote, and rewrote, her novel in loyalty to her noble theme and to the characters she had invented to dramatize it. She was to write in *Atlas Shrugged*: "To hold an unchanging youth is to reach, at the end, the vision with which one started."[19] In *We the Living*, Ayn Rand wrote her book until it was entirely hers. And now, of course, it is ours as well.

NOTES

1. Michael S. Berliner, ed., *Letters of Ayn Rand* (New York: Dutton, 1995), 23.

2. Berliner, *Letters*, 19.

3. Berliner, *Letters*, 18.

4. The drafts of *The Fountainhead*, by contrast, consist of a nearly complete, handwritten first draft (missing only one chapter); a typed second draft beginning in part 2, chapter 7, and continuing to the end; two sets of 1943 galleys; and a set of 1968 galleys. For a discussion of some aspects of the revisions in those drafts, see Shoshana Milgram, "Artist at Work: Ayn Rand's Drafts of *The Fountainhead*," *The Intellectual Activist* 15, nos. 8–9 (August–September 2001).

For the *We the Living* material, each reference to the first draft and to the second draft will be followed by "first draft" and "second draft" respectively, plus the page number(s). The "Airtight Notebook" is not paginated or dated. "1936" plus page number(s) refers to the first published edition of *We the Living* (New York: Macmillan, 1936); and, following the format for chapters in this collection, page numbers on their own refer to the 1959 revised edition of *We the Living*, as found in its currently most accessible form: the 1996 sixtieth anniversary paperback edition. However, in a few cases, it was necessary to give " *We the Living*" followed by page number(s), to make clear that I refer to this paperback edition, and not to one of the drafts.

The "Airtight Notebook" is located at the Ayn Rand Archives. The drafts are located at the Library of Congress, though the Ayn Rand Archives have copies of these drafts in bound volumes (which I consulted).

5. David Harriman, ed., *Journals of Ayn Rand* (New York: Dutton, 1997), 60–62.

6. Leonard Peikoff, ed., *The Early Ayn Rand: A Selection from Her Unpublished Fiction* (New York: New American Library, 1984; Signet paperback edition, 1986), 195–200.

7. Harriman, *Journals*, 61.

8. Peikoff, *Early Ayn Rand*, 194.

9. Page 514 cuts off at this point, and page 515 is omitted. The manuscript continues with page 516.

10. See Ayn Rand, *The Art of Fiction: A Guide for Writers and Readers*, Tore Boeckmann, ed. (New York: Plume, 2000), 97.

11. Harriman, *Journals*, 89.

12. Ayn Rand, *The Romantic Manifesto: A Philosophy of Literature*, revised edition (New York: Signet, 1975), 72.

13. For more on Kira's laughter, see Robert Mayhew, "Kira Argounova Laughed: Humor and Joy in *We the Living*," in the present volume.

14. Ayn Rand, *The Fountainhead* (New York: Bobbs-Merrill, 1943; Signet fiftieth anniversary paperback edition, 1993), 15.

15. Peikoff, *Early Ayn Rand*, 203.

16. As discussed in Robert Mayhew, " *We the Living*: '36 & '59," in the present volume, pp. 201–203.

17. The 1959 version omits "of right or wrong, for no reason at all" (89).

18. Berliner, *Letters*, 463.

19. Ayn Rand, *Atlas Shrugged* (New York: Random House, 1957; Signet thirty-fifth anniversary paperback edition, 1992), 669.

2

Parallel Lives: Models and Inspirations for Characters in *We the Living*

Scott McConnell

Ayn Rand wrote in her foreword to *We the Living*: " *We the Living* is as near to an autobiography as I will ever write. It is not an autobiography in the literal, but only the intellectual sense. The plot is invented, the background is not" (xvii). Ayn Rand was born Alisa Rosenbaum in St. Petersburg, Russia, in 1905, and lived there until 1926, living under the Soviets for more than eight years. Since one of her purposes in writing *We the Living* was to tell the world the truth about Soviet life, it was natural that she would use events and ideas from her own life and from the lives of people she knew.

In fact, one of the reasons she wrote *We the Living* as her first novel was that it would not require any research, because she knew life in Russia so well. But Ayn Rand was not a journalist or historian merely recording life under the Soviets. She was a fiction writer who used her experiences and observations as background only, as a means to an end: to dramatize her theme, characters, and completely invented plot situation. This chapter focuses on the ways in which some of the characters of *We The Living* were inspired by or modeled on actual people and names in Russia. The first and most significant of these models is Kira Argounova's "twin."

KIRA ARGOUNOVA AND AYN RAND

Kira is the heroine and protagonist of *We the Living*, but "Kira" also wrote the novel. In the book's introduction, Ayn Rand writes: "The specific events of Kira's life were not mine; her ideas, her convictions, her values were and are" (xvii). Although the events of Kira's life—and especially those pertaining to the novel's main conflict—were generally not based on Ayn Rand's own life, the author of *We the Living* did draw upon her own life and character in creating Kira.

Alisa and Kira are twins in spirit, especially in their attitude to life. Both passionately believe in the importance and great possibilities of their lives. While in prison, Irina Dunaeva tells Kira (her cousin) about her life: "they don't know what it means, that treasure of mine, and there's something about it that they should understand" (350). In the novel's foreword, Ayn Rand notes that at Irina's age (eighteen) she did not know much more about this question than did Irina, but adds that later she did complete her answer in *Atlas Shrugged*, where she dramatized what she then called the "meaning of the men who value their own lives and of the men who don't" (xiv). Kira and Alisa did value their own lives—they were among "the living" referred to in the novel's title—as Kira says when addressing Andrei: "God—whatever anyone chooses to call God—is one's highest conception of the highest possible. And whoever places his highest conception above his own possibility thinks very little of himself and his life. . . . You see, you and I, we believe in life" (117).

Alisa and Kira's prolife convictions are also found in their anticommunism. In an interview in the early 1960s, Ayn Rand recalled that at the age of twelve, "I realized what's wrong with the Russian revolution, it was the communists' principle of living for the state."[1] Kira expresses to Andrei her reason for loathing communism this way:

> For one reason, mainly, chiefly and eternally, no matter how much your Party promises to accomplish, no matter what paradise it plans to bring mankind. Whatever your other claims may be, there's one you can't avoid, one that will rise to the surface as a deadly poison to turn your paradise into the most unspeakable of all hells: your claim that man must live for the state (89).

Because Alisa and Kira shared so many ideas, values and attitudes, there are strong similarities in their personalities. Both were passionate man worshippers (one specifically in regard to Leo, the other in regard to his real life counterpart—more on him shortly), and both were eager to find man at his best (whether loving engineering and building or the United States). Both desired to create (one, buildings and bridges, the other, novels). Both were valuers who desired to experience great art (foreign movies and operetta). Neither could surrender to the conditions surrounding them. Both lived and loved in extremes; "all or nothing" could have been their anthem. Both approached life fully focused, whether trying to understand the man they loved or the Russian Revolution. Both had a passionate sense of justice regarding the evil they saw around them, speaking out against communism, in student lecture halls or to family. Both expressed scathing irony toward fools and cowards (if they noticed them), such as the Russian masses or corrupt Party toadies. Both yearned and fought to be free, in spirit and in body, which could only mean to go "abroad." Both Kira and Alisa loved their lives.

The list of Kira and Alisa's value similarities could run pages, but to clarify the point, I offer two examples. First, their attitude to work. When Kira is looking at a building under construction, she thinks of "the only work she wanted." Kira is suffocating, denied the freedom to pursue her career as an engineer and builder, her reason for being. For Kira and Alisa the only way to achieve this was "Some day . . . Abroad" (324). Alisa was equally passionate toward her work, creating fiction. She kept a journal of her ideas, wrote scenarios, began her first novel and carried in her head to America the ideas for seventeen scenarios, novels and plays. She was later to write two hymns to work, *The Fountainhead* and *Atlas Shrugged.*

The second example concerns art and aesthetics: Kira and Leo are watching the operetta *Die Bajadere.* Ayn Rand wrote, "They sat, solemn, erect, reverent as at a church service. . . . It was very gay nonsense. It was like a glance straight through the snow and the flags, through the border, into the heart of that other world . . . a promise that existed somewhere, that was, that could be" (208). Years afterwards, Ayn Rand described how operetta (and later movies) were the "oxygen" from abroad that kept her soul from suffocating in Soviet Russia.[2]

Reading Kira's story is a first-hand view of the young Ayn Rand. And who to better express this view than Ayn Rand, who could have been describing herself when writing about Kira in her journals: "Dominant Trait: an intense, passionate hunger for life. Beautifully sensitive to the real meaning and value of life." And: "Proud and definite. Unbreakable. . . . A sane, healthy individual thrown into the very depths of abnormal, inhuman conditions." And: "No religion whatsoever. Brilliant mind. Lots of courage and daring. Only her calm exterior poise hides her tempestuous emotional nature. A sort of graceful restraint under which one can feel the storming fire."[3]

Not only did Alisa and Kira share important values, Ayn Rand also took experiences from her own life and gave them to Kira. Both Alisa and Kira suffered the terrible economic conditions of the new Russia. Of her family's economic position after the communist revolution of 1917, Ayn Rand said:

In this particular respect, *We The Living* was very much the paraphrase of our factual history. That is, when we came back [to Petrograd from the Crimea in 1921], our apartment was occupied by somebody who had some of our furniture and some of it was in the basement. So we got back only what he couldn't use. I think he was a sign painter. . . . And so we were living in real squalor of the same kind I describe in *We the Living.* This is autobiographical as background.[4]

The Argounov family's journeys to and from the Crimea were also based on the travels of Alisa and her family, as Ayn Rand later reported: "And then we started back for Petrograd, and the way we traveled was exactly described in *We the Living*, so that is practically naturalistic autobiography. I mean the conditions and the trains and the bundles."[5]

Alisa and Kira were educated under the Soviets, and although Alisa was interested in engineering, which Kira studied at the Leningrad Technical Institute, Alisa instead studied history at Petrograd State University. She later explained that Kira's first year at university was practically "autobiographical, in the sense of background. I was taking chronologically the exact events as they were happening at that time."[6] Regarding one of these events, she said,

> In my first year in college [1921–22], I was somewhat reckless. I made all kinds of anti-Soviet remarks and was very much afraid afterwards because I realized that I could have gotten my whole family in trouble. . . . Kira is of that same period. And in that time, the dictatorship wasn't fully tightened yet. And there was quite a lot of anti-Soviet sentiment among students. Well, I was very vocal.[7]

An example of her "recklessness" was telling a communist student that soon he and his ilk would be hanging from lampposts.[8] In the novel, Kira is reckless when she loudly tells a fellow student, while *The Internationale* is playing: "When all this is over, when the traces of their republic are disinfected from history—what a glorious funeral march this will make!" (74). In fact, Alisa and Kira had the same reaction to the communist anthem: they both loved the music but loathed its lyrics and meaning.[9]

Alisa witnessed the purging of the anticommunist students at Petrograd University, which she used in *We the Living* (209–13) and years later commented on: "In the first year . . . the students were quite outspoken and I attended my first student meeting, just as I described in *We the Living*."[10] At one such meeting, a young man was very "outspoken against the communists," and Ayn Rand uses some of his words in the scene of Kira's first student meeting (70–75).[11] Ayn Rand ends this man's story dramatically as follows:

> By the end of that first year [1922], there was a purge of students. They [the Soviets] began to tighten. And that same young man, plus a lot of others whom I knew, and girls who had gone out with them but weren't political in any sense, were all sent to Siberia. By the second year there were no more political speeches.[12]

In 1923–24, Kira and Alisa experienced another purge:

> [T]he conditions of the purge were as I described in *We the Living*. It applied to all institutes of higher learning in Petrograd. And you had to fill questionnaires

about your parents and grandparents, and if your father owned a business before the Revolution, you would be thrown out as a socially undesirable element, therefore not to be educated.[13]

Kira and Alisa *were* both purged, but unlike Kira, Alisa was soon reinstated. She later learned that she had purely by luck been saved by visiting foreign scientists who had complained about the purge. To "make a good impression on visitors," the Soviet authorities let the purged students in their last year complete their degrees.[14] According to Alisa's academic record from Petrograd State University, she was expelled on December 12, 1923, and later readmitted.[15]

Both Alisa and Kira worked as tour guides. Alisa (as did her mother) gave talks on the history of the Peter Paul Fortress, a former prison dedicated to communist martyrs. Kira gave tours at the former Winter Palace, which became The Museum of the Revolution (258).

When Kira and Leo begin living together, she tells him: "When I cook—you're not to see me. When you see me—you're not to know that I've been cooking" (135). This advice is very similar to that in a 1929 letter to Ayn Rand from her mother: "If a husband sees his wife work in the kitchen, their relationship loses its magic."[16]

Andrei's funeral was most probably based on Alisa Rosenbaum's witnessing, from her family's apartment window, the January 1918 funeral procession of the delegates to the Constitutional Assembly, who had been murdered by the Bolsheviks.[17]

Keep in mind that Ayn Rand was not a naturalistic writer, or as she puts it in the novel's introduction: "I would never be willing to transcribe a 'real life' story" (xvii). She used herself as an inspiration for Kira because of their shared values, ideals, age, and the similar period and circumstances in which they lived; but there were also significant differences. The most important is the plot situation central to Kira's life and story: a woman caught between two lovers. Alisa Rosenbaum had never lived with a man nor had a communist (or any other) lover in Russia.

Less significant, Alisa did not much resemble Kira, who was medium height, slender, with gray eyes, brown hair, and was born on April 11, 1904 (44–45). Ayn Rand was born, by the old (Julian) Russian calendar, on January 20, 1905,[18] and was (according to her Russian passport) 5 feet 4 inches tall, and had a slender to medium build with a broader face than Kira's. Her eyes, though appearing black, were actually brown.

Finally, a more significant difference between Alisa and Kira concerns their respective fates. On January 20, 1926, Alisa Rosenbaum legally crossed the Russian border, never to return. In the winter of 1925–26, Kira was murdered trying to cross the same border illegally. Ayn Rand escaped the system that regarded her as a worthless slave to the state, and she fought it and its ideals for the rest of her life, and achieved all her important goals. Kira died, her values still a distant possibility, but her spirit lives on through this novel and the life and success of her older self and successor, Ayn Rand. Kira's life is Alisa's in spirit.

LEO KOVALENSKY AND LEV BEKKERMAN

Arguably the most fascinating model for a *We the Living* character is the model for Leo Kovalensky. Many years after leaving Russia, Ayn Rand noted the result of her having written this novel: "I was glad to do it. I found that it got Russia out of [my] system in the sense that I was through with it by the time I finished." This was true, with one exception (which she noted): There was always the matter of Leo Kovalensky.[19] Toward the end of the novel's climax, after Leo has been arrested, he tells Kira: "I have only one last favor to ask, Kira . . . I hope you'll forget me" (400). Kira does not reply, and she does not forget. At the end of *We the Living*—shot, dying, but forcing herself to continue through the snow—she thinks of "the Leo that could have been" (463). And Ayn Rand never did forget the man on whom Leo was based. While Andrei Taganov, as "pure invention,"[20] was perhaps the hardest character for her to write literarily, Leo must have been the most difficult psychologically, for with him Ayn Rand had struggled to understand the first man she ever loved.[21] His name was Lev Bekkerman.

Ayn Rand once said of Lev Bekkerman: "He was the symbol and the focus of my whole life in Russia, and if I were to project any kind of story, he had to be the hero of it."[22] She modeled Leo Kovalensky on Lev Bekkerman, from the broadest abstraction of his motivation to the detail of his first name, using the name Leo in the novel (a name she disliked and whose Russian equivalent is Liolia or Lev) and his "habit of saying 'allo' when greeting people."[23]

Alisa Rosenbaum met Lev Bekkerman in a social group of young men and women called Uno Momento, whose social leader was her cousin Nina Guzarchik. Ayn Rand later reported the following about one of their gatherings, when she was an eighteen-year-old university student:

> The first time I saw him, I remember being very startled by how good-looking he was. He entered the room and I couldn't quite believe it. He didn't look quite real in the sense that he was too perfectly good looking. . . . What was unusual is that he was my type of face, with one exception, he had dark hair rather than light hair. But he had light gray eyes, was very tall. . . . It's that type of face, very sharp. . . . Of all my heroes, he would be the nearest to Francisco. And, it's his looks that I liked enormously. Very intelligent face, very determined, kind of clear-cut, self-confident. And the quality that I liked about him most was arrogance. But the Francisco kind of arrogance—not boastful, not vanity, but actually what he projected was pride, with a kind of haughty smile. I tried to get the

style of his appearance or outward personality in Leo in *We the Living*. There was always a smile behind his attitude, and an arrogant smile of, "Well, world, you have to admire me." That sort of attitude . . . like some fantastic aristocrat.[24]

Commenting further on Lev's "enormous self-confidence," she said:

I would say of all the young men or girls that I knew there, he was the only one who seemed to value himself. You see what he projected was an authentic self-esteem. . . . He projected that he was something enormously important. I would forgive a lot of minor flaws for that. He never projected that he is unimportant to himself or that he is a mediocrity. And that I think I conveyed in Leo in *We the Living*.[25]

Alisa also admired some of Bekkerman's ideas and one particular act of heroism where "he hid some young students, that were wanted by the police, in his house for the longest time. And he was literally taking a chance on his life." There were, however, also things she did not like about him: his over-flirtatious ways with women, his softness toward communism, and some of his "lightweight" and naturalistic literary and aesthetic preferences. She later stated: "I did not really understand him and . . . some day I very much [wanted] to know what is he really like."[26] She was torn between her admiration for his enormous self-confidence and her doubt and dislike of his dubious activities and attitudes.

Unlike Kira and Leo's first meeting, Alisa and Lev's was not love at first sight. But two or three months later, after another meeting, Lev escorted her home and, as Ayn Rand later noted, "By the time he got me home, I was madly and desperately in love." Bekkerman would take Alisa to parties or the theater, but their "relationship" did not last long. She remembered: "the trouble was that progressively I would show openly how I felt and I knew he didn't like it."[27]

The story of Lev Bekkerman's influence on *We the Living*—most importantly, Leo's motivation and final choice—continued and deepened after Alisa Rosenbaum left Russia in January 1926. This influence was a result of what she learned about him in letters from her immediate family and her cousin Nina.

Revealed in the letters is an event that confirmed Ayn Rand's projection of the motivation of Leo Kovalensky in the novel. First, here is what Alisa's mother wrote (on August 3, 1933) about Lev Bekkerman's first marriage, to Lili-Maria Palmen: "Liolia [Lev] B. (whom I have never regarded as a hero) and his wife divorced (don't know which one of them initiated it). He stole another man's wife, and thus acquired a new family."[28] Ayn Rand's cousin Nina Guzarchik also wrote about this divorce:

He [Bekkerman] and his wife Lilya [Lili] got divorced, it was painful for both of them. A little while later Liolia married again. Do you remember a certain Ata

Ris? Well, he married her. They seem to live well, they have a family hearth and pretty doilies; they call each other Lyoka and Atia. Despite all this, he once told me that the purpose of marriage is to make one appreciate the joys of bachelor-hood.[29]

Here is Ayn Rand's reaction to Bekkerman marrying a mediocrity:

I was shocked particularly in this sense: that the whole issue in my mind is still an unfinished story, like a mystery story, to which I may never know the ending. Because I was fully aware even by the time I came to America that I did not really understand him and that some day I very much would like to know what is he really like. And this was just one more, and horrible, touch of mystery. And in spite of this I still couldn't, even then, think that he was a total mediocrity and that I just invented everything. Because he wasn't. Of that I am sure. But my only explanation, as hypothesis, not as knowledge, would be what I wrote about Leo in *We the Living*, that it was deliberate self-destruction, deliberately consigning himself to mediocrity because he couldn't care for anything. Because whichever higher values, if he were capable of them, were not possible there.[30]

So who was Lev Bekkerman, and how did he more concretely influence the characterization of Leo Kovalensky? Although the historical record is slim, there are some Soviet records on Bekkerman. They reveal interesting similarities (and differences) between him and Leo Kovalensky, and possible evidence of minor inspirations for the latter's characterization.

The main source of information comes from Bekkerman's student file at The Leningrad Technical Institute, where he studied engineering from 1918 to 1925. His file reveals that Bekkerman had a brilliant scholastic record at a boy's gymnasium (high school), graduating in April 1918 with honors and the gold medal for his "consistent excellent performance." His subjects included Latin, German, French, history, and philosophy. His fictional counterpart, Leo, spoke English, German, and French (171) and studied philosophy (155).

In 1923–24, Lev was secretary of the publishing house Atheneum (or Agent; the record is contradictory) and in May 1924 Lev gave the following answer in a university questionnaire: "Since April I have no job, live on accidental earnings." He was translating technical works to earn an income. Similarly, Leo translated English, German, and French books into Russian (for the main Soviet publisher Gossizdat) (136).

In June 1924 Bekkerman reported: "During the current year, due to the illness of my sister, who had to go to the Crimea, I found myself in dire financial straits. Also due to my own illness and service." It seems that both Leo and Lev (and Lev's sister) had tuberculosis and lived in the Crimea to help cure it.[31]

Like Leo, Bekkerman was investigated during the student purge of 1923–24. A sheet in his file is headed "Technological Institute, Form Sheet for students being investigated. 1924." As in the novel, Bekkerman filled out questionnaires that asked for such information as his parents' occupations and his party membership (cf. 209–10). Unlike the novel, however, while Kira and Leo were expelled, Lev was allowed to graduate, but was ordered to do so by January 1, 1925.[32]

The only other uncovered historical evidence concerning Bekkerman comes from a less benign source.

The fate of Lev Bekkerman is now known; but first, the fate of Leo. At the end of the novel, Leo Kovalensky is taking the steps necessary to commit spiritual suicide. Believing that under the Soviet dictatorship his life is not worth fighting for, Kovalensky lets the communist system "choke" the life from him, and he leaves Kira for an old, shallow, and promiscuous manipulator, Antonina, fully knowing her true nature and what their relationship means. Leo tells Kira: "You'll be better off without me." In real life, this turned out to be true for Ayn Rand and Lev Bekkerman. Many years later, when asked if she would have stayed in the Soviet Union if Lev Bekkerman had returned her feelings, Ayn Rand replied: "I would have. Almost certainly."[33] (This was the fate of her sister Nora. In 1931, Nora married Feodor Drobyshev—just as Ayn Rand was arranging for her to come to America to study and become an artist.[34] Nora stayed in the Soviet Union, and was destroyed spiritually.)

The most tragic irony concerning fictional events in *We the Living* and real life events involves the final fate of Lev Bekkerman. During the climax of *We the Living,* Leo is arrested by the G.P.U. for black market activities (395–400). Lev Bekkerman was arrested three times by the secret police, either the G.P.U. or the N.K.V.D.

His first arrest was in 1924, along with many other students (and professors). A search of his apartment found nothing, and he was released.[35] He was subsequently released after his second arrest as well.

Bekkerman was arrested a final time in 1937, the Year of Terror under Stalin. The Leningrad Martyr Log for 1937–38 lists the following:

Bekkerman, Lev Borisovich, b. 1901 in Leningrad. Resided in Leningrad. Jew. Non-party member. Manager of the motor group of Voroshilor factory. Residence: 6 7th Soviet Street, apt. 9. Arrested January 18, 1937. Sentenced to the highest form of punishment, according to statute 58:7-8-11 UK RSFSR, on May 5, 1937 by the temporary session of the military committee of the Supreme Court of the USSR. Executed by shooting on May 6, 1937.[36]

Statute 58:7-8-11 refers to several "crimes" according to the Soviet criminal code. One was for black market activities, another for "The commission of

terrorist acts against representatives of the Soviet State or members of revolutionary worker and peasant organizations, and the participation in the commission of such acts."[37]

During his "interrogation," Bekkerman "admitted" being a member of a
counterrevolutionary organization and sabotaging tanks in the factory where
he worked. Witnesses described Bekkerman as "sharply hostile" to Soviet
authority and quoted him as saying: "All Soviet authority is constructed on
sand and kept by bayonets." As a member of this organization he was also
accused of the December 1934 assassination of the Secretary of Central Committee, Sergei Kirov, who was second in power to Stalin. For these "crimes,"
Bekkerman was shot on May 5, 1937. On October 10, 1957, he was "rehabilitated" and declared innocent.

These are the final notes in tragically similar lives: of the man who was
Ayn Rand's main source of happiness in Russia and the one crucial to her
being able to write *We the Living* and its hero.

VASILI DUNAEV AND ZINOVY ROSENBAUM

Vasili Dunaev is another character heavily modeled on a real person who
was close to Ayn Rand. She once said: "I copied Uncle Vasili in *We the Living*
from [my father, Zinovy Zacharovich Rosenbaum], both in appearance and
in essential characteristics, not in every literal detail. But if you have an idea
of what that man was, omitting the slight exaggeration of fiction, that would
be my father."[38]

Ayn Rand also noted the following about her father: "the unbending character, the enormous, what I today would call somewhat repressed, integrity.
He was a man who held ideals which I didn't discover until I was fifteen.
Very strong ideals, a man of very firm conviction."[39] Vasili Dunaev was very
much like this in the way he built his fur trading business and led his family
and ran his life.

Ayn Rand said that her father "had an exaggerated mid-Victorian attitude,"
notably in regard to women and romantic relations. Uncle Vasili was similar,
once expressing this attitude by walking out of the room when Kira visits,
because she is now living with, though not married to, Leo Kovalensky.
Upon exiting the room, Vasili, as Zinovy would also have done, says, "There
are things with which one does not compromise" (139).

Vasili and Zinovy were both well-read and enjoyed Russian literary classics. In *We the Living* Vasili is seen reading Chekhov, and he says: "Old classics are still the best. In those days, they had culture, and moral values . . .
and integrity" (214). In interviews Ayn Rand has spoken of her father's enjoy-
ment of such minor Russian individualist writers as Vladimir Korolenko and
of his desire to be a writer.[40]

Zinovy Rosenbaum and Uncle Vasili were ardent anticommunists. Ayn
Rand said her father "would have been for a constitutional monarchy. His
ideal of government was England."[41] Both men believed, at great cost to

themselves, that the Soviet regime would soon fall. At one point, Vasili says: "We're all turning into beasts in a beastly struggle. But we'll be saved. We'll be saved before it gets us all" (257). While Vasili waited for that day, Zinovy Zacharovich, also expecting the Soviet system to collapse, refused in 1918 to take the opportunity to flee the country.[42]

Further evidence of Zinovy Rosenbaum's anticommunism is found in letters from his wife, Anna, to Ayn Rand. In one such letter Anna wrote that her husband had ended his relationship with his sister because she had married a communist, but that they had later reconciled.[43] In an earlier letter, Anna Rosenbaum reported her husband calling the rest of the family "socialists," presumably because they weren't strong enough in their anticommunism.[44] In the novel Vasili rails against the communists and is furious when they visit his home (115).

This anticommunism is reflected in both men's attitude toward working for the Soviets. Ayn Rand said of her father:

> He wouldn't do anything. To begin with, he wouldn't have been accepted, as a former owner, into any Soviet job and he didn't want to do it. In that sense he was very much like Vasili. He was enormously on strike. Only about the time when I was leaving Russia, he finally decided that he would go to work. And since the regulation kind of relaxed a little, he got a job as an employee in some drug store, somewhere way at the other end of the city.[45]

Zinovy worked for the Soviets only a few years in the second half of the 1920s; after this, there was no work for him, and like Vasili, he became the homemaker of the family. One letter from Anna Rosenbaum reports his doing the family cooking, shopping, and other household work.[46] Vasili Dunaev never worked for the Soviets.

Ayn Rand had one later use for the Zinovy-Vasili connection. In early 1944 she began working at Warner Bros. Studio, writing the screenplay for *The Fountainhead*. When completing an application for Social Security, she wrote that her father's name was "Vasili Rand."[47]

Uncle Vasili is a fascinating glimpse into the soul of Ayn Rand's father, and of two men of integrity who were trapped in an evil system choking life from them. Nora Rosenbaum said of her father: "Papa was tall and handsome, but not energetic. He was broken by the Revolution. . . . Everything was taken away from us. And Papa was unable to withstand the tragedy."[48] At the end of the novel, Uncle Vasili is without a future, standing forlornly on a street corner, still hopelessly waiting to be rescued from communism, while struggling to survive with his daughter. This picture is a dramatic symbol of the fate of the man he was modeled on: Ayn Rand's father, a man of great integrity, trapped in a slave camp that embodied the antithesis of that virtue.

GALINA ARGOUNOVA AND ANNA ROSENBAUM

Ayn Rand used not only her father but also her mother as a model for a *We the Living* character. She once said of Anna Borisovna Rosenbaum:

We really did not get along and, if anything, she was my exact opposite. She was by principle and basic style, and sense of life, extremely social. Her sole interest, in fact, was to have parties, to be an intellectual hostess, to be surrounded by people, to be very active. And she was much more interested in the social aspects of activity than in the subjects. For instance, she would be, by the standards of that time, considered intellectually avant garde. She would consider herself a revolutionary. She was much too tolerant, for instance, of the communist revolution, in a kind of a vague, liberal attitude. Parts of it I used for Galina in *We the Living*."

She continued, however, that she did not use her mother for Galina as much as she used her father for Vasili. "But that one aspect, if you remember in which way Galina was kind of socially being a snob about the Revolution ultimately. . . . Well that's my mother. That attitude."[49]

Ayn Rand's comment on her mother was echoed by Nora. When asked, "What were your mother's views?" she replied: "she was a 'pink'—she would occasionally talk about 'beautiful ideas.' "[50]

Galina and Anna were both schoolteachers. Ayn Rand said: "My mother was teaching languages in high schools. And she had several [schools] on her list and she was really the main supporter of the family."[51] Anna Rosenbaum knew at least three languages (German, French, and English) and also taught social studies and "political literacy" at high schools and language seminars.[52] Galina taught sewing, mostly to high school students (163, 271).

Ayn Rand later used the connection between Anna Rosenbaum and Galina Argounova when filling in the Social Security application mentioned above: she wrote her mother's name as "Galina Ivanova."

IRINA DUNAEVA AND NORA ROSENBAUM, AND SOME OTHER PARALLELS

An important part of Ayn Rand's literary technique is that all her characterizations are integrated to the work's theme. Her working title for *We the Living* was *Airtight*, which stresses the suffocating nature of dictatorships while expressing the novel's theme: "the individual against the state, and, more specifically, the evil of statism."[53] We have already seen how this theme is applied to the lives of the novel's characters and their real life models, but there is no more tragic example of this than Sasha Chernov, the man Irina loves. Ayn Rand explains the real-life basis for this character:

> There was the incident when one young man, who incidentally is the model for the character of Sasha in *We the Living*, he was a friend of my cousin's [Nina] actually. . . . He came suddenly to ask me whether I would let him hide anti-Communist pamphlets in my house. . . . I didn't want to refuse him, but I knew

that I had absolutely no right to take it upon myself, so I told him I'd have to ask Father. Because if I smuggled it in without telling the family, I was risking their lives. Father absolutely forbad it. . . . And so I had to refuse him.[54]

Several months later, engaged to be married to a girl also in the underground, this man was arrested. Ayn Rand tells the climax of his story:

> He had a mother. And the story of Irina and Sasha is [based on] what his mother did. She went through every possible Soviet bureau and commissars' offices, begging to let them be sent to the same prison in Siberia. . . . And she succeeded in getting them married but not in being sent to the same place. They were sent to two Siberian prisons miles apart. That was a true story.[55]

Ayn Rand did not tell us the fate of the real Sasha and Irina, but it was probably the same as in *We the Living*: slow death in Siberian camps (341–43).

Although Irina was partly modeled on "Sasha's" wife, she was also based on a person very close to Ayn Rand.

Ayn Rand once described her youngest sister Eleonora (Nora) as "the one that wanted to be an artist." In fact, Nora Rosenbaum was a significant model for the character Irina Dunaeva, Kira's cousin. The key similarity between Irina and Nora is that they were both artists with a similar style. A 1935 letter to Ayn Rand from Anna Rosenbaum reported the following criticism by Soviet teachers of Nora's drawings: "Nora having trouble at work. She draws thin, aristocratic ladies with proud faces, whereas she is required to draw stout peasant women."[56] In the novel this same complaint is directed against Irina: "I've been reprimanded twice in the Wall Newspaper. They said my peasant women looked like cabaret dancers and my workers were too graceful. My bourgeois ideology, you know" (256).

When Sasha and Irina are being shipped to the labor camps, he asks her to put drawings in her letters to him. In Nora's letters to Ayn Rand in America, she drew pictures on the pages, with her first letter (in February 1926) including seven drawings.[57] Another artistic similarity between Irina and Nora was that Irina wanted to work designing fashion and stage sets (336–37), and Nora did in fact become a theatrical artist.[58]

Although the following two inspirations for *We the Living* characters were based on people known to Ayn Rand, they also represent a class or type of person. The first involves Ayn Rand's other sister, Natasha. Of her middle sister, Ayn Rand recalled that while having "friendly relations," they "had nothing in common." She explained:

> Because she was . . . my exact opposite. She was not intellectual particularly, she was very feminine. She is the one who took great interest in personal appearance at a time when we were really in rags. She was more interested in

young men than I was. And she had girlfriends in school, which neither I nor my little sister ever had. And she was much more conventional.[59]

While on the surface this description seems to fit Lydia in *We the Living*, Ayn Rand explicitly stated that she was not the model for Lydia: "Lydia is total invention. She [Natasha] was not religious nor mawkish like Lydia. Lydia is the projection of my idea of the collective Russian soul. . . . The typically Russian young ladies."[60] Or, as she put it more specifically in her journals, Lydia was a "representative of the older half of the younger generation."[61]

Natasha does, however, appear to have influenced some minor aspects of Lydia's characterization. Natasha, like Lydia, was very feminine, as evidenced in Natasha's letters to Ayn Rand in America, which focus on fashion, clothes, her appearance and men.[62] Although Natasha was feminine, she was also well-educated, very modern, and somewhat ambitious, especially in her career. The most significant similarity between Natasha and Lydia is that both were pianists and worked hard to be successful musicians. In *We the Living*, Lydia played Chopin, Tchaikovsky and Bach (93, 117, 446), as Natasha did, and they both practiced long hours. While Lydia practiced three hours a day (93), Ayn Rand said of Natasha: "She practiced eight to ten hours a day, driving everybody and herself crazy, but she practiced. She had marvelous technique and very little expression. She was a strictly virtuoso pianist."[63]

It is plausible that when writing of Lydia's fate in *We the Living*, Ayn Rand was echoing her sister's fate: never becoming a concert pianist, playing at Communist Party functions or parties, not playing at home except for the rare, violent outbursts of beloved songs smashed from the keys (446).

There were also important differences between Lydia and Natasha. Unlike Natasha, Lydia was ten years older than Kira and a Christian, whereas Natasha was younger than Alisa and Jewish, though nonreligious.[64] While Lydia's denunciation of others for not being religious enough indicates a somewhat nasty personality (see 114–15), Natasha wasn't like this. Ayn Rand's comments about Natasha, and Natasha's letters to her, support this view.[65]

Another character who also was representative of a class or type is Antonina Pavlovna Platoshkina, the promiscuous middle-aged woman with whom Leo Kovalensky begins a self-destructive affair at the end of the novel. In her journals Ayn Rand wrote that Antonina was "the condensed low female of all times. Selfish like a dumb, brutal monster. Vain. Conceited. Eager for everything that flatters her ego. But mainly: a loose creature out to satisfy herself. . . . Vulgar in her sex affairs. She has many of them—some for profit, some for animal desire . . . the animal desire of an oversexed creature for the gorgeous male that he [Leo] is."[66]

Antonina, too, was based on a real person:

> I went to Paris [in route to America, in 1926]. And there, one acquaintance that I had was the woman whom I used as the model for Antonina. Not quite as bad,

but she was one of those Russian widows. . . . She had two children. And I'm afraid she was living by her wits, more or less, barely respectable. We had known her in the Crimea. And that's the only address I had for Paris and she helped me to select which stores to shop in.[67]

While Antonina and all the character inspirations discussed above were based on real people, not all were; some are pure invention. Ayn Rand wrote of the character Ivan Ivanov (the Russian equivalent of John Smith), the border guard who kills Kira: "That solder is a symbol, a typical representative of the average, the dull, the useless, the commonplace, the masses—that killed the best on earth. . . . Citizen Ivan Ivanov was guarding the border of the Union of Socialist Soviet Republics. And that Union killed Kira."[68]

Some of the character names Ayn Rand created for *We the Living* were also symbolic—and comical. She applied a technique she used in other fiction works: undercutting negative or villainous characters with silly, ironic names, sometimes in a foreign language. The humor is Ayn Rand's private joke about Soviet types. In *We the Living* the mediocrity and power-luster Pavel Syerov has a surname meaning "gray." Syerov's friend Valka Dourova has a last name meaning "idiot" or "fool" (288). Comrade Sonia's last name, Presniakova, means "bland" (72); the non-entity Kolya Smiatkin has a family name deriving from "v smiatku," or "runny egg" (153). When the *upravdom* (a Soviet apartment building manager) of the Argounov's apartment building visits the Argounovs to collect money, he is holding a list of the building's tenants. On the list are the names Doubenko, which also comes from the word for "idiot," and Rilnikov, which means "pig's snout" (68).[69]

CONCLUSION

A little-known figure from history is the last *We the Living* character inspiration. Nestor Makhno is mentioned when Kira is remembering her family's journey to the Crimea (27–28). Kira remembers the fear of the travelers—that they would be attacked by the bandit Makhno. (They were not.) Though not strictly a bandit, Nestor Makhno was a real person of that time and place. Born in 1889 in the Ukraine, Makhno was an anarchist and revolutionary who from 1917 to 1921 was a military commander in the Ukraine, first against the Central Powers of Germany and Austria, then against the White Russians, and finally against his former allies, the Reds, who had betrayed him. Makhno fled Russia in 1921 and died in France in 1934.

In 1918, the Rosenbaums traveled to the Crimea through the Ukraine, and—unlike Kira's family—they were attacked and robbed by bandits (though not political ones). They were released and made it to their destination, Odessa.[70]

From this minor example of a character influence to major ones such as
Ayn Rand herself, the lives of real people can be seen woven by Ayn Rand
into the fabric of a larger, more dramatic cloth, a fictional plot. This principle
can be seen in one last real-life scene that she wove into *We the Living*.

At Alisa Rosenbaum's farewell party in St. Petersburg, a man told her to
"tell the rest of the world that we are dying here."[71] This became one of Ayn
Rand's motives for writing *We the Living*, and she gave the man's plea to the
novel's heroine. At the novel's end, Kira has a chance farewell meeting with
Uncle Vasili, who is standing on a street selling saccharine. Kira says good-
bye to the man who has lost everything except his daughter Acia. Vasili tells
Kira that change will come to Russia, and Kira replies: "Uncle Vasili . . . I'll
tell them . . . over there . . . where I'm going . . . I'll tell them about everything
. . . it's like an S.O.S. . . . And maybe . . . someone . . . somewhere . . . will
understand" (451).

Ayn Rand kept her promise to the man at the party and Kira's promise to
Uncle Vasili, in fact to all the admirable characters who were inspired by real
people and who were victims of communism. Ayn Rand wrote her Russian
novel and essentially got the Soviet Union "out of her system." But she did
not forget those she loved, who were not only an important part of her life,
but were also influential in the creation of the "autobiographical" *We the
Living*.

NOTES

1. Biographical interviews (Ayn Rand Archives).
2. See Michael S. Berliner, "Music in *We the Living*," in the present volume,
p. 119–21.
3. David Harriman, ed., *Journals of Ayn Rand* (New York: Dutton, 1997), 50.
4. Biographical interviews (Ayn Rand Archives). Cf. *We the Living*, 52–53.
5. Biographical interviews (Ayn Rand Archives). Cf. *We the Living*, part 1,
chapter 1.
6. Biographical interviews (Ayn Rand Archives).
7. Biographical interviews (Ayn Rand Archives).
8. Biographical interviews (Ayn Rand Archives).
9. Biographical interviews (Ayn Rand Archives).
10. Biographical interviews (Ayn Rand Archives).
11. Biographical interviews (Ayn Rand Archives).
12. Biographical interviews (Ayn Rand Archives).
13. Biographical interviews (Ayn Rand Archives).
14. Biographical interviews (Ayn Rand Archives). Cf. *We the Living*, 209–13.
15. From a copy (in the Ayn Rand Archives) of Alisa Rosenbaum's (Ayn Rand's)
academic transcripts, in her student file at Petrograd State University. The Ayn Rand
Institute's St. Petersburg researcher Alexander Lebedev reports: "In the 1923–24 academic year there was an especially thorough 'cleansing,' resulting in the expulsion of

about 4,000 students, i.e., about a third of the entire student body. The 'cleansing' was conducted by a committee created by the university administration and its Party organization. The students expelled were not only those who actively spoke out against the Soviet regime, but also the children of the so-called 'socially alien elements,' and students who were not members of the Party."

16. Letter from Anna Rosenbaum dated October 22, 1929. For more information on the letters Ayn Rand received, while in America, from her family in Russia, see Dina Schein Garmong, "*We the Living* and the Rosenbaum Family Letters," in the present volume, p. 67–68.

17. Biographical interviews (Ayn Rand Archives).

18. By the later Gregorian calendar, adopted by the Soviets in 1918, she was born on February 2, 1905.

19. Biographical interviews (Ayn Rand Archives).

20. See Leonard Peikoff's introduction to the sixtieth anniversary edition of *We the Living*, vi.

21. See Leonard Peikoff's introduction to the sixtieth anniversary edition of *We the Living*, vi.

22. Biographical interviews (Ayn Rand Archives).

23. Biographical interviews (Ayn Rand Archives).

24. Biographical interviews (Ayn Rand Archives).

25. Biographical interviews (Ayn Rand Archives).

26. Biographical interviews (Ayn Rand Archives).

27. Biographical interviews (Ayn Rand Archives).

28. Russian Letter from Anna Rosenbaum, no. 276a.

29. Russian Letter from Nina Guzarchik, no. 308, dated February 9, 1934.

30. Biographical interviews (Ayn Rand Archives).

31. From Ayn Rand Institute researcher Alexander Lebedev, and the Leningrad Technical Institute records.

32. Leningrad Technical Institute record.

33. Biographical interviews (Ayn Rand Archives).

34. Russian Letter from Nora (Rosenbaum) Drobysheva, no. 218, September 15, 1931.

35. From the Ayn Rand Institute researcher, Alexander Lebedev.

36. The Leningrad Martyr Log for 1937–38, vol. 4: 1937 (St. Petersburg, 1999), 44.

37. From the Penal Code of the USSR of that period. It is interesting and ironic that Bekkerman was charged with black market "crimes," similar to Leo in the novel.

38. Biographical interviews (Ayn Rand Archives). Judging by the letters between Ayn Rand and her family, they called her father "ZZ," the initials of his first name and patronymic.

39. Biographical interviews (Ayn Rand Archives).

40. Biographical interviews (Ayn Rand Archives).

41. Biographical interviews (Ayn Rand Archives).

42. Biographical interviews (Ayn Rand Archives).

43. Russian Letter from Anna Rosenbaum, no.294c AB, November 10–11, 1933.

44. Russian Letter from Anna Rosenbaum, no. 260e, May 6 1933.

45. Biographical interviews (Ayn Rand Archives).

46. Russian Letter from Anna Rosenbaum, no. 250a, February 26, 1933.

47. I presume the lie was to protect her Russian family's identity and safety, especially in a studio and government riddled with communists. On the same form, Ayn Rand gave her own birth name as Alice Rand.

48. From Eleanora (Rosenbaum) Drobysheva's oral history interview for the Ayn Rand Archives.

49. Biographical interviews (Ayn Rand Archives).

50. From Eleanora (Rosenbaum) Drobysheva's oral history interview for the Ayn Rand Archives. Ayn Rand was always careful to qualify her criticisms of her mother, because Anna, unlike Galina with Kira, ardently encouraged and arranged for Alisa to go to America, thus saving her from being destroyed in Soviet Russia. (Biographical interviews [Ayn Rand Archives].)

51. Biographical interviews (Ayn Rand Archives).

52. Revealed in a letter in Natasha's Rosenbaum's Conservatory record, and Russian Letter no. 12d, April 8, 1926.

53. Ayn Rand, *The Art of Fiction: A Guide for Writers and Readers*, Tore Boeckmann, ed. (New York: Plume, 2000), 17.

54. Biographical interviews (Ayn Rand Archives).

55. Biographical interviews (Ayn Rand Archives). Cf. *We the Living*, part 2, chapter 8.

56. Russian Letter from Anna Rosenbaum no. 358-A, February 6–7, 1935. Cf. *We the Living*, 256.

57. Russian Letter from Nora Rosenbaum, no. 4.5c, February 21, 1926.

58. From Nora Drobysheva's Soviet work record.

59. Biographical interviews (Ayn Rand Archives).

60. Biographical interviews (Ayn Rand Archives).

61. Harriman, *Journals*, 55.

62. Russian Letters from Natasha (Natalie) Rosenbaum, nos. 44b, June 18, 1926, 53b, June 30, 1926, 49b, June 27, 1926, and 41a, June 8, 1926.

63. Biographical interviews (Ayn Rand Archives). Letter from Natasha Rosenbaum no. 85.b, November 28, 1926, reveals that she played Bach.

64. No member of the Rosenbaum family was a theist, and at most they observed some of the Jewish holidays for purely social reasons.

65. Biographical interviews (Ayn Rand Archives). E.g., letter to Ayn Rand no. 50, June 28, 1926. Nora supported this positive opinion of Natasha: "Natasha was cute, a good person with a heart." Nora (Rosenbaum) Drobysheva's oral history interview with the Ayn Rand Archives.

66. Harriman, *Journals*, 55. Ayn Rand's stress on Antonina Pavlovna Platoskina animal desires could be deliberate irony, because the name Pavlovna brings to mind Pavlov, the famous researcher of drooling dogs and other animals. If Ayn Rand intended any irony concerning Antonina's family name it is unclear. Platon is the Russian equivalent of the name of the Greek philosopher Plato, whose philosophy Ayn Rand opposed in all its fundamentals.

67. Biographical interviews (Ayn Rand Archives).

68. Michael Berliner, ed., *Letters of Ayn Rand* (New York: Dutton, 1995), 18.

69. In her play *Think Twice*, the villain, a Soviet spy, is called Sookin—Russian for "son of a bitch."

I am indebted to Dina Schein Garmong for these examples and for her translation of all the Russian material used in this chapter.

70. Biographical interviews (Ayn Rand Archives).

71. Isabel Paterson, "Turns with a Bookworm," *New York Herald Tribune*, 29 June 1941. Newspaper clipping in Ayn Rand's papers (Ayn Rand Archives).

3

We the Living and the Rosenbaum Family Letters

Dina Schein Garmong

> "I'll tell them . . . over there . . . where I'm going . . . I'll tell them about everything . . . it's like an S.O.S. . . . And maybe . . . someone . . . somewhere . . . will understand." (451).

Ayn Rand's heroine Kira Argounova was speaking for the author when she promised to tell the free world about the evils of communism and the horrors of Soviet life. It is a vow Ayn Rand made before she left Russia. As a persuasive and passionate champion of freedom, she kept her word. And *We the Living* was the first weapon in her arsenal. In 1934, in a letter to her agent, Miss Rand said: "The conditions I have depicted [in *We the Living*] are true. I have lived them. No one has ever come out of Soviet Russia to tell it to the world. That was my job."[1]

The letters that she received from her family in Russia provide vivid evidence that the living conditions depicted in the novel were ones that she had lived through herself and that they were in no way exaggerated.[2]

Ayn Rand (born Alisa Rosenbaum) left Russia in January 1926, shortly before she turned twenty-one. She and her family, the Rosenbaums, corresponded regularly for about ten years after she left. Most of the letters to her were written by her mother, father, and two younger sisters, Natasha and Nora. She also corresponded with her cousin and good friend Nina Guzarchik. Her correspondence with them ceased circa 1936, prior to the height of the Stalinist terror. At a time when people disappeared without a trace and were shot without trial, it was potentially fatal for a Soviet citizen to correspond with persons living abroad. Ayn Rand knew this; she stopped writing to her family in order to protect them.

Most people wait for something noteworthy to happen before writing a letter; the Rosenbaums, however, wrote frequently and at length. (The Ayn Rand Archives contain approximately 900 multiple-page letters to Miss Rand from her family.) The family's purpose in writing so often and so much was to keep in close contact with their daughter and sister. So, many of their letters describe their day-to-day lives, thus providing an excellent picture of the conditions under which they lived.

This chapter shows the great similarity between the background of *We the Living* and the actual living conditions as gleaned from her family's letters. Its main purpose is to support Rand's statement that the sort of life described in her novel is one that she had experienced herself. To this end, the Rosenbaum letters are an invaluable resource, for which no work of scholarly research on the Soviet Union could offer a substitute: they are the only source, outside of her own statements, that provide information on Rand's actual experiences in Russia. They are from the persons who were closest to her while she lived there, who shared many of her experiences; after she left, they continued living in the same apartment, holding the same jobs, interacting with the same people, going through the same daily trials as she went through.

In light of the stark realism of the novel's background, some readers might wonder if *We the Living* is a naturalistic novel, and thus if it was written in a way contrary to its author's conviction that romanticism is superior to naturalism. Ayn Rand held that writers of fiction should not merely copy people or events that they happen to observe in real life; instead, they should project an ideal conception of how life (and men) ought to be. I conclude this chapter by showing that there is no tension between her rejection of naturalism as a literary method and her use of Soviet reality as the background for *We the Living*.

FACTS OF LIFE UNDER THE SOVIETS[3]

"You came and you forbade life to the living" (404).

After the Bolshevik Revolution, private property was abolished. In *We the Living*, the Argounovs' textile factory was nationalized, leaving Kira's family in dire financial straits. The same was true of the Rosenbaums, when Mr. Rosenbaum's pharmacy was nationalized shortly after the communist takeover. People like the Argounovs (and the Rosenbaums) thought the ideology of the new regime was so obviously absurd and barbaric that it could not last for long. So, shortly after the revolution, the Argounovs left Petrograd for the Crimea to wait for the communist craze to burn itself out. They expected to be gone a few months. They returned to Petrograd five years later, when it became clear that, despite their predictions, communism was there to stay. The same was true of the Rosenbaums, as were the living conditions that Kira and her family experienced after their return: poverty, chronic shortages, starvation, and ubiquitous fear and hopelessness.

Let us examine *We the Living*'s presentation of the problems that Soviet citizens suffered, and compare it to similar accounts in the Rosenbaums' letters. I group these problems into four categories: housing, poverty and shortages, Soviet jobs, and hopelessness.

Housing Woes

> "God knows where you'll find an apartment, Galina. People are crowded like dogs" (36).

The first problem that Kira's family faced upon returning to Petrograd at the start of the novel was finding a place to live, for their old house had been taken from them after the revolution. Ayn Rand has made it clear that the details of the novel concerning the Argounovs' finding an apartment were autobiographical.[4] In *We the Living*, a sign painter lived in the Argounovs' house when they returned to Petrograd; he allowed them to take back some of their own furniture—broken pieces which he found useless—which they then carted to the small apartment they were lucky enough to rent. The Rosenbaums had a similar experience. They managed to rent a dilapidated apartment in the overcrowded city, were able to salvage a few pieces of furniture from their old home—which was occupied by a sign painter at the time—and were forced to live in squalor from then on. The Argounovs' apartment had no hot water; neither did the Rosenbaums'. When Ayn Rand was married and living in California, she described some aspects of her Los Angeles apartment to her family. Responding to her letter, her mother summed up their reactions: "We do not know what to be most amazed about. I am most impressed by your gas stove [and] real hot water" (255d/April 14, 1933).

The overcrowding of Soviet cities and lack of upkeep of buildings led the state to institute a "Domicile Norm," according to which each citizen was allowed only a small amount of space in which to live. Any apartment whose square footage was larger than what was allowed by the Domicile Norm would have more people moved into it. Henceforth, the apartment's owners had to share their living space with people who were usually total strangers.[5] As the years passed and the city's population grew while inhabitable housing dwindled, the allotted square footage per person continued to shrink. In the early 1930s, the upper limit on living space legally allowed per person was approximately 80 square feet (93d/January 3, 1927; 96c/January 14, 1927; 288b/ October 5, 1933). In *We the Living*, nearly every apartment is occupied by many unrelated people.[6] By the time we first meet Leo, four of the seven rooms of his apartment had already been confiscated by the state and given over to "tenants." Later, Leo and Kira are further forced to give up two of their remaining rooms, after which they had to work, cook, and sleep in one small room.

The Rosenbaums, too, fell victim to the Domicile Norm. New tenants had been moved into their apartment some months after Ayn Rand's departure; a couple of years later, the Rosenbaums had yet another room and their kitchen taken away from them, which meant they had to cook in a bedroom. Mrs. Rosenbaum commented in one of her letters to Ayn that she was glad she wasn't required to feed their tenants, too! (84d/November 23, 1926; 171.5c/November 29, 1928). One of Miss Rand's cousins, a medical student, lived in a tiny, cold and damp storage closet. But he was fortunate, Mrs. Rosenbaum wrote, for at least he had a roof over his head (199a/July 2, 1930).

Moreover, skyrocketing rents left many people no choice but to sublet the little space they were allotted. For instance, the Guzarchiks, the family of one of Mrs. Rosenbaum's sisters, had to give up their daughter's room to tenants, forcing Ayn Rand's adult cousin Nina to sleep in a corner of her parents' former living room.

When a young couple married, they typically continued to live with their parents, because it was usually impossible to obtain a separate apartment. After Natasha and Nora married, both husbands came to live with the Rosenbaums, because there was nowhere else for the newlyweds to go. But they were fortunate: each couple had a room to themselves in their parents' apartment.[7] Still, the result was that three families had to live in a total of three rooms, and the Rosenbaums' unrelated "tenants" continued to occupy a part of their apartment (218.5a/ November 4, 1931; 250a/ February 26, 1933).

The sheer number of persons crammed into tiny spaces led to chronic tension and unceasing hostility among an apartment's residents, particularly among unrelated persons sharing the kitchen and bathroom. The tenants in the Guzarchiks' apartment were rude to them and played nasty tricks on them. The Konheims, the family of another of Mrs. Rosenbaum's sisters, lived in constant fear of being evicted as a result of their tenants' machinations. The Rosenbaums' tenants—whom Mrs. Rosenbaum referred to as thieves and prostitutes—were not much better. As a result of their tenants' destructive actions, the Rosenbaums tried to get them evicted, but were unsuccessful (199a/July 2, 1930; 260e/May 6, 1933).

In *We the Living*, the tension and hostility among an apartment's residents is less intense than it perhaps was in real life. In real life, crime, including murder, was not unusual, as people fought desperately and ruthlessly for living space. In March 1930, Mrs. Rosenbaum reported:

You simply cannot imagine the extent of our housing crisis. . . . Everyone tries to take away rooms from everybody else, people do all kinds of dishonest things, all for the sake of a few square feet. . . . Anyone who moves into a room and lives there for a little while can no longer be evicted. So any person with an "excess" of rooms hides this fact, tries to prevent it from leaking out, because everyone knows what it means to have a tenant who knows that he cannot be evicted. Usually such tenants show their beastly nature right away; their goal is no longer simply to hang on to their own living space, but to force out the others who already live in the apartment. This horror is everywhere. There are many court cases over this; there are many cases of violent crimes and murders over housing. While I myself have been fortunate not to go beyond a consultation with a lawyer, I have heard of much worse cases.

For example, in order to get one more person into an apartment, a certain citizen passed off a male friend of his as his wife. He and the buddy got married, and he lived with his "wife" in that apartment for more than a year. This "wife" used to kick the owner of the apartment, a lady schoolteacher, in the stomach. The schoolteacher could never understand how a woman could have such strength. Eventually, the schoolteacher got sick and died from the beatings. And it was only a year and a half later, when the husband and "wife" got drunk and had a fight, that the police came and the "wife" was finally exposed. But since the "wife" lived there for some time, it was impossible to evict him, so his goal was accomplished.

In the same building, another group of tenants locked the owner of an apartment, an elderly lady, inside and set the apartment on fire. Afterwards, since the owner was "missing," they got the apartment (193/March 20, 1930).

The Rosenbaums themselves had one such brush with death when some residents of their apartment building set it on fire. They managed to escape down the back stairs, and firemen succeeded in putting out the fire before the building burned down. "Thank God we got away with only a bad scare, commotion and mess. We could have been left without a roof over our heads, and that is a catastrophe these days" (193/March 20, 1930).

In a country where people felt fortunate simply to have a roof over their heads, remodeling a residence was a difficult achievement. The Soviet version of remodeling often consisted largely of a painstaking restoration of old collapsing furniture and decor. The Rosenbaums attempted such redecoration twice: the first time some months after Ayn's departure, and again shortly before Natasha's wedding (84d/November 23, 1926; 177b/March 18, 1929).

The Rosenbaums considered American living conditions (even modest ones) incredibly luxurious compared to their own—to be wistfully yearned for, but never attained. When Ayn Rand wrote from California that she and her husband were moving out of their one-bedroom apartment because it had become too small for their needs, her Russian relatives were amazed at her freedom to make such a move. By Soviet standards, a one-bedroom apartment for only two persons was a spacious residence. When told that in America people owned houses, Natasha could not believe that one couple could live in a house all by themselves.[8] In Russia, every room of such a home might have housed a separate family (245/January 27, 1933; 255b/ April 14, 1933).

Starvation and Poverty

> "You stand in line for three hours at the co-operative and maybe you get food" (24).

The desperate shortage of housing in Soviet cities reflected Russia's wider shortage of all other goods. The entire nation was starving. In *We the Living*, at a party in the home of Kira's wealthiest acquaintance, the hostess offered her guests such "delicacies" as cookies made of potato skins and slices of bread "with a suspicion of butter" (158). Ayn Rand and her family were not exempt from the consequences of the famine that ravaged the country after the Soviets took over. When the communists nationalized her father's business and the last of the family's savings was gone, the Rosenbaums were in danger of starving to death. Mrs. Rosenbaum recalled their years of hunger: "we ate cakes made of potato peelings, which to our hungry stomachs had seemed more delicious than the nectar of the Olympic gods" (359c/January 22, 1935).

In their letters to Ayn Rand, her family would occasionally note the deteriorating material conditions. (See, e.g., 190a/January 7, 1930.) Like all Soviet citizens, the Rosenbaums spent hours scouring stores all over the city in search of food. Once Mrs. Rosenbaum managed to buy a bag of apples. She noted that Natasha's and Nora's joy at such a find was beyond measure (250a/February 26, 1933; 284b/September 14, 1933). Another time she reported that onions had become a luxury item in Russia (274a/July 24, 1933). Mr. Rosenbaum was amazed to learn from one of Ayn's letters that in America "they have fresh tomatoes, fresh all year round" (255d/April 14, 1933).

We the Living reports that the revolution brought to Russia the kerosene-burning Primus—a smelly, messy, sooty cooker, whose use carried the risk of explosion. The Primus became the new Soviet stove, to cook citizens' hard-won food (134). Fifteen years after the revolution, Mrs. Rosenbaum mentioned that everyone in Russia still used Primuses, the only cooking implement widely available. They were one of the worst aspects of Soviet domestic life, because they generate dirt, filth and smoke, and can explode (260e/May 6, 1933).

With even the basic food staples so difficult to obtain, sweets became something of a rare delicacy in Russia. When Ayn Rand mentioned in a letter that she eats chocolate covered ice-cream bars for dessert, her family replied that they do not have them in Russia. Mrs. Rosenbaum remarked that people refrain from mentioning sweets at all, to avoid torturing themselves and others (274a/July 24, 1933). What passes for ice cream in Russia, she reported, is fruit-flavored frozen water between two paper-thin wafers—a confection very popular with children, for lack of anything better. She also mentioned ersatz "chocolate" candy made of soybeans (260e/May 6, 1933). The only decent desserts were available from the "international trade" stores, which sold foreign food items and accepted only foreign currency—i.e., shops out of reach to the vast majority of Soviet citizens (272.5a/July 21, 1933). Mrs. Rosenbaum sometimes sent Ayn recipes for delicious Russian dishes, from borscht and pirogies to delicate desserts, noting that they could no longer prepare them in Russia, since many of the ingredients—such as meat, eggs, butter, and sugar—were impossible to obtain.

Given that in Soviet Russia the mere satisfaction of basic needs took up the bulk of one's time, it is no wonder that what we in the free world regard as banal had been a cause for celebration in the USSR. *We the Living* shows people rejoicing when they obtain non-moldy millet for dinner or lentils or bread: "Next week, they say, we are going to get lard. That will be a holiday, won't it? That's something to look forward to, isn't it?" (425; see also 24, 57, 146). Indeed, with the struggle for survival in the forefront of every Soviet citizen's mind, it is normal life that had become an unattainable ideal: "Abroad . . . I heard . . . they say they don't have provision cards, or cooperatives, or anything, you just go into a store just when you feel like it, and just buy bread or potatoes or anything, even sugar. Me, I don't believe it myself" (154).

Food was not the only thing that was difficult to find. Soviet shortages spread to all items of production. The wistful longing for lard, bread, and potatoes was matched by a wistful longing for toilet paper, stockings, shoes that fit, etc. From time to time, the Rosenbaums mentioned their struggles to obtain footwear or clothing. Mr. Rosenbaum once reported his unsuccessful, weeks-long search all over Leningrad for a light bulb (254d/April 6, 1933; 310c/February 21, 1934).

We the Living shows that such articles of clothing that were available in stores served merely to protect oneself from the elements. Finding something attractive and fashionable was an almost unattainable dream. Kira had a single dress in which to attend social occasions, a plain gray dress with short sleeves and a shirt collar, remade from one of her mother's old dresses. On another occasion, Kira spent three weeks painstakingly turning an old dress inside out, thus acquiring a "new" dress: "the blue wool was smooth and silky on the inside; it looked almost fresh" (95, 183). The rags that people wore contributed to taking the joy out of get-togethers: "The guests sat huddled in corners, shivering in old shawls and sweaters, tense and self-con-

scious. . . . They kept their arms pressed to their sides to hide the holes in
their armpits; elbows motionless on their knees—to hide rubbed patches;
feet deep under chairs—to hide worn felt boots" (152).

This aspect of life in *We the Living* was also autobiographical. Ayn Rand
once mentioned that in Russia she had only one dress to go to parties in,
which was remade from her mother's old summer coat. Natasha once jok-
ingly reminisced that her elder sister's dress was so old and worn out that it
was a museum piece (4.5b/February 21, 1926). When a dress became so old
that it was shiny with wear, it might have been turned inside out, as Kira had
done; material to make a new one was hard to come by. The teenage Ayn
Rand wore dresses made out of her mother's old garments, and these were
in turn handed down to her sisters: Natasha reported going to a party in a
"new" outfit made from one of Ayn's old dresses (84a/November 23, 1926).
Mrs. Rosenbaum remarked that she, like everyone else, is "wearing ugly and
shapeless felt boots," but that at least they keep her feet warm. Nora remembered that in Russia, Ayn used to wear things "which bore a vague resemblance to boots" (96c/January 14, 1927; 103d/February 14, 1927).

Old clothes shiny with wear and shapeless felt boots were an ugly reality
for women, who yearned for fashion. For the Rosenbaum women, that ugliness was partially relieved for a few years, when Ayn sent them American
fashion plates (40c/June 4, 1926). Her mother and sisters could sew themselves clothes in the latest American fashion, whenever they could buy some
material. She once sent Natasha and Nora each a set of pajamas, as a gift.
Compared to their regular clothing, these pajamas were luxury items, which
her sisters did not want to use for such a mundane purpose as sleeping.
Natasha refashioned her pajamas into a dress, and Nora wore hers when she
entertained her friends, as an exotic party outfit.

Mrs. Rosenbaum once explained to Ayn that they were not writing to her
often enough because of certain obstacles set in their way, such as the
unavailability of envelopes for mailing abroad (17a/April 21, 1926). The condition of the Rosenbaums' letters themselves serves as mute testimony to the
lack of quality products in Soviet Russia. The contrast between the faded,
thin and crumbly scraps of paper their letters were written on, and the thick
sheets of stationery Ayn Rand's American relatives used to write to her at
about the same time, is staggering.[9]

Jobs, Not Careers

"What is my life? I have no career. I have no future" (284).

We the Living presents the kind of hand-to-mouth jobs that Soviet citizens
held. A person did not have a career, that is, a long-range pursuit of goals in
one's chosen field of endeavor. Instead, people clung to any jobs they could

find with the desperation of animals hanging by their claws over an abyss: only Soviet employees had ration cards, which were one's passkey to food, and one could lose one's job at any moment. Those who were denied employment were condemned to starve. Kira clung to her secretarial position in the House of the Peasant despite the rotten work environment, for it was the only thing keeping her and Leo alive (192–99). And she eventually lost that job because of her boss's fear and Comrade Sonia's whim:

> Comrade Sonia roared with laughter: "Well, well, well! A loyal citizen like Comrade Argounova in the Red 'House of the Peasant'!"
>
> "What's the matter, comrade?" Comrade Bitiuk [Kira's boss] inquired nervously, obsequiously. "What's the matter?"
>
> "A joke," roared Comrade Sonia, "a good joke!"
>
> Kira shrugged with resignation; she knew what to expect. When a reduction of staffs came to the "House of the Peasant" and she saw her name among those dismissed as "anti-social element," she was not surprised (225).

A person rarely liked his work; jobs were simply what one did to keep one's head above water. This remained true in the late 1920s and 1930s. Judging by the Rosenbaums' descriptions of their work and that of other individuals they knew, people often did not work in their specialty. Rather, they took whatever job they could find and hung on to it for as long as they could. Mrs. Rosenbaum summed up the situation: "All the older people are sick and dying and are making room for the younger generation. But the younger generation has nothing to look forward to. They grab whatever job they can find, but none of them likes his job" (173b/December 27, 1928). She herself typically held several jobs at the same time, each bringing in a little bit of money to help keep the family afloat. The other family members were in a similar situation (173b/December 27, 1928; 238/November 25, 1932; 250c/ February 26, 1933).

A number of jobs mentioned in *We the Living* were ones that Ayn Rand and/or her relatives held at one time or another. For instance, Kira's mother, Galina Petrovna, became a teacher in a workers' school. So was Mrs. Rosenbaum, who had been employed in a school for workers' children since 1921, and who continued to hold that position throughout the years of her correspondence with Ayn. The only difference is that in the novel Galina Petrovna taught sewing, whereas Mrs. Rosenbaum taught foreign languages. But Ayn's mother could not survive on this salary alone, even though more than one school employed her at a time. She complained that her workload was huge while her wage was very low (12c/April 8, 1926; 72a/August 24, 1926; 194/ March 31, 1930). She needed another source of income, which she managed to secure for a few years: translation.

In *We the Living*, when Kira and Leo first started their life together, Leo had been making a living translating English, German, and French books into Russian for the Gossizdat (the state publishing house). It was work he could do at home, and it paid relatively well (136–37). Translation was Mrs. Rosenbaum's favorite job for the same reasons (25/May 3, 1926, 29c/May 11, 1926): "You work at home, you set your own hours, and you earn almost twice the annual pay in a workers' school" (40c/June 4, 1926). When the teenage Ayn Rand still lived in Russia, she secured translation jobs for her mother by submitting American movie magazines and other literature to the publishing house for translation.[10] For the first few years after she left, she sent her family American novels, which her mother then offered to translate for the state publishing house. Mrs. Rosenbaum marveled at Ayn's skill in selecting just the right books: many of the ones that she sent over a period of about two years were accepted, keeping Mrs. Rosenbaum in work that paid well. In *We the Living*, Ayn Rand describes the kind of foreign novels the Soviet publishing house was likely to accept:

> [in these novels] a poor, honest worker was always sent to jail for stealing a loaf of bread to feed the starving mother of his pretty young wife who had been raped by a capitalist and committed suicide thereafter, for which the all-powerful capitalist fired her husband from the factory, so that their child had to beg on the streets and was run over by the capitalist's limousine with sparkling fenders and a chauffeur in uniform (136–37).

What she sent were novels with communist themes. Her mother urged her to send books "with a social message," as those almost certainly would be accepted (12.5b/April 11, 1926).

Because translators could earn decent money by Soviet standards, Mrs. Rosenbaum taught some English to Natasha and Nora, who helped out with her translation projects. The entire family would pitch in to translate a book in the short amount of time allowed for by the publisher's deadline. Mrs. Rosenbaum was the chief translator, with Natasha as her assistant. They would divide up the pages of a novel to be translated, and each work independently. Nora's job was copying down translated sentences that her mother and sister would say out loud and looking up unfamiliar words in the dictionary. Mr. Rosenbaum, who did not know English, was often recruited to recopy translated pages, but Natasha complained that he was not much help: he would read the material and start discussing its philosophical and literary worth, which slowed them down.[11]

In *We the Living*, Kira gave private lessons in French for a while to make ends meet (173, 178). There is some evidence that Mrs. Rosenbaum, too, gave private foreign language lessons (7b/March 7, 1926; 12c/April 8, 1926).

In the novel, another job Kira held was lecturer and excursion guide at the Museum of the Revolution (formerly the Winter Palace). When the excursion center called, she would go to the museum to lead a tour, and receive a few rubles for her effort (258). This detail was autobiographical. Ayn Rand, in her last couple of years in Russia, worked as a tour guide, a job she got with the assistance of her mother, who herself had led tours through the Peter-Paul Fortress and around many of Leningrad's other points of interest (96c/January 14, 1927; 120c/ June 3, 1927; 124e/July 14, 1927). Mrs. Rosenbaum continued to guide tours throughout the years of their correspondence. She found tour guide jobs for her other daughters as well. A few years later, she reminisced about the days when Ayn used to work as a tour guide: the excursion center was a place of petty quarrels and intrigue, a "hornets' nest," where everyone was at each other's throat (288b/October 5, 1933).

It is doubtful that any of these jobs was something that Mrs. Rosenbaum and her daughters would have chosen as a career. They were simply a means of putting food on the table. Mrs. Rosenbaum from time to time lamented about the availability of new work and the danger of losing the job one had. She reported that if you missed a day of work and did not have a doctor's note explaining your absence, you would be dismissed and barred from further employment. And if you lost your job, you would lose your ration card and starve (254a/April 3, 1933).

Because keeping a job was necessary for bare survival, no one was immune from the fear of "reduction of staffs." In *We the Living*, everyone from Kira to Kolya Smiatkin (a minor character) lived in dread of this disaster (e.g., 153–55). One of Natasha's friends, who dropped in for a visit while Natasha was writing Ayn, added a few lines to Natasha's letter, conveying her worry that there might soon be a reduction of staffs where she worked (49c/June 27, 1926). When Nora was awarded a prize for being the most "socially active" at the school where she worked, it allayed her and her family's fears, because winning that prize guaranteed her continued employment—at least temporarily (270/July 8, 1933).

In *We the Living*, no one—including Kira—dared ignore a notice about oneself in the wall newspaper at work. A negative reference could lead to dismissal; a positive one increased one's job security. Kira's mother was praised in the wall newspaper for being one of the best teachers at her school (260). So was Mrs. Rosenbaum, who was pleased by the praise primarily because it guaranteed that she would not be dismissed yet (96c/January 14, 1927; 215b/July 1, 1931; 374a/ August 11, 1935).

Kira and the other excursion guides had to pass periodic political examinations, requiring the memorization of much useless information, such as the numbers allegedly reflecting coal production in the Don Basin, the latest decree of some commissar on schools for illiterates in Turkestan, and the state of some strike of British textile workers (324–25, 327). Those examined lived in mortal fear of their performance; some suffered nervous breakdowns, because failing an exam was likely to lead to dismissal. This, too, was taken from real life. Mrs. Rosenbaum, as a schoolteacher, was required to be "politically conscious." She reported that the Education Commission sat in on her class—a fact that cost her many long, stressful days of preparation, for her teaching "had to be ideal in terms of methodology, subject, grammar, *and ideology*" (255d/ April 14, 1933, emphasis added).

In *We the Living*, Irina, Leo, and others were forced to work without pay on extra projects or risk losing their jobs, and everyone had to be active in the Marxist clubs at work for the same reason. They thus lost countless hours in political meetings or on Marxist thesis writing (69–70, 145, 154, 166, 202, 205–6, 256). Natasha, who studied piano at the conservatory, complained that the number of mandatory political meetings left little time for piano practice. She later mentioned that she had to attend many political club meetings in order to keep her job (172c/ December 9, 1928; 292/October 23, 1933).

We the Living shows how the Soviets replaced the legitimate pursuit of a long-term career with mindless work performed unwillingly to avoid starvation. Every minute of a citizen's life was regulated so as to destroy his ability to determine his own career and make other important decisions. Kira wanted to be an engineer, but was expelled from the Technological Institute because of her "social origins" and so had to make ends meet by leading tours of uninterested peasants and filing unread documents. Leo wanted to be a philosopher, but was expelled from the University and condemned to starve. This same pattern characterizes the lives of Irina, Sasha, and the other positive characters (212–14, 254).

This, too, was drawn from real life: Soviet citizens were condemned to a purposeless existence, with their basic survival needs as their most pressing concern, leaving little room for anything else. Consequently, countless lives were wasted. People did not flourish, but dragged themselves through their days. In the Rosenbaum family, Natasha is a particularly poignant example of this waste of talent. She studied piano, was one of the best students in her class at the conservatory, and—according to her mother's letters—passionately loved her work (20b/April 25, 1926; 23a/April 28, 1926, 41b/ June 8, 1926). Her mother commented, after watching Natasha's solo performance at a concert, that "when she is playing the piano, she looks like a leopard about to pounce on its prey," and added with a wistful longing that "if Natasha were to fall into the hands of some exploiter, her talent would really blossom and the world would know of her" (7b/March 7, 1926; 85c/ November 28, 1926). Unfortunately, in Soviet Russia this dream was not to be realized. Instead, Natasha had to give up the piano and work as a tour guide, a job she loathed, for the rest of her short life. (She died in the summer of 1942 during an air-raid.) On the job, she frequently led tours outdoors, walking for two hours at a time in the freezing cold of Leningrad (136c/ November 21, 1927; 197a/May 17, 1930; 218.5/November 4, 1931; 219.5/January 17, 1932; 300/December 24, 1933).

Nora followed the same pattern. Her career passion was costume design; during Nora's years of correspondence with her sister, she sent her many drawings of beautiful and elegant ladies wearing exquisite clothes. Sometimes she made drawings directly on the paper on which she and the other family members wrote their letters (see 20b/April 25, 1926 for a particularly spectacular example of the latter). Her joyful and graceful artistic style was constantly criticized in Russia. She was told to bring her goddesses down to earth (358/February 6, 1935; 359.3a/March 12, 1935). Instead of designing costumes and stage sets, as she wanted to, she was forced to do work that did not make use of her talent. Like her mother and Natasha, she made ends meet as a tour guide. She also worked as a teacher of graphics and as an architect. And she loathed these jobs and the fact that they prevented her from pursuing her desired career (189/December 28, 1929; 197a/May 17, 1930; 218.5/November 4, 1931; 219.5/January 17, 1932; 310a/February 21, 1934).[12]

Nina Guzarchik (Ayn's cousin and friend) suffered a similar fate to Natasha's. Her interests lay in cinematography, but she was prevented from such a career, spending her life swimming from job to job. During the ten years of her correspondence with Ayn, she worked (often for a very low wage) as a dancer, a teacher of graphics, and an architect (188/October 22, 1929; 229/June 30, 1932).

Pursuing a long-term career was often impossible, so people attempted to give themselves the illusion of such a pursuit. To this end, the Rosenbaums, their extended family, and a number of their acquaintances enrolled in courses that taught skills that they did not care to acquire and knew they would never use. For instance, Natasha studied Latin and engineering; Nora studied drafting and engineering; Nina studied architecture. Although a waste of time, working on course assignments gave one the illusion of being busy and moving toward a goal. In reality, there was nothing awaiting any of them. Mrs. Rosenbaum spoke for many Russians when she complained about their pointless lives (293/October 27, 1933).

Drab, Joyless Existence

> "[Kira] found suddenly that the mere fact of keeping alive had grown into a complicated problem which required many hours of effort, the simple keeping alive which she had always haughtily, contemptuously taken for granted. She found that she could fight it by keeping, fiercer than ever, that very contempt; the contempt which, once dropped, would bring all of life down to the little blue flame of the Primus slowly cooking millet for dinner" (135).

Kira never drops that contempt; she is the only character in *We the Living* who does not surrender. Although she is forced to endure ugly living conditions, she never allows the ugliness into her soul. She never, even temporarily, accepts that kind of existence as *normal*, as all that one can hope for in life.

But those around her do accept such an outlook. Their ambitions since the revolution never rise above trying to buy buckwheat at the co-operative before it runs out; their conception of ecstasy is being able to take a "nice, hot bath with soap" (432–33, 24). Soviet living conditions made life meaningless. Nina Guzarchik summed it up best: "Nothing here. No prospects for the future" (55/July 3, 1926). A common theme running throughout the family's correspondence is the drabness and joylessness of their lives and their consequent depression.[13] Mrs. Rosenbaum frequently commented that their lives were dull and monotonous—which she regarded as a *positive*, because change usually heralded a turn for the worse. "Same daily grind, day in and day out, and I often thank god for that, because frequently I'm afraid things will get worse, since any changes are more likely to be negative than positive" (7b/March 7, 1926). She was happy whenever a day went by without misfortune. The daily battles to acquire food, clothing and medical treatment, she complained bitterly, made them unwilling to generate the energy to go on living (7b/March 7, 1926; 247/February 5, 1933; 248/February 5, 1933; 251b/March 6, 1933).

Resignation infected every area of life, even that which is normally the most joyful: romantic love. *We the Living* shows love falling victim to the gray rot of daily Soviet existence. It mentions divorces for the sake of a bread card and describes marriages for the sake of Party standing (155, 298–305). Vava Milovskaia, a stylish young woman in love with Victor Dunaev and eager about her future with him, eventually gives up and settles for a marriage to Kolya Smiatkin, a dull, nerdish drudge. She mutters in justification: "What is there to wait for? What can one do with oneself, these days?" (314–15). In letters written a few months after her daughter's departure, Mrs. Rosenbaum reported on a flurry of marriages—or "registrations," as they were called—devoid of celebration or joy. She noted that "everyone is getting married, everyone is unhappy," and predicted that none of the newlyweds would enjoy his or her married life (36a/May 21, 1926; 74a/end of August, 1926; see also 13/April 13, 1926 and 14/April 14, 1926). This was not said out of malice; it was a prediction based on wide observation. Indeed, a few years later, she and Nina reported that all those people were divorcing or already divorced (229/June 30, 1932; 276a/August 3, 1933; 308/February 9, 1934).

A Soviet citizen could not count on taking a vacation from the dreariness of Soviet life. Going out of town was fraught with difficulties, owing to the multitude of permits and other documents one had to obtain to travel and to stay in another town temporarily. Here is a relevant scene from *We the Living*:

Once, Kira and Leo attempted to spend a night in the country.

"Certainly," said the landlady. "Certainly, citizens, I can let you have a room for the night. But first you must get a certificate from your Upravdom as to where you live in the city, and a permit from your militia department, and then you must bring me your labor books, and I must register them with our Soviet here, and our militia department, and get a permit for you as transient guests, and there's a tax to pay, and then you can have the room."

They stayed in the city (162–63).

Natasha and Nora described similar struggles to arrange for summer vacations with their husbands. In Nora's case, this included, among other things, waiting in line for twelve hours to buy a train ticket. And Natasha described the hoops she had to jump through in order to obtain permission to go on holiday with her husband (271/July 18, 1933; 282b/September 5, 1933).

Even when successful, the sisters and their husbands did not have much to look forward to. Some Soviet citizens could take a vacation at a "rest home," in which one could secure a spot through one's place of employment. One summer, Nora and her husband went on such a "holiday" by the seashore. But it turned out that they had to live in separate rest homes, and Nora was assigned to a room with five other women. The rest home had no indoor plumbing; one cardboard outhouse had to serve the needs of the entire building. Since no baths or showers were available, one had to wash in the sea (347b & c/October 2, 1934).

If one was unsatisfied with such an arrangement, one could choose a different Soviet vacation option: In the summer, rows of tents were set up on hard ground in a wooded area outside the city. These tents, along with makeshift outdoor cooking facilities, made up a "tent town"—an arrangement reminiscent of an American Civil War army camp. Citizens could rent a tent, as Mr. Rosenbaum did for a couple of weeks in the summer of 1932 (261/May 12, 1933).

In the years before Ayn Rand left Russia, Mrs. Rosenbaum and her daughters sometimes rented a room in a small house in a town outside of Petrograd, for a few weeks over the summer. During these vacations, the teenage Ayn slept on a mattress whose springs stuck out (37a/May 26, 1926), and as there was no indoor plumbing, she had to carry water up to the house in buckets. Nevertheless, in contrast to the kinds of vacations they had to contend with in later years, Natasha had fond memories of these outings (59b/July 14, 1926).

If vacations failed, people could still attempt to escape the drabness, if only for the span of an hour or two. *We the Living* mentions crowds that flocked to plays and movies, with an eagerness disproportionate to the mere pursuit of an evening's entertainment (97). The same was true for Ayn Rand's family. Mrs. Rosenbaum summed it up for all of them when she said that because they disliked their work, they went to the theater to escape (316b/ April 6, 1934).[14] During her last couple of years in Russia, Ayn Rand herself attended hundreds of films in local theaters.[15]

Because they lived like animals trapped in a cage, people dreamed of the free West. *We the Living* projects the reverence felt for "abroad."[16] Kira's family and her acquaintances regarded foreign-made objects, and listened to stories of life in the West, with breathless wonder. Kira's cousin Irina sat through two showings of a foreign film in order to catch a single shot of New York at night.[17] So did the young Ayn Rand herself. All of this, too, was autobiographical (250c/February 26, 1933). In the 1930s, the Rosenbaums listened to the radio frequently, because they could occasionally catch foreign broadcasts. In 1934, they saw their first American "talkie." This was their only chance to get a glimpse of the American way of life; for the first (and only) time they heard how Americans speak, and they saw on the screen a "black jazz band singing, and the sounds of life of an American city" (332/August 8, 1934). The Rosenbaums had yet another source of information about life in America: letters from Ayn Rand. Her mother responded to one of her letters describing the joyousness of Americans: "What a people! Everyone is so happy. When living conditions are good, people are benevolent" (59b/July 14, 1926).

Nora dreamed for years of getting out of Russia and going to America; the rest of the family wished to go as well (see, e.g., 12.5a & b/April 11, 1926). Unfortunately, that fervent wish could not be realized. Although Miss Rand attempted in the 1930s to get her family out of Russia, she did not succeed: the Soviet government refused to let them emigrate. Like Kira, most of Ayn Rand's family would never make it out of Russia. Mr. and Mrs. Rosenbaum, Natasha, and Ayn's cousin Nina all perished before or during World War II.[18]

The background of *We the Living* was not invented; it was taken from real life—from the daily life that the young Ayn Rand had lived, and that nearly a thousand letters from her family reflected.

WE THE LIVING: REALISM *AND* ROMANTICISM

> "As far as literary schools are concerned, I would call myself a Romantic Realist."[19]

In the *Art of Fiction* Rand says:

> In today's literature, many books do not have any abstract theme, which means that one cannot tell why they were written. An example is the kind of first novel that relates the writer's childhood impressions and early struggle with life. If asked why the particular events are included, the author says: "It happened to *me*." I warn you against writing such a novel. That something happened to *you* is of no importance to anyone, not even to you (and you are now

hearing it from the arch apostle of selfishness). The important thing about you is what you *choose* to make happen—your values and choices. That which happened by accident—what family you were born into, in what country, and where you went to school—is totally unimportant.

If any author has something of wider significance to say about them, it is valid for him to use his own experiences (preferably not too literally transcribed). But if he can give his readers no reason why they should read his book, except that the events happened to him, it is not a valid book, neither for the readers nor for himself.[20]

Rand rejected the literary school of naturalism, which presents people as they are, not as they should be, and in place of plot and stylized characterization chronicles the actions of "average" people. As a romanticist, she held that the better novelists are not passive, uncritical reporters of the people and events they see around them; instead, she adhered to a literary principle that she argued was first formulated by Aristotle and adopted by the romanticists, namely, that unlike history, which represents things as they are, fiction should represent things as they might be and ought to be.[21]

But in *We the Living*, Rand certainly made use of "things as they are" in the Soviet Union—i.e., the people and events of 1920s Russia that she and her family observed. As she points out: "the living conditions, the atmosphere, the circumstances which make the incidents of the plot possible, are all true, to the smallest detail."[22] I have provided ample evidence for this in the present chapter. In addition, most of the songs that figure into the story—e.g., "You Fell As a Victim" and "John Gray"—are real;[23] and the University purges (in which Kira, Leo, Irina, and other students were expelled) actually took place. Ayn Rand was a victim of the purges, expelled from the University of Petrograd in December 1923.[24] And I could go on.

Does the fact that the background of *We the Living* has been taken from real life, recording the exact sorts of things that its author had seen and experienced herself during her youth in Soviet Russia, contradict her esthetic convictions? Did Rand choose the events of her first novel simply because they happened to *her*, and the location simply because that is where *she* grew up?

No. As she writes, *We the Living* "is not a novel about Russia. It is a novel about the problem of the individual versus the mass . . . and a plea in defense of the individual. . . . I have selected Russia as my background merely because that problem stands out in Russia more sharply, more tragically than anywhere on earth."[25] In her foreword to the 1959 edition of *We the Living*, she says that:

> *We the Living* . . . is a story about Dictatorship, any dictatorship, anywhere, at any time, whether it be Soviet Russia, Nazi Germany, or—which this novel might do its share in helping to prevent—a socialist America. What the rule of brute force does to men and how it destroys the best, will be the same in 1925,

in 1955 or in 1975—whether the secret police is called G.P.U. or N.K.V.D., whether men eat millet or bread, whether they live in hovels or in housing projects, whether the rulers wear red shirts or brown ones, whether the head butcher kisses a Cambodian witch doctor or an American pianist (xv).

In her introduction to Victor Hugo's *Ninety-Three*, Rand points out that "Hugo's story is not devised as a means of presenting the French Revolution; the French Revolution is used as a means of presenting his story."[26] In the same way, her story is not devised as a means of presenting life in 1920s Soviet Russia; the details of life in 1920s Soviet Russia are used as a means of presenting her story. Her use of her own experiences in Soviet Russia, which the letters from her family confirm, does not dull her theme or make her story merely journalistic; instead, these details help her to create an even more accurate picture of totalitarian existence.

The realism of *We the Living* is perfectly consistent with Ayn Rand's romanticism. In order to present things "as they might be and ought to be," a writer need not shun things that actually happened. The theme of *We the Living* is the evil of dictatorship; the events of the plot show that dictatorship crushes human lives, that such a system makes impossible the pursuit of human values. The real-life conditions, events, or persons that she included were all carefully selected to convey that theme. For instance, including the University purge, a policy that denies young people an education, thus destroying their chances for a future, supports her message.

The concrete details of Soviet existence recorded in the novel are true to life: they are the conditions that Ayn Rand herself and other Russian citizens were forced to endure. But these details are neither the focus nor the essence of her novel, nor do they make the point of her story inapplicable to other people, places and times. They were an excellent means of presenting her theme, which is universal. The ethical-political theme of *We the Living*—that man's life is sacred and that dictatorship destroys it—is relevant in any society and era, and is one that we cannot afford to ignore.[27]

NOTES

1. Michael S. Berliner, ed., *Letters of Ayn Rand* (New York: Dutton, 1995), 18.

2. These letters, written in Russian, are housed in the Ayn Rand Archives. When I cite a letter, I usually indicate both its archive file number and its date (e.g., 93d/ January 3, 1927). Translations from the Russian are my own.

3. The letters from her family date from 1926 to 1936; *We the Living* is set in the mid-1920s (in her foreword to the revised edition, Ayn Rand speaks of 1925 [xv]). For further information on the nature of life in the Soviet Union at this time, see Stéphane Courtois et al., *The Black Book of Communism: Crimes, Terror, Repression.* Trans. by Jonathan Murphy and Mark Kramer (Cambridge, Mass.: Harvard University Press,

1999), chapter 6. Also see Sheila Fitzpatrick, *Everyday Stalinism: Ordinary Life in Extraordinary Times: Soviet Russia in the 1930s* (New York: Oxford University Press, 1999). The period Fitzpatrick covers is the thirties, but much of what she describes is applicable to the twenties.

4. Biographical interviews (Ayn Rand Archives).

5. See *We the Living*, 164, 177.

6. See *We the Living*, 33, 135, 164, 177–82, 187, 198, 202, 218–19, 315, 355.

7. This was fortunate by Soviet standards. The housing shortage wreaked havoc with marriages. Some spouses were forced to live apart, because of a lack of living space (282a/September 5, 1933). Divorces, too, were often impossible, owing to the difficulty of finding separate housing (211b/April 2, 1931).

8. In *We the Living*, Irina says to Sasha: "I'll draw two dozen pictures—there, abroad—and you can stick them all over the walls of our house. Sasha, *our house!*" (337). In Rand's novella *Anthem* (written in 1937, revised edition, in 1946), the hero and heroine—recently escaped from a collectivist dictatorship—discover a house from "the Unmentionable Times," and are astonished: "We found no other beds in the house, and then we knew that only two had lived here, and this passes understanding. What kind of world did they have, the men of the Unmentionable Times?" Ayn Rand, *Anthem*, fiftieth anniversary edition (New York: Signet, 1996), 103.

9. This comparison is based on letters to Ayn Rand from her relatives in Chicago written around the same time. Unfortunately, her letters to her family in Russia have not survived.

10. In her final year or so in Russia, Ayn Rand was a student at the Leningrad Cinema Institute, studying scenario writing and other skills for working in the movies. While a student there, she wrote reviews of and essays about American films. My translation of two of these essays can be found in Ayn Rand, *Russian Writings on Hollywood*, Michael S. Berliner, ed. (Marina del Rey, Calif.: The Ayn Rand Institute Press, 1999). It is most likely that she obtained her information about the American film industry from American movie magazines, to which she subscribed. (See, e.g., 7d/March 7, 1926; 8a & c/March 12, 1926.)

11. A completed translation might have been submitted to the publishing house in handwritten form. Hence, a manuscript had to be neatly recopied for submission. Many of the earlier letters in the correspondence mention or discuss this translation work. See, e.g., 3.5; 7b; 8b; 10a, b, & d; 12b & d; 12.5b; 15a, b & c; 17a & c; 23c; 25; 27a, b & c; 29c; 31a; 33; 35b; 37a & b; 38a, b, & d; 40c; 43; 45c; 58d; 59c; 60; 61a, b, & c; 64a & b; 65c; 66a; 67c; 68a & c; 70a; 71.5a; 74b; 75b & c; 77c; 78b; 79a; 80b; 83a, b, & c; 84d; 85a; 87b & c; 88a & c; 92c; 94e; 98c; 188; 194.

12. Unlike Natasha, who was barred for the rest of her life from the work she loved, Nora was later able to find employment closer to her calling.

13. See, e.g., letters 5a, 7b, 14, 38d, 69, 82c, 84d, 97, 102b, 103e, 176a, 195, 222b, 229, 247, 248, 251b, 280b, 289, 308, 315, 341.5—among others.

14. See also 94d/January 10, 1927 and 310c/February 21, 1934.

15. A diary she kept of the movies she saw is reprinted, with my translation, in Rand, *Writings on Hollywood*. See also *We the Living*, 91, 95, 96, 146, 381, 383.

16. On the meaning of the word "abroad" for a Soviet citizen, see Ayn Rand, "The 'Inexplicable Personal Alchemy,'" in *Return of the Primitive: The Anti-Industrial Revolution*, Peter Schwartz, ed. (New York: Meridian, 1999), 125.

17. See *We the Living,* 79–80, 142–43, 153–55, 174–75, 184–85, 208, 337, 357–58, 444, 447–48, 457.

18. Correspondence to Ayn Rand from Nora, 1973; correspondence from one of Ayn Rand's cousins to another, December 1946.

19. Ayn Rand, "The Goal of My Writing," in *The Romantic Manifesto: A Philosophy of Literature,* revised edition (New York: Signet, 1975), 167.

20. Ayn Rand, *The Art of Fiction: A Guide for Writers and Readers,* Tore Boeckmann, ed. (New York: Plume, 2000), 16. Emphases in the original.

21. Ayn Rand, "Basic Principles of Literature," in *Romantic Manifesto,* 80; Aristotle, *Poetics,* 1451a36–b5, 1460b8–11, 1460b32–35, 1461b11–13.

22. Berliner, *Letters,* 4.

23. See Michael S. Berliner, "The Music of *We the Living,*" in the present volume.

24. See: *We the Living,* 209–15; Berliner, *Letters,* 636–37; Ayn Rand's University of Petrograd student file (Ayn Rand Archives), and Biographical interviews (Ayn Rand Archives). Soviet law allowed expelled students who had less than a year before graduation to complete their studies. This amendment was provided in response to pressure from a delegation of foreign scholars angered at the injustice. Since Ayn was in her final year at the University, she was readmitted three months later and graduated in July 1924. Most children of nonproletarian parents were not so fortunate.

25. Berliner, *Letters,* 12–13.

26. Ayn Rand, "Introduction to *Ninety-Three,*" *Romantic Manifesto,* 156.

27. I wish to thank Robert Mayhew for his comments on earlier versions of this chapter.

4

Russian Revolutionary Ideology and *We the Living*

John Ridpath

"Russia has a long revolutionary history."

—Sasha Chernov in *We the Living* (258)

Ayn Rand began work on *We the Living* in 1930 at age twenty-five, having left Communist Russia only four years earlier. The manuscript was completed by March 1934, before she turned twenty-nine.[1] Soon after this and over the next thirty years, she entered into a lively dialogue with readers, editors, fans, and others over aspects of *We the Living*. And on at least five occasions, she specifically addressed one issue: the "background" in *We the Living* as contrasted with the plot.[2]

Repeatedly, she stressed the fact that while the plot, as her own artistic creation, is fictional, the background for the novel was "true," "true to the smallest detail," "real," and "exact." Further, in an October 17, 1934, letter, she states that the "background is more essential than the plot itself," as it "creates the characters and their tragedy." And in a February 2, 1936, note to her publisher, she writes that "the background and circumstances which make the plot possible are entirely true."[3]

The background to *We the Living* is the setting within which the plot development occurs. As such, it includes the following. First, there is the myriad of people (family, friends, students, bureaucrats, etc.). Second, there is the existential world in which they all live (decaying cities, bureaucratic indifference and cruelty, fanatical adherence to communism, omnipresent hardship and doom, etc.). And third, there is the ideology of the communist revolution, which motivates several of the central characters, is the unacknowledged cause of the spreading material and spiritual disaster portrayed in the novel, and is omnipresent in the culture of *We the Living*.

The background to which Ayn Rand refers consists, in essence, of the ideology as the cause, and of the characters (other than the heroes) and the existential setting, as the effects.[4]

The focus of this chapter is the ideological background to *We the Living*.[5] That background, as we shall see, is in the first instance Lenin's and Stalin's versions of Marxism as "adapted" by them to the Russian situation of the early twentieth century. In what follows, I present the essentials of Marxist-Leninism, and reveal the accuracy with which Ayn Rand portrays this ideology in the action of *We the Living*.

Marxist-Leninism was the ideological *cause* of the Russian Revolution of 1917. It was also the *effect* or result of a century-long revolutionary movement within Russia, without which its rise to prominence and domination never would have occurred. In addressing the ideological background of *We the Living*, therefore, the primary goal of this chapter is to present the long period of fermentation during which the old wine of elitist tyranny was poured into the new bottle of Marxist-Leninist ideology that dominates *We the Living*. This ideology is the background to *We the Living*, and this chapter will present the background to that background.[6]

REVOLUTIONARY IDEOLOGY AS PRESENTED IN *WE THE LIVING*

The revolutionary ideology that pervades *We the Living* is presented to us in several ways. It appears in speeches and lectures, it is present in posters, banners, and slogans. And it underlies the myriad of pronouncements and denouncements that appear constantly, throughout the story, as rationalizations for the robotic actions of the young revolutionaries. That tyranny in Russia is necessary, what its "lofty" goals are, and why sacrifice is virtuous, are constant mantras in the background of Kira's struggle to live.

With some exceptions—Pavel Syerov's speech at Andrei's funeral being the best example (435)—the ideological background is sprinkled throughout *We the Living* in seemingly disconnected and unsystematic fragments. For this chapter, I made note of over seventy of these.

It is possible, however, to take each instance of ideological rhetoric and identify the idea or theme it presents. This, in turn, reduces the isolated instances into a set of general propositions, and this set constitutes the ideological background in *We the Living*. Finally, these propositions can be placed in hierarchical order from the philosophically broadest to the more narrow and derivative. When this is done, the ideological "fragments" in *We the Living* coalesce into a comprehensive viewpoint, and this revolutionary ideology surfaces as a set of abstract "visionary speculations," plus an asserted set of narrower implications for human life of these speculations.

The ideological background of *We the Living* is no fictional concoction, tailored to fit the novel. Ayn Rand, as we have seen, repeatedly insisted that the background to *We the Living* was factual and true in every detail. This chapter will demonstrate that, in regards to the ideological aspect of the background to *We the Living*, her claim to factual accuracy is completely justified.

IDEOLOGY IN *WE THE LIVING*: THE ABSTRACT VISION

The first component of the ideology in *We the Living* consists of seven abstract propositions that are so broad and "visionary" that they could and have been applied to historical processes and events throughout human history.[7] These propositions themselves have a long history, and it is in examining this history that this chapter presents the background to the background of *We the Living*.

The world that both Ayn Rand and Kira Argounova lived in arose out of the following philosophical framework.

1. *There are profound and inescapable forces at work in history* (38, 58, 109, 174, 189, 295).

This notion, that the world is a stage on which a drama of human, if not cosmic, proportions is being played out, has a long history. In various forms, it has appeared in all of the Western religions, and it reappears here in an allegedly materialistic, scientific, and secular form. Throughout its long history, this "vision" presents some version of the Christian redemption saga: man, cast out and alienated from the good, struggling to return in order to be redeemed.

In *We the Living*, we find this notion repeatedly asserted in claims that "history is on the march," and a "historical drama of gigantic importance" is underway and will "sweep the earth."

2. *These forces must not be resisted or impeded* (38, 58).

The claim here is that the successful completion of this drama is the highest good. To participate in it and help to further it, is the most important purpose to which a life, and all human life, can be devoted. To not understand and not accept this, and thus to resist it or act to impede it, is the hallmark of the "lost soul," and is intolerable.

3. *These forces work through a specific process of first generating and then overcoming contradictions* (32, 170–71, 254, 308–9).

This necessarily mysterious process, known as "the dialectic," will be discussed later.[8] It appears in *We the Living*, for example, in Lenin's infamous New Economic Policy. This "policy," which is in place throughout the novel, involved the contradiction of freer markets within the embrace of a totally state-controlled economy. It also appears in Irina's observation that Sasha has been expelled from university for trying to think in a country of free thought. And again, it appears in the denouncement of Trotsky for his "purity," i.e., his unwillingness to embrace contradictions, when circumstances required it.

4. *These historical forces work through and, therefore, necessitate conflict and violence* (30–31, 38, 73, 128, 162).

The dialectical process, as we shall see later, involves three steps. (It has been described as a "weird waltzlike contortion."[9]) In this process, an integrated situation, known as the thesis, arises. With time, an "opposite" or "contrary" to this thesis, known as the antithesis, develops within the thesis, and as a result of this contradiction, stress or tension builds. Finally, the tension, becoming no longer sustainable, is released in a cataclysm of conflict and violence (a revolution!), and a higher stage of historical development, known as the synthesis, is reached. This becomes a new, "fuller" integrated thesis, from which, inevitably, the process begins again. This process does not stop until the final goal of redemption is reached.

We see this view of the necessity of violence in *We the Living*: when Kira is told she is living in a "historical cataclysm"; in posters showing proletarian boots stomping on bourgeois necks; and, in little children singing of their "world of fire and blood."

5. *The goal being sought by history is "humanity," the releasing of "the truly human life," "the redemption of man"* (31, 58, 270, 426).

This is the supposed "goal" or "speculative vision" that justifies the violence, the cruelty, and the tyranny, both in the fiction of *We the Living* and in the 20th century horrors perpetrated by communists around the globe. Thus, when Kira first arrives at the Petrograd railroad station, she is greeted with a poster stating "Comrades! We Are the Builders of a New Life!" Following this, and throughout the novel, Kira is bombarded with the claim that the revolutionaries are building "a new humanity."

6. *These deep historical forces work through collectives* (42, 162, 166, 193, 270, 435–36).

The great historical forces have "mankind" or even "God" as their beneficiary, and work through the most potent agencies on hand. Be it "the Church," "the wretched of the Earth," "the laboring people," "the State," or whatever, it is such collectives that are most potent, and the significance of individuals lies exclusively in their participating in these collectives. "Society, Kira, is a stupendous whole"; there must be a "tight welding of the collective," a "clamping of the workers and the peasants." All must serve "the eternal collective."

7. *The achievement of the goal history is seeking requires that individuals must sacrifice, or be forced to sacrifice, to the collective* (42, 46, 51–52, 70, 89–90, 145, 155, 176, 270, 355, 436).

This is the moral implication of all the foregoing and is the most pervasive philosophical dictate throughout *We the Living*.[10] Kira is bombarded at every turn with her duty to society, her good fortune at having many years to give to the cause, the notion that "the brotherhood of workers and peasants should be the goal of her life," and that she and all other individuals are "human resources" to be used by the state.

IDEOLOGY IN *WE THE LIVING*: THE NARROWER MARXIST-LENINIST APPLICATION

The second and more predominant component of the ideology in *We the Living* consists of five specifically Marxist-Leninist propositions. These are the form in which the wider vision we have covered is adapted, by Lenin, to the needs of the Russian revolutionaries. By examining the actual evolution of Marxist-Leninism in Russia, we will come to see the impressive accuracy with which Ayn Rand presents this in *We the Living*.

1. *The Industrial Working Class is the historical force through which history's goal will be achieved* (391).

As we shall see later, in detail, the industrial working class is the potent collective agency which, as the antithesis formed up within the capitalist thesis, will, through revolution, transcend the conditions that prevent a truly human life, and usher in man's truly human future.

2. *A person's consciousness (the ideas, hopes, and values held) is a determined by-product of the economic class to which he belongs* (25, 70, 73, 174, 179, 196–97, 209–11, 296–97).

This is Marx and Engel's materialist version of human consciousness, and Kira is constantly being bombarded with this. She is told that she suffers from her "bourgeois prejudices"; she is warned about her "arrogant bourgeois attitudes." Those who are "from bourgeois descent" are incorrigible; factory owners and their children are the worst class enemies of man. Those who are "from the workbench or the plough," on the other hand, are pure and on the side of mankind.

3. *The class is all. You must fight your private self and narrow ego* (71, 311).

Individuals are significant only in their participation in the collective force.

The "slobbering egoism of the bourgeois whiners" must be outgrown, to the point where no one will have any individualist thoughts at all.

4. *The proletarian revolutionary force will be incapable of grasping its own best interest, let alone organizing and acting to achieve it. An elite group, therefore, will have to control them, and lead them down the path to their fulfillment* (55, 308–9).
This is the premise behind the training, at the university, of the young zealots who will be "the vanguard of the world revolution." All of them, in turn, will be slavishly obedient to the dictates of the elite vanguard party, as will it, in turn, be to its dictatorial leadership.

5. *The revolution is not limited to Russia alone; it is worldwide* (162, 166, 173, 200, 268, 308).
Thus we see, throughout *We the Living*, the visits from foreign labor agitators, utterances about "the world revolution," and children singing of their "world fire of blood."

This, in brief, is the ideology presented in *We the Living* as part of the background to the story. This is "what created the characters and their tragedy." Every one of these tenets was behind the actual Russian Revolution; and all of it is false. It is no mere coincidence that the total and brutal imposition of such ideas upon a society produces nothing but decay, destruction, inhumanity, suffering, and death. To observe such a catastrophe, as Ayn Rand did in her own life, and as readers do through *We the Living*, is a wrenching experience. But it must be faced if we are to learn from history. In the real world of communist Russia, as in *We the Living*, the roofs did in fact leak, the houses collapsed, the railroads were in chaos, the public clocks had no hands, the doctors had no phones, and the people were starving. They did hoard bread crusts and fight over the bodies of dead horses. They did walk stooped over, lose their children in crowds, descend into bestiality, and watch helplessly as all their hopes, and even their lives, shrank to nothing before them.

Why did this happen? What reduced Czar Peter the Great's St. Petersburg—his "jewel of the West"—to this? Ideas did this—false ideas. Not only is Ayn Rand's fictional description of existential life in *We the Living* true to reality, her portrayal of the dominant ideology is also true—it *was* the actual ideology that fueled Lenin's revolution.

We turn now to the historical context behind the ideology and events as portrayed in *We the Living* in order to see that the disaster of communist Russia has a longer and deeper history than the portrayal Ayn Rand was able to offer in *We the Living*.

SETTING THE STAGE: RUSSIA BEFORE 1825

Revolutionary ideology in Russia developed in three stages. First came the "Russian Jacobins" of the 1850s and 1860s; then came the Marxist stage of the 1870s and 1880s; and finally, there is the Leninist version of Marxism featured in *We the Living*. While the Russian Jacobins and the Marxists are the background to the background, they in turn grew out of an earlier history. We begin, therefore, with a brief sketch of this history in order to understand the context that would eventually give rise to the Russian revolutionaries.

Russia has had a long, tortuous, and dark history, dominated for centuries by three institutions. The first of these was despotic autocracy—absolute rule by one. The roots of this lie in the thirteenth century, when all of the lands to the west of the Ural Mountains, including the vibrant and relatively civilized area around Kiev, were invaded and conquered by the Mongols. Everyone was subjected to the absolute, unlimited, and unchallengeable rule of the Khan. Asiatic despotism took hold, and would last for 250 years. In order to control this vast conquered territory, the Khans relied on the help of those who ruled over various principalities. These were the Khan's loyal and trustworthy grand dukes.

By the fifteenth century, the Mongol grip over these territories and these dukes began to erode, and in 1480, the grand duke of Muscovy (Ivan II) gained independence from the Khan, took control of the territory, and adapted the Mongol term for leader: czar. With this, Asiatic despotism in new Russian garb became a central institution in Russia's history.

The second institution dominating Russia's history—the Russian Orthodox Church—has even earlier roots. In the fifth century A.D., Rome collapsed and the Catholic Church fled to Constantinople—the center of an alien Byzantine culture that had begun to penetrate what would later become Russia. This culture was primitive, agrarian, and communal, and obsessed with the mystical power of the soil. When the Catholic Church returned to Rome, the Constantinople "eastern" branch continued, led by its own patriarch. In the centuries that followed, disputes between Rome and Constantinople grew— particularly over what was the correct (i.e., "orthodox") form of worship. This ended in 1054, with the Roman pope excommunicating the Eastern patriarch who, claiming a monopoly on the proper form of Christian worship, founded the Eastern Orthodox Church. This church spread slowly, eventually reaching Muscovy. When the Mongols, retreating from the West, sacked Constantinople, the patriarch there granted independence to the Moscow church, and the Russian Orthodox Church was born.

This church maintained that it alone (and certainly not the Roman Church) followed the proper form of worshipping God. Therefore, it saw as its mission to show all Christians, even all of mankind, the true path to redemption. This involved proper forms of worship and proper forms of work, the latter being voluntary collective labor on the soil. This type of labor, they believed, would generate a mystical process out of which God's truth would emanate to all. Salvation would follow the grasping of God's truth, and could only be achieved collectively, as a "people." The "toilers of the soil" are God's "royal priesthood." The people and the soil together make Mother Russia holy.[11]

The third institution dominating Russian history is serfdom. Early in Russia's czarist history, Czar Ivan IV (1547–84) embraced the mission of the Russian Orthodox Church. Already the owner of all the land in Russia, he extended his ownership by binding to him all those who worked his land. Serfdom, the Russian form of slavery, arrived and was later formalized in 1649 by Czar Alexis Romanov, in his infamous Russian Code of Law, which was based on the principle that every individual belongs, first and foremost, to the Czar.

By the middle of the seventeenth century, as the scientific revolution in the West accelerated, and the basis for the enlightened eighteenth century was being laid, Russia was sinking into despotism, Christian mysticism, collectivism, and human slavery.

When Czar Alexis died, and his son Peter became czar (Peter the Great, 1689–1725), it seemed that he would bring secularism, Western ideas, industry, customs, and institutions to Russia. His interest in this, however, was undercut by his financing of a huge military, his wasteful building of St. Petersburg, and his organizing the state into a powerful institution which, assisted by new organs of repression and terror, would see to it that his will was done.

Hope resurfaced again under Czarina Catherine (1762–1795), who, because of an early fascination with Western ideas, was known as "the philosopher queen." She was a study in contradictions, however, and as she aged, she lost interest in the West, and turned to extending serfdom to 90 percent of the Russian population.

Hope resurfaced for a third time when Catherine's grandson, Alexander I, became czar (1800–1825). He also admired Western ideas and accomplishments. He urged the Russian nobility to seek Western knowledge, and developed around him a coterie of Western-thinking advisors.

Like Peter and Catherine before him, however, he turned away from the West as he aged, thus precipitating a true tragedy in Russia's history. Advisors, nobles, and army officers had followed his lead, and had turned to the West for guidance. They had read Locke, Smith, Bentham, and other Western liberal thinkers, and had become open advocates of liberalism in Russia, and outspoken admirers of the American Revolution and the Founding Fathers. Finally, they had observed successful uprisings against autocracy in Spain, Italy, and Greece. Consequently, they began to plan an uprising against the turncoat Czar Alexander; but in December of 1825, he died suddenly—and his even more reactionary son, Nicholas I (1825–55), took the throne.

The tragedy of "the Decembrists" followed. These heroic officers confronted the new Czar on the very day he took the throne, at the Winter Palace in St. Petersburg. Nicholas met their pleas with bayonets, personally interrogated them all, and had them executed, announcing a few days later: "I cannot permit that any individual should dare defy my wishes, once they are known. The slightest infringement will be punished with all the force of the law. No pardon will be granted."[12] With this, Nicholas I began a thirty-year reign of warfare abroad, and the embracing at home of Russia's holy mission to lead mankind to God. All opposition to czarism was to be crushed. He censored ideas, alienated the educated, distrusted the people, and increasingly relied on a growing state police bureaucracy. He openly suppressed universities, and drove the intellectuals underground where, like poisonous mushrooms in the cellar, the seeds of the Russian revolutionary movement were sown and nourished.

TWO SHUNNED FUTURES: RUSSIA 1825–1855

In the face of the 1825 murder of the Decembrists, and Nicholas's subsequent policies, it became obvious to Russia's intellectuals that Russia would have to climb out of its dark past by abandoning czarism and serfdom. But to what end? In favor of what new type of social system?

In the first half of the nineteenth century, Russian intellectual life came to be dominated by two competing schools of thought on this, both trying to steer Russia away from czarism and onto the right path. In neither case, however, was that path to be the one followed by the Decembrists. Russia's future, both schools agreed, did not lie down the road to Western liberalism, freedom, and capitalism. According to one school, it lay back down the road to the past, to the Russian Church and agrarian collectivism. According to the other, it lay ahead, down the road to the future, as discovered by the nonliberal Western thinkers: the road to industrial socialism.

The first of these two schools were the *Slavophiles*.[13] The Slavophiles were so named because when faced with Russia's dilemma (to Westernize or not), they chose to shun the lure of the West, and to return to Russia's Slavic past. This school was to some extent influenced by Western ideas, notably those of Schelling and the early German Romantics. Their deepest roots, however, lay in the Russian Orthodox Church: the mystical soil of Holy Mother Russia and the simple, communal, agrarian peasant life. To them, Russia's backwardness was its strength, not its weakness. Czars Peter, Catherine, and Nicholas I were seen as imposers of alien ideas and goals on Russia, like the Mongols before them. Russia's czars, nobles, bureaucracy, and intellectuals, it was claimed, were all caught up in this, and thus had "lost their souls" and become "wanderers in their own land," as they sought to divert Russia from her divine historical mission.[14]

In the Slavophile view, Russia should shun Western secularism, individualism, liberalism, industrialism, and wealth. Instead, Russia should re-embrace the village commune (the *obschina*) and simple cooperative agrarian labor governed by councils of appointed elders (the *mir*). Once this life is reestablished, and with the Orthodox Church as a guide, the mystical transformation of the people (*sobornost*) will occur. Thus, fused as a "people" into one group consciousness, the path to redemption will become clear. Faith in the "visionary speculations" of the church and the Slavophile thinkers will lead Russia to nonviolent, nonstatist communism, under which alienation will end and man will be redeemed.

The second school, the *Westernizers*,[15] like the Slavophiles, were also struck by the great contrast between Russia and the West. But they did not conclude that Russia should shun the West. Quite the opposite. They believed that Russia's intellectuals must learn from the West—not from the Western liberals who had led the Decembrists to their doom, however, but from the French socialists (e.g., St. Simon, Fourier, Proudhon) and the German idealists, with heavy emphasis on the philosophy of Hegel.[16] From these sources, the Westernizers were led to the transformation of Hegel's thought flowing out of the young Hegelians at the University of Berlin in the 1830s and 1840s.[17]

Guided by these sources, the Westernizers were appalled by the "unmitigated horrors" of early Western capitalism.[18] They were also appalled by the mysticism and backwardness of the Russian Orthodox Church. Their conclusion, therefore, was that Russia needed socialism. Not mystical, rural, cooperative socialism, but scientific, industrial, state-guided socialism, supported by the populace but guided by the intelligentsia.

By this stage in her history, Russia's intellectuals had already embraced all of the general philosophical propositions to be found in *We the Living* (outlined above, pp. 89–91). There is an historical struggle underway to redeem humanity. Private property, individualism, and capitalism are now holding back this process. Russia needs communal work and collectivized property, guided by the intelligentsia. Czarism and serfdom must be abolished. But how is this to be done?

Driven by Nicholas I into underground journals and discussion groups, the Westernizers, led by a young Alexander Herzen, came to view themselves as Russia's "new men," whose destiny it was to lead Russia in overthrowing czarism and serfdom (cf. Herzen's *From the Other Shore*). With time and maturity, however, Herzen's group turned against the false guidance of philosophical abstractions that, with Moloch-like[19] power, could absorb and destroy actual men. They turned instead to "the people," the rural populace—to working with them, and being guided by their simple wisdom, in order to achieve reform of Russia through gradual, nonviolent means. This group was the forerunner of a later nineteenth-century movement in Russia known as "Populism," with its slogan "to the people."

Not all of the young Westernizers, however, followed this path. A different group, led by Vissarion Belinsky, was driven by its peculiar psychologies to remain loyal to the need for violent revolution. This was not to be revolution *by* the people, but revolution *for* the people, who were themselves unable to understand their plight or take action on their own behalf. This group took as their slogan not "to the people," but "to the axe." Russia's revolutionaries had arrived.

In Ivan Turgenev's influential and famous novel *Fathers and Sons* (1862), we encounter the "fathers": decent, intellectual, concerned men who hope for gradual nonviolent change in Russia. By contrast, the "sons," epitomized by Arcady Kirsanov and the nihilist Eugene Bazarov, are superficial, impatient, and angry, and welcome the prospect of violent upheaval in Russia. These "sons," whom Herzen would come to characterize as "the syphilis of our revolutionary passions,"[20] are the prototypes of Russia's revolutionary movement. They are the "new men" who alone understand "what is to be done," and have the motivation to do it.

RUSSIA'S FIRST REVOLUTIONARIES: THE JACOBINS

Social history is replete with examples of the fate that was now to descend on Russia.[21] False philosophical ideas seep slowly from books and lectures into the culture—propounded and spread by seemingly intellectual, patient, civilized men. From this process, the "fathers" are born. These are men who have integrated into their subconscious some valid ideas and values and are, consequently, able to retain intellectuality, patience, and decency, despite undermining their basic outlook by the inconsistent and/or false ideas they have absorbed. Characteristically, such men are horrified by incivility, emotionalist rage, murder, and destruction. While they turn to dialogue, consultation with others, journal writing, and civilized discourse in pursuit of their mistaken philosophical goals, they meet with frustration and intolerance, and become bewildered, apathetic, defeatist, fatalistic, and, in the end, irrelevant.

The "sons," on the other hand, experience no such restraint. If, when young, they have absorbed false ideas—such as those propagated by the church or Hegel, and encouraged by the tragedy of serfdom—they develop early psychologies of anxiety, impotence, self-loathing, and anger. As they develop intellectually through their adolescence, they are easily persuaded to embrace a more consistent pseudophilosophical framework that will serve to rationalize their anger and scorn, turning it outward against the external world they now hold responsible for their suffering. And most importantly, these pseudophilosophical "speculations," which are in fact mere emotionalist assertions, provide them with the perspective within which their lonely and troubled lives are transformed into the agency through which great redemptive historical change is going to come to fruition. In essence, early childhood philosophical error produces a psychology that, in turn, seeks out a grander philosophical rationalization that, once in place, is immune to any further challenge.

Out of this process, the characteristic personality of the revolutionary emerges. He is full of abstract "justification" for his views and actions; he is impatient with dialogue, anxious to "act, not talk," and unconcerned with—in fact, even relishing—the violence, power, and destruction he deems necessary to the fulfillment of the great redemptive mission.

These are the mentalities that were developing in the dark cellar groups of Czar Nicholas' Russia, and who were about to bring revolutionary ideology and action into Russian life as a prelude to Marx and Lenin.

When Czar Nicholas I died in 1855, his successor, Alexander II, having witnessed the rising tide of opposition to czarism, announced his intention to reform and liberate Russia. He lifted the ban on university philosophy departments, reformed the judiciary, emancipated the serfs (1861), and set about reviving local government agencies (*zemstovs*) throughout Russia.

As the result of this "liberalization," Russia's universities reached out into the broader populace, offering subsidized education. Students from all parts of Russia, and all walks of life, came to Moscow and St. Petersburg. They were known as "the *raznochintsy*," the "people of diverse ranks." Cut off from their rural roots, eager to make their mark on Russian history, and bearing guilt and anger over the conditions from which Russia's peasantry suffered, they were easy prey for the radicalized branch of the Westernizers, and were soon co-opted into the underground revolutionary movement. Thus, when Alexander II abandoned his flirtation with liberalism in the early 1860s, and clamped down once again on the universities and the private discussion groups, the *raznochintsy*, prepared by their professors and intellectual leaders, were, despite not having yet encountered Marx, ready to act. The crop of poisonous cellar mushrooms was ready for harvest.

In 1862, as part of the repression of the intellectuals, Alexander II ordered the arrest and imprisonment of a prominent journalist, a leader in underground discussion circles, and hero of the *raznochintsy*: Nikolay Chernyshevsky. He was sent to Peter and Paul prison in St. Petersburg, where he immediately set about writing what would become an historic novel: *What Is to Be Done? Tales about a New People*, published in 1863. Joseph Frank, a noted scholar of nineteenth-century Russian literature, writes of this work: "If one were to ask for the title of the nineteenth-century novel that has had the greatest influence on Russian society . . . Chernyshevsky's novel, far more than Marx's *Kapital*, supplied the emotional dynamic that eventually went to make the Russian revolution."[22] Frank is both correct and insightful in his focus on the "emotional dynamic" of the revolutionary movement. With this novel—a lauding of Turgenev's "sons" as the needed "new people"—the revolutionary fires in Russia were lit to burn for fifty-five years, right up to the lecture halls and parading zealots of Kira Argounovas's world in *We the Living*.

Who were these early revolutionaries, and what did they stand for?[23]

The leading lights in this dark epoch in Russian intellectual history were: Mikhail Bakunin (1814–1876), Nikolay Chernyshevsky (1829–1889), Dimitri Pisarev (1840–1868), Pyotr Zaichnevsky (1842–1896), Pyotr Tkachev (1844–1886), and Sergei Nechayev (1847–1882).

My focus is on Chernyshevsky, the undisputed leader, and idol, of the group.

Nikolay Chernyshevsky, son of a Russian orthodox priest, was "educated" at home until age fourteen. He was then sent to a theological seminary where he demonstrated his intelligence and mastered eight foreign languages. In 1846 he arrived at the University of St. Petersburg where his Orthodox Church upbringing was challenged by the ideas of the Westernizers. Within two years he was won over, and by the age of twenty was immersed in the study of the French utopian socialists, Hegel, and the ideas of the young Hegelians, most notably Ludwig Feuerbach. (More on Hegel and Feuerbach shortly.) Chernyshevsky abandoned religion, accepted materialism, and committed himself to achieving the good of mankind as revealed to him by these mentors.

Another mentor was Mikhail Bakunin (1814–1876), who in his twenties had left Russia to study in Berlin. Studying in Berlin at this time meant studying Hegel and offering revisions, called "critiques" or "transformations," of Hegel's views. Bakunin's revisions included a rejection of Hegel's view on the process of change whereby historical advance occurs through transcending, while also preserving, the present. In its place, Bakunin insisted that advance occurs through the destruction, not the preservation, of the present.

By 1855, Chernyshevsky—now twenty-seven, committed to revolution and destruction and known in intellectual circles as a teacher and literary critic—was ready to take advantage of Alexander II's leniency. He denounced both Western liberalism and czarism, and sought to rally the people of Russia in support of rural, communal, agrarian life. By the time Alexander clamped down on the intelligentsia, Chernyshevsky had lost confidence in the people's ability to discern their true interests or muster the commitment to act for themselves. Thus, as his own imprisonment loomed, Chernyshevsky turned to the French revolution—notably to Maximilien Robespierre—for guidance. With this, the Russian Jacobin[24] movement was born.

Jacobism, as characterized in the final bloody stages of the French revolution, stood for those "visionaries" who alone knew the destiny that man must seek. They also knew that they alone, and certainly not the masses, knew this, and thus they must lead their world through a bloody revolution, cringing at nothing, in order to reach this destiny.[25]

In Turgenev's *Fathers and Sons*, Bazarov is a defeated and aimless nihilist, waiting and longing for social destruction. He has no idea of or passion for what might follow the destruction. Chernyshevsky's *What Is to Be Done? Tales about a New People* goes much further. Here we find the blueprint for what is to be done, the portrayal of those who must do it, and the plan for carrying it out. Throughout Chernyshevsky's writings, we find the following themes which, it will be apparent, include many of the ideological themes found in *We the Living*.

In a secular version of his youthful religious outlook, Chernyshevsky was obsessed with the theme of a suffering mankind, cut off from "the full life of organic and psychical unity." One's highest calling—the most meaningful life a person could live—is to work "for the good of mankind." The achieving of such a life is only possible by merging oneself with the whole of mankind through sacrifice of oneself to the cause.[26]

This lofty goal cannot, and never will be, achieved naturally and spontaneously by the populace. "The mass of the population knows nothing, and cares about nothing, except material advantages."[27] Nor will it be achieved by waiting passively for some process of natural evolution to occur. Achieving the good of mankind, therefore, requires the leadership and action of those select few (the "new people") who do understand what is at stake, and what needs to be done. He writes: "The appearance of strong personalities has a decisive influence on history. They impose their character on the direction of events . . . the new type has been born . . . it does not matter what one thinks of them . . . whatever they say *will be obeyed by all.*"[28] As for the general populace, "The mass is simply the raw material for . . . political experiments. Whoever rules it tells it what to do, and it obeys."[29] These "new people," the "elite cognicenzy" who will take on this historic responsibility, are "those able to realize the correct principles," those who are "rare specimens," "the flower of the best people."[30]

Obviously, the "weak" common people cannot be allowed to struggle against or oppose their leaders. "Therefore, I believe that the only good form of government is dictatorship . . . aware of its mission." The "strong" must realize that there will be resistance from the "weak." They must be prepared to crush this ignorant barrier to man's fulfillment. "Only the axe can save us, and nothing but the axe. . . . Summon Russia to take up the axe." And they must be resolute, and not shy away from the violence and destruction they will cause: "the high road of History is not the sidewalk of the Nevsky Prospect . . . [do not] shrink from dirtying one's boots." Finally, they must stop at nothing, until the final goal of man's fulfillment is reached: "This organization of new men must usurp government through dictatorship, and stop at nothing. We shall be more consistent than the great [Jacobin] terrorists of 1792 . . . [our] enemies must be destroyed by all possible means."[31]

For the more moderate Westernizers, this was a horror, and they turned away from revolution to working with and learning from the people. But to no avail. In their conflict with the more irrational, vicious, and consistent

Jacobins, they were pushed aside, as a whole generation of fanatics followed Chernyshevsky's lead. Among these, the following stood out.

Dimitri Pisarev (1840–1868) presented the movement with a role model of what it meant to be a dedicated revolutionary. Totally committed to destruction by the age of twenty-two, and armed with the requisite dialectical rationalizations for his self-loathing and anger, he joined Chernyshevsky's revolutionary cell. He was arrested along with his idol, went to prison, suffered a series of mental breakdowns, and twice attempted suicide. Released from prison in 1866, he drowned in 1868, and became a martyr to their cause.

Pyotr Zaichnevsky (1842–1896) supplied the revolutionaries with exact guidelines as to what kinds of actions the "new people" must be prepared to take. In his *Young Russia*, written when he was nineteen, he presents in blatant blood-curdling language the manifesto of the Russian Jacobin. The only escape from the "monstrous, oppressive condition" from which Russia suffers is "revolution, bloody and merciless revolution." The elite revolutionary party "must seize the dictatorship into its own hands, and stop at nothing." Opponents must be "massacred," and in this, the revolutionaries must "be more consistent than . . . the great terrorists of France."[32]

Sergie Nechayev (1847–1882) showed the revolutionaries, by his own life, what it would mean to be a revolutionary. Later an idol of the American Black Panther Party, and referred to by Lenin as "the titan of the revolution," he came to prominence at age twenty-two (1869) when he orchestrated the murder of a disobedient young follower.[33] In the same year, he cowrote with Pyotr Tkachev a manifesto entitled *Program of Revolutionary Action*, devoted to methods for recruiting and molding "new people." In 1870, Nechayev faked his own arrest and snuck off to join Bakunin in Switzerland, where they wrote *Principles of Revolution*, which advocated the assassination of the czar and his minions.[34] This tract was followed by *Catechism of the Revolutionary* stressing the selflessness, necessary coldness, and fanatical commitment to the cause characteristic of the true revolutionary. To drive the message home, Nechayev snuck back to Moscow, set up a conspiratorial student group, murdered a faltering member in 1871, implicated members of his own group in the murder to further revolutionize them through prison terms, and then fled back to Switzerland. Arrested soon after, he was sent to Peter and Paul Prison for the rest of his life, where, from his cell, he organized the infamous terrorist group, the Narodnaia Volya or "The People's Will."[35]

Finally, Pyotr Tkachev (1844–1886) deserves mention for contributing three things to the revolutionary movement: an operating manual for revolution; an elaborate theoretical rationalization for revolution; and an introduction to the works of Marx and Engels. Tkachev addressed the mechanics of actually seizing power. He faced the fact that after seizing power, a long period of indoctrination of the populace would be needed. By teaching them the rudiments of "progressive communism," the revolutionaries "would breathe new life into society's cold and dead forms." And he argued in his *Revolution and the State*, contrary to the orthodox Marxist view, that the Russian state, not being an agent of any capitalist class, "floats in the air" and is there for the Jacobins to seize and use in the prosecution of the revolution.[36]

RESPECTABILITY AND GUARANTEED SUCCESS: THE ROLE OF HEGEL AND MARX

While in Europe the left studied the growing corpus of works by Marx and Engels, in Russia Chernyshevsky's "new people" turned to violence, disruption, and assassination. On March 1, 1881, the People's Will succeeded in assassinating Czar Alexander II.

Not surprisingly, Czar Alexander III turned on them. Claiming that God had instructed him to reinstate total autocratic, czarist rule (weakened by Alexander II), he built the government institutions necessary to this end: a police-state to dominate culture; a state bureaucracy to manage the economy; and an organ for the persecution of Russia's Jewry. Revolutionary fervor and activity appeared to diminish. As Alexander III's grip on Russia tightened, the revolutionary movement—not lacking in passion and notoriety, but losing credibility—struggled on in increasingly desperate need of four things.

First, while the ideology of the movement was sufficient to generate moral fervor and desperate action, it failed them in other respects. It offered them only abstract "speculation" on which to build, not scientific rigor. And it offered them the vision of a battle to be waged, but no guarantee that they would win. Second, they lacked credibility to outsiders. Their ideology was viewed as the dreams of misfits, rather than genuine social theory with proven historical relevance. Third, they had no developed following or power base outside the ranks of their own devotees. And finally, they had very little internal organizational structure or plans on how actually to conduct a revolution.

Starting in the 1880s, Marxism seeped into Russian revolutionary circles to cater to the first two of these needs. Later, at the turn of the twentieth century, as we shall see, Lenin's "revisions" of Marxism would fulfill the rest of their needs. And with this, the Russian revolution, and the "background" world of *We the Living*, would descend on Russia.

Marxism is the allegedly scientific demonstration of the fact that the inescapable laws of history necessitate an imminent revolution in which capitalism will be displaced and replaced by socialism, and that under socialism, humanity will at last be fulfilled.

These views were developed by Karl Marx (1818–1883) between 1836 and 1848 as he wrestled with the philosophy of Hegel. To understand the essentials of Marxism, therefore, an extremely brief essentialized overview of Hegel's philosophy is necessary.[37]

Hegel is a candidate for the title of philosophy's most profound and comprehensive "visionary speculator," as well as a good example of the importance of Protestant Pietism in eighteenth- and nineteenth-century thought.[38] Initially trained in a Protestant theological seminary, as a young man he was tortured by his separateness from God, and by the threat of sin and damnation. Never has a more elaborate resolution to this dilemma appeared in print! In long, torturous tomes, Hegel presents the following.

The universe, which is the creation of an omnipotent but not omniscient God (the Absolute or Reason), appears to us to be an independent, material reality. This, however, is an illusion. The universe is not only God's creation; it is in fact a manifestation of God in evolution, the cosmic mind (e.g., Reason) in action.[39] For what purpose? Hegel's God, not being omniscient, lacks crucial knowledge. This cosmic consciousness is ignorant of its own nature, of the fact that it is everything (the "totality," "infinitude," the "absolute"). In Hegelian terminology, the Absolute is "alienated" (i.e., separated) from its own identity, and is, therefore, incomplete, unfulfilled—in not knowing itself—and suffers from this self-ignorance. To end this suffering and return to itself fulfilled, the Absolute enters into a course of action, of struggle, out of which the end awareness of itself as "totality" will be achieved.

To engage in this struggle, the Absolute sets up a foil, an illusion of limitedness, for it to then confront and overcome, and thereby discover its own unlimitedness or "infinitude." This foil is the appearance to it of an independent, material universe that confronts the Absolute as "objectivity," "limit," "the other." Out of the origin ("pure Idea" as the thesis) appears its apparent opposite ("pure Nature," the antithesis). Out of "Idea" (mind unconscious of itself) comes "Nature" (matter, apparently separate from and opposing mind). And then, in the form of idea-in-nature, as "Spirit" or "Geist," the Absolute confronts the apparently objective world, engages it, and proceeds with the idealist struggle to overcome the seeming opposition of idea versus nature (thesis versus antithesis). Out of this struggle to "smash objectivity" arises the insight (the higher synthesis) that the Absolute is everything. The purpose of the illusory material world is fulfilled, and the Absolute, as Cosmic Ego, rests fulfilled in its discovery of its own true nature.

This triadic process of achieving fulfillment through a series of thesis-versus-antithesis clashes, which end in higher syntheses, each of which then unfolds into new "fuller" theses-antitheses-syntheses triad, is Hegel's famous dialectical process. This is why Hegel's philosophy is called "dialectical idealism." This process is one of seemingly stable "moments" in history, generating within itself its own opposite or contradiction, followed by a struggle or conflict between them. The resolution of this conflict constitutes an advance—a higher "moment"—from which the process of internally gener-ated tension, and then release of that tension in another advance re-occurs. This goes on until the ultimate goal is reached.

All of this applies to human history as follows. Geist (Spirit, Idea *in* Nature) appears in the form of man. Man's history, therefore, is the record of Geist's struggle through historical time to achieve its goal. This struggle is furthered, first, in individuals, but then, more powerfully, in families, or com-munities, or nations, or closely-knit "volk" or nation-states. Virile nation-states engage in this struggle in the form of warfare with other states, down through the "slaughter-bench" of human history. At crucial stages in the dia-lectic of human history, agents of the Absolute appear, as World-Historical Individuals (Alexander, Caesar, Napoleon), who lead Geist to ever-higher awareness. Hegel believed that his philosophy, conjoined with Napoleon's advance and the rise of the Prussian state, had brought Geist to the long-sought goal!

This, in essentials, is the Hegelian "speculative vision" that Marx encoun-tered when he arrived at the University of Berlin in 1836.

Karl Marx was raised in a Jewish family that had converted to Protestant-ism.[40] Consequently, in his youth he sought the path to a Christian life of serving, and even saving mankind, writing high school essays on these top-ics. By age eighteen, however, having wandered into a more dissolute and angry life at the University of Bonn, his father transferred him to a "serious" university—the University of Berlin. When Marx arrived there, the great Hegel had been dead for five years, and the campus was dominated by dis-cussion and criticism of Hegel's ideas.

Marx was drawn into this, immersed himself in study, and "converted" to Hegelianism in 1841, at age twenty-three. But which Hegel?

When Hegel died, his followers disagreed over what his ideas implied for any action they should or should not take in their own lives. One group held that the goal of the Absolute, to reach awareness of its own infinitude, seemed to have been fulfilled, both in the march of the Prussian Volk-state, and in the mind of Hegel himself. Nothing further being required, these "qui-etists" retired from activism to await the end of history. To other young schol-ars, however, bent on their need to act, fight evil, and serve mankind, quietism was not merely wrong, it was disreputable. When the young Marx arrived, newly distanced from religion and looking for a redemptive life of action, he was immediately drawn to this group, known as the "left" or "young" Hegelians.

Led by David Strauss and Ludwig Feuerbach, they accepted Hegel's notion of the dialectical processes of "advance" as the great kernel of truth in Hege-lianism. But they believed that this kernel had been hidden within Hegel's mystical, idealist, cosmic shell, thereby diverting attention from the real struggle here on earth to end man's alienation from his own true nature. Their mission, therefore, was to demystify Hegel, to "transform" his ideas into guidance for the real struggle, namely, to end human alienation here, not holy alienation in the cosmos.

Strauss and Feuerbach led the way, focusing attention on religion, which gave all man's attributes of productivity, justice, goodness and love to God. In doing this, religion was the true source of alienation. What men needed to do was abandon God, re-orient their focus on themselves, and engage in communal labor and love of mankind. If we reorient ourselves and see that Hegel's philosophy is, in truth, "esoteric psychology," alienation will be overcome.

Marx was excited by this. Feuerbach had succeeded in overcoming Hegel's mystifications, thus showing that alienation is man's problem, not God's, and that to overcome this, man must act, not philosophize. But Feuerbach had not gone far enough. He had not located the fundamental source of human alienation. He had condemned religion, but failed to see that there are "unholy forms of alienation" that are deeper than religion. Feuerbach was (in a pun) the "brook of fire" that had to be crossed to arrive at the true root of alienation, which lay in man's economic life.

In a burst of activity, from 1842 to 1848, Marx wrote a series of tracts, culminating in the *Communist Manifesto*, in which he believed he had laid bare the true source of alienation in man's life, and the actual arena within which the dialectic operates. The true source of alienation is the separation of the economic laborer from the instruments with which he labors. The proletariats, as a class, face the owners of the means of production, the capitalists, in a dialectical clash of interests. This situation, driven on by deterministic forces, drives both the proletariat and the bourgeois further and further from the fulfillment possible through communal, voluntary labor. At the same time, this situation steadily drives the two classes (the thesis and the antithesis) into deeper conflict, which, by 1848, Marx believed had reached its breaking point. Thus the *Communist Manifesto's* call to revolution: "Workers of the world, unite. You have nothing to lose but your chains." In 1848, Marx and Engels believed that the "nodal point" of history had arrived, a revolutionary clash of interests would occur, the dialectical tension between thesis and antithesis would be released in a social revolution, and after a brief transitional period, human alienation would come to an end as the communist era—heaven come to earth—began.

When the expected revolution did not occur, Marx set to work to prove "scientifically" that his prediction of the overthrow of capitalism was backed up by necessary dialectical laws of economics and history. Thus, Marxism is referred to as dialectical historicism. He worked on this unsuccessfully for the rest of his life, in his famous *Das Kapital*, trying to prove that his theoretical "laws of capitalist development" were actually at work, and that the inevitable socialist revolution was at hand. The capitalist institutions of exploitation, dominance, and alienation were about to be overthrown in a violent revolution. The exploited would achieve a common understanding of their plight and of what they must do, and they would then rise up *en masse* in revolution, temporarily seize political power, use the state to "expropriate the expropriators," and prepare a short-lived dictatorship *of* the proletariat, following which the state would "wither away" and communist utopia would arrive. And then the long-awaited reuniting of man with his alienated essence would occur, and the "pre-human history" that man has suffered through would end.

MARXISM COMES TO RUSSIA

These Hegelian and Marxist "visionary speculations" bolstered the struggling Narodniks by offering them pseudoscientific respectability, the moral certitude of rightness, and the historical guarantee of success that they needed. When Marxism came to Russia, most of the ideological propositions in *We the Living* fell into place.

Marx's early writings first came to Russian attention in the late 1840s primarily through translations and other efforts on the part of Herzen and Bakunin. In 1869, a Russian translation of the *Communist Manifesto* appeared, followed by *Das Kapital* in 1872.

Russian intellectuals, led by the "father of Russian Marxism," Georg Plekhanov (1857–1918), immediately recognized the value of Marxism to the Russian situation, and in 1883, the explicitly Marxist organization, "The Liberation of Labor," was formed. Early Russian Marxists embraced the seeming "scientific respectability" Marxism gave to their cause. But they faced a major difficulty with Marx's theories. This was the claim—central to Marxism—that the laws of social history, rooted in economic forces and relations, dictate that the development of capitalism is indispensable in generating the conditions for revolution.

To Plekhanov and other orthodox Russian Marxists, this meant that they must work to foment capitalism in Russia. Some of them, therefore, set out to promote Western liberal ideas and capitalism in Russia. Even the Decembrists of 1825 were rejuvenated as heroes.

In 1871, the Paris Commune socialist uprising in France collapsed. Marx and Engels were crushed. Revealing their ultimate commitment to be to revolution above theory, they went back to the theoretical drawing board and "discovered" that, under some circumstances, the capitalist stage of history could, in some societies on the capitalist periphery, be sidestepped. Russia exhibited these circumstances. When these views appeared in print,[41] Plekhanov and Russia's orthodox Marxists were displaced to the sidelines of

Russia's revolutionary movement, as the Jacobins moved to the fore. Released from the need to experience capitalism before revolution, they set to work on two fronts. They began "revising" other aspects of Marxism (as Marx had done with Hegel) to fit their Russian situation. And they began to organize discipline within their ranks, as they began to prepare for the overthrow of czarism and the bringing of revolution and communism to Russia. Their leader in this was Vladimir Ilyich Ulyanov (Lenin).

LENIN APPEARS AND ADAPTS
MARXISM TO HIS NEEDS

Following the assassination of Alexander II in March 1881, Alexander III intensified the hunt for terrorist cells. Assassination attempts continued. In 1887, Alexander III's secret police uncovered another plot, arrested the leaders, and executed them. One of them was Alexander (Sasha) Ulyanov, a biology and chemistry student, and maker of bombs.

Sasha's execution traumatized his seventeen-year-old brother, Vladimir, who was still living at home. Vladimir took his brother's favorite book, Chernyshevsky's *What Is to Be Done?*, and read it five times over the summer of 1887. The die was cast. It gave him, he later recounted, a "charge" that lasted a lifetime.[42] In 1888, Vladimir (later to take the pen name Lenin) joined the People's Will, and began reading Marx. By 1893 (age twenty-three), he announced that on all fundamental questions, his mind was made up. He would no longer tolerate in his company any criticisms of Chernyshevsky, Marx, or Engels. Convinced of his destiny as a leader of the "new people," and guided by Marx as to where to seek support, he became a revolutionary agitator within Russia's growing industrial and unionized workforce. For this, he was arrested and sent to Siberia.

In 1894, Alexander III died unexpectedly from kidney failure. The "last czar," Nicholas II, took the throne amidst artificial expansion of Russian industry, agricultural collapse, labor unrest and growing unionization, and widening student and peasant revolt.

Released in 1900 from exile, Lenin fled to Europe to write and to foment agitation in Russia from abroad. His own *What Is to Be Done?* appeared in 1902—endorsing the Jacobin elitist approach to revolution. Other works soon followed, "adapting" Marxism to the Russian situation and, at the same time, he worked toward building up the ranks of his party and organizing mobs of dissatisfied Russian factory workers.

It is with Lenin's "adaptations" of Marxism that the ideology of Russia's revolutionaries finally reaches the particular form so accurately portrayed in *We the Living*. What changes did Lenin have to make[43] to Marx's own views?

At one point in *We the Living*, we find Kira reading from her thesis, "Marxism and Leninism":

> Leninism is Marxism adapted to Russian reality. Karl Marx, the great founder of Communism, believed that Socialism was to be *the logical outcome of Capitalism in a country of highly developed Industrialism and with a proletariat attuned to a high degree of class-consciousness.* But our great leader, Comrade Lenin, proved that . . . (205, emphasis added, the passage from Kira's thesis ends here).

What had Lenin "proved"? That this italicized line is wrong!

Lenin made five "necessary" changes to Marx's views in order to justify the revolution that he was working to bring about in Russia.

1. Lenin's first change to Marx's theory had to do with socialism having to follow capitalism, because it is under capitalism that the necessary dialectic develops, as the precondition to revolution. When Marx revised his views on this, after the Paris Commune, he did so only as a special case and within the context that capitalism had developed in other countries. Lenin went much further in defense of this notion in his *Imperialism: The Highest State of Capitalism* (1917). Here, he develops the view that capitalism, in its most advanced state, will succeed in co-opting its own proletariat into the ranks of the exploiters. Capitalism spreads to the underdeveloped periphery of the world, exporting its exploitation abroad. These outer arenas, Lenin argues (and Russia is one!), are where the exploited will first rise up and supply the spark to a revolutionary fire that will sweep into the capitalist center.

2. Lenin also challenged Marx's claim that a revolution would require, as a precondition, that the mass of the proletariat, as a class, had attained a collective class consciousness of its condition. In *What Is to Be Done?* Lenin portrayed the proletariat as unaware, lethargic, conservative, "asleep," and incapable of grasping the need for, let alone acting for, revolution. Therefore, the proletariat and the revolution must be led by "new people," by a "vanguard party" of knowledgeable and committed revolutionaries. And the masses, if they prove to be hesitant or squeamish about what is to be done, will be indoctrinated and forced into the service of the revolutionary cause.

3. Marx expected the revolution to be relatively short-lived, to be followed by a gradual "withering away" of the state. In *State and Revolution* (1917), Lenin asserts that the revolution will be a long, drawn-out affair, with the state, now in revolutionary hands, persisting and even growing in power as the revolution proceeded.

4. Marx had also portrayed the revolution as a continuously progressing event, without interruption or reversal. Lenin's New Economic Policy of 1921, where elements of capitalism were reintroduced in the economy (cf.

We the Living, 308–9) was a result of his rejection of Marx's linear view of revolutionary progress.

5. While Marx understood that the revolution would require violent destruction of factories, machines, and other forms of capital, he believed—with the model of the Paris Commune in mind—that within the ranks of the proletariat there would be discussion, free press, and cooperation. No personality cults or any internal authoritarianism would occur, as the proletarians, with mass collective awareness, prepared the way for communism. Given Lenin's dismissal of the masses as "asleep," he could not hold this view of the revolution. Describing it as "toy democracy," he brought to the revolution the cruel elitism of the earlier Russian Jacobins.

WITH THE IDEOLOGY IN PLACE, REVOLUTION FOLLOWS

In 1863, Chernyshevsky offered the first comprehensive answer to the question, "what is to be done," accompanied by a portrayal of the "new men" whose historical mission it was to do it. In 1917, armed with a fuller development of revolutionary ideology, tailored to the Russian situation, and with history and science allegedly on their side, the revolutionaries were poised to act. It is a tragedy, and a lesson in the destructive nature of attempted compromise, that they were able to succeed. It could have been otherwise.

As Nicholas II half-heartedly led Russia into the twentieth century, unrest and economic dislocation led intellectuals to reject czarism and socialism, and to turn, one last time, toward Western liberalism. As Lenin's Bolsheviks worked steadily for revolution, Russia, with no opposition from the czar, turned to the idea of local, representative governing bodies—the *zemstovs* rehabilitated by Alexander II—as the basis for a free Russia. A "Union of Liberation" organization was formed to guide this, and plans were begun for calling a nation-wide assembly at which the groundwork for genuine constitutional representative government would be laid. The beacon of the 1825 Decembrists was raised once again, but these new would-be liberals had no agreed-upon coherent philosophy to guide them. The possibility for a free Russia, undercut from the outset in this way, was doomed.

Thus, as Lenin from abroad, and Leon Trotsky from within, carried on their preparations, the Russian reformers argued, failed to unify, and frittered away precious time. Repeatedly, assemblies of *zemstov* representatives met (known as *Dumas*), but produced little. Then Russia was drawn into the First World War. Amidst confusion, the fourth Duma was taken by surprise when their demand for the abdication of the czar was accepted. Nicholas stepped down, and as the war neared its end, a provisional government was set up by the current Duma.[44] The primary objective of this government was to complete plans for a nationwide constitutional assembly where *zemstov* representatives from across Russia would meet and vote—for the first time in Russia's long, tortured history—for a nationally elected government.

As the Duma squabbled over details, and maneuvered for position in the upcoming Assembly, Lenin finally succeeded from abroad in bringing his Bolshevik organization, led by Trotsky, into action. In the autumn of 1917 with Lenin now in charge, his "Red Guard" storm troopers took control of St. Petersburg and forcefully disbanded the sitting provisional government. The next day, Lenin announced to Russia that the Bolsheviks were now in charge, and would proceed with the revolution by nationalizing all land, banks, and factories, and by arresting all who opposed them. Amazingly, however, at a meeting of the Bolshevik Central Committee in Lenin's and Trotsky's absence, the Committee voted to allow the planned-for national constitutional assembly to meet, and to be bound by the votes cast at this meeting.

The meeting took place in January 1918. The result of the election, to the shock of the Bolsheviks, showed massive support across the country for the social democrats, as against the Bolsheviks and the liberals.[45] In the face of this, the long tradition of Chernyshevsky, Nechayev, Tkachev, and Lenin came to the fore. Trotsky and Lenin ordered out the Red Guards, who forcefully disbanded the Assembly, arrested many delegates, and executed some on the spot. The world of *We the Living* descended like a funeral cloak over Russia.[46]

From early 1918 until early 1926,[47] Lenin, Trotsky, and then Stalin[48] proceeded with the revolution, creating all of the state organizations and initiating all of the repression that appears as background in *We the Living*. Factories and buildings *were* nationalized, grain harvests *were* expropriated. Civil war *did* follow, and families *did* flee the "red north" for the "white south." All of the background in *We the Living*, both ideological and existential, was in fact now present in, and pervasive throughout, Russia. It *was* all true, as Ayn Rand repeatedly insisted it was.

CONCLUSION

In the foreword to the 1959 edition of *We the Living*, Ayn Rand writes that its basic theme is "the sanctity of human life" (xiii), and that the essence of this theme is contained in the words of Irina to Kira from her prison cell the night before being sent by train to Siberia (349–50). Irina is puzzled, as she faces doom, over what it is about human life that people, including herself, do not understand. "What is it? What?" she asks, that we need to understand in order to explain why every life is "precious," "rare," a "sacred treasure."

Ayn Rand then comments: "At that time,[49] I knew little more about this question than did Irina" (xiii).

Thus, when Ayn Rand promised in real life, and Kira promised in *We the Living*, to "tell the world" about conditions in Soviet Russia, neither of them could then fully explain what made life so sacred.[50] Thirty years later, Ayn Rand writes, "I reached the full answer to Irina's question" (xiv).

She certainly did—in an incomparably profound and comprehensive grasp: of what human life is; of why it is a "sacred treasure"; of how it is successfully lived; and of what its needs are. Had Ayn Rand, with this fuller understanding of human life and of the central role in human life of philosophical abstractions, returned to the Petrograd railway station (as Kira does at the beginning of *We the Living*), what would she then have known?

She would have known fully not only *that* Petrograd smelt of carbolic acid, but also *why*.[51]

She would have known that the revolutionaries we have discussed, and the ideas that fueled them, were the ultimate cause of the destruction of Petrograd, and of human life as such.

She would have known that these ideas were the epistemological lice and pestilence that had infected Russia, and that the revolutionaries were the human vermin that had carried these ideas into the Russian culture. And she would have known that her own ideas would be the philosophical carbolic acid that is needed to definitively combat such scourges wherever and whenever they may arise.

NOTES

1. See Michael S. Berliner, ed., *Letters of Ayn Rand* (New York: Dutton, 1995), 4.

2. See: Berliner, *Letters*, 4 (March 23, 1934), 17 (October 17, 1934), 637 (August 21, 1965); David Harriman, ed., *Journals of Ayn Rand* (New York: Dutton, 1997), 65 (February 2, 1936); and the foreword to the revised edition of *We the Living* (xvii).

3. Ayn Rand had every right to make this claim, having herself lived in the place (Petrograd) and the time (1922–1926) depicted in *We the Living*.

4. The *Oxford English Dictionary* defines "ideology" as "manner of thinking characteristic of a class or individual; ideas at the basis of some economic or political theory or system; *visionary speculation*" (emphasis added). In the cases discussed in this chapter, "ideology" refers to the "ideas" that serve as rationalizations for deeply held emotional-psychological reasons. As such, "ideology" is not a manner of *thinking* in any precise sense. Intellectual history is replete with brilliant and passionate minds who have, at a young age, "discovered" the answers to profound questions (both Marx and Lenin being classic examples). Not being the product of actual thinking, however, these ideologies are not, and cannot be, knowledge, and to follow them necessarily leads to the undermining and destruction of life.

That ideology, whether rational (and thus beneficial) or irrational (and thus destructive) *is* inescapable, and the primary cause of social history, is not something

Ayn Rand fully understood when writing *We the Living* (see her foreword to the revised edition, xiii–xiv), and will not be addressed here. On this issue, see Leonard Peikoff, "Philosophy and Psychology in History," *The Objectivist Forum* 6, no. 5 (October 1985). The present essay offers further evidence for a central conviction of the Objectivist philosophy of history, namely, that philosophical ideas are the primary cause of social history.

5. Puzzlingly, this aspect has received almost no critical comment in reviews of *We the Living*, as if it were either irrelevant or too obvious to warrant attention.

6. There is reason, in addition to the accuracy of her portrayal of Marxist-Leninist ideology in *We the Living*, to believe that Ayn Rand understood this ideology. At the University of Petrograd (later University of Leningrad), she took nine courses that would have been saturated in the official Marxist-Leninist perspective. There is much less information on the extent to which she had studied the earlier revolutionaries.

7. Given the true nature of "visionary speculation," it is not surprising that very little is said in *We the Living* and in the actual revolutionary literature about the epistemological methods that lead to these "insights." Rooted as they are in the psychological needs of the visionaries, they are profoundly subjective; and they are considered convincing (to them) because of needs they cater to, rather than any evidence reality offers in their support; and they are held for this reason to be "true" and beyond challenge. Thus, those who dare to disagree face not counter-evidence and logical refutation, but prison camps and firing squads.

8. For our purposes, the relevant view of this process is the one held by G. W. F. Hegel and "transformed" by Marx, Engels, and Lenin.

9. Leonard Peikoff, *Objectivism: The Philosophy of Ayn Rand* (New York: Dutton, 1991), 33.

10. This focus on morality rather than on deeper philosophy is in part explained by the early stage in her life and thought Ayn Rand was at when she wrote *We the Living*.

11. For a synopsis of the mission of the Russian Orthodox Church, see Tibor Szamuely, *The Russian Tradition* (New York: McGraw-Hill, 1974), 67–73.

12. Constantine de Grunwald, *Tsar Nicholas I*, translated by Blight Patmore (London: Futura, 1954), 74.

13. The leading intellectuals of this movement included: Peter Chaadayev (1794–1856); Alexis Khomyakov (1804–1860); Ivan Kireevsky (1806–1856); Konstantin Aksakov (1817–1860); and Yuri Samarin (1819–1876). Leo Tolstoy was, in significant respects, influenced by this school.

14. Cf. *We the Living*, where a philosopher comments: "Russia's destiny has ever been of the spirit. Holy Russia has lost her God and her Soul" (154). Similarly, later in the novel Lydia exclaims to Kira: "It has been revealed to me. . . . Holy Russia's salvation will come from faith" (272–73).

15. The leading intellectuals of this movement included: Vissarion Belinsky (1811–1848); Alexander Herzen (1812–1870); to some extent, Mikhail Bakunin (1814–1876); and Nicholas Stankevich (1813–1840). Ivan Turgenev and Fyodor Dostoevsky were influenced by this school.

16. Hegel played a central role in the genesis of Russian revolutionary ideology and, through his influence on Marx, on the ideology of the Russian revolution. More on this shortly.

17. Leaders in this group included David Strauss and, particularly, Ludwig Feuerbach. One of the early converts was Karl Marx.

18. "Horrors," it should be noted, that led to the greatest advances in population, material production, and life span in human history.

19. The Moloch was a tyrannical Canaanite idol to whom children were sacrificed.

20. Isaiah Berlin, *Russian Thinkers* (London: Penguin, 1979), 206.

21. For example, the French Revolution (from Rousseau to Robespierre), Nazi Germany (from Luther and Hegel to Hitler), and twentieth-century communist tyranny (from Hegel, Marx, and Lenin, to Stalin, Mao, Castro, and Pol Pot).

22. Joseph Frank, "N. G. Chernyshevsky: A Russian Utopian," *Southern Review* 3 (1967), 68.

23. The following sources will offer a doorway into the large literature on these men and their "ideas": Berlin, *Russian Thinkers*; Fredrick Copelston, *Philosophy in Russia* (South Bend, Ind.: University of Notre Dame Press, 1986); Eugene Methvin, *The Rise of Radicalism* (New Rochelle, N.Y.: Arlington House, 1973).

24. The label "Jacobin" was taken by the furthest left, most fanatical wing of the opposition to monarchy in late eighteenth-century France—ultimately to be dominated by Robespierre and Antoine St. Just. This group had used a Jacobin monastery for their meetings.

25. This they "learned" from Jean-Jacques Rousseau's notions of the General Will, and the Legislator who alone knows this Will and has the authority and power to impose it in order that "men be forced to be free"!

26. See Szamuely, *Russian Tradition*, chapter 10: "The Intelligentsia."

27. Quoted in Szamuely, *Russian Tradition*, 156.

28. Quoted in Methvin, *Rise of Radicalism*, 181.

29. Quoted in Szamuely, *Russian Tradition*, 156. In Hegel's terms, this is the World Historical Figure (e.g., Caesar, Napoleon) who tells his age what time it is (see Hegel's *Phenomenology of Spirit*).

30. Quoted in Methvin, *Rise of Radicalism*, 187.

31. Quoted in Methvin, *Rise of Radicalism*, 184–85. From *We the Living*, cf. Comrade Sonia: "We've got to stamp our proletarian boot into their white throats" (73), and Stepan Timoshenko: "you don't make a revolution with white gloves on" (128).

32. Quoted in Szamuely, *Russian Tradition*, 233.

33. Reports of this murder prompted Fyodor Dostoevsky to write his famous novel, *The Demons*, a condemning portrayal of the fanatic revolutionary, published in 1872. (See Richard Pevear's foreword to his and Larissa Volokhonsky's translation of *The Demons* [New York: Vintage, 1995], which states that the victim, Ivan Ivanov, was beaten, strangled, and shot in the head.) This novel has, as a front piece, the following quote from the Bible (Luke 8:32–36): "Then the demons came out of the man, and entered the swine, and the herd rushed down the steep bank into the lake, and were drowned." Out of what man? Chernyshevsky. What demons? Chernyshevsky's ideas. Into what swine? The Russian Jacobins. Tragically, as *We the Living* portrays, the swine did not rush to a quick death.

On Nechayev's fanaticism, see Szamuely, *Russian Tradition*, 247–71 (and especially 265–66, in regard to Dostoevsky).

34. Bakunin early on referred admiringly to Nechayev as "the young savage."

35. This name is intentionally misleading. The cell, as "new people," had disdain

for the common people and what they might will. The model for this "people's will" was Rousseau's infamous "General Will," which he used to refer to a mystic, universal "Will" representing what the people should will, but were too ignorant of their true interests to do so. Pol Pot used the same dishonest terminology.

36. Quoted in B. Eissenstat, *Lenin and Leninism, State, Law, and Society* (Lexington, Mass.: Lexington Books, 1971), 16. See also Szamuely, *Russian Tradition*, chapter 16: "Tkachev and The Roots of Leninism."

37. Hegel's central works include *The Phenomenology of Spirit* (1807), *Science of Logic* (1812–1813), and *Philosophy of Right* (1821). Introductions to Hegel's thought include W. T. Stace, *The Philosophy of Hegel: A Systematic Exposition* (New York: Dover, 1955), and chapters in Karl Popper, *The Open Society and Its Enemies*, vol. 2, *Hegel and Marx*, 5th ed. (Princeton, N.J.: Princeton University Press, 1971), and W. T. Jones, *A History of Western Philosophy*, vol. 4, *Kant and the Nineteenth Century*, 2d ed. (New York: Harcourt Brace Jovanovich, 1975).

Although only the barest summary of his ideas, this will give evidence of the purely subjective and disreputable nature of the "visionary speculations" that ideologies often embrace, and connect them to their true source in the psychologies of the speculators and to their earlier roots in mystical (and therefore false) philosophy accepted when young. It is easy to understand why very intelligent young "speculative visionaries" come to an unshakeable truth while still quite young. It is because their method is merely quasi-logical inference from deeply felt premises. No patient observation, gathering of evidence, rejecting of error, or integrating of the warranted is required as it characteristically was by history's honest philosophical minds.

38. Hegel is the pivotal thinker in Russia's revolutionary history in that his philosophy lies at the deepest level of the many revolutionary neo-Hegelians who followed him, most notoriously, Marx.

39. This is the collapsing of Kant's distinction between the noumenal and phenomenal realms into one all-encompassing universe as phenomena. Hegel's philosophy is an example of *idealism*.

40. Protestantism, particularly in its more extreme Pietist form, was an important undercurrent in the thought of eighteenth- and nineteenth-century dissident thinkers (e.g., Rousseau, Kant, Hegel, Schopenhauer, and several of the German romantics).

41. This change in Marx and Engel's position appeared in 1882, in their preface to Plekhanov's Russian translation of the *Communist Manifesto*.

42. Lenin's use of this term is clear evidence that the psychological processes mentioned earlier, as underlying a revolutionary's "discovery" of the "truth," are at work here.

43. By "have to make," I mean what changes he had to make to turn Marxist theory into a fuller rationalization for power-lust, and to eliminate any opposition Marxism may contain to Lenin's plan for Russia.

44. This government came to be led by their justice minister, Alexander Kerensky, who became a hero for a twelve-year-old resident of St. Petersburg, Ayn Rand. (Biographical interviews [Ayn Rand Archives].)

45. In the nationwide election, the social democrats received approximately 21 million votes, the Bolsheviks 9 million, and the liberals 5 million.

46. Ayn Rand would later recount that in January of 1918, nearly thirteen years old, she witnessed, from her apartment window, the funeral procession of murdered

delegates. In particular, she recalled the body of a beautiful black-haired young woman, in an open coffin, her hair framed by a red pillow. (Biographical interviews [Ayn Rand Archives].) Perhaps the young Ayn Rand realized that if she remained in Russia, she would share the same fate.

47. Ayn Rand left Russia in 1926. A comparison of the date and details of Ayn Rand's departure from Russia, with the date and details of Kira Argounova's attempted escape from Russia, and her death on the border with Latvia, seems to indicate that these two events occurred within a few days of each other. With "poetic licence," we could even say they happened on the same day, at the same border, 200 miles southwest of Petrograd.

48. Lenin, after a series of strokes, died in early 1924 (cf. *We the Living*, 291). Following this, Stalin maneuvered to the top of the leadership dung heap, displacing Trotsky on the way (cf. *We the Living*, 309). Note that Stalin is never mentioned in *We the Living*.

49. That is, the early thirties, when she wrote *We the Living*.

50. At a party in early 1926 before she left for America, Ayn Rand promised to tell America that Russia was a huge cemetery, where everyone was slowly dying. See Leonard Peikoff's introduction to the sixtieth anniversary edition (v). At the end of *We the Living*, Kira promises her Uncle Vasili: "I'll tell them . . . where I'm going . . . about everything . . . like an S.O.S." (451).

51. "Petrograd smelt of carbolic acid" are the opening words of *We the Living*. Carbolic acid is a powerful disinfectant used to fight the spread of disease born by lice and other carriers.

5

The Music of *We the Living*

Michael S. Berliner

We the Living is like no other Ayn Rand novel. It takes place amid actual historical events and ones that are essential to the story. As she wrote in her 1959 foreword to *We the Living*, it is

> as near to an autobiography as I will ever write. It is not an autobiography in the literal, but only in the intellectual, sense. The plot is invented; the background is not. . . . The particulars of Kira's story were not mine. . . . The specific events of Kira's life were not mine; her ideas, her convictions, her values were and are (xvii).

In theme and content, *We the Living* is a novel about the individual versus the state, but in background, it is very definitely a novel about Soviet Russia: scores of events and places are real, drawn from the times and from Ayn Rand's own life.

During her lifetime, she said very little about those years, concealing her birth name (Alisa Rosenbaum) from even her closest friends. It wasn't until after her death in 1982 that a study of her papers and other effects (now residing in the Ayn Rand Archives) revealed the autobiographical elements in *We the Living*, details of which are explored elsewhere in this volume. One aspect that merits special attention is music. The approximately seventy musical references, most drawn from her life, give *We the Living* a distinctly musical aura.

At the age of nine, Ayn Rand decided to become a writer, and she devoted her life to that activity—once calling herself "a writing engine."[1] She produced screenplays, theatrical plays, short stories, best-selling novels, and books on technical philosophy. But music played a very important role in

117

her life. On a 1937 biographical entry in *Leading Women of America,* she listed "music" as her only "recreation."[2] And in the late 1950s, she prepared what she called "My Musical Biography," a list of the seventeen songs from 1911 to 1959 that were her favorite ones at various ages.[3] After moving to America in 1926, she began acquiring a collection of phonograph records, of which about 100 albums and 140 singles (mostly 78 rpm) have survived. The collection contains primarily classical, operetta and what she termed "tiddlywink" music. The latter is fast-paced, light-hearted, popular music primarily from the early part of the twentieth century and exemplified by such tunes as "Get Out and Get Under" (1913) and "Canadian Capers" (1915).

It was tiddlywink music that, she often said, best exemplified her "sense of life," a term which she defined as "a preconceptual equivalent of metaphysics, an emotional, subconsciously integrated appraisal of man and of existence."[4] Unlike other art forms, she explained, "music is experienced as if it had the power to reach man's emotions directly."[5] This explains the importance of music in general and its role in conveying the atmosphere of a particular scene in her fiction. Music evokes a wealth of subconscious material, including "images, actions, scenes, actual or imaginary experiences."

> The process is wordless, directed, in effect, by the equivalent of the words: "I would feel this way if . . ." if I were in a beautiful garden on a spring morning . . . if I were dancing in a great, brilliant ballroom . . . if I were seeing the person I love . . . if I were on the barricades. . . .[6]

That is why music is used throughout *We the Living*; it conveys (to those who know the music) the emotion of the scene and the emotion of the events in the lives of the characters.

Music can also convey the sense of life of a whole culture, and it did for the young Alisa Rosenbaum. She was born in mystical Mother Russia, which underwent the Bolshevik revolution when she was fifteen years old. Despising both cultures (she once described Russia as "an accidental cesspool of civilization"[7]), music became her door to Western civilization, to a world that ought to be.

Describing one of her earliest experiences with music, at a Finnish summer resort, she said:

> We spent practically every day either on the beach or in the park. And that is a very happy memory as far as I'm concerned, because it was my introduction to music. They had this military band playing in the park, all day long almost. And that's when I discovered all my early favorites, from the age of six or earlier.[8]

Of her musical tastes at the age of seven, she said:

In music I would always be in trouble with all the adults. All the older people thought that I had a very uncultured taste, because what I liked was what today is the tiddlywink [music] and military marches. And it's in this music that I would pick out things at first hearing and decide: it's mine or it isn't. . . . I remember the first record players that ever came to Petrograd. One of the first was one my grandmother bought. So that in our family or our circle, that was the great foreign innovation. She had an enormous pile of records, and they were predominantly operas or lighter classics, not symphonies. I would literally run out of the room and pout when they played other kinds of music, like tragic opera or Russian songs.[9]

With that as a background, let us now turn to the music of *We the Living*. The dozens of musical mentions in the novel comprise a wide range of classical, popular and folk music, jazz bands, fox trots, and gypsy love songs. But the specific music mentioned by Ayn Rand is worthy of special attention.

NON-RUSSIAN MUSIC

Die Bajadere

Shortly before Leo's departure for the sanitarium to treat his tuberculosis, he and Kira attended an operetta, *Die Bajadere*, by Emmerich Kálmán. It had been advertised, wrote Rand, as "the latest sensation of Vienna, Berlin and Paris." It was

the most wanton operetta from over there, from *abroad*. It was like a glance straight through the snow and the flags, through the border, into the heart of that other world. There were colored lights, and spangles, and crystal goblets, and a real foreign bar with a dull glass archway where a green light moved slowly upward, preceding every entrance—a real foreign elevator. There were women in shimmering satin from a place where fashions existed, and people dancing a funny foreign dance called "Shimmy," and a woman who did not sing, but barked words out, spitting them contemptuously at the audience, in a flat, hoarse voice that trailed suddenly into a husky moan—and a music that laughed defiantly, panting, gasping, hitting one's throat and breath, an impudent drunken music, like the "Song of Broken Glass," a promise that existed somewhere, that *was*, that could be (208).

This same operetta makes a later appearance, when Kira and Andrei dance to its fox-trots at the roof garden of the European Hotel (275–76).

Ayn Rand and her sister Nora attended operettas at the Mikhailovsky Theater on Nevsky Prospekt, but the references to *Bajadere* have a deeper biographical significance: they are Rand's homage to a genre and to a particular operetta whose importance to her cannot be overestimated. Operetta was, in fact, a psychological lifesaver.

At the age of sixteen, Ayn Rand found what she called a "spiritual escape" from Soviet Russia. That escape was the world of Viennese operetta. "Here is the way in which I discovered operettas," she recalled.

> The theaters—some were private, some were semi-private—were enormously expensive that showed foreign operettas, and I couldn't even dream of attending them. But the three state theaters presented operas and ballet. One of the three [the Mikhailovsky] put on lighter operas and some classical operettas. They had four balconies, and the back row of the fourth balcony, which was about ten seats, was very cheap and hard to get. They opened the box office for each week's performances on Saturday at ten o'clock. I made it a point to get up at five in the morning to be at that theater at six, and I waited for three hours, first in the street for an hour and then in the unheated lobby—and you know what Russian winters are. By ten o'clock there would be lines around the block waiting for all the cheap seats. For my first two years of college [at Petrograd State University], I was there every Saturday, and every time I would be either first or second. The money for it came from what my parents gave me for tramway tickets for the university. I would walk the three miles to the university to save the money and spend it on operas and operettas. Verdi was the first opera I saw.[10] And the whole spectacle of that sort of glamorous, medieval existence, the productions were still of the pre-revolutionary days, so the sets and costumes were marvelous. And to see that after coming in from a Soviet reality, that was worse than anything. It's precisely for that sense of life that I worked that hard to get into that theater. Then I discovered operettas. They began by doing certain classical operettas of the nineteenth century and ended up by doing some [Franz] Lehar, which was unprecedented in a serious, academic theater. That was my first great art passion. That really saved my life. It was the most marvelous, benevolent universe, a shot in the arm, practically narcotic. Only it wasn't narcotic in the sense of escape, because it was the one positive fuel that I could have. My sense of life was kept going on that. A life-saving transfusion.[11]

From one unnamed operetta she described a scene that epitomized the West:

> There was one scene where they had some kind of ballroom and a huge window showing the lighted street. They do it with transparencies, black backdrop with the lights cut out so that the lights shone from behind. It was a very good imitation of a foreign city, which was all lights. That was more important to me than Nietzsche and the whole university. That set something in my sense of life. My love for city streets, city lights, skyscrapers, it was all that category. That category of value, and that's what I expected from abroad. . . . What it all meant to me, I don't have to repeat. You can see it from *We the Living*. . . . That was the world I had to reach.[12]

After she graduated from college in 1924, she could afford to attend the private theater, and it was here that she discovered the composer who was to become her favorite operetta composer; in fact, in a 1936 publicity questionnaire for Macmillan publishing company, she listed him as her favorite composer overall: Emmerich Kálmán (Kálmán Imre in his native Hungary).[13] Kálmán, along with Franz Lehar, were the preeminent composers of Viennese operetta. Born in Siofek, Hungary in 1882, Kálmán

> received an excellent musical education at the Budapest Academy of Music, where his fellow students included [Bela] Bartok and [Zoltan] Kodaly. As a young man he wrote music criticism for a Budapest paper and tried to establish himself as a serious composer. The popularity of his humorous cabaret songs, however, prompted his friends to urge him to try his hand at operetta.[14]

Kálmán soon moved to Vienna, where his first major work *Der Ziguenerprimas* (*The Gypsy Virtuoso*) opened in 1912. Then came his biggest hits, *Die Csardasfurstin* (*The Gypsy Princess*) in 1915, *Die Bajadere* in 1921, *Gräfin Mariza* (*Countess Maritza*) in 1924, and *Die Zirkusprinzessin* (*The Circus Princess*) in 1926. After the Anschluss, and despite being offered honorary Aryan status by Hitler, Kálmán moved to America and became an American citizen. He ultimately moved to Paris, where he died in 1953.

Kálmán's operettas, particularly *The Gypsy Princess* and *Countess Maritza,* are still performed in America and widely throughout Europe. A weeklong Kálmán Festival was held at the Budapest Operetta Theater in 2002, whose resident company is generally recognized as the world's leading performers of Viennese operetta. The festival included a rare performance of *Die Bajadere,* which had received its first American performance three years earlier at the Ohio Light Opera—although an adaptation renamed *The Yankee Princess* had a short run on Broadway in 1922.[15] Like all the great Kálmán operettas, *Die Bajadere* is replete with lush melodies, from operatic to music hall to gypsy. One can well understand that this was Ayn Rand's favorite operetta.[16] The operetta tells of the romance between an Indian prince and an operetta star, whom he sees starring as a Bajadere or Indian dancer. It is during a nightclub scene with supporting characters that the "Shimmy" song is performed. A wildly popular dance during the flapper period of the 1920s, the shimmy inspired a Kálmán piece that has achieved a life well beyond its place in *Die Bajadere.* It is often interpolated into performances and recordings of other Kálmán operettas—otherwise it would have all but disappeared, since the English-language recording of *Die Bajadere* in 1998 is the only recording in print and the first in decades. As the composer's daughter, Yvonne Kalman, put it: "The Shimmy song travels well."[17]

"Song of Broken Glass"

This is a particularly intriguing inclusion because it is the only fictional piece of music in the novel and—as a consequence—has elicited considerable curiosity as to its origins.

There are seven mentions of this song in the novel, and it is clear that it represents an ideal: promise, benevolence, an image of life as it ought to be. For Kira, it evoked the West—the spirit of a free, productive society, which stood in stark contrast to the grayness and horror of life in Soviet Russia.

The first two mentions of the "Song of Broken Glass" describe the music and thereby convey its importance. In the first, Ayn Rand is describing Kira—probably a young Kira—as she sits on a hill above the city, gazing at a casino below and thinking about her life and goals. The casino orchestra played

> gay, sparkling tunes from musical comedies. . . . [These tunes] had a significance for Kira that no one else ever attached to them. She heard in them a profound joy of life, so profound that they could be as light as a dancer's feet. . . . And because she felt a profound rebellion against the weighty, the tragic, the solemn, Kira had a solemn reverence for those songs of defiant gaiety. . . .
>
> She had selected one song as her, Kira's, own: it was from an old operetta and was called "The Song of Broken Glass." It had been introduced by a famous beauty of Vienna. There had been a balustrade on the stage, overlooking a drop with the twinkling lights of a big city, and a row of crystal goblets lined along the balustrade. The beauty sang the number and one by one, lightly, hardly touching them, kicked the crystal goblets and sent them flying in tingling, glittering splinters—around the tight, sheer stockings on the most beautiful legs in Europe.
>
> There were sharp little blows in the music, and waves of quick, fine notes that burst and rolled like the thin, clear ringing of broken glass. There were slow notes, as if the cords of the violins trembled in hesitation, tense with the fullness of sound, taking a few measured steps before the leap into the explosion of laughter (50–51).

Then, just a few pages later, Kira is walking through the "dead city" when she hears a gramophone playing the "Song of Broken Glass." It now seems more like the song of what might have been:

> It was the song of a nameless hope that frightened her, for it promised so much, and she could not tell what it promised; she could not even say that it was a promise; it was an emotion, almost of pain, that went through her whole body.
>
> Quick, fine notes exploded, as if the trembling chords could not hold them, as if a pair of defiant legs were kicking crystal goblets. And, in the gaps of ragged clouds above, the dark sky was sprinkled with a luminous powder that looked like splinters of broken glass (60).

Later, Kira is walking with Leo, who is imagining life outside of Soviet Russia. "Over there," he tells Kira, there are automobiles, boulevards, lights, champagne, radios, jazz bands. Whispers Kira: "like the 'Song of Broken Glass'" (120).

She is reminded of the song again when she dances with Leo (156) and when she hears the "Shimmy" song in *Die Bajadere* (208). And late in the novel, at a nightclub with Andrei, she asks him to request that the orchestra play the "Song of Broken Glass." Responding to his concern about her looking so sad while listening to "the gayest music he had ever heard," she replies:

> It's something I liked . . . long ago . . . when I was a child. . . . Andrei, did you ever feel as if something had been promised to you in your childhood, and you look at yourself and you think "I didn't know, then, that this is what would happen to me"—and it's strange, and funny, and a little sad? (277).

Fittingly, the promise and the tragedy of that song follow Kira to the end. As she lay dying in the snow,

> she heard a song, a tune now loud enough to be a human sound, a song as a last battle-march. It was not a funeral dirge, it was not a hymn, it was not a prayer. It was a tune from an old operetta, the "Song of Broken Glass."
>
> Little notes of music trembled in hesitation, and burst, and rolled in quick, fine waves, like the thin, clear ringing of glass. Little notes leaped and exploded and laughed, laughed with a full, unconditional, consummate joy.
>
> She did not know whether she was singing. Perhaps she was only hearing the music somewhere.
>
> But the music had been a promise; a promise at the dawn of her life. That which had been promised then, could not be denied to her now (463).

The "Song of Broken Glass" remains until the end the emotional equivalent of Kira's life and of the West—but now it is a life that will end too soon and a West that she will never reach.

What is the source of this song? Various candidates have been offered over the years. Acquaintances of Ayn Rand have reported her telling them that it was based on "Mucki aus Amerika," a lively song written in 1919 by Viennese operetta composer Robert Stolz; "Mucki" was also Ayn Rand's 1923 entry in her "Musical Biography." Musician Duane Eddy[18] reports that Miss Rand told him that "Will O' the Wisp" by Herbert Küster was the song. But that would have to have been a later realization, since "Will O' the Wisp" wasn't copyrighted (as "Irrlicht") until 1934, after *We the Living* was written.[19] The most likely candidate for a song that inspired her is the "Shimmy" song from *Die Bajadere*, with its spirit of defiance and a series of "quick fine notes" that "burst" and sound like someone kicking crystal goblets. However, Ayn Rand is on record as denying that any one song is the basis for the "Song of Broken Glass": "What I had in mind for it was my kind of tiddly-wink music, as an abstraction of that. . . . I used one particular record at the time as inspiration, but I never held it literally as that song, but only as the prototype. And that [was the] Drdla serenade"[20] (i.e., the Serenade for Violin and Piano no. 1, by Franz Drdla). And once, during a question period following a lecture I attended, when she was asked whether "Song of Broken Glass" was based on anything in particular, she answered "no."

"Destiny Waltz"

This music is played on the piano by Lydia. Rand describes it as "slow and soft; it stopped for a breathless second once in a while and swung into rhythm again, slowly, rocking a little, as if expecting soft, billowing satin skirts to murmur gently in answer, in a ball-room such as did not exist any longer" (157). Composed in 1912 by Sidney Baynes, "Destiny Waltz" was the "Musical Biography" entry for the 17-year old Ayn Rand in 1922. It gained renown as the theme music for the popular radio soap opera *One Man's Family.*

RUSSIAN MUSIC[21]

"The Internationale"

Not surprisingly, for a novel set in Soviet Russia, "The Internationale" is mentioned more than any other piece of music, a total of twelve times. Originally a French Communist march, it was written to celebrate the Paris Commune of 1871. The music was by Pierre Degeyter, and the lyrics by Eugene Potlier, a member of the First International. The song was adopted by the Bolsheviks as the official anthem of the revolution after the 1917 revolution, but was dropped by Stalin in 1941 when the Soviets turned away from internationalism in favor of "socialism in one country."

In the novel, it is first mentioned as an accompaniment to the raising of the red banner upon the final Communist victory in 1921 (22). It is also mentioned as the Communist students' answer to the singing by non-Communist students of "Days of Our Life" (aka "Swift as the Waves") at a student council election meeting at the Technological Institute (73). At this point, Rand provides a lengthy description of the melody:

> [I]n the magnificent goblet of the music, the words were not intoxicating as wine; they were not terrifying as blood; they were gray as dishwater.
> But the music was like the marching of thousands of feet, measured and steady, like drums beaten by unvarying, unhurried hands. The music was like the feet of soldiers marching into the dawn that is to see their battle and their victory; as if the song rose from under the soldiers' feet, with the dust of the road, as if the solders' feet played it upon the earth.
> The tune sang a promise, calmly, with the calm of an immeasurable strength,

and then, tense with a restrained, but uncontrollable ecstasy, the notes rose, trembling, repeating themselves, too rapt to be held still, like arms raised and waving in the sweep of banners.

It was a hymn with the force of a march, a march with the majesty of a hymn. It was the song of soldiers bearing sacred banners and of priests carrying swords. It was an anthem to the sanctity of strength (73–74).

After noting that the "Internationale" is "the first beautiful thing I've noticed about the revolution," Kira provides her estimate of the piece: "When all this is over, when the traces of the revolution are disinfected from history—what a glorious funeral march this will make!" (74)

In addition to being played at important events, for example, the visit of a British Trade Union delegation and Andrei's funeral, it also appears as a reminder that the Bolsheviks are always there: it is even heard being played on a piano just before Kira and Andrei make love (248).

"The Days of Our Life" (aka "Swift as the Waves")

Mentioned once, as sung at the end of the election meeting of the university student council, "Days of Our Life" was described by Ayn Rand as

an old drinking song grown to the dignity of a students' anthem; a slow, mournful tune with an artificial gaiety in the roll of its spiritless notes, born long before the revolution in the stuffy rooms where unshaved men and mannish women discussed philosophy and with forced bravado drank cheap vodka to the futility of life (73).

One version of this pre-Soviet student song begins:

> Swift as the waves
> Are the days of our lives
> If you die, you won't arise
> To join your friends' merriment.
> So pour me a toast-cup,
> Dear friend,
> God only knows what
> Will become of us.[22]

"God Save the Czar"

The unofficial Russian Imperial anthem, it was composed in 1833 by Alexei Lvov (the Czar's personal composer), with lyrics by Vasili Zhukovsky. It had been commissioned by Czar Nicholas I and first performed on December 6, 1833. It is still famous because of its use by Tchaikovsky near the conclusion of his *1812 Overture*.

It has one appearance in the novel: Leo (who was not a Czarist) derisively whistles it in the face of a Communist who calls him "comrade" at a pre-1917 secret meeting of young revolutionaries (138).

"The Fire of Moscow"

Composed by A.A. Gairabetov, this is a song about Napoleon's defeat in Russia. It was played on the gramophone by Marisha Lavrova and Victor Dunaev, both Communists (180). Here is one of its verses (in the voice of Napoleon):

> All the battalions that I called up
> Will perish here in the snow,
> Our bones will turn to dust in the fields
> Without burial or coffins.[23]

"Your Fingers Smell of Incense"

As part of the entertainment at a party she gave, Vava Milovskaia "sang a song about a dead lady whose fingers smelt of incense" (159). This was an actual song, entitled "Your Fingers Smell of Incense." Composed by Alexander Vertinsky in 1916, it was dedicated to the Russian silent film legend Vera Kholodnaya. A song that can best be characterized as a lament, the chorus is:

> Your fingers smell of incense,
> Sadness slumbers in your eyelashes.
> Now you no longer need anything,
> Now you no longer feel sorry for anyone.[24]

"You Fell As a Victim"

The Red funeral march, this dates from c. 1883 and was played at all important funerals, including that of Lenin and of the fictional Andrei Taganov in *We the Living*. In a 1997 review of Giya Kancheli's "Light Sorrow/ Mourned by the Wind," *Gramophone* magazine referred to "You Fell As a Victim" as "the famous Russian revolutionary lament."[25] "Many years ago," wrote Rand in *We the Living*,

in secret cellars hidden from the eyes of the Czar's gendarmes, a song had been born to the memory of those who had fallen in the fight for freedom. It was sung in muffled, breathless whispers to the clanking of chains, in honor of nameless heroes. It traveled down dark sidelanes; it had no author, and no copy of it had ever been printed. The Revolution brought it into every music store window and into the roar of every band that followed a Communist to its grave. The Revolution brought the "Internationale" to its living and "You fell as a victim" to its dead. It became the official dirge of the new republic. . . . The music began with the majesty of that hopelessness which is beyond the need of hope. It mounted to an ecstatic cry, which was not joy nor sorrow, but a military salute. It fell, breaking into a pitiless tenderness, the reverent tenderness that honors a warrior without tears. It was a resonant smile of sorrow (431–32).

The song begins:

> You fell as a victim in a fateful fight
> Of devoted love to the people.
> You gave all you could for them,
> For their life, honor and freedom.
> At times you had languished in damp prisons,
> Your enemies, tormentors, having long ago passed
> Their merciless judgment on you.
> So you walked, clanking your fetters.[26]

The lyrics (apparently translated by Miss Rand) in *We the Living*:

> You fell as a victim
> In our fateful fight,
> A victim of endless devotion.
> You gave all you had to the people you loved,
> Your honor, your life and your freedom (431).

And then a further verse (also from the novel):

> The tyrant shall fall and the people shall rise,
> Sublime, almighty, unchained!
> So farewell, our brother,
> You've gallantly made
> Your noble and valiant journey! (432).

"Song of the Little Apple"

Although mentioned in only two places, this song is one of the most evocative in the novel. Also known as "The Apple," the lyrics have had many variants, presumably to fit any situation. The melody is a well-known Russian gypsy folk tune that was used for "The Russian Sailor's Dance" by Reinhold Glière in his ballet *The Red Poppy* (1927). Its first appearance in *We the Living* is early in the book, when Kira hears it on the train the Argounov family was taking from the Crimea back to Petrograd. It was sung by a soldier accompanying himself on the accordion.

> No one could tell whether his song was gay or sad, a joke or an immortal monument; it was the first song of the revolution, risen from nowhere, gay, reckless, bitter, impudent, sung by millions of voices, echoing against train roofs, and village roads, and dark city pavements, some voices laughing, some voices wailing, a people laughing at its own sorrow, the song of the revolution, written on no banner, but in every weary throat, the "Song of the Little Apple." . . . No one knew what the little apple was; but everyone understood (26).

It was also sung "softly, monotonously" by a young boy on the train taking Irina and Sasha to a Siberian prison camp (350, 352). The message of the song and its use in these scenes seems to be that of inevitability and resignation.

The lyrics of the first stanza in *We the Living* are:

> Hey, little apple,
> Where are you rolling?
> If you fall into German paws,
> You'll never come back (26).

Another variant is:

> Hey, little apple
> Green on one side
> A Kolchak is not allowed
> To go across the Urals.[27]

"John Gray"

"Historians," wrote Ayn Rand,

> will write of the "Internationale" as the great anthem of the revolution. But the cities of the revolution had their own hymn. In days to come, the men of Petrograd will remember those years of hunger and struggle and hope—to the convulsive rhythm of "John Gray." It was called a fox-trot. It had a tune and a rhythm such as those of the new dances far across the border, abroad. It had very foreign lyrics about a very foreign John Gray whose sweetheart Kitty spurned his love for fear of having children, as she told him plainly. Petrograd had known sweeping epidemics of cholera; it had known epidemics of typhus, which were worse; the worst of its epidemics was that of "John Gray" (155).

And she describes that epidemic, a song played and sung at school recesses, while standing in line at stores, at dances, after Marxist lectures. And the meaning was obvious: "Its gaiety was sad; its abrupt rhythm was hysterical; its frivolity was a plea, a moan for that which existed somewhere, forever out of reach. Through winter nights red flags whistled in the snowdrifts and the city prayed hopelessly with the short, sharp notes of 'John Gray'" (156). The song is mentioned throughout the book, played on the piano or on the gramophone as a haunting reminder of what cannot be. "It flung brief, blunt notes out into space, as if tearing them off the strings before they were ripe, hiding the gap of an uncapturable gaiety under a convulsive rhythm" (368).

There are no standard lyrics to this song, with various—though similar—stories being told about John Gray. In one version, the first stanza reads:

> In a faraway southern land
> Where blizzards do not blow
> There once was a handsome man
> John Gray, the cowboy,
> John Gray, strong and rakish
> As tall as Hercules
> As brave as Don Quixote.[28]

The *We the Living* version (possibly translated by Ayn Rand) begins:

> John Gray was brave and daring
> Kitty was very pretty.
> Wildly, John fell in love with Kitty.
> Passion's hard to restrain
> He made his feelings plain,
> But Kat said "No" to that! (156).

CLASSICAL MUSIC

Ayn Rand did not "learn to like" classical music until she came to America and began hearing it on the radio: "It took me quite a long time, that is, listening very often and repeatedly before I would begin to really hear or properly appreciate the classical music"—by which she meant concertos and symphonies.[29] By 1936, she had become a fan of Ev Suffens' classical music program on WEVD in New York City,[30] but classical music had already found its way into the manuscript for *We the Living*, completed in March 1934.

Of particular importance were the operas of Giuseppe Verdi and the piano music of Frederic Chopin. Chopin is played (usually by Kira's cousin Lydia), at various events in the novel, as it was played often by Rand's sister Natasha during Ayn Rand's childhood and teenage years in Russia.[31] Although it was Chopin's "Butterfly Etude" that was a particular Rand favorite (it was the 1917 listing on her "Musical Biography"), it was his "Dog's Waltz" (more commonly known as the "Minute Waltz") that received mention in the novel (180). Lydia also played Bach and Tchaikovsky, whose *Sleeping Beauty* and *Swan Lake* ballets are also mentioned (146, 189, 446).

Verdi played a special role in Ayn Rand's musical life, and provides the right note on which to end a study of the music in *We the Living*. One of his operas, as we have seen, was the first opera she saw in Petrograd, in 1921. Just as it did in her life, opera in the novel represents one of the few vestiges of luxury and glamour in the USSR. Kira's Uncle Vasili put it this way: "Yes, old classics are still the best. In those days, they had culture, and moral values, and . . . and integrity" (214). In the novel are mentions of *Aïda* (194) and *La Traviata* (214–15), the first act Prelude (misnamed by her as the "Overture") to which was Ayn Rand's 1912 entry in her "Musical Biography."

But it was *Rigoletto* that came in for special mention. Kira and Andrei attend a performance at the Mikhailovsky Theater, which

> smelt of old velvet, marble and moth balls. Four balconies rose high to a huge chandelier of crystal chains that threw little rainbows on the distant ceiling. Five years of revolution had not touched the theater's solemn grandeur; they had left but one sign: the Imperial eagle was removed from over the huge central box which had belong to the royal family (96).

Here is Rand describing the opening of the opera:

> And when the curtain went up and music rose in the dark, silent shaft of the theater, growing, swilling, thundering against walls that could not hold it, something stopped in Kira's throat and she opened her mouth to take a breath. Beyond the walls were linseed-oil wicks, men waiting in line for tramways, red flags and the dictatorship of the proletariat. On the stage, under the marble columns of an Italian palace, women waved their hands softly, gracefully, like reeds in the waves of music, long velvet trains rusted under a blinding light and, young, carefree, drunk on the light and the music, the Duke of Mantua sang the challenge of youth and laughter[32] to gray, wary, cringing faces in the darkness, faces that would forget, for a while, the hour and the day and the century (97).

To Kira and to Ayn Rand, that was the glamorous, prerevolutionary spectacle.

CONCLUSION

Although music played a significant role in Ayn Rand's first novel, *We the Living*, it did not play such a role in her two major novels, *The Fountainhead* and *Atlas Shrugged.* In *The Fountainhead,* there are references to the Rachmaninoff Second Piano Concerto and the Tchaikovsky First Piano Concerto. And one of the minor characters in *Atlas Shrugged* is a composer, whose views on "The Nature of an Artist" are reprinted in *For the New Intellectual.*[33] But it was in her planned—but never written—novel (tentatively entitled "To Lorne Dieterling") that music would once again achieve a dominant role, one well beyond that in *We the Living.*

The story was to feature a dancer, and the *"real essence"* of the story would be musical: "the universe of my 'tiddlywink' music, of the 'Traviata Overture' and 'Simple Confessions,' of *my* sense of life."[34] In fact, according to her working notes, she would "build the whole novel" on the *La Traviata* prelude.[35]

The notes for "To Lorne Dieterling" were written over an eight-year period, from November 30, 1957, to January 2, 1966, but the project never got beyond those notes. In a 1977 answer to a question about her lack of fiction writing in the previous twenty years, Ayn Rand replied: "I don't like to write historical fiction or fantasies, and it is impossible to write about heroic characters, or a romantic story, in today's setting. The world is in such a low state that I could not bear to put it in fiction. . . . If I don't write another novel, that would be the reason. Look around you."[36] Like the "Song of Broken Glass," her projected novel would be only a promise, as she turned her attention to writing and developing the philosophy that makes possible the ideal man.

NOTES

1. David Harriman, ed., *Journals of Ayn Rand* (New York: Dutton, 1997), 48.

2. See form accompanying June 26, 1937, letter to editor Virginia Tompkins, Ayn Rand Archives.

3. "My Musical Biography," Ayn Rand Archives.

4. "Philosophy and Sense of Life," in Ayn Rand, *The Romantic Manifesto: A Philosophy of Literature*, revised edition (New York: Signet, 1975), 25.

5. Ayn Rand, "Art and Cognition," in *Romantic Manifesto*, 50.

6. Rand, "Art and Cognition," 51.

7. Biographical interviews (Ayn Rand Archives).

8. Biographical interviews (Ayn Rand Archives).

9. Biographical interviews (Ayn Rand Archives).

10. Probably *Rigoletto.*

11. Biographical interviews (Ayn Rand Archives).

12. Biographical interviews (Ayn Rand Archives).

13. Ayn Rand Archives.

14. Michael Miller, program notes for the Ohio Light Opera production of *Die Bajadere*, 1998.

15. Richard Traubner, *Operetta* (Oxford: Oxford University Press, 1983), 267.

16. Personal communication from Leonard Peikoff.

17. Personal communication.

18. In a 1999 interview for the Ayn Rand Oral History Project.

19. See Friedrich Hofmeister, *Hofmeisters Handbuch der Musikliteratur*, 1934–40 (Leipzig, 1943).

20. Biographical interviews (Ayn Rand Archives).

21. I would like to thank Professor Robert A. Rothstein, University of Massachusetts, for providing the lyrics and music for most of the Russian songs discussed in this chapter and for the prior point that all of these songs were, unlike the "Song of Broken Glass," real and not fictional.

22. Russian lyrics translated by Dina Garmong, from *Chanson des etudiant* #3206 (Northern League publishers, n.d.).

23. Russian lyrics translated by Dina Garmong, from *A Collection of War Songs of the Russian Imperial Army and the Civil War Period* (Chicago: no publisher information, 1969).

24. Russian lyrics translated by Dina Garmong, from *Songs of the Russian People*, A. Ivanov, ed. (Leningrad: State Musical Publishing House, 1948).

25. See www.iclassics.com.

26. Russian lyrics translated by Dina Garmong, from a book of Vertinsky songs published by the Center of Song of the Soviet Culture Reserve, Moscow, 1990.

27. "Kolchak" refers to Aleksandr Vailiyevich Kolchak, an anti-Bolshevik admiral executed by the Bolsheviks in 1920. Lyrics translated from the Russian by Dina Garmong, from A. Ivanov, ed., *Songs of the Russian People* (Leningrad: State Musical Publishing House, 1948).

28. Russian lyrics translated by Dina Garmong, from *Songs: Ships Entered Our Harbor* (Moscow: Omega, Denis Alpha, 1995).

29. Biographical interviews (Ayn Rand Archives).

30. Michael S. Berliner, ed., *Letters of Ayn Rand* (New York: Dutton, 1995), 26.

31. Biographical interviews (Ayn Rand Archives).

32. The aria referred to is "Questa o Quella."

33. Ayn Rand, *For the New Intellectual* (New York: Random House, 1961; Signet paperback edition, 1963).

34. Harriman, *Journals*, 710. "Simple Confessions" was composed in 1878 by Francois Thomé and titled (in French) "Simple Aveu," and was Ayn Rand's 1924 entry in her "Musical Biography."

35. Harriman, *Journals*, 712.

36. Question period following Ayn Rand's 1977 Ford Hall Forum talk, "Global Balkanization," in Boston.

6

Publishing *We the Living*

Richard E. Ralston

FINDING A PUBLISHER

Ayn Rand energetically involved herself in every detail of publishing and promoting her books. She early on discovered that this was necessary, if she was to reach what she later called "my kind of readers."[1]

She met a Hollywood writer, Gouverneur Morris, who liked her screen treatment, *Red Pawn* (which she sold to Universal), and her play *Night of January 16th*. She showed him the manuscript of *We the Living*, which he also liked, and sent to Jean Wick, his agent in New York.

Ayn Rand soon tired of hearing nothing from this agent but occasional news of rejection without explanation. She did not leave matters in her agent's hands. She knew how the unique characteristics of her novel should be presented to publishers, and so gave her ideas to Wick in great detail, as in this letter of March 23, 1934:

> When I first began work on *Airtight* [*We the Living*], the quality which I hoped would make it saleable, quite aside from any possible literary merit, was the fact that it is the *first* story written by a Russian who knows the living conditions of the new Russia and who has actually lived under the Soviets in the period described. My plot and characters are fiction, but the living conditions, the atmosphere, the circumstances which make the incidents of the plot possible, are all true, to the smallest detail. There have been any number of novels dealing with modern Russia, but they have been written either by émigrés who left Russia right after the revolution and had no way of knowing the new conditions, or by Soviet authors who were under the strictest censorship and had no right and no way of telling the whole truth. My book is, as far as I know, the first one by a person who *knows* the facts and also *can tell* them.

I have watched very carefully all the literature on new Russia, that has appeared in English. I do not believe that there has been a work of fiction on this subject, which has enjoyed an outstanding and wide popular success. I believe this is due to the fact that all those novels were translations from the Russian, written primarily *for* the Russian reader. As a consequence, they were hard to understand and of no great interest to the general American public, to those not too well acquainted with Russian conditions.

Airtight, I believe, is the first novel on Russia written *in English by a Russian.* Throughout the entire book, I have tried to write it *from the viewpoint of and for the American public.* I have never relied on any previous knowledge of Russia in my future readers, and I have attempted to show a panorama of the whole country as it would unfold before the eyes of a person who had never heard before that such a country as Russia existed. It is not, primarily, a book for Russians, but a book for Americans—or so I hope.

I have also attempted to show, not the political struggles, theories and ideals of modern Russia, of which we have heard so much, but the everyday human lives, the everyday tragedies of human beings who are not or try not to be connected with politics. It is not a story of glamorous grand dukes and brutal Bolsheviks—or vice-versa—as most of the novels of the Russian Revolution have been; it is the story of the middle class, the vast majority of Russian citizens, about whom little has been said in fiction. It is not the usual story of revolutionary plots, of GPU spies, of secret executions and exaggerated horrors. It is the story of the drudgery of life which millions have to lead day after day, year after year. Our American readers have been crammed full, too full, of Russian aims, projects and slogans on red banners. No one—to the best of my knowledge—has spoken of what goes on every day in every home and kitchen behind the red banners. . . .

I would like to mention that the qualities I have described are not the aim, theme or purpose of the book, but I have gone into them in such detail only because I believe they are valuable sales points. I may be quite mistaken and these suggestions may have no value. But since you were kind enough to express the desire to hear them and since these "sales points" have been in my mind all through the writing of the book, I felt that I should share them with you and let you judge their worth. . . .[2]

These suggestions were valuable, but their value was probably lost on Wick. It took many years for Ayn Rand to find an agent with any understanding of whom they were dealing with. Her agents tended to be more understanding of the misconceptions of publishers than of the insights of their client, Ayn Rand.

Ayn Rand experienced the challenges facing any first-time author in finding (1) an agent willing and able to present the book to publishers and (2) a publisher. H. L. Mencken read a copy of *We the Living* sent to him by Gouverneur Morris, and identified another problem, which Ayn Rand passed along to Wick on June 19, 1934:

Mr. Morris has received a letter from Mr. Mencken in regard to my book *Airtight*. I am quoting from his letter: "I agree with you thoroughly that it is a really excellent piece of work, and I see no reason whatever why it shouldn't find a publisher readily. The only objection to it, of course, is the fact that it is anti-Communist in tone. Most of the American publishers, who print Russian stuff lean toward the Trotskys. However, that is an objection that is certainly not insuperable."

In view of this, Mrs. Morris has suggested that we try to submit the novel to Dutton, for they have just published a nonfiction book entitled *Escape from the Soviets*, which is violently anti-Soviet and, from what I hear, a great best-seller. Evidently, Dutton are not pro-Communist and I am very happy to know that neither is the public, and therefore an anti-Soviet book has a chance of success.

In his letter, Mr. Mencken has offered to send the book to any other publisher we name, if Knopf have not taken it, and Mr. Morris has written to him, suggesting Dutton. If it is convenient for you, you may get in touch with him about this.

I have been waiting to hear about Knopf's decision and, if they have rejected the book, I will appreciate it if you would let me know the reasons they gave.

I realize that we have to take into consideration the publisher's political views when submitting the book. But, if Mr. Mencken is right and the political angle is the only one that stands in the way of a sale, I certainly refuse to believe that America has nothing but Communist-minded publishers. I will appreciate it if you will let me know the reactions to the book from this angle.[3]

The contact with Mencken, whom Ayn Rand had admired for some time, resulted in an exchange of letters, one of which places her tactical difficulties in finding a publisher in the context of what was, in 1934, a remarkable confidence in the enduring impact her writing would have. On July 28, she wrote to him:

I am sure you understand that my book is not at all a story about Russia, but a story of an individual against the masses and a plea in defense of the individual. Your favorable opinion of it was particularly valuable to me, since I have always regarded you as the foremost champion of individualism in this county.

This book is only my first step and above all a means of acquiring a voice, of making myself heard. What I shall have to say when I acquire that voice does not need an explanation, for I know that you can understand it. Perhaps it may seem a lost cause, at present, and there are those who will say that I am too late, that I can only hope to be the last fighter for a mode of thinking which has no place in the future. But I do not think so. I intend to be the first one in a new battle which the world needs as it has never needed before, the first to answer the too many advocates of collectivism, and answer them in a manner which will not be forgotten.

I know that you may smile when you read this. I fully realize that I am a very "green," very helpless beginner who has the arrogance of embarking, single-handed, against what many call the irrevocable trend of our century. I know that I am only a would-be David starting out against Goliath—and what a fearful, ugly Goliath! I say "single-handed," because I have heard so much from that other side, the collectivist side, and so little in defense of man against men, and yet so much has to be said. I have attempted to say it in my book. I do not know of a better way to make my entrance into the battle. I believe that man will always be an individualist, whether he knows it or not, and I want to make it my duty to make him know it.

So you can understand why I appreciate your kindness in helping me to put my book before the public, for—if you will excuse my presumption—I consider myself a young and very humble brother-in-arms in your own cause.[4]

Mencken answered her a few days later: "I sympathize with your position thoroughly, and it seems to me that you have made a very good beginning in *Airtight*. I see no reason whatever why it should not find a publisher and make a success. Certainly the time has come to turn back the tide of Communist propaganda in this country."[5] On August 8, she replied and asked him to send the book to Dutton. Dutton turned it down with a routine rejection letter (which still exists in the Ayn Rand Archives). (In one of the many ironies of her relations with publishers, Dutton, as a part of Penguin, became the publisher of *We the Living* fifty-five years later.)

Knopf also rejected the manuscript. Writing to Wick on July 19, 1934, in response to this news, it appears that the problem was ideological:

I quite agree with your suggestion about my coming to New York. I do believe it would be advisable and very much to my advantage. But as I mentioned in my last letter, I am at present working at the Paramount Studio on an original story of my own and I do not know how long I am going to be held here. As soon as I finish this assignment, I will try to arrange to go to New York, if I find it possible. Frankly, the financial angle is the only circumstance that is keeping me from it, for I have been anxious to move to New York for a long time.

As to the opinion of Mr. Abbott at Knopf's I can see his point of view and I can understand his hesitation, particularly in regard to the length of my novel. However, if I had a chance to do it, I would like to point out to him that he is greatly mistaken on the subject of the book being "dated." In the first place, the book does not deal with a "temporary" phase of Russian life. It merely takes place in the years 1922–1925, instead of the immediate present, but it deals with the birth of conditions which are far from gone, which still prevail in Russia in their full force, which are the very essence of the revolution. In the second place—and this may sound paradoxical—*Airtight* is *not* a novel about Russia. It is a novel about the problem of the individual versus the mass, a problem which is the latest, the most vital, the most tremendous problem of the world today, and about which very little has been said in fiction. I have selected Russia as my background merely because that problem stands out in Russia more sharply, more tragically than anywhere on earth.

However, I quite agree with you that it would not be advisable to press that point with Knopf's at present, and I mention this only in case you find yourself confronted again with the same objection.[6]

Abbott, the editor at Knopf, was undoubtedly following the standard line of "Red Decade" intellectuals (noted by Ayn Rand and others) that any unfortunate incidents in Soviet life were "temporary" and in the past—and that *now* everything was fine and progressive. This line was faithfully reported from Moscow by the *New York Times* during this period (i.e., from the early 1930s, when millions of Ukrainian and Russian peasants died during Stalin's collectivization of agriculture, to the purges and show-trials of the late 1930s).

Other publishers who read and rejected the manuscript included Little Brown & Co., Longmans Green, Viking Press, Bobbs-Merrill, Farra & Rinehart, and Simon & Schuster. The reader for Simon & Schuster was Clifton Fadiman, who reported: "It has its points, but it is far too long and tortuous. I read parts of it with interest but as a whole it did not grip me." A literary magazine, *Forum*, rejected the book for serialization because it was "much too gloomy."[7]

Appleton-Century-Crofts came close to taking the book. Their editor-in-chief, Barry Benefield, was a novelist himself. In comments to Wick and later at a luncheon with Ayn Rand in New York City, he explained at length how he would rewrite the novel. Ayn Rand's point-by-point response is included in an October 27, 1934, letter to Wick:

> I have received your letter today and I have thought it over carefully from every angle. I greatly appreciate all the details of the matter which you have given me. Here is what I have to say: I certainly would not go so far as to demand the book be published exactly as it is or not at all. I am quite willing to make all the cuts and changes that may be required to improve it. But I do insist that the theme and *spirit* of the book be kept intact. Therefore, I must explain in detail exactly what I mean.
>
> I am afraid that I cannot agree with Mr. Benefield's idea of the book. It is *not* a love story. It never could be. In fact, I believe, personally, that the love story is the least interesting thing about it. Mr. Benefield may be right about the fact that I have too much background in it and I am willing to cut it some. But that background is more essential than the plot itself for the story I want to tell. Without it—there *is no* story. It is the background that creates the characters and their tragedy. It is the background that makes them do the things they do. If one does not understand the background—one does not understand them.
>
> And Mr. Benefield is completely mistaken about the fact that the American reader "has a fair knowledge of existence in Leningrad during the time covered by the novel." The American reader has no knowledge of it whatsoever. He has not the slightest suspicion of it. If he had—we would not have the appalling number of parlor Bolsheviks and idealistic sympathizers with the Soviet regime,

liberals who would scream with horror if they knew the truth of Soviet existence. It is for them that the book was written.

The principal reaction I have had from those who have read the book is one
of complete amazement at the revelation of Soviet life as it is actually lived. "Can
it possibly be true? I had no idea that that's what it was like. Why were we never
told?"—those are the things I have heard over and over again. Those are the
things I wanted to hear. Because the conditions I have depicted *are* true. I have
lived them. No one has ever come out of Soviet Russian to tell it to the world.
That was my job.

I repeat, I may have too much of it in the book and I am willing to cut it
down some. But I also repeat that it must stand as a most important part of the
novel—*not* merely as a setting for a love story. I have never heard one person
say that he was *bored* while reading the book. I have tied my background firmly
to the structure of the plot. But that background *has to* be there.

Furthermore—and here we come to the most important point—has Mr. Benefield understood the idea of the book? *Airtight is not* the story of Kira Argounova. It is the story of Kira Argounova *and* the masses—her greatest enemy.
Those masses—and what they do to the individual—are the real hero of the
book. Remove that—and you have nothing but a conventional little romance to
tell. The individual against the masses—such is the real, the only theme of the
book. Such is the greatest problem of our century—for those who are willing to
realize it.

I feel I must explain one point to Mr. Benefield—a point of the greatest
importance. Mr. Benefield wonders why I stop in the last chapter to present the
biography of the soldier who kills Kira Argounova. That stop, in my opinion, is
one of the best things in the book. It contains—in a few pages—the whole idea
and purpose of the novel. After the reader has seen Kira Argounova, has learned
what a rare, precious, irreplaceable human being she was—I give him the picture of the man who killed Kira Argounova, of the life that took her life. That
soldier is a symbol, a typical representative of the average, the dull, the useless,
the commonplace, the masses—that killed the best there is on this earth. I
believe I made this obvious when I concluded his biography by saying—
quoting from the book: "Citizen Ivan Ivanov was guarding the border of the
Union of Socialist Soviet Republics." Citizen Ivan Ivanov *is* the Union of Socialist
Soviet Republics. And that Union killed Kira Argounova. Kira Argounova against
citizen Ivan Ivanov—that is the whole book in a few pages.

I am willing to do some cutting and I believe I could cut out about fifteen
thousand, perhaps even twenty-five thousand words. That would be the most.
Cutting it down to 100,000 words would be impossible.

I agree that the title may not be a good one and I am entirely willing to
change that.

As to the matter of a suggested collaborator, I give you full authority to refuse
at once, without informing me, any and all offers that carry such a suggestion. I
do not care to hear of such offers. I consider them nothing short of an insult.
Anyone reading my book must realize that I am an individualist above everything else. As such, I shall stand or fall on my own work. I hope you do not
consider this as a beginner's arrogance. It is merely the feeling of a person who

takes pride in her work. At the cost of being considered arrogant, I must state that I do not believe there is a human being alive who could improve that book of mine in the matter of actual rewriting. If anyone is capable of improving *that* book—he should have written it himself. I would prefer not only never seeing it in print, but also burning every manuscript of it—rather than having William Shakespeare himself add one line to it which was not mine, or cross out one comma. I repeat, I welcome and appreciate all suggestions of changes to improve the book without destroying its theme, and I am quite willing to make them. But these changes must be made *by me.*

The time is certainly ripe for an anti-Red novel and it is only a question of finding the right party to take an interest in it. I do not believe that we will get very far with publishers who disapprove of or try to diminish the political implications of the book. These implications are its best chance of success. If you remember, Mr. Morris in his letter to Mr. Mencken, referred to the book as the "*Uncle Tom's Cabin* of Soviet Russia." That is exactly what the book was intended to be and exactly the angle under which it must be sold.[8]

Whether Benefield "understood the idea of the book" or not, it was becoming clear to Ayn Rand that Wick did not. In late 1934, Ayn Rand moved to New York City in preparation for the Broadway production of *Night of January 16th*. After meeting with Wick—who was primarily an agent for magazine writers—she was even more dissatisfied, and decided to make a change. Mary Inloes, the Hollywood agent for her play, had recommended New York agent Ann Watkins, and Ayn Rand went to see her. Watkins represented a number of prominent writers, including Sinclair Lewis. She read the novel, liked it, and agreed to represent it.

Watkins sent *We the Living* to Macmillan. Stanley Young was enthusiastic about the book and fought for it, but associate editor Granville Hicks (who turned out to be a member of the Communist Party) fought strongly against it. But the president of Macmillan, George P. Brett, read the book, and recommended its publication. Years later, Ayn Rand recalled that Brett had said that he did not know if they would make money on it or not, but that it was a novel that should be published. This represented a short window of opportunity for Rand during the "Red Decade." Two years later, Brett was dead, and Macmillan rejected Rand's novella *Anthem*, because "the author does not understand socialism."[9] Twenty-one years later, Hicks wrote a vicious review of *Atlas Shrugged* for the *New York Times*.

SELLING *WE THE LIVING*

We the Living was well down on Macmillan's "list" in 1936. They did little to market it and only included it in a couple of advertisements with other books. As should come as no surprise, Ayn Rand did not leave marketing and promotion to her publisher. Although she was not yet comfortable at public speaking, she took on a heavy schedule of lectures (including one at the Talk of the Town Club on West 67th Street in Manhattan). Further, she tirelessly provided interviews: on May 5, 1936, the *New York Post* published a substantial interview with a photograph; on June 15, the *New York American* published a prominent interview with a photograph of her with her husband, Frank O'Connor; and, on September 6, the *Boston Post* published a full-page interview with a rotogravure color illustration of a scene from *We the Living*. In all of these interviews, Ayn Rand painted a picture of the realities of daily life in Soviet Russia.

The April 1936 issue of *Book-of-the-Month Club News* contained a promotional paragraph about the book—not at all usual for a first novel:

> *We the Living*, ($2.50), is another book which is at once a good story and the picture of an unfamiliar world—the chaotic world of Russia immediately after the Revolution. It deals with an aristocratic family, reduced to abject poverty, but still keeping up its old allegiances and ideals, until the daughter falls in love with a young man of her own class but of less strength of character, who breaks under the strain of post-revolutionary conditions and involves her in tragedy as well. The book does justice to the virtues of revolutionists of the best type, but it goes farther than most in portraying the insincerity and brutality of the Red government in its struggle to establish itself; and it carries the conviction of being a faithful picture.[10]

This favorable, if inaccurate, description (Kira's family was middle-class) is revealing in the defensive wording employed for the benefit of "revolutionists of the best type," and outright comic in the understatement that the book "goes farther than most in portraying the insincerity and brutality of the Red government." Such were the times.

The first printing of 3,000 copies sold out in 18 months—with most sales at the end of this period. By that time Macmillan had destroyed the plates, although by contract they were obligated to keep the book in print for two years. Ayn Rand discovered this when she tried to get more copies for her own use. She immediately put Watkins on the case. Because Macmillan let the book go out of print, all rights reverted to Ayn Rand. They offered to issue a second edition, but only if Ayn Rand signed a contract for her next novel on the same terms—a $250 advance. Ayn Rand considered this, but after the failure of Macmillan to support the first edition of *We the Living* with significant advertising, she wanted a publicity guarantee for the next novel. Watkins asked for a publicity guarantee of $1,200, but Macmillan would not agree to this. Thus Macmillan lost *We the Living* and, as it turned out, *The Fountainhead*. Unfortunately, this resulted in *We the Living* remaining out of print in the United States for more than twenty years.

EUROPEAN EDITIONS

Curiously, *We the Living* received a better welcome from Ayn Rand's British publisher, Cassell & Co. Ltd., who published it in 1937, and kept it in print for many years. They also went on to publish *Anthem* in 1938—for which no American publisher was found for many years. Desmond Flower of Cassell was eagerly awaiting her next novel (*The Fountainhead*) before it had a U.S. publisher, as seen in his January 22, 1940, letter to Ayn Rand's London agent, Laurence Pollinger:

> I am returning to the attack on the subject of Ayn Rand not because I think there is anything you can do which you have not already done, but because I want her to be fully cognizant of the facts which led me to say in my last letter that there was a good market for her next novel going begging.
>
> *We the Living*, published in January 1937, is the only novel in our list which is still selling at the original price—exactly three years later. This is remarkable. We reprinted it again in the early summer last year, still at 8/6d, and the copies are steadily going out. Simpkins were in for more again last week. This shows an astonishing and gratifying interest on the part of the public, and I know I am not wrong in saying that we could have a really big success if we could get a new book from her.
>
> I should be grateful if you would let her know these facts, because they may encourage her to get on with the job![11]

As an indication of how well *We the Living* did in Europe, consider the circa 1948 document, entitled "The Publishing History of *We the Living*," that Ayn Rand wrote for an agent attempting to sell the U.S. motion picture rights to the book. After recounting the story of the Macmillan sales in the United States in 1936–1937, she summarized foreign sales:

> In England, *We the Living* was a huge success. It went into edition after edition. I kept receiving royalties for it for *ten years*, up to about a year ago, when it went out of print due to the paper shortage in England. Cassell's, my English publishers, informed me that they intend to reissue the book, still in its full-price, original edition, as soon as they get the paper.
>
> In Denmark, *We the Living* has been selling for ten years, was interrupted for a year during the war and is now selling again. Recently, I received a $4,500 check for Danish royalties. For a country as small as Denmark such royalties are an eloquent indication of the extent of the book's success.
>
> In Italy, *We the Living* was a smash hit. That was the reason for the piracy of the book by an Italian movie company. The first report which I received about this piracy, from an American connected with the American Embassy in Italy, stated that the picture of *We the Living* was sensationally successful in Europe. I have no exact information about the details of this as yet.
>
> Now, this is what the book has done to-date. Can you name another obscure

novel—which went unnoticed in this country and so could be considered a flop—that had a history of this kind? If not, isn't this worthy of some serious thought and aren't there some conclusions to be drawn from it, as I shall presently point out?

Against the above, there is one fact which may be listed as a real failure, and that is the stage production of this novel, titled *The Unconquered.* I shall take just half the blame for that; the book was not proper stage material. As to the way it was produced—anyone who saw it on the stage would have to judge for himself whether what he saw had any relation to the book or not.

I have not mentioned the political aspects of the history of *We the Living*, and of what was done to kill it. The time has now come for you to realize for yourself the kind of secret sabotage that anti-Communist writers have had to endure for years. The rest of the country is realizing now.

The conclusions I have made about *We the Living* and its possibilities are as follows:

Just as *The Fountainhead* was rejected by *twelve publishers* who considered it non-commercial and predicted that it would not sell, until I found one editor who had the intelligence to understand the value of the book—so *We the Living* needs to find one man who is capable of forming an independent judgment about its actual merit and to act accordingly. *We the Living* may be a lesser book than *The Fountainhead*—but, on a smaller scale, it has potentialities which have not been touched and I intend to see that it gets its full chance.

The time is right for it now, and the political opinion of this country is overwhelmingly on my side. I want to find one person in the picture industry who would be the equivalent in mental stature, of the editor of Bobbs-Merrill. If such a person can be found and will make a picture of *We the Living*, I will have the book re-issued, and we would have—before the picture is released—a ready made best-seller to help the screen version. The demand for the book is huge right now, I get requests for it from readers constantly, and I understand that it is almost impossible to get a copy of the book in the second-hand market. If no picture is made now, I will probably re-issue the book after my next novel.

What I should like you, as my agents, to consider is this: my entire career has been and will probably always be on this same pattern. All the rules, judgments and estimates which apply to and are derived from the experience of other writers, work in reverse in my case. I shall probably always find most of the pseudo-intellectuals among the average editors or producers, against me—but I have the public. The things I write are not the trite, easily-obvious successes that remind people of ten other best-sellers. I will always be met with doubt from the safe-playing, standard-minded persons, and will always need to find one independent man to deal with. The public will do the rest for me, as it has invariably done before, when given the chance.

I fully realize that this is a difficult and unconventional undertaking for you—to attempt to sell, merely on its merit, a book which has been tagged as a failure. The history of *The Fountainhead* is my reason for insisting that it has to be done, and my illustration of the possible consequences of the potential rewards involved for both you and me.[12]

PUBLICATION AND SALE OF THE SECOND EDITION

While she hoped for a production of a motion picture,[13] Ayn Rand did not look for a new publisher for the book after *The Fountainhead* was published, as she explained in a progress report on the writing of *Atlas Shrugged* to her agent Alan Collins at Curtis Brown on December 30, 1950:

> I would like very much for you to take over certain properties, as I have not been too happy about the manner in which they were handled by the Ann Watkins office. The most important one of them is my first novel, *We the Living*. It was published by Macmillan in 1936, but the American publishing rights have reverted to me. There is now a great demand for this novel. I keep getting letters about it constantly, and Bobbs-Merrill have been after me for several years to let them issue a new American Edition of it. I have refused, because I don't want to have it issued as a follow-up to *The Fountainhead*, since, being an earlier novel, it would be an anticlimax at present. But I want it to be reissued shortly after my new novel is published, and I would like to make arrangements for it at the time I sign the contract for the new novel, whether it will be with Bobbs-Merrill or another publisher. Therefore it will be much better if both novels are handled by you.[14]

After the publication of *Atlas Shrugged* by Random House in 1957, there was understandably no difficulty in securing the new (revised) edition of *We the Living* from Random House in 1959.[15] In 1960, the first paperback edition was published by New American Library—now a part of Penguin Putnam, Inc., which since 1989 has also been the hardcover publisher.

By this time a "new" novel by the author of *The Fountainhead* and *Atlas Shrugged* effectively sold itself. Three million copies of *We the Living* have been sold since 1959. A remarkable sale for a book whose plates had been destroyed by Macmillan before the first printing of 3,000 copies sold out in 1937.

Translations in Spanish and Italian have gone in and out of print in recent years. The book is currently in print in French and Greek. But perhaps the most eloquent refutation of those who tried to smother the book in America during the "Red" 1930s occurred in 1993, when *We the Living* was published for the first time in Russian, in the city in which the story was set, St. Petersburg. It has had a good sale.

NOTES

1. Biographical interviews (Ayn Rand Archives).
2. Michael S. Berliner, ed., *Letters of Ayn Rand*, (New York: Dutton, 1995), 4–6.
3. Berliner, *Letters*, 10.

4. Berliner, *Letters*, 13.

5. Quoted in Berliner, *Letters*, 14.

6. Berliner, *Letters*, 12.

7. Unpublished material in the Ayn Rand Archives.

8. Berliner, *Letters*, 17–19.

9. Biographical interviews (Ayn Rand Archives).

10. *Book-of-the-Month Club News*, April 1936.

11. Unpublished, in the Ayn Rand Archives.

12. Unpublished, in the Ayn Rand Archives.

13. This hope was never realized. On the pirate Italian version of the novel, see Jeff Britting, "Adapting *We the Living*," in the present volume.

14. Berliner, *Letters*, 488.

15. On the differences between the 1936 and 1959 editions, see Robert Mayhew, "*We the Living*: '36 and '59," in the present volume.

7

Reviews of *We the Living*

Michael S. Berliner

A study of the reviews of a book provides a variety of insights. It is a cultural barometer of the times in which the book is published. It tells us something about the ease or difficulty a book has reaching its audience (e.g., some books such as Ayn Rand's *The Fountainhead* become bestsellers despite being ignored by reviewers). Such a study also provides important biographical information about the author. In the case of *We the Living*, this first novel, widely and positively reviewed, did *not* presage similar treatment of her later novels or nonfiction works. As she became more radical in her writings, the reviewers turned either silent or antagonistic.

It is of particular interest that Ayn Rand paid close attention to reviews of her works. Philosophically, she was a staunch advocate of individualism, whose essence is the reliance on one's own independent judgment. One might, therefore, expect her to have had little interest in the opinions of reviewers. Such, however, was not the case. She kept extensive collections of reviews, clipping many herself or filing those sent to her by clipping services. And she discussed reviews at some length in her unpublished biographical interviews of 1960–61.[1]

The explanation for her interest in reviews is not difficult to discover. She held that reviews—even negative ones—helped book sales and helped her reach her audience. She also knew that they provided a bargaining point for future publishing and performance contracts. Ayn Rand was not ethereal, either in her writing or in her life. She carefully monitored and directed every aspect of her career. She kept careful track of print runs of her books and of book sales, and she vetted and even wrote advertising copy.

Her attitude toward reviews reveals an analytic approach to opinions about her works. She expected little from reviews because, she said,

I had read too many book reviews of books that I had read and I had seen the terrible contradictions and no standards nor reasons given. For instance, I thought [Clifton] Fadiman's reviews [in *The New Yorker*] were intelligent, and I tried once or twice to read books that he recommended. Well that ended Fadiman for me. Then, Alexander Woolcott was very prominent. He had a radio program where he reviewed books and did it so interestingly, really intelligently, that for awhile he had an enormous following—anything he recommended people would read, and it became a best seller. His reviews impressed me, so I tried to read some of his selections. The result was I stopped listening to him. And, incidentally, the same happened with all of his following. He had recommended too many bad books and he lost his influence. I knew that the field of reviewing was not fully rational; however, I would not have expected it to be totally irrational.[2]

Nor did she blame herself for bad reviews:

If they had given me justice for what was good, and said something like "the style was rough or uneven," then I would have taken the blame; not otherwise. If anybody praises me I want to know why. And, particularly, if anybody criticizes me I want to know why. If I see arbitrary statements I discount them immediately, particularly if they're distorting statements. Because there I would be totally objective. I often thought that's [the same point as] in [my] story "The Simplest Thing in the World"[3]: that I wished I could find some serious flaw in the book, because that would make the situation more benevolent, in effect more just. And I knew damn well there wasn't.

But reviews could and did have a positive effect on Ayn Rand. As she wrote to Lorine Pruette, after Pruette's *New York Times* review of *The Fountainhead* in 1943:

If one reviewer had missed the theme, it could be ascribed to stupidity. Four of them can be explained only by dishonesty and cowardice. And it terrified me to think our country had reached such a state of depravity that one was no longer permitted to speak in defense of the individual, that the mere mention of such an issue was to be evaded and hushed up as too dangerous. That is why I am grateful to you in a way much beyond literary matters and for much more than the beautiful things you said about me and the book, although they did make me very happy. I am grateful for your integrity as a person, which saved me from the horror of believing that this country is lost, that people are much more rotten than I presented them in the book, and that there is no intellectual decency left anywhere.[4]

That review was especially important to her because it was in a New York newspaper. As she later said, "professionally nothing counts except the New York reviews."

The source of what follows is primarily the material in the Ayn Rand

Archives, though I've supplemented these slightly. It should be noted that this is a history of reviews only, for example, formal reviews that came out when the book and movie were released; it is not a history of all commentary on *We the Living*.

THE REVIEWS

We the Living, published in 1936, was Ayn Rand's first novel. The Ayn Rand Archives contains a very large collection of reviews of this book, because the reviews were supplied by a clipping service. There are approximately 125 different reviews ("approximate" because it is sometimes difficult to tell if a review is original or cribbed from another review—a surprisingly common practice at that time). Since some reviews were syndicated, the number of publications carrying reviews was more than 200. In addition, there were hundreds of short feature stories and mentions in columns, some of which were quasi reviews.

In her biographical interviews, she said that *We the Living* was not widely reviewed in important publications. That is an intriguing remark, because it was the most reviewed of any of her works, certainly the most positively reviewed, and in such major publications as the *New York Times*, the *Nation*, *Saturday Review of Literature*, *Time* magazine, the *Sunday Times* of London and the *Manchester Guardian*. Both the number and quality of publications reviewing the book would seem to indicate significant response to a first novel.

Let us look first at the major U.S. reviews—beginning with those she believed really counted: the New York City reviews. The *New York Times'* Harold Strauss praised it for "remarkably fluent English" and narrative skill. But, he warned, "the dice are slavishly warped to the dictates of propaganda," and thus the novel blunders into artistic improbabilities. The book, he warned, might seem impartial to the unwary, but it's loaded in favor of Leo Kovalensky. However, he did allow as how the "improbabilities" pertained only to the plot: "We cannot here hold in question the facts upon which Miss Rand's political attitude is based."

The second major New York paper was the *Herald Tribune*. Its reviewer, Ida Zeitlin (April 19), called the book "passionate and powerful" and—most impressively—"primarily a wild cry for the right of an individual to live for what he wants to live for." Only secondarily, she thought, was it an indictment of the Soviets. And she quotes the novel's heroine: "I want to live for myself—for the something sacred and untouchable within me that makes me myself. Who gave you the right to forbid it?" However, she concluded with the hope that the USSR of 1936, more firmly established than that of 1925, has found it possible and desirable to make life bearable for the everyday people like Uncle Vasili.[5]

The lesser New York papers were more positive: for example, in the *Sun* (April 17), James C. Grey called it a "masterpiece" and used many anticommunist quotes from the novel; the *Evening Journal*'s Elsie Robinson (July 8) said that, because it's not a fantasy, it is more convincing than Sinclair Lewis's *It Can't Happen Here*, and that it is not the usual exaggerated, shrill propaganda. Robinson wanted to "put it in the hands of every young person in America, knowing that they would never be as happy or carefree again."

Positive reviews came from the *Book of the Month Club News* (April) and *Variety* (May 6), both of which recognized the philosophic content to some degree. Other magazines were less positive: *Time* (April 20) in its two-sentence review, rode the fence, describing *We the Living* as the story of the younger generation in Russia during the early years of Soviet rule. "Communist sympathizers," it said, "would find it annoying, Whites heartening." The *Nation*'s Ben Belitt (April 22) snidely retold the story and carped that it was "out to puncture a bubble with a bludgeon" and that Ayn Rand's "excessive theatricality invites suspicion about her politics." The prestigious *Saturday Review of Literature* chose as its reviewer a Russian émigré, Irina Skariatina, author of *First to Go Back* (to Soviet Russia).[6] Her review (April 18), which treated *We the Living* as just a graphic story of what could and did happen in 1922, thoroughly disgusted Miss Rand—especially its ending: "Thank God that period for my people has passed." (This was written in 1936, three years after the murder of 6 million kulaks, when Russia was at the height of Stalinist terror.)

In other major papers, J. C. Rogers, in the *Washington Post* (April 26) found it "entertaining" and "beautifully written," but suffering "from deliberate exaggeration and aristocratic bias." One comment by Rogers indicates the more conservative moral climate of the 1930s: he opined that Ayn Rand's love scenes would cause Boccacio to "writhe with jealousy" and make Erskine Caldwell (author of the rather trashy *Tobacco Road*) "seem like a producer of Gospel mission tracts." The *Los Angeles Times* (April 12, by H. C.) thought it "the best novel to come out of Russia since the World War," praising it for creating real people with mixed motives, rather than cardboard saints and sinners. Then, showing the contradictions pervading the history of book reviews, the *Toronto Globe*'s J. P. C. (May 9) wrote the opposite: that it was bad literature *because* there were no "real people." Incidentally, Ayn Rand said in her biographical interviews that reading wildly contradictory reviews of other books had armed her against this phenomenon.

Reviews in major papers were not the only ones to come to Ayn Rand's attention. In an April 11 review in the *Deseret News* (the main paper in Salt Lake City), Ayn Rand circled the following: "It tears the front covering from the puppet show and shows the inner workings of Soviet rule. . . . A great book, one that should go down as an epic of one of the greatest struggles the world has ever seen, the struggle between individualism and collectivism." Thus, some reviewers got the point of the book, writing that it shows what communist theories mean in practice (e.g., Carleton Cady's May 10 review in the *Grand Rapids Herald*), calling it anticollectivist (e.g., Adrian Rose's May 3 review in the *Dallas Times-Herald* and John Cummings' June 21 review in the *Detroit Free Press*) and "a plea for the individual against the collective, for the right to the pursuit of happiness" (the *Topeka State Journal* on May 2).

But many didn't understand, considering *We the Living* to be a story about the Russian middle-class (e.g., the *Indianapolis Times* on May 1). Some reviews (e.g., the *Cincinnati Times-Star* on July 25) saw it as biased against the Soviet "experiment" (a headline in the *Oklahoman* on April 26: "Reactionary Russian"), but many (e.g., the *Dallas News* on May 10 and Ivar Spector in the *Seattle Post-Intelligencer* on May 5) repeated the idea (bizarrely included in a Macmillan press release) that the book is "impartial" and leaves the reader to decide for himself. In this vein was a review by Bruce Catton (who later gained fame as a Civil War historian) syndicated to seventy papers. Wrote Catton:

> Most novels about post-war Russia describe either the heroism and triumph of the proletariat or the heroism and escape of the aristocrats. Ayn Rand takes a middle course and tells about the middle-class folk who stayed in Russia and tried to make a go of things. It makes a tragic story, packed with significant overtones for those vague dreamers who think that a revolution would be an interesting experience.

Here is another circled passage, an insightful one from the *Albany News* (April 13): "The end is very tragic and helps to drive Miss Rand's point to her logical conclusion. But one loses the sense of frustration that tragedy sometimes engenders, by the magnificence of the presentation." Circled from the *Syracuse Post-Standard* (April 12): " *We the Living* probably provides a more true and devastating picture of the Communist government in Russia than all of the intellectual analyses that have been written about it. . . . It has all the earmarks of great literature." Finally, here are two insightful philosophic points: Georgiana G. Stevens in the *San Francisco Chronicle* (June 28) wrote that the theme is "that men have a sacred right to life and to a personal ego." And the *Washington Star*'s Margaret Germond (May 6) deemed Soviet Russia (as described by Rand) to be "the most amazing experiment in the regimentation of human souls that the world has ever witnessed," and she recommended the novel to those who refuse to relinquish their view that communism is ideal.

In the British Isles, where it was widely reviewed in 1937, *We the Living* was received quite positively. *The Sunday Times'* Ralph Straus (January 17), though generally ignoring the ideas, called it "remarkable" writing, a vivid picture of life, a thrilling but believable story. The *Times Literary Supplement* (January 17) said that Ayn Rand wrote in "irreproachable English" but thought that the material at the author's disposal afforded the opportunity for a more interesting and revealing story. Harold Brighouse in the *Manchester Guardian* (January 12) wrote that Ayn Rand had an "extraordinary" command of English and had written an immensely readable description of life in the 1920s. Reviewer Young Marlow in the *Reynolds News* thought the story "first-rate" and doubted that the author was really a foreigner: "The style of the writing is that of an old hand." Not recognizing Rand's anti-altruist moral position, Howard Spring, who succeeded J. B. Priestly as reviewer at the *Evening Standard*, thought the message to be that the best way for the individual to serve the masses is for the masses to let the individual alone (January 14).

The *New Statesman and Nation* (January 6) called it "bitter" and "aggressive," but good to see after all the Left-wing adulation of pro-Soviet novels. The reviewer for *Irish Press* (January 19) wrote that *We the Living* presented a picture of misery "as convincing as a Rembrandt drawing." *Time and Tide's* John Brophy (January 23) was encouraged by the USSR "transforming itself" from a dictatorship and wished that Ayn Rand had waited for this development and "excised some of the criticisms of Communism," for "she might have seen this novel a best seller in Russia." William Plomer in *The Spectator* (January 15) opined that the book was so counterrevolutionary that it will "annoy people of Reddish sympathies." *Current Literature's* Dennis Wheatley (January) called it "one of the most terrible indictments of utter failure that world communism has ever been called upon to answer." *Books of the Month* (January) branded it a consistently virulent piece of anti-Soviet propaganda. And Arthur Porritt, in *The Baptist Times* (August 19) after quoting the "air-tight" passage near the end of the novel (see 404–405, cf. 407), wrote that *We the Living* gives a "vivid picture of the slavery of the individual to the collective."

Australian reviews (in early 1937) went from the sublime to the ridiculous: The *Adelaide Advertiser* (February 27) saw *We the Living* as a book against "all forms of state tyranny," Communist or Nazi, an indictment of the state that claims all, an appeal for "the right of the individual to live his own life." In contrast to the British praise of her writing ability, the *Melbourne Argus* reviewer (February 13) thought it read like "translated Scandinavian." However, the *Sydney Morning Herald* (January 22) thought it brilliantly written, with a remarkable flair for portraiture. But the prize for absurdity goes to Leslie Haylen, in the *Sydney Women's Weekly* (one of Australia's most prominent magazines). Haylen called it a magnificently told story of Kira's courage, but thought that Ayn Rand's message was: "Revolution and change may be ancient things, but woman and her emotions are as old as the world. . . . Body and soul may belong to the new social order, but a woman's heart is her own."

There were a number of foreign-language editions of *We the Living* during Ayn Rand's lifetime, and she collected some reviews (though there is no evidence that she read English translations of them). For example, there were a number of reviews in Denmark, though none from major papers, and they echoed the contradictions in other countries: some said the book doesn't apply to today's Russia, while others warned that the executions continue and hoped that the novel would shut the mouths of Danish parlor Communists. The most interesting historically were the reviews in Italy, when the book came out in 1938. This was, of course, Fascist Italy, and the reviews are predictable: High praise for *We the Living*'s attack on Communism and Soviet Russia. Echoing Mussolini's party line, two reviews (*Nero Su Bianco* of Rome on May 8, 1938, and *Corriere Mercantile* of Genoa on June 15) praised the book for revealing the weakness of Communism: its annihilation of the Fascist values of country, family, and religion. Two reviewers (in *Il Nuovo Geornale* on May 7 and *Corriere del Tirreno* on July 9) were sufficiently attuned to Fascism that they deplored Kira's "excessive" individualism, but none identified Kira's philosophy, the philosophic conflict or even why Ayn Rand condemned communism.

We the Living was reissued in both hardback and paperback volumes in 1959. That it did not attract major reviews is somewhat curious, even though reissues and paperbacks are often ignored by reviewers. However, in 1959, *We the Living* was virtually new to American readers, having been out of print for two decades. In the interim, Ayn Rand had gained considerable fame with *The Fountainhead* book and movie and with *Atlas Shrugged*, which had been on the bestseller lists for more than five months, ending in March 1958. Furthermore, the Cold War with Soviet Russia was in full swing, with revelations by Khrushchev of the Stalin purges. The reissued novel wasn't totally ignored, however. Paul Clark (*Miami Herald*, January 25, 1959) quoted extensively from Ayn Rand's new foreword about the belief that Communism is a noble ideal and opined that the book "will make a greater impact than 20 years ago." The *Detroit Jewish News* (February 6) said that it "exposes the horrors of dictatorial rule, its dangers to human freedom" and quoted from the foreword about unchanged living conditions in 1959 compared to the book's setting in 1925.

THE MOVIE REVIEWS

Upon its release in Fascist Italy in 1942, the four-hour Italian-made film was popular with both audiences (probably for its implied anti-Fascism) and critics (who awarded it a Biennale prize at the 1942 Venice Film Festival). The film starred Alida Valli, Rossano Brazzi, and Fosco Giachetti and was directed by Goffredo Alessandrini. Critic Guido Gualassini wrote in *Primi Piani* (September 1942) that the film "can truly be defined as a giant." And Umberto de Franciscis, also in *Primi Piani* (August 1942), said:

> [This film] continues the theme of Italian faith. . . . [It] is an attack on Bolshevik civilization. An attack that does not stop at the visible manifestations of the New World but also exposes the torment that the free spirits of the Russian people are subjected to. The Russian machinery works with tragic results, like a grinder that crushes and pulverizes everything that comes close to its grindstone.[7]

The 1988 release of the 2-hour 50-minute subtitled version attracted dozens of reviews in the English-speaking world. Reviews varied considerably regarding both the content and production values. The *Dallas Morning News* (Bill Cosford, April 28, 1989) found it to be "a grand old Hollywood-style weeper" that succeeds because "the over-wrought Randisms are submerged in the melodramatics." In the *Milwaukee Journal* (February 2, 1989), Douglas Armstrong thought the movie inspiring and, with a revisionism found in other reviews, admired Rand's "feminist" heroine. *Weekly Variety* (February 4, 1988) stressed the oft-published history of the movie: "Fascist authorities quickly got wise that the film's anti-authoritarian message directed at the communists could just as easily be meant for them." *Newsday*'s Mike McGrady (November 25, 1988) wrote: "Individual rights—that's the subject of the film. Though the setting is vital, the film is neither about Russia or communism; it is about any human being whose freedoms have been curtailed by the state."

Major U.S. publications were less kind and indicated that the leftist attitudes of the 1930s Red Decade were alive and well in the late 1980s. The *Los Angeles Times'* left-leaning Michael Wilmington (November 12, 1988) sneered at the ideas and called the movie an adventure in "triple-think," taking it to task for rewriting the dialogue and redubbing the hero's climactic speech (ignoring the fact that it was Ayn Rand who rewrote the dialogue to conform to the book, which had been changed by the Italian filmmakers). The *New York Times'* Caryn James (November 25, 1988) found it to be "a simplistic paean to the lost wealth and freedom of upper-class individuals," and thought that it made "Doctor Zhivago look like the Communist Manifesto." In the *New York Post* (November 25, 1988), David Edelstein branded Ayn Rand a "fanatic" and "loony" and wrote that her "vision seems crazed." The *Village Voice*'s J. Hoberman thought the movie "not quite nutty enough to qualify as camp" and snickered that it was "worthy of its source," "a unique combination of Adam Smith, Friederich Nietzsche and Jacqueline Susann." He wrote that "Rand is a triumph of political kitsch" and even doubted the story's anti-Fascism.

The rest of the English-speaking world was kinder. Reviews in the major Australian papers ranged from mildly positive to glowing, with the *Weekend Australian*'s Evan Williams (November 26–27, 1988) calling it "among the greatest love stories the cinema has given us." The British reviews were much more positive and generally more intellectual than the U.S. reviews. None considered the story to be outdated, and most stressed the implicit anti-Fascism of the story, although Sheila Johnston in the *Independent* (July 20, 1989) liked the movie despite its "standard Red-bashing propaganda." In the *Monthly Film Bulletin* (July 1989), Geoffrey Nowell-Smith thought that the story was not really a political film, and he discussed at length his thesis that "the most obvious message opposes the individual to the collective. But this front line of opposition covers for one between personal integrity and those demands on the individual which threaten it."

SUMMARY AND CONCLUSIONS

What are we to make of these reviews? Given that *We the Living* was published in the middle of the Red Decade, the reviews are both predictable and surprising. On the one hand, they reflect a widespread sympathy with Communism that would be unheard of among mainstream reviewers by the 1950s. That sympathy was manifested in pro-Soviet reviews in mainstream publications, but also in the wonderment that any writer could be as anti-Soviet as was Ayn Rand in *We the Living*. Numerous reviews also accepted the Marxist notion that any anti-Soviet writer must be an apologist for the aristocracy. That said, a more dominant—and surprising—thread in the reviews is that they aren't more pro-Soviet. In fact, most reviews are generally positive regarding Ayn Rand's ideas and her warnings about the destruction of the individual. None contested her facts, though some thought they no longer applied. Particularly surprising was the lack of objections to her characterization of Marxist ideology, which she portrayed as favoring the sacrifice of the individual to the collective. Yet nowhere do the reviewers cry out that Ayn Rand misrepresented a glorious ideal as anti-life. Perhaps her characterizations were just too obviously true to be dismissed.

In retrospect, the *We the Living* reviews do not seem very negative. Most were positive, certainly about the story and Ayn Rand's writing; but also the majority was positive about the ideas, which is surprising in the Red Decade. But Ayn Rand was just coming to realize that the individualistic ideas she brought from Russia were not only not welcome but were considered anathema by the intellectuals of the freest country on earth. Unfortunately, this attitude would only grow through the years.

NOTES

1. Clippings are held at the Ayn Rand Archives. All quotes of Ayn Rand, unless otherwise indicated, come from the biographical interviews (Ayn Rand Archives).

2. For more on her views regarding book reviews, see Ayn Rand, *The Art of Non-fiction: A Guide for Writers and Readers*, Robert Mayhew, ed. (New York: Plume, 2001), chapter 9.

3. See Ayn Rand, *The Romantic Manifesto: A Philosophy of Literature*, revised edition (New York: Signet, 1975), 173–85.

4. Michael S. Berliner, ed., *Letters of Ayn Rand* (New York: Dutton, 1995), 74.

5. Ironically, on the page facing this review was a review of a biography of John Reed (the American who moved to Russia and was so pro-Soviet he was eventually buried in Red Square): *John Reed: the Making of a Revolutionary* (New York: Macmillan, 1936), by Granville Hicks, reviewed by Floyd Dell, a Reed colleague. The previous year, Macmillan had published Hicks' *The Great Tradition*, an explicitly Communist work, and published it jointly with International Publishers, the official Communist publishing firm. The New York literary world was indeed Moscow West. On Hicks' involvement with the publishing of *We the Living*, see Richard Ralston, "Publishing *We the Living*," in the present volume, p. 139.

6. Irina Skariatina, *First to Go Back, An Aristocrat in Soviet Russia* (New York: Bobbs-Merrill, 1933).

7. Translated by Alberta Miculan.

8

Adapting *We the Living*

Jeff Britting

We the Living is unique among Ayn Rand's fiction for two reasons. First, it is the only work adapted and produced during her lifetime as both a stage play and a motion picture. Second, *We the Living* is her first novel—the first of any of Ayn Rand's works—to have a major impact on current events, which it did as a result of its adaptation.[1]

The theme of *We the Living* is: "the individual against the state; the supreme value of a human life and the evil of a totalitarian state that claims the right to sacrifice it."[2] In 1940, *We the Living* was adapted and produced as a Broadway play called *The Unconquered*.[3] The theater critics of the time, however, ignored or failed to grasp its theme and the work slipped into theatrical obscurity. In 1942, during World War II, *We the Living* was adapted and released as a two-part film in Italy called *Noi Vivi* and *Addio Kira*.[4] Italy's besieged public grasped its theme immediately and the film inspired a national protest against the Fascist government.

These two adaptations of *We the Living*, and their production histories, are case studies of Ayn Rand's early intellectual impact in the twentieth century.[5]

WE THE LIVING AS THEATER: THE UNCONQUERED

By the mid-1930s, Ayn Rand was at the start of a promising career. She had written and sold three works: a screen scenario entitled *Red Pawn*, a successful Broadway play, *Night of January 16th*, and a first novel, *We the Living*. The works showed promise and accomplishment, but they were not professional breakthroughs. *Red Pawn*, a story set in Russia, was sold to Universal Pictures in 1932. It never went into production and remains unproduced to this day. *Night of January 16th* ran successfully for twenty-nine weeks on Broadway during the 1935–36 season, but Al Woods, its producer, disfigured the play with inappropriate changes.[6] In 1936, Macmillan published *We the Living*. Despite the novel's considerable coverage in the press and slow but accelerating sales, the book went out of print prematurely and vanished.[7]

Adapting *We the Living* was proposed shortly after the novel's publication in 1936, a time when Rand's early successes were most evident. The proposal did not originate with Rand; rather, Jerome Mayer, a producer and writer, originated the idea.[8] Mayer had read and admired *We the Living* and offered to option the novel while Rand adapted the work. Unlike Al Woods, producer of *Night of January 16th* and a successful producer of "hit" melodramas, including *The Trial of Mary Dugan*, Mayer was a modest producer of intellectually orientated plays with no major financial successes.[9] Nevertheless, the idea appealed to Rand as a way to stimulate the slow domestic sales of the novel. As she later said, her motive was legitimate but "it was not a literary motive. My primary goal and interest were not in the play as such."[10]

Rand was a successful Broadway playwright and published novelist and her next theatrical effort warranted newspaper coverage. A July 1936 headline in the *New York Mirror* announced: "Mayer Buys Play From Girl Who Fled Soviet."[11] The *New York Times* reported that Ayn Rand was spending the summer writing a play based on her novel, a "bitter attack of Soviet Russia" published that spring.[12] In a September follow-up report, the *New York Times* wrote "Ayn Rand has been toiling through the summer on a dramatization of her own novel, 'We, the Living.' By this morning she should have finished two acts of it. By November, she expects, Jerome Mayer will be ready to produce it—a bitter and anti-Soviet note that will not make Union Square very happy."[13] By January 1937, *Publishers Weekly* reported that Ayn Rand had completed her adaptation.[14]

In March 1937, a year after the publication of the novel, the production was delayed. "First announced last July for production last February," the *New York Times* reported, "Ayn Rand's dramatization of her novel, *We the Living*, is now listed for a spring [1937] tryout. All being well, [Mayer] would bring it here in the autumn."[15] However, all was not well. Mayer's effort to raise sufficient money to capitalize his production proved daunting and casting the role of Kira Argounova caused further delays. In June 1937 theater columnist Jack Stinnett reported that Mayer was in Hollywood searching for actors for a spring 1938 production of *We the Living*. The play, he wrote, "will undoubtedly start a siege of picketing, being strongly anti-communist."[16] Casting troubles continued. A year later in July 1938 Leonard Lyons' column "Broadway Melody" reported "Ayn Rand, author of *Night of January 16th* is having difficulty casting her new play. Its theme is anti-communist."[17]

Rand's own assessment of the situation concurred with the published reports. The underlying cause of Mayer's casting troubles was the play's openly anticommunist theme. It was the height of the 1930s "Red Decade," an aptly named period when American intellectuals sympathetic to Soviet Russia struggled to dominate Hollywood and Broadway.[18] Leonard Peikoff, Rand's literary executor, relates there was

> a tremendous amount of opposition from Hollywood stars, who would profess to her—Bette Davis is one example—that they would be honored to do the part of Kira and suddenly, two weeks or two months later, they would say, "I'm sorry. My agent says [appearing in an anti-communist play] will destroy my career."[19]

Without Bette Davis or an equivalent star, Mayer was unable to capitalize his production and his option lapsed. Meanwhile, Rand focused on other writing projects, completing her novella, *Anthem*, and the plotting of her next novel, *The Fountainhead*.

Rand was well into the writing of *The Fountainhead* when her agent called with news of yet another offer on *We the Living*, this time from the Broadway star Eugenie Leontovich.[20] Leontovich read the novel, learned that a theatrical adaptation existed, and requested a script. Leontovich then sent the play to George Abbott, a personal friend and one-time director, who was also a major Broadway producer.[21] Eager to direct a serious drama, Abbott read the play and agreed to proceed with Leontovich in the role of Kira Argounova.

Rand described Abbott as a "scrupulously" honorable man primarily interested in musical comedy and farce, but who aspired to a more serious type of theater. Financially speaking, Abbott was a significant advance over Mayer: he was one of Broadway's most successful producers and was backed financially by Warner Bros. Studios in Hollywood. Abbott's interest in *We the Living* was auspicious—a Broadway success might generate further interest on the part of Hollywood.[22] Meanwhile, in 1937, Rand had made a disturbing discovery, which underscored the urgency of a Broadway production. Much to Rand's surprise, Macmillan failed to keep *We the Living* in print, having destroyed prematurely the book's typeset. Abbott's theatrical venture, virtually the only way to keep the memory of the novel alive in the public's mind, could not be ignored.

Abbott scheduled *We the Living* for the 1939–1940 New York theatrical season. By fall 1939 Abbott began casting *We the Living* around Eugenie Leontovich and preparing the play's out-of-town tryout in Baltimore. The play would open on Christmas evening and run for one week, thereafter coming to New York at the beginning of January 1940. *We the Living* would be Abbott's fourth Broadway production that season and his most costly, ambitious production ever.[23]

Meanwhile, Rand began revising *We the Living* under Abbott's supervision and, in the weeks before the Baltimore opening, came to realize at the last minute that the whole venture was a mistake. Abbott, she recalled, was a "very nice person" but "totally inept about drama." As a director, he was

> totally un-stylized. And he wanted the folks next door. . . . [He] tried to suggest that if a line was simple, you must use ten words instead of three. . . . [For instance] something as simple as Kira saying, "I will try to cross the border." . . . He wanted her to say . . . : "Well, if I have a chance, and I think I might try, what I really would like is to cross the border." . . . And I asked him, "What for?" And he said, "Because when it's too brief, people don't talk that way."

Unlike Woods, who sought to make script changes in *Night of January 16th* without her permission, Rand had final say over all changes in *The Unconquered*. Abbot requested changes and Rand refused constantly: "I usually like to permit them changes, if there's any reason for it, and even when it's dubious, once in awhile to permit it, simply not to be too arbitrary about it, because he had to direct. But it was one succession of flat 'No's' after another."[24]

By November 1939 Rand and Abbott's script troubles surfaced publicly. Under the headline, "Author, Actor Trouble Hits Coming Play," the press reported that

> Miss Rand's play, "We, The Living" was to go in rehearsal immediately under George Abbott's sponsorship. The play is an indictment of Soviet Russia and Abbott has decided that one character needs to be made more sympathetic. Miss Rand doesn't think so, and the contretemps threatens to become serious. Also, Eugenie Leontovich, the play's star is reported in the throws of reconciliation with her husband, Gregory Ratoff, and is anxious to return to Hollywood and abandon her stage career. [25]

The controversy, however, was quickly diffused by the *News*. It reported that a story "floating around Broadway" concerning a disagreement between Abbott and Rand over a "leading character" was false. On the contrary, both producer and author were "in complete agreement and of equal enthusiasm as to the drama's chances." The play was "scheduled to go into rehearsals early next week."[26] In December 1939, the *News* announced a new cast member and a name change: "With John Emery as her leading man, Eugenie Leontovich is en route East for 'The Unconquered,' new title of Ayn Rand's play George Abbott is doing."[27]

In November 1939, newspaper coverage of *The Unconquered* began to widen beyond casting and writing controversies. Several months earlier in August 1939, the USSR signed a controversial nonaggression treaty with Nazi Germany.[28] As a result, newspaper reports about the play began to include references to the Soviet Union and other current topics. The *World-Telegram* wrote that the "George Abbott show is going to be a local Ninotchka—ridiculing the pro-Soviet plotter. . . . *The New Masses*, incidentally, stations men to guard its editorial offices against vandals."[29] The press also tied the play back to Hollywood. According to *Woman's Wear*, the new Ayn Rand play in rehearsal "will mark the first time Mr. Abbott has given any actor or actress precedence in billing over the name of a play he has produced. Miss Leontovich's reputation, however, and the magnitude of her role in the forthcoming production have moved him to change his traditional attitude toward the star system."[30]

By mid-December 1939, the play left New York for its Baltimore tryout, and a major problem surfaced in Eugenie Leontovich's portrayal of Kira. Rand recalled:

> You could do nothing with her. She would play it in the old Moscow Art Theater style, ham all over the place, and she wouldn't take direction. Abbott, literally, couldn't do anything with her. He would work and he'd explain and he would show lines. She would say yes, and when it comes time to perform, she does it her way.[31]

Despite leading-lady problems, the press remained oddly silent. Instead, the press appeared diverted by the enormous size of the production loading-in to the Maryland Theatre and the elaborate theatrical vision of scenic designer Boris Aronson. The *Baltimore Sun* announced that the new Abbott show was "one of the most elaborate productions he has ever presented" and reported that "fourteen van loads of equipment, properties, electrical fixtures and setting were hauled to the theatre Tuesday night and Wednesday" in anticipation of a Christmas opening.[32]

As described by the *Baltimore Evening Sun,* the production was enormous:

> The twin turntables, each eighteen feet in diameter, have been placed side by side on stage. Although each of the play's seven major scenes is being played out front, stagehands at the rear will be setting up the backdrops and properties for the next scene on the rear halves of the two turntables. A curtain will drop momentarily, the twin tables will spin then halt with the new set facing the proscenium and the action will be resumed with but the briefest of delays.

As to the set design, the report continued: "The action takes place in and around the Kremlin, the massive and gloomy stone citadel of Czarist origin in Moscow, and the massive sets were designed by Boris Aronson, to recreate the atmosphere that surrounds that grim building."[33]

In an interview with Aronson, the *Baltimore Sun* reported extensively on the designer's vision:

Aronson uses the color red as the predominant theme in the sets for *The Uncon-quered*. . . . "Of course red is the revolutionary color," Mr. Aronson explained, "but it is used here as the connecting theme between the two regimes." Its backgrounds are a rich, wine red velour and against them he projects the splendor of Czarist palaces, and the upsurge of the proletariat. For one, red symbolizes richness of color and decoration; for the other, red symbolizes a movement overtaking an older one.

Even the last scene, an exterior, has the same red background, except that the red is black. Better let Mr. Aronson explain this: "Plain black is flat," he said, "but red-black is different from green-black. Look at the difference . . . the use of emulsions of the lights changes the red to black, only it's red-black and carries out the artistic sense of red which runs through the other scenes." He doesn't believe in making sets the duplicates of actual rooms. Sets, to him, should express the mood of the play, the essence of the environment. He takes special interest in the current production because it is Russian. Most of his other plays have been 100% American. . . . "I got so I knew more about American hotel bars than I did about Russian houses so I had to study up before I started this one."

There are seven sets in the latest Abbott play and thirteen changes, any of which can be done in forty seconds. Eight men came with Mr. Abbott, and about two dozen from Baltimore are needed to operate the sets. Three banks of switches—where one alone sufficed for the other Abbott shows—are used. . . . "Nineteen hundred and twenty-four was a dynamic period," he said. "It was the time I last remembered Russia. The old was being taken over by another order. That's what I tried to do in the sets. Show the former period and contrast it sharply with the new." Executed on a massive scale by Boris Aronson . . . [t]heir decadent tone is in keeping with the author's underlying inference—the decay of the human character and the destruction of the human soul by the Moloch of the all-powerful state, which denies even the primary rights to humanity.[34]

In addition to press mentions of the sets, a Baltimore paper reported on a new production aspect: "Special music is being arranged by Alexander Haas to be played during performances of *The Unconquered*. . . . The selections will be made from post-revolutionary music now popular in Russia. . . . Mr. Haas is also preparing an unusual program of music to be played during the entr-actes." [*sic*][35]

In a summary statement, another Baltimore paper wrote that *The Uncon-quered* will be "Mr. Abbott's first appearance hereabout as a director of romantic drama . . . an impassioned love story [that] deals with the way in which individual liberty was crushed by the tyranny of communist bureau-cracy."[36]

The Unconquered opened on the evening of December 25, 1939. The curtain rose upon a massive production, which included its own artificial snow—as well as a flurry of theatrical jinxes. The *Baltimore Sun* reported that

Howard Freeman, character actor in the cast of George Abbott's *The Uncon-quered*, fell fifteen feet from a second-floor tier of the dressing rooms at the

Maryland Theater just before the curtain was scheduled to rise on the world premiere of the play. . . .

John Parrish, who had never rehearsed Freeman's role, went on in his place and read the part from the script. The accident was not announced before the play began. . . .

A wondering Baltimore audience, many of whom could not remember a read performance at a premiere in this city, at first received the substitute coldly. There was much grumbling when the curtain fell on the first act. . . . In the lobby outside, the news of the accident spread quickly. And as the audience awoke to the situation the whole feeling changed from distaste to warm sympathy. This spirit was evident throughout the rest of the play.[37]

Unfortunately, the Baltimore critics were not of a unanimously warm spirit. Norman Clark wrote that one "hesitates to pass judgment upon George Abbott's newest play, *The Unconquered*, after viewing the hesitant, out-of-key performance given at the Maryland Theatre last evening." The play was

a jerky melodrama—there are thirteen scenes—with its locale in Red Russia. But, barring some jibes at the inefficiency and hypocrisy of Communism, the plot could have been laid anywhere at all. . . . Whether or not *The Unconquered* presents a true picture of affairs in Russia, we honestly cannot say. We once had dinner in a Russian cafe in New York, but that hardly qualifies us to pose as an expert on Soviet conditions.

In conclusion, Clark wrote: "may we wish Mr. Abbott a most happy and prosperous New Year."[38]

The *Baltimore Evening Sun*, however, disagreed and referred to *The Unconquered* as a "Gripping Abbott Tragedy." The review said the producer of "'Brother Rat' and 'Room Service' . . . has taken an excursion into heavy drama—powerful, gripping tragedy with a trio of emotional stars whose Herculean wrestling with their several cosmic problems present some of the most effective dramatic acting seen here in many months." Calling the play a "ringing indictment of communism," the reviewer referred positively to the plot, especially "Andrei's speech on Communistic principles after his disillusionment in which a wooden repetition of Reed platitudes becomes a ringing indictment of Sovietism."[39]

The mixed Baltimore reviews had a sobering effect. Abbott now explained to Rand that if they went to New York, they would have to fire Leontovich. Rand agreed completely. However, Abbott's dilemma was how to fire Leontovich—after all, the entire production had been developed with her in mind. Rand recalls Abbott's solution:

[H]e asked me: Would I permit him to tell her that it's my decision, not his? And since I have the okay on the cast, he can do nothing about it. And I said, "Most certainly," kind of [astonished]. And it took me several days to realize what a cowardly thing it was on his part. He had said, "You see, we're old friends with her, and can I tell her that it's you, and that I'm giving in." I said, "By all means." . . . [And] that's how he got rid of Eugenie Leontovich.[40]

When the Baltimore tryout closed, the *Journal-American* reported that Leontovich had "retired gracefully from the recent Abbott play when it was discovered she wasn't the type, [and] will retire from the stage, too, and resume as Gregory Ratoff's hausfrau. . . ."[41] Immediately, Abbott began to revise his production. The *Sun* reported that "Broadway won't see its first production of 1940 until the second week in January due to the shelving by George Abbott of Ayn Rand's play *The Unconquered*, which has been due to come to the St. James a week from this evening"[42]

Anticipating the next round of battles between producer and author, the Baltimore *Eagle* reported that the play was "not without its comic situations."[43] In early January, the *News* announced "George Abbott has made up his mind to go ahead with the revised edition of Ayn Rand's *The Unconquered*. The drama already has been drastically rewritten with Abbott submitting several ideas and sequences. The producer is searching for an actress to replace Eugenie Leontovich."[44] The revisions, recalled Rand, resulted in "sacrificing everything for comedy": "[T]here was a scene in the Home of the Peasant, with Comrade Bitiuk and Kira. . . . And he played it for a farce in the most ridiculous way, with the girls marching in and out of the office almost in goose step. . . . It's the only kind of thing that he felt at home in."[45]

Abbott's direction, according to Rand, was "miserable." However, during the recasting of Kira Argounova in New York, Abbott at last discovered "how to really direct" the play:

[T]here was one English actress that some agent had sent insisting very much that he wanted us to hear her. She was sort of late thirties, very homely. She was really a young character woman type that would have done much better for Comrade Sonia than Kira, so that Abbott had not even wanted to give her a reading but did it as a courtesy for the agent. She was marvelous. Now that was really heartbreaking, in a way, for both Abbott and me. The reading was magnificent. But she was just so much not the type that it was impossible. She was short, stocky, somewhat piano legs or on that order or, you know, which would have been really impossible. Why the incident remains in my mind is this: Abbott told me afterwards, he said, "Do you know," in a kind of a sad manner, "I only now realized what your writing is like or how this play should have been done." He said "that actress made me realize." He said, "You know, your style is the same as Bernard Shaw's. Bernard Shaw is considered very difficult to stage, for the same reason. I only realized it by the way she read it." . . . [Abbott] didn't mean style in the full literary sense of the word. He meant the method, the purposeful and intellectual. In other words, lines that had to be understood and not projected emotionally. That's what he got out of that girl. But imagine a director telling you that, when it's too late. I don't think he could have done it, anyway.

Helen Craig was cast as the new Kira. Although not ideally suited for the part, Rand considered Craig, an admirer of *We the Living*, a hard-working, "rather good," and politically conservative actress.[46]

With script changes completed and a new Kira in place, Abbott announced his opening date: Tuesday, February 13. A reporter noted "Tuesday is a departure for Mr. Abbott, who has long favored Wednesday openings on Broadway. Now he has picked not only a Tuesday, but a Tuesday the 13th!"[47] During February 1940, seven new and competing Broadway productions would open, including plays by Clifford Odets and Ernest Hemingway.[48]

By February the play was a truncated 102-page adaptation of the novel in three acts comprising ten scenes in seven settings.[49] In Act I, Leo Kovalensky is released from G.P.U. custody following his father's execution for counter-revolutionary activities. Kira arrives at his apartment indicating she will now join him. In the opening thematic statement of the play, Kira turns from her parents' disappointment with her decision to live with Leo, and addresses her future:

> KIRA: I think they hate me because I want a future—any future. They've given up. Father's crying for the factories they've taken away from him, mother's crying for the diamond necklaces she's had to sell. They can't understand why I laugh about it. There's so much ahead of me!
> LEO: Is there?
> KIRA: To build, Leo. To build, to shape, to raise girders in a net against the sky, to watch the sunrise from the top of a steel skeleton and to know that it's mine, every beam of it!
> LEO: Of the building—or of the sun?
> KIRA: Of the building. That's more important, because it's I who will have created it. . . .[50]

By February 11, 1940, the week of *The Unconquered*'s Broadway opening, over 300 blurbs, column mentions, preview pieces, and features articles including photographs and drawings of cast members had prepared the New York theatergoing public for the premiere.[51] On February 11, two days before the opening, the *New York Times* placed an Al Hirshfeld caricature announcing *The Unconquered* across page one of the Sunday arts section. The headline read: "This Week Gives Broadway Only One Drama Opening." The pen and ink drawing foretold a drama involving the Soviet state, the proletariat, propaganda posters, and a defiant girl.[52]

On Monday, February 12, the first preview performance hosted a fund-raising event for the Young Folks Auxiliary of the Home for Hebrew Infants.

On February 13, *The Unconquered* opened at the Biltmore Theatre.

On February 14, roughly between the hours of midnight and early morning, the New York critics completed twenty-six full-length reviews of *The Unconquered*.

On February 17, George Abbott closed *The Unconquered* after six performances.[53] The production was a complete failure.

The reviews were almost entirely negative. The critics were unanimous in their negative assessment of the play's structure, Abbott's direction, the comedy-satire, and the character motivations. The critics praised the acting, especially performances by Dean Jagger as Andrei Taganov and Helen Craig as Kira Argounova, and the settings of Boris Aronson. Politically, the reviewers divided into three camps: those on the left, who rejected the play's politics; those in the middle, who rejected the play's lack of entertainment value; and those on the right, who rejected the play's diluted attack on the evil of Soviet Russia.

Leading the attack from the political left was Alvah Bessie, screenwriter and future member of the Hollywood Ten. Under the headline, "One for the Ashcan . . . ," Bessie wrote in the *New Masses*:

> if you were a smart, capitalistically inclined impresario and were anxious to produce a vicious and effective diatribe against the USSR, wouldn't you hire the finest playwright you could lay your hands on, who could write a brilliant, incisive, subtle, and above all *moving* play, that would damn the hell out of all those awful Bolsheviks? Or would you toss onto the stage a deadly dull 10-20-30 meller written by a fourth-rate hack?

After summarizing the play, Bessie concludes with a nod to his fellow reviewers:

> To quote the capitalist press: "Not only does Miss Rand's melodrama make a GPU man its most attractive character, but its loudest eloquence seems devoted to the contention that what the Russians needed (in 1924–25) was more and better purges. The idealistic agent of the secret police is surrounded by shrewd, Tosca-like heroines, decadent aristocrats, corrupt politicians and fat speculators, and the most violent charge the play brings against the Communist regime is that the GPU refuses to shoot more of them." (New York *Herald Tribune*) Soviet papers please copy.[54]

Theatre Arts expressed a more politically liberal viewpoint: "*The Unconquered* by Ayn Rand, a dramatization of her novel, *We the Living*, . . . suffered from the lack of perspective that recent experience makes inevitable. Reputed to be founded on actual events, Miss Rand's story of life in present day Russia smacked more of nineteenth-century melodrama, French Revolutionary style, than reality," by which was meant the current events involving the USSR.[55]

The nonpolitical, nonintellectual middle-of-the-road commentators included the following: a gossip column in the *Post* wrote " *The Unconquered* is a story of White Russian in a Red Sea of trouble, and if Mr. Abbott cares, or doesn't, I like him better when he's in more of an 'Abbott' and Costello mood."[56] The *Bronx Home News* wrote that although " *The Unconquered* was heralded as an expose of the terrible GPU, Ayn Rand O'Connor actually has written about poor Russians in the dreadful clutches of SEX."[57]

From a politically more sympathetic but still theatrically critical mode is the *Morning-Telegraph's* review. After apologizing to George Abbott for attacking his efforts to fill a "feeble" season with an "astounding" four new plays, the reviewer wrote: "The truth of the matter is Mr. Abbott should stick to his last [comedy] and Miss Rand should stick to her knitting. For not only is the play an absurd and improbable one, but it is produced and directed . . ." without any subtlety, which makes the play's "gem of an idea" a "gross caricature of Miss Rand's philosophy and an immense bore to the public at large." Conceding that a play about a philosophy that "refuses to recognize the importance, or even the existence of individual desires" is a valid theme, the paper writes that the only valid way to attack the wrongness of such a philosophy "is to demonstrate that even under ideal conditions such a philosophy only brings disastrous results, while Miss Rand, on the contrary does her best to convince us that all Soviet officials are venal and self-seeking grafters, and that idealism has been corrupted by the basic pettiness of human nature, which is unable to use power for constructive purposes." The *Morning-Telegraph* repeated objections expressed by the critical establishment: the play's "characters are completely unreal; the comedy is unbearably caricatured; its plot is melodramatic and unconvincing. The tale of a couple who because of bourgeoisie descent and a desire for personal freedom are unable to exist under the Soviet Government, turns into a lurid story of a pair of food speculators."[58]

From the other side of the country, Hollywood's representative in New York filed the following with the *Hollywood Reporter*:

> George Abbott unveiled Ayn Rand's anti-Soviet play, *The Unconquered*, at the Biltmore Theatre last night, and no matter how you look at it politically, dramatically it's sabotage, comrades.
>
> In adapting this bit of anti-entertainment to the stage from her novel, "We, the Living," Miss Rand has succeeded only in boring from within—for [its] three acts are as interminable as the five-year plan. Neither John Emery's noble struggle with a plot that thickens every time it should be liquidated, nor Boris Aronson's eye-blinking settings can save *The Unconquered* from being an anti-Red excursion that will put Mr. Abbott in the red.[59]

The regional *Philadelphia Record* took a broader, more cultural view-point. The paper noted that the "isms" sweeping Europe and spreading into this country periodically transformed Broadway into "a rostrum either to defend our form of democracy, or to reveal the flaws of the ideologies of dictators." Writing that *The Unconquered* might have been "inspired by the front pages" and by a recent speech by President Roosevelt's about "the dictatorial qualities of the Soviet Government," the play was "far more a political document than it is entertainment expected from a night in the theatre."[60]

Lewis Nichols of the *New York Times* wrote that the drama was "confusing, not going into the matter of the individual man in Russia, 1924—where there would be a play—and not adding to the theatre's already expert knowledge of the state of romance." Abbott tried to "pull together the sentimental melodrama that was almost old Hoboken and the discussion of the rights of man, of which there was not nearly enough."[61]

Completing the spectrum of political commentary was the voice of the political right. Sidney B. Whipple criticized the play because it diluted the presentation of Soviet Communism's evil with trivializing theatrics. Whipple wrote that, opposing Andrei Taganov, a character who

> is tragic and noble rather than a symbol of Bolshevik ruthlessness, [Ayn Rand] gives us [in Leo] a decadent aristocrat, a weakling whose liquidation would not be a matter of concern to the bitterest of Red-baiters. Certainly this cannot be the "civilization" Miss Rand hopes to save! . . . The other characters are too petty—too unimportant, in fact, to be considered horrifying examples of the rotten fruits of Stalinism.

Whipple concludes that the "unadorned facts are stronger than any of the imagined situations created by dramatists however sincere they may be and however hotly they burn with crusading fervor."[62]

Virtually the only semi-sympathetic review came from *Woman's Wear*, which wrote that the play is "an anti-Soviet melodrama with scattered moments of compelling interest" and that the "play is well acted in the main. . . . Dean Jagger is a bit stagy in his portrayal of Taganov, until his big scene where he addresses the Marxist club. The scene he plays brilliantly."[63]

Within days of *The Unconquered*'s closing, the production's physical properties were dispersed, its personnel dismissed, and the play slipped into theatrical obscurity.[64]

What was Ayn Rand's own critical reaction to the production? On this she commented at some length. She regarded the venture as a total and expensive disaster. First of all, the book was not proper play material. Its plot involved too much well-connected action and was better suited for film adaptation.[65] By the Baltimore tryout, she also realized Abbott's production, including her own script, was bad. By the play's February opening, the script was a compromise encompassing ten or more versions. Even the expensive sets were wrong for the play. Abbott, to his credit, had expended his best, most honorable effort, which made the failure worse.[66]

"It was," Rand recounts, "a total flop. . . . I had a terrible time writing the play, and I disliked every version of it, from the original to the many rewrites. I became acutely aware of the fact that my purpose in writing it did not originate with me." And, in a candid insight from an author who had interrupted writing *The Fountainhead* to write and rewrite *The Unconquered*:

> The play never was—and I came to realize, never could be—good. It grew out of somebody else's suggestion plus my own irrelevant motive. So, no matter how conscientiously I tried, I could not make it good. . . . This taught me never to write anything that was not my own idea. Even if it is a good idea, if it does not come out of my own context, I will be unable to integrate it. It will not be *first-handed.*[67]

The Abbott production marked the end of Ayn Rand's career as a playwright.[68] The promising decade of the 1930s—which included her first financial successes—ended in professional disappointment. In 1940, Rand returned to freelance employment, reading and summarizing stories for the film industry. But most importantly, she returned to writing and securing a publisher for *The Fountainhead*. Ayn Rand's own theatrical adaptation of her novel failed to stimulate domestic sales of *We the Living*. But in 1942, a film adaptation made without her knowledge did, in an unexpected way, stimulate foreign recognition of the importance of the novel's philosophy. *We the Living*'s film adaptation ignited an international protest a year and a half before the phenomenal success of *The Fountainhead* in 1943 established Ayn Rand's worldwide fame.

WE THE LIVING AS FILM:
NOI VIVI AND ADDIO KIRA

In March 1940, a month after the Broadway closing of *The Unconquered*, Benito Mussolini and Italy agreed to join Germany in declaring war against Britain and France. In December 1941 Italy declared war on the United States.[69] These events, while seemingly removed from the matter of dramatic adaptation, actually account for the second adaptation of *We the Living*: a 1942 two-part film called *Noi Vivi* (*We the Living*) and *Addio Kira* (*Good-bye Kira*) sanctioned by the Italian government as anti-Russian/anti-Bolshevik propaganda.

In 1947, Ayn Rand characterized communist propaganda in motion pictures as any content or film technique "that gives a good impression of communism as a way of life . . . that sells people the idea that life in Russia is

good and that people are free and happy."[70] As understood by one of the
Axis powers, anticommunist propaganda in motion pictures presented a bad
impression of communism, suggesting—in a description attributed to Nazi
Minister of Propaganda Joseph Goebbels—that the Russian people were
"inhuman animals."[71] Propaganda was used by Germany and Italy to justify
or sustain their ideologies while, simultaneously, discouraging or crushing
intellectual dissent with police force.[72]

In Italy, the ideology was Fascism and motion pictures were developed to
disseminate it.

"The foundation of Fascism," wrote Mussolini,

> is the conception of the State, its character, its duty, and its aim. Fascism con-
> ceives of the State as an absolute, in comparison with which all individuals or
> groups are relative, only to be conceived in their relation to the State. . . . The
> Fascist State is itself conscious and has a will and personality—thus it may be
> called the "ethic" state. . . .[73]

The "ethic" required the subjugation of the interests of the individual
before the interests of the collective. In the Italian version, the collective was
a syndicate of labor, management and nominal private property owners
united by an all-embracing ideology articulated by the Fascist Party and
enforced by the police.[74]

Since motion pictures appealed to a mass audience, "for us," Mussolini
concluded, "cinema is the strongest weapon."[75]

The development of Mussolini's cinema-weapon occurred, albeit inconsis-
tently, over nearly two decades of Fascist intervention in the Italian film
industry. After coming to power in October 1922, the Fascist movement took
over the Institutio Nazionale LUCE, or *Il'Unione Cinematographica Educat-
iva* (Union of Cinematography and Education) in 1926 in order to control the
dissemination of documentaries and newsreels. Over the next thirteen years,
the Fascist government created a public distribution and exhibition network
for narrative feature films, established motion picture studios, influenced the
funding of films through government approved bankers, created a film
school under the supervision of the Ministry of Popular Culture, and encouraged the development of the world's first film festival, "First International
Exhibition of Cinematic Art," which was held for the first time in conjunction
with the eighteenth Venice "Biennale" exhibition of figurative arts in 1932. [76]

Although Mussolini's regime monitored "foreign ideologies," it was not
fully effective in doing so. Unlike Soviet Russia and Nazi Germany, which
arrested and executed entire intellectual and artistic communities, Italy's
approach was less monolithic. The regime might silence dissenting intellectuals—or, on pragmatic grounds, might reverse this effort by looking the
other way. The latter appears to have been the case with the Italian translation and publication of Rand's *We the Living.*

In 1937, fifteen years into the development of the Fascist State, Rand signed a contract for an Italian translation of *We the Living*. No such contract was ever signed with Soviet Russian or Nazi German publishers.[77] That same year Mussolini instituted production goals for the Italian film industry, ordering one hundred films, out of which only thirty-two were eventually completed. By 1938, sales of Ayn Rand's novel were growing. Baldini & Castoldi of Milan, publishers of *We the Living*, issued a second edition of the novel.[78] Simultaneously, Italian legislation restricted the importation of American motion pictures, which resulted in the boycott of the Italian market by Metro-Goldwyn-Mayer, Warner Bros. Pictures, Twentieth Century Fox Motion Picture Corporation, and Paramount Pictures. The resulting scarcity of Hollywood films caused the Fascists to increase their production quota to eighty-seven films in 1940.[79] As the demand for filmable literature grew, the literary works of foreign authors were seized.

"The Italian war law authorized the Italian Government to seize the copyrights of enemy authors, more or less on the same basis as the American law did. The procedure consisted of making a request to the Ministry of Propaganda. Same would grant the permit, against a token payment, that went to a special fund."[80] Prior to the war, Fascist film authorities had encouraged the development of propaganda genres, including revisionist European costume dramas featuring idealized proto-Fascist historical figures. Once the war effort was underway, in 1939 the Fascist authorities created a new propaganda category consisting of anti-Russian/anti-Bolshevik films whose objective was to portray the Soviets as unfavorably as possible.[81]

Following 1939, Bruna Scalera, daughter of Michele Scalera, owner of Scalera Film Studios, proposed adapting *We the Living* into a motion picture, and recommended the project to Massimo Ferrara-Santamaria, General Manager of Scalera. After reading a treatment of the novel, Ferrara-Santamaria was impressed favorably and decided to arrange for a production, hiring writers Corrado Alvaro and Orio Vergani to prepare a script. Ferrara-Santamaria also attached the services of director Goffredo Alessandrini, and cast the actress Alida Valli as Kira Argounova, and actors Rossano Brazzi as Leo Kovalensky and Fosco Giachetti as Andrei Taganov. In addition, Antonio Giulio Majano, Alessandrini's assistant director, was appointed by Ferrara-Santamaria as the production's "fiduciary."

After assembling his cast and crew, Ferrara-Santamaria's next step was to request permission from the Ministry of Culture to proceed with the production. At first, the Fascist Minister of Culture, Corrado Pavolini, ruled against it, regarding the prospective screenwriters as "outside the fascist ideology." Undaunted, Ferrara-Santamaria appealed the Minister's ruling before Vittorio Mussolini who, besides being Ferrara-Santamaria's friend, was himself a film producer and the son of Benito Mussolini. Pavolini was overruled and the production was able to proceed.[82]

Under Italy's wartime conditions, the production appeared to have an official stamp of approval as anti-Soviet propaganda. However, Goffredo Alessandrini regarded the basic situation in *We the Living* as "perfect" film material, apart from its alleged value as propaganda. Alessandrini said,

> there was this girl from a well-to-do family; the serious and idealistic commissar; and the young son of an admiral. . . . The two men were very different, but both interesting, and between them a young woman, in love with one because he is handsome and romantic, and with the other because of his almost "religious" political commitment.

After reading *We the Living*, Alessandrini informed Scalera that he would like to work "without a script—just bring out from the book all the parts that should be brought on the screen." This meant directing a film of unusual length. Alessandrini said "we could make for the first time in Italy a film longer than three hours, and then see what happens."[83]

During the preproduction period, Majano and Alessadrini left for Africa to work on a production there, leaving the completion of the script in the hands of the "two writers." When Majano and Alessadrini returned to Italy, they discovered the script was unusable: the writers had transformed Kira Argounova from an engineering student into a ballet dancer.[84] With an imminent starting date and no time to draft another script, Alessandrini and Majano decided to write and film the script simultaneously. The night before each day's shooting, new dialogue was prepared and distributed the next morning by Majano's assistant.[85]

Alessandrini was unable to shoot on location because of the war. "At that time," he recalled, "we had to shoot everything in the Scalera Studios, everything, the winter too, with artificial snow, and Petersburg and its bridges. The film was held back by all that. . . . [T]he result was a narration that you could call "for television: all close-ups." As to the casting and directing of Alida Valli, Alessandrini said ". . . . while reading how Kira was described in the book, I saw Valli in the description of the woman. . . . I couldn't imagine any other actress." Alessandrini's minimal direction consisted of blocking and lighting her. He relayed to Valli: "I won't tell you how to interpret Kira, because you *are* Kira. What you'll do will be fine."[86] As Alessandrini's assistant director, Majano directed the film extras, significant numbers of whom were former Russian nobles and members of the Russian émigré community.[87]

Andrei Taganov as portrayed by Fosco Giachetti was the most controversial casting choice and, from the perspective of anti-Soviet propaganda, the most ambiguous character during the production. Taganov was an idealist who commits suicide after realizing his Communistic beliefs undermine not only human life in general but his new found self-assertiveness in particular.

According to Giachetti, Majano's dialogue diminished Taganov's character and Giachetti fought against it throughout the filming. It was a continuation of a battle begun by Giachetti at an earlier and politically riskier stage. Giachetti recalled a meeting he had with Vittorio Mussolini several days before the commencement of filming. *Il Duce's* son requested that Giachetti accept changes in Andrei's character in order to bring it in line with Fascist ideology. Giachetti recalled:

> [Vittorio] asks me to do him a personal favor, to give up Andrei as presented in the book because of cuts they had to make due to "political reasons. . . . With such an artistic personality as yours," [Vittorio] says, "you can take part in a film as a lesser character and not be diminished."
> So I answered: "Well, I don't do favors to anybody, my artistic personality is mine, and if in the film I don't find the novel's Andrei, on whom we have based everything and signed the contract, I won't do the film."

In a few hours, the Minister of Popular Culture Pavolini proposed a second meeting with Giachetti, scheduled for the following day. Upon Giachetti's arrival, Pavolini planned to ask him for a favor, which Giachetti had anticipated and then politely refused. When asked why, Giachetti answered:

> Because I have signed a contract. I like Andrei because he is an idealist, not only a communist, he could be a Christian, he could represent—and why not?—your 1919 program. . . . "But you see," [the minister] says, "I'm afraid that in the little theatres, in the low-class theatres, when they see this character, people may applaud and give me headaches." So I say, "Your excellency, if I'm to play Andrei as he is written in the novel, I'll use my modest artistic talent, whatever I have, to receive that applause rather than lose it."[88]

The production of *We the Living* was a matter of official concern. Majano recalled further encounters with the authorities who reviewed the film footage at sudden intervals. However, scenes removed at the direction of the Fascist censors were subsequently edited back into the film.[89] There were two especially offensive sequences: the first showed Leo unable to secure employment because of his lack of Communist Party membership; the second showed Andrei denouncing communism before an assembly of party members.[90]

The first public exhibition of *Noi Vivi* occurred during the 1942 Venice Film Festival. The film's running time was now three hours and fifty minutes. As to the public's reaction, *La Stampa* reported that the Venice Film Festival ended with *Noi Vivi* and *Addio Kira*, based on the novel by Ayn Rand, and that Alessandrini had successfully condensed the material from Rand's novel, creating an appealing film. The Volpi Cup for Best Actor was awarded to Fosco Giachetti for his performance as Andrei and the film received the prestigious Biennale Prize.[91] The screening audience gave *Noi Vivi* a standing ovation.[92]

Certain reviewers concurred. Raffaele Calzini wrote that *Noi Vivi* was the most elaborate and lengthy film production in the history of Italian filmmaking. The story of a sensual and tragic heroine, Giachetti's interpretation of Andrei was superb. And in comparison to other frenzied portrayals of the Russian Revolution like *October* by Eisenstein or *The End of Petrograd* by Pudovkin, *Noi Vivi* appeared civilized.[93] Others, such as Diego Calcagno, noted that the film did not invent anything new but did well in reproducing the novel. The novel itself was propagandistic and of relatively low quality. It did not have enough elements to make it totally noble and satisfying. Yet, for the most part, the actors were well selected and the parts were well performed. The positive response among festival audiences suggested that such responses would only increase in the future.[94]

As director Alessandrini recalls, summarizing the issue of propaganda:

> We never considered making an anti-communist film, even Scalera never asked me to do such a thing. In any Italian reader's eye, there were similarities between the Russian situation and ours. As the fact that you couldn't obtain a job without being a party member. . . . Because of this, *Noi Vivi* came to be unofficially called "the film of elbowing in the dark," as people recognized the present conditions in the film.

Alessandrini thought the "even-handed" story explained the public reaction. "I mean," he recalled, "it was not anti-communist, other than in the official party line, despite all the propaganda; and the same fascists admitted there were characters on the other side worthy of respect. This was exactly the case with Giachetti's character."[95]

The audience reaction at the Venice Festival was repeated nationwide. Majano described the reaction to the release and singled out an aspect that horrified the Fascist officials: "It was an extraordinary success, almost a fanatical success. . . . People would get up from their tables along the street and embrace me and say, 'At last you've begun to go against the tide.' People who saw it, who were intelligent enough, did realize what we were doing."[96]

During the first six months of its release in Italy, the film earned an estimated $631,043 in profits. It became a rallying point for the besieged Italian population. After the film's successful Italian opening, Massimo Ferrara-Santamaria turned to foreign film market sales and arranged a screening for German Minister of Propaganda Goebbels and his family in Berlin. Goebbels objected to the film as "too mild" in its portrayal of the Russian people.[97] The film was exhibited in Denmark, Switzerland, Slovakia, Rumania, Hungary, Belgium, Greece, and Vichy France.[98] What was manifestly clear to the Italian public during the fall and winter of 1942–1943 gradually became clear to the

Ministry of Popular Culture. The film attacked dictatorship and praised the individual, thus criticizing both communism and fascism with an attack on both. Benito Mussolini was reported to be furious and, after six months, Nazi Germany pressured the Fascists to withdraw the film from release.[99]

The Secretariat of the National Fascist Party issued an injunction seizing the negative and the exhibition prints. Ferrara-Santamaria was ordered to appear before the Roman headquarters of the Director of the Fascist Party, accused of making an anti-totalitarian film and "waging a war against the wishes of the majority of the Italians." In his defense, Ferrara-Santamaria argued that he had made a "beautiful love story" and was "not responsible for the Italian public sentiment."[100]

Alida Valli and Rossano Brazzi protested the film's confiscation by refusing to work in Italy for the duration of the war. In addition, "Scalera's legal counsel was blacklisted by the government for having allowed [*Noi Vivi*] to be produced. Alessandrini and Majano had to flee the country because of their other anti-fascist activities. Fittingly, when they crossed the Allied lines, what they used for identification were publicity pictures of themselves taken on the set."[101]

In 1945, the Axis powers were defeated.

In 1946, Armitage Watkins, Rand's agent from the office of Ann Watkins, received a letter from Donald Downes, who revealed news of an Italian piracy of *We the Living*:

Scalera made not one, but two movies from the book; the first was called NOI I VIV [*sic*] and the second called ADIO KIRA [*sic*]. Both were extremely successful during the war years, not only, I am informed, in Italy but had a big box office in Germany and Vichy France. This is in part accounted for by the fact that my informant who used to work in Scalera advises me both were made in cooperation with the Ministry of Popular Culture as semiofficial, fascist, anti-Russian and anti-leftist propaganda.[102]

In reaction to the news, Rand wrote to Watkins:

Your letter of May 24th was certainly a bombshell to me. I am extremely indignant at the piracy of WE THE LIVING by the Italian producers, and at the use which they made of it. Thank you for finding this out for me. I shall now blast them with the kind of lawsuit which they deserve.[103]

Rand wrote to her attorney John C. Gall, and advised him of the situation:

I should sue not only for whatever royalties are due me, but also and primarily for the damage to my reputation as a writer, damage caused by the fact that a book of mine was used as Fascist propaganda. WE THE LIVING is a story laid in Soviet Russia, and it is anti-Soviet but, above all, it is anti-dictatorship. Therefore, it is as much anti-Fascist as anti-Communist, and I resent, more than the financial piracy, the use of my material or the distortion of my message into a pro-Fascist picture.[104]

In another development, a March 1947 letter from Rand to Gall mentions David O. Selznick's possible interest in acquiring film rights to *We the Living*. Selznick's office "called my literary agent here, asked whether the movie rights to WE THE LIVING were available, and said that he was interested in the book and knew about the Italian picture. . . . Selznick has not made any definite offer for the movie rights as yet."[105]

Two courses of action were possible: one was to re-make the film entirely and the other was to re-edit and re-release the Italian film. Alida Valli, now in Hollywood, attempted but failed to persuade Selznick to produce a re-make. Thereafter, the most promising avenue appeared to be editing and sub-titling a version for release in the United States, but certain literary and political problems remained to be solved.

Rand's initial reaction to the film was positive. She elaborates in a May 1947 letter to her attorney:

> I have now seen the two pictures. I had an Italian interpreter present, who trans-lated for me the general action of every scene and the key lines of dialogue. But it was impossible for her to translate literally every single line. So I was able to form only a general opinion of the two pictures.
>
> The cast, direction and production are excellent. The adaptation follows my novel closely—until the last part of the picture, at which some point changes have been made.

As to presence of any political propaganda,

> as far as I can judge . . . the story has not been distorted into Fascist propaganda in any major way, but it does contain some lines of dialogue stuck in without relation to the story, which are most objectionable and offensive to me. . . . The interpreter caught one blatantly Fascist, anti-Semitic line—and I do not know how many other lines there may be, which she did not get.[106]

Apart from cutting the film, the remaining issue was the damage to Rand's political reputation. The film had been exhibited in Europe during the war, a fact that might enable American Communists to smear her as pro-Fascist. By July 1947, this danger was resolved in favor of releasing the picture. Valli apprised Rand of the film's history: both its reception by the Italian public and its suppression by the government as anti-Fascist propaganda. "If this story is true," Rand wrote in a letter to John Gall,

> I think it is wonderful. It would make the greatest kind of publicity in this coun-try, not just publicity for my book, but an important proof to demonstrate con-

cretely the similarity of Soviet Russia and Fascism, which even Mussolini recognized, though some of the fools in this country refuse to.[107]

In a February 1948 letter to Isabel Paterson, Rand related her plans for the film:

> We are still in the process of negotiating. . . . If I let them release it in this country, I will have to change the ending by means of new English dialogue, and extra film footage. That will be quite a job, but if we reach an agreement, I will have a writer of my own choice to do it for me; I cannot take time off from my novel for this work.[108]

That same day Rand wrote to Jack Warner about releasing a re-edited version of the film. She admired Warner's stand against communism and thought he might want to exhibit an anti-Soviet picture in the United States. Still, remaking the picture was not entirely out of the question. In 1947, Rand put down her thoughts on the matter by answering the objection that the novel was "dated," an objection also raised against the novel and its earlier theatrical adaptation. She wrote:

> The *theme* of "WE THE LIVING" is: *the Individual against the State.*
>
> It is a much wider theme than merely the presentation of any particular period of Soviet life. It is a picture of Communism and of every other kind of dictatorship, anywhere, at any time. It is a denunciation of the doctrine of dictatorship—and this is the most timely and crucial question in the world today.
>
> The three leading characters of "WE THE LIVING," who carry the entire plot and action of the story, do not belong to any particular period of Soviet history. Their story could take place at any time, under any dictatorship. The specific, superficial details of the year in which their story might be played do not affect it any more that would a change of clothes styles.
>
> The elements of the central conflict are:
>
> A girl, who is a born individualist, who has so independent a spirit that she can never compromise with any form of compulsion, can never exist under slavery, and can never be broken. A young man who is a stern, incorruptible idealist, who believes in Communism and devotes his whole life to its service—only to learn, in tragic disillusionment, the real nature of his cause and of its monstrous evil. And a young man of reckless pride and violent temper, who cannot adjust himself to a life of servility, who is too strong to compromise, but too weak to withstand the pressure; who cannot bend, but only break.
>
> The essence of their story is their desperate desire to live, their blind struggle for a human being's right to life and happiness—under a system that recognizes no such right. Kira understands the issue and fights for happiness passionately, ruthlessly, against terrible odds, never giving in. Andrei, who has renounced all thought of a personal life, considering it evil, discovers—through his love for a girl who is his political enemy—the nature, the beauty and the supreme importance of personal happiness, discovers it to be a higher right and a nobler cause

than the inhuman Collectivism of the State—but discovers it only to find tragedy and to learn that it was he who brought it upon himself and upon the girl he loves. Leo, who was born with a great capacity to enjoy life and would have been a man of great energy in any normal, human society, turns his own nature against himself; his bright gaiety becomes bitterness, his courage becomes cynicism, and he breaks in spirit, losing all desire to live.[109]

By 1948, unable to interest Hollywood in a remake, Rand began making notes on future cuts and revisions. Although the public remained interested in the film—in February 1949 the Federated Italo-Americans of Los Angeles held a screening of it—Rand was no longer interested in Hollywood. By 1951, she returned to New York City and devoted her full energy to writing her next novel, *Atlas Shrugged*.

The legal battle to recover damages from the Italian film piracy proved long and protracted. According to actors who worked on the film, the picture was released in Italy under the Allied occupation.[110] In 1961, Rand's fifteen-year effort to collect damages resulted in an out-of-court settlement of 14,000,000 Italian lire (US$22,778).[111] Thereafter, an abbreviated version of the film was exhibited in Europe. Alessandrini recalled seeing a ninety-minute version of the film in an Italian cinema specializing in film revivals. The shorter version was titled *Noi Vivi* (with *Addio Kira* added underneath in parenthesis). At a later point, Alessandrini considered directing a ninety-minute remake of *Noi Vivi* for Italian television.[112]

After the settlement of Rand's legal claims, another effort to re-edit the film began. In 1966, Henry Mark Holzer, Rand's lawyer at the time, initiated a search for the film after Rand informed him of its existence. In 1968, Holzer located and purchased the nitrate negative in Rome and then, with the assistance of a young editor named Duncan Scott, began the long process of assembling the film. In New York, Rand reviewed and orally edited the film footage on a Moviola while the English translation of the script was read aloud. As assistant editor, Scott, who would later become producer of the final project, carefully recorded Rand's instructions. In recalling those editorial sessions, he remarked that Rand was "very perceptive, like someone who had been studying the movie for weeks before. . . . She displayed no hesitation. She would say to cut this scene out or to put these two together. Whatever made her a good editor of writing made her a good film editor too."[113]

During Rand's lifetime, the major editorial revisions were recorded under her supervision but never enacted fully. She died in 1982, leaving the reassembly of *Noi Vivi* and *Addio Kira* unfinished.[114]

CONCLUSION

The United States was—and remained—Ayn Rand's political refuge from communist dictatorship. She was free to write as she pleased even if, during

America's 1930s Red Decade, American critics dismissed or misunderstood her treatment of her first major theme: "the individual against the state" and "the supreme value of a human life and the evil of the totalitarian state that claims the right to sacrifice it." Ultimately, the importance of her message, or at least the evidence of its impact, found its way to America from abroad. The history of theater and film adaptations of *We The Living* is not simply a case study of Rand's early intellectual impact on the twentieth century—it also confirms that she not only developed her philosophical ideas, but throughout her life succeeded in communicating them to the world's stage.

NOTES

1. I would like to thank the following institutions and individuals for assistance in preparing this chapter. Any errors or omissions are my own. For primary and secondary materials: the Ayn Rand Archives, a collection of the Ayn Rand Institute; the Richard J. Riordan Main Branch of the Los Angeles Public Library; the Billy Rose Theatre Collection at the Lincoln Center Branch of the New York Public Library; Internet Broadway Database; and the Margaret Herrick Library at the Academy of Motion Picture Arts and Sciences. For editorial comment and research assistance: Michael S. Berliner, Scott McConnell, and Sharyn Blumenthal. For English summaries and translations of Italian sources: Anu Seppala.

Special thanks are due the Billy Rose Theatre Collection at the New York Public Library, whose preservation microfilming of *The Unconquered* press book made this chapter possible.

2. Ayn Rand, *For The New Intellectual* (New York: Random House, 1961; Signet paperback edition, 1963), 60.

3. Producer: George Abbott; From the novel *We The Living* by Ayn Rand; Adapted by Ayn Rand; Staged by George Abbott; Principal cast: Helen Craig as Kira Argounova, John Emery as Leo Kovalensky, Dean Jagger as Andrei Taganov; Additional opening night cast: Georgina Brand, Arthur Pierson, Edwin Philips, Lea Penman, Ludmilla Toretzka, Paul Ballantyne; Scenic Designer: Boris Aronson; Incidental Music: Alexander Haas. Biltmore Theatre, New York, N.Y. *Ayn Rand Papers*, Ayn Rand Archives.

4. Production Company: Scalera Films, Rome; Producer: Massimo Ferrara-Santamaria; Director: Goffredo Alessandrini; Principal cast: Alida Valli as Kira Argounova, Rossano Brazzi as Leo Kovalensky, Fosco Giachetti as Andrei Taganov; Production Manager: Franco Magli; Screenplay: Anton Giulio Majano; From the novel by Ayn Rand; Adapted by Corrado Alvaro and Orio Vergani; Editor: Eraldo da Roma; Director of Photography: Giuseppe Carracciolo; Music: Renzo Rossellini; Art Direction: Andrea Beloborodoff, Giorgio Abkhasi, Amleto Bonetti; Costumes: Rosi Gori; Sound: Piero Cavazzuti, Tullo Parmegiani; Associate Director: Anton Giulio Majano; Assistant Director: Giorgio Cristallini; Camera Operator: Leone Bioli. Included in Angelika Films media kit prepared in conjunction with the 1986 release of *We The Living*, a condensed version of *Noi Vivi* and *Addio Kira*. See note 114.

5. For further details about Ayn Rand's life and intellectual development, see the short biography: Jeff Britting, *Ayn Rand* (New York: Overlook Press, 2004).

6. Rand disavowed the play's amateur version and subsequent Hollywood film adaptation. For an explanation, see her 1968 introduction to the play, in Ayn Rand, *Night of January 16th*, final revised version (New York: Plume, 1987).

7. Biographical interviews (Ayn Rand Archives).

8. Biographical interviews (Ayn Rand Archives).

9. Biographical interviews (Ayn Rand Archives).

10. Ayn Rand, *The Art of Nonfiction: A Guide for Writers and Readers*, Robert Mayhew, ed. (New York: Plume, 2001), 81. Rand is known primarily for her work as a novelist. However, she developed an early interest in theater, motion pictures, and, later in her life, television. As a child in Russia, she appreciated the dramatic inventiveness of Victor Hugo's plays and the visual stylization of Fritz Lang's silent films. Her second novel, *Anthem*, was originally conceived as a play while she was a college student in Russia.

11. *New York Mirror*, July 10, 1936, found in "Press Book, Warner Bros. Pictures *The Unconquered*, November 24, 1939–February 1940, Books A and 1," available on microfilm, Billy Rose Theatre Collection, New York Public Library. (As a result of the press book's deteriorated condition, the authorship and publication information of some clippings have been lost.)

12. *New York Times*, July 10, 1936, Press book, *The Unconquered*.

13. *New York Times*, September 6, 1936, Press book, *The Unconquered*. The comma in the play's title reflects the original spelling of the book's name as used in promotional materials at the time of the novel's publication in 1936. The date and reason for the comma's discontinuation is not known. However, it remained a common journalistic practice until 1939.

14. *Publishers Weekly*, January 1937, Press book, *The Unconquered*. Rand's adaptation under Mayer is no longer extant, and the evolution of the drafts is unknown. Among the *Ayn Rand Papers* (at the Ayn Rand Archives) are eleven typescripts, which appear to have been prepared and/or revised under George Abbott, including extensive revisions in Rand's hand and miscellaneous notes on speeches.

15. *New York Times*, March 13, 1937, Press book, *The Unconquered*.

16. Malone, N.Y. *Telegram*, June 19, 1937, Press book, *The Unconquered*.

17. *Chicago Times*, July 13, 1938, Press book, *The Unconquered*.

18. Biographical interviews (Ayn Rand Archives). See also Eugene Lyons, *The Red Decade* (New Rochelle, N.Y.: Arlington House, 1971).

19. Michael Paxton, *Ayn Rand: A Sense of Life* (Layton, Utah: Gibbs Smith, 1998), 101.

20. Biographical interviews (Ayn Rand Archives). According to a profile in the *Baltimore Evening Sun* (December 26, 1939), Eugenie Leontovich first appeared before New York theater audiences portraying a ballerina in the Broadway production of *Grand Hotel* and had most recently portrayed the Grand Duchess in a London production of *Tovarich*, a comedy that toured subsequently in the United States. A native of Russia, Leontovich studied dance at the Imperial School of the Theatre and was later a member of the Moscow Art Theatre Company. Both her father and her husband died in street fighting during the Russian Revolution and, after Lenin's assumption of power, she fled Russia disguised as a peasant. She met her future hus-

band, actor-director Gregory Ratoff, in Constantinople, later joining him in a series of dramatic performances that brought her to the United States and to the attention of George Abbott. Abbott first directed Leontovich in his 1932 Broadway production of *Twentieth Century*.

21. George Francis Abbott (1887–1995). Born in Forestville, N.Y., Abbott studied at Harvard's distinguished 47 Workshop and went on to a career as coauthor, director, and producer of over one hundred theatrical productions including *Chicago* (1926), *The Boys from Syracuse* (1938), *Pal Joey* (1940), *The Pajama Game* (1954), *Damn Yankees* (1955), and numerous revivals. (Gerald Bordman, ed., *The Concise Oxford Companion to American Theatre* [New York: Oxford University Press, 1987], 3.) "Combining an astute business sense and a rare flair for the stage, George Francis Abbott has become one of the most remarkable men of the American theater. Thoroughly schooled in a dozen branches of stagecraft, he is an admitted expert playwright, actor, director and producer." Quoted from "Theatre," Cue [?], no date, Press book, *The Unconquered*.

22. Under the standard production contract, investors in Broadway plays earn a set percentage of the future market created by a successful theatrical run. Warner Bros. reportedly invested $50,000 in *The Unconquered* (*World-Telegram*, December 28, 1939) and provided the use of the Biltmore Theatre, which it owned at the time (Internet Broadway Database).

23. "When the rest of Broadway was trembling before threats of war in Europe and staged a general walkout, Abbott calmly announced four productions for the new season with possibility of others to come. True to schedule, he opened *See My Lawyer* (starring Milton Berle), *Too Many Girls*, and *Ring Two*. We the Living, due in January, rounds out the list." Quoted from "Theatre," Cue [?], no date, Press book, *The Unconquered*.

24. Biographical interviews (Ayn Rand Archives).

25. Author and publication unknown, c. November 1939, Press book, *The Unconquered*. Gregory Ratoff would eventually direct *Song of Russia* in 1943 at Metro-Goldwyn-Mayer. In 1947, Rand testified before the House Committee on Un-American Activities, analyzing *Song of Russia* as communist propaganda.

26. Author unknown, *News*, November 23, 1939, Press book, *The Unconquered*.

27. Author unknown, *News*, December 1, 1939, Press book, *The Unconquered*. John Emery (1905–1964) portrayed Leo Kovalensky in *The Unconquered*. Emery first appeared on Broadway in *Mrs. Patridge Presents* (1925) and made his film debut in *Spellbound* (1945) directed by Alfred Hitchcock. He was married briefly to Tallulah Bankhead who, at the time of *The Unconquered*, was appearing as Regina Giddens in the 1939 Broadway production of Lillian Hellman's *The Little Foxes* (Biographical File, Margaret Herrick Library).

Completing the principal cast of *The Unconquered* was Dean Jagger (1903–1991) in the role of Andrei Taganov. Jagger's acting career began in the New York regional theater followed by his Broadway debut in *Tobacco Road* (1933). In 1949, he received an Academy Award for Best Supporting Actor for his portrayal of Major Stovall in *Twelve O'Clock High* (1949). He appeared in over 125 films (*Variety* (w), 11 February 1991).

28. Arthur M. Schlesinger Jr., ed., *The Almanac of American History* (New York: Barnes & Noble Books, 1993), 477.

29. G. Ross, *World-Telegram*, November 27, 1939, Press book, *The Unconquered*.

30. *Woman's Wear*, December 6, 1939, Press book, *The Unconquered*.

31. Biographical Interviews (Ayn Rand Archives).

32. Boris Aronson (1900–1980) was a native of Russia who studied art and design in Kiev and Moscow before coming to New York in 1923. He became one of the leading scenic designers in American theater history. His work was featured in such productions as: *Awake and Sing* (1935), *Cabin in the Sky* (1940), *Bus Stop* (1955), *The Diary of Anne Frank* (1955), and *Cabaret* (1966). "His stylization, free placement of form, and use of bright colors were heavily influenced by his admiration of Marc Chagall. He was one of the first to employ projections against neutral backgrounds to effect changes of mood and place." (Bordman, *Oxford Companion to American Theatre*, 25.)

33. *Baltimore Evening Sun*, December 22, 1939, Press book, *The Unconquered*.

34. *Baltimore Sun*, December 23, 1939, Press book, *The Unconquered*.

35. *Baltimore* [?], n.d. "Abbott Play at Maryland Dec. 25," Press book, *The Unconquered*.

36. Author and publication unknown, c. 1939, Press book, *The Unconquered*.

37. *Baltimore Sun*, December 16, 1939, Press book, *The Unconquered*.

38. Norman Clark "Unconquered, New Abbott Play, Now at Maryland," Press book, *The Unconquered*.

39. R. B. C., *Baltimore Evening Sun*, Press book, *The Unconquered*.

40. Biographical Interviews (Ayn Rand Archives).

41. D. Kilgallen, *Journal-American*, January 29, 1940, Press book, *The Unconquered*.

42. *Sun*, "The Holiday Stage" column, December 27, 1940, Press book, *The Unconquered*.

43. "Abbott Play," *Eagle*, December 19, 1939, Press book, *The Unconquered*.

44. *News*, January 7, 1940, Press book, *The Unconquered*.

45. Biographical Interviews (Ayn Rand Archives).

46. Biographical Interviews (Ayn Rand Archives). Helen Craig (1912–1986), married to actor John Beal, was born in San Antonio, Texas, but moved to South America as an infant, where she spent her early childhood in Chile and Mexico, learning English upon her return to the United States at the age of eight. An aspiring actress since childhood, she created the role of the deaf-mute in the Broadway production of *Johnny Belinda*. Her film work included *The Snake Pit*, *They Live By Night*, and *War and Peace*. On television she appeared in episodes of *Kojak*, *The Waltons*, and *The Bionic Woman*. (Perry Lieber, *RKO Studios Press Release*, c. 1940s; *Variety*, July 23, 1986.)

47. Author and publication unknown, Press book, *The Unconquered*.

48. "Producers List 7 Opening for Month; Fontanne and Lunt Play Head Schedule; . . . plays consisted of: "The Taming of the Shrew," Alfred Lunt and Lynn Fontanne; "For the Show," a review by Nancy Hamilton and Morgan Lewis; "The Unconquered," by Ayn Rand; "Another Sun," by Dorothy Thompson and Fritz Kortner; "Night Music," by Clifford Odets; "The Burning Deck," by Andrew Rosenthal; "Leave Her to Heaven," by John van Bruten; "The Fifth Column," by Ernest Hemingway." As quoted in "News of the Theatre," *New York Herald Tribune*, February 2, 1940, Press book, *The Unconquered*.

49. The final version of the play as produced and directed by Abbott is not known. The observations made here are based on a reconstruction of the play prepared by Rand's literary estate and intended for (but not used in) Leonard Peikoff, ed., *The Early Ayn Rand: A Selection from Her Unpublished Fiction* (New York: New American Library, 1984; Signet paperback edition, 1986). For a brief description of the extant drafts of *The Unconquered* among the *Ayn Rand Papers* (at the Ayn Rand Archives), see note 14.

50. Ayn Rand, *The Unconquered*, "final draft," unpublished xerography of typescript, 1–9, *Special Collections*, Ayn Rand Archives.

51. Press book, *The Unconquered*.

52. *New York Times*, Sunday, February 11, 1940, Press book, *The Unconquered*.

53. Press book, *The Unconquered*.

54. Alvah Bessie, *New Masses*, February 27, 1940, Press book, *The Unconquered*.

55. Review, *Theatre Arts*, April 1940, Press book, *The Unconquered*.

56. Dixie Righe [?], "George Abbott Presents," *Post*, February 14, 1940, Press book, *The Unconquered*.

57. The Playviewer, "New Plays, The Unconquered," *Bronx Home News*, February 14, 1940, Press book, *The Unconquered*.

58. "The Stage Today" column, "Ayn Rand's Play at Biltmore Theatre Came, Was Seen, Failed to Conquer," *Morning-Telegraph*, February 15, 1940, Press book, *The Unconquered*.

59. "The New York Play" column, *Hollywood Reporter*, February 14, 1940, Press book, *The Unconquered*.

60. Mark Barron, "Spying on Gotham—'Unconquered' Changes Stage Into 'Anti-isms' Rostrum," *Philadelphia Record*, February 18, 1940, Press book, *The Unconquered*.

61. Lewis Nichols, "The Play" column: *The Unconquered, New York Times*, February 14, 1940.

62. Sidney B. Whipple, "Events Too Rapid For Dramatist," Press book, *The Unconquered*.

63. Kelcey Allen, "The Unconquered," *Woman's Wear*, February 14, 1940, Press book, *The Unconquered*.

64. Certain records of organizations involved with the production are on deposit with the New York Public Library. Besides a small collection of Van Dame Studio promotional photographs, Boris Aronson's set renderings, and a Warner Bros. Pictures Press Book on *The Unconquered* and related ephemera, nothing of the production is known to remain. A single script of *The Unconquered* was available until the late 1970s or early 1980s but is now lost.

65. Biographical Interviews (Ayn Rand Archives).

66. Biographical Interviews (Ayn Rand Archives).

67. Rand, *The Art of Nonfiction*, 80–81 (emphasis added).

68. *Ideal*, a novella written by Rand during her first Hollywood period, was subsequently adapted for the stage in New York City and revised intermittently until 1941. A second play, *Think Twice*, was written in the years 1939–1940. Neither work was produced in Rand's lifetime. See: Rand, *The Early Ayn Rand*, 205–90, 293–377.

69. Arthur M. Schlesinger Jr., ed., *The Almanac of American History* (New York: Barnes & Noble Books, 1993), 479, 486.

70. Ayn Rand, "Testimony," October 20, 1947, "Hearing Regarding Communist Infiltration of the Motion Picture Industry," House Committee on Un-American Activities as reprinted in Dave Harriman, ed., *Journals of Ayn Rand* (New York: Plume, 1997), 371–81.

71. Massimo Ferrara-Santamaria to Duncan Scott, February 20, 1988, Angelika Films media kit.

72. For an analysis of the philosophical underpinnings of twentieth-century totalitarianism, see Leonard Peikoff, *The Ominous Parallels* (New York: Stein and Day, 1982; Meridian paperback edition, 1993), 13–99. For the Objectivist view of the fundamentality of philosophical ideas in explaining human history, see Leonard Peikoff, "Philosophy and Psychology in History," *The Objectivist Forum* 6, no. 5 (October 1985).

73. Benito Mussolini, *What is Fascism,* in Paul Halsall, translator, *Internet History Sourcebooks Project* (New York: Fordham University, 1997).

74. James B. Whisker, "Italian Fascism: An Interpretation," *The Journal of Historical Review* 4, no. 4 (Spring 1983).

75. Mussolini's statement is similar to Lenin's view of film as quoted in *We the Living*: "Of all the arts, the most important one for Russia is the cinema" (382).

76. Morando Morandini, "Italy from Fascism to Neo-Realism," in *Oxford History of Western Cinema* (Oxford: Oxford University Press, 1986) 353–61.

77. Rand to Gall, June 24, 1946, *Ayn Rand Papers*, Ayn Rand Archives. For information about Italian critical reaction, see Michael S. Berliner, "Reviews of *We The Living*," in the present volume.

78. Rand to Gall, 24 June 1946, *Ayn Rand Papers*, Ayn Rand Archives.

79. Morandini, "Italy from Fascism to Neo-Realism," 357.

80. Graziadei & Scipioni to Gall, October 21, 1945, *Ayn Rand Papers*, Ayn Rand Archives.

81. Morandini, "Italy from Fascism to Neo-Realism," 355.

82. Ferrara-Santamaria to Duncan Scott, February 20, 1988.

83. "Goffredo Alessandrini," interview conducted by Francesco Savio from *Cinecittà Anni Trenta: Parlano 116 Protagonisti del Secondo Cinema Italiano* [*Cinecittà in the 1930s: 116 Voices from the Italian Secondo Cinema*] (Roma: Bulzoni, 1979), 48. New English translations and review of unidentified translation: Anu Seppala.

84. Duncan Scott, "An Interview With Anton Giulio Majano, Associate Director, *We The Living*" (May 6, 1986), Angelika Films media kit.

85. Peter Schwartz, "We The Living—The Movie," *The Intellectual Activist* 4, no. 16 (September 1986).

86. Goffredo Alessandrini," *Cinecittà Anni Trenta*, 48.

87. Scott, "An Interview With Anton Giulio Majano."

88. "Fosco Giachetti," *Cinecittà Anni Trenta*, 584.

89. Scott, "An Interview with Anton Giulio Majano."

90. Schwartz, "We The Living," 3.

91. Mario Gromo, Correspondent, Venice Film Festival, *La Stampa*, September 16, 1942.

92. Author unknown, " *We The Living—A Film Discovered"* Press release in con-

junction with *We The Living* (New York: Angelika Films, May 6, 1986), 2, Angelika Films media kit.

93. Raffaele Calzini, *Film Anno* 5, no. 39, September 26, 1942. English summary Anu Seppala.

94. Diego Calcagno, *Film Anno* 5, no. 45, November 7, 1942. English summary Anu Seppala.

95. Goffredo Alessandrini," *Cinecittà Anni Trenta*, 49.

96. Scott, "An Interview with Anton Giulio Majano."

97. Ferrara-Santamaria to Scott, February 20, 1988.

98. Foreign Claims Settlement Commission of the United States, Washington D.C., In the matter of the Claim of Alice O'Connor [Ayn Rand] Under the International Claims Settlement Act of 1949, as amended, Filed September 27, 1956, *Ayn Rand Papers*, Ayn Rand Archives.

99. Schwartz, "We The Living," 3.

100. Ferrara-Santamaria to Scott, February 20, 1988. The producer was found guilty of anti-Fascist propaganda and expelled from the party.

101. Schwartz, "We The Living," 3.

102. Downes to Watkins, May 16, 1946, *Ayn Rand Papers*, Ayn Rand Archives.

103. Rand to Watkins, May 28, 1946, *Ayn Rand Papers*, Ayn Rand Archives.

104. Rand to Gall, May 28, 1946, *Ayn Rand Papers*, Ayn Rand Archives.

105. Rand to Gall, March 13, 1947, *Ayn Rand Papers*, Ayn Rand Archives.

106. Michael S. Berliner, ed., *Letters of Ayn Rand* (New York: Dutton, 1997), 368–70.

107. Berliner, *Letters*, 370.

108. Berliner, *Letters*, 196.

109. Ayn Rand, "Line of Treatment for: 'We the Living,'" 7 typewritten pages with markings, December 2, 1948, *Ayn Rand Papers*, Ayn Rand Archives.

110. Biographical Interviews (Ayn Rand Archives).

111. Berliner, *Letters*, 488–89.

112. Goffredo Alessandrini," *Cinecittà Anni Trenta*, 48.

113. Schwartz, "We The Living," 4.

114. After Ayn Rand's death, the revisions of *Noi Vivi* and *Addio Kira* were finished and a single "author's version" with English subtitles entitled *We the Living* was completed. Duncan Scott Productions produced *We the Living*, in association with Henry Mark Holzer and Erika Holzer, and with the cooperation of the Estate of Ayn Rand. Angelika Films distributed the film theatrically in 1986.

The Scott revision of *Noi Vivi* and *Addio Kira* falls outside the scope of the present chapter and merits its own separate study. *We The Living* debuted at the Telluride Film Festival in Colorado in 1986. During its North American release, the *New York Times* called *We The Living* an ". . . ambitious and ingenious film."

9

We the Living: '36 and '59

Robert Mayhew

We the Living was published by Macmillan in 1936, and during the following year, owing to the publisher's neglect, it went out of print.[1] After the publication of *Atlas Shrugged* in 1957, Rand prepared a revised edition of *We the Living*, which was published in 1959. Here is what she had to say about her changes (in her foreword to the revised edition):

> I want to account for the editorial changes which I have made in the text of this novel for its present reissue: the chief inadequacy of my literary means was grammatical—a particular kind of uncertainty in the use of the English language, which reflected the transitional state of a mind thinking no longer in Russian, but not yet fully in English. I have changed only the most awkward or confusing lapses of this kind. I have reworded the sentences and clarified their meaning without changing their content. I have not added or eliminated anything to or from the content of the novel. I have cut out some sentences and a few paragraphs that were repetitive or so confusing in their implications that to clarify them would have necessitated lengthy additions. In brief, all the changes are merely editorial line-changes. The novel remains what and as it was (xvi–xvii).

In what follows, I illustrate and explain the kinds of changes she made.

When I started comparing the first edition of *We the Living* to the revised edition (for which I made use of the 1996 sixtieth anniversary paperback edition, though the hardcover 1959 edition was always within reach), I was surprised by the number of changes Rand made. As a brief indication of the extent of her revisions, note that she made over 900 changes in punctuation and well over 2,000 changes in wording (in which I include deletions, additions, the replacing of individual words and the rewording of phrases and sentences). According to my examination of these changes, only one page (of the 1996 edition) went without a single change (namely, 105).

I begin with the less interesting changes—for instance, punctuation—then move to changes in wording, before finally turning to some of the more substantial and substantive changes.

PUNCTUATION, CAPITALIZATION, AND PARAGRAPHING

In her *Art of Nonfiction*, Ayn Rand states:

> Although there is a great deal of latitude in English, it is a language in which punctuation is particularly crucial. Incidentally, the other two languages I know—Russian and French—are not quite so prone to equivocation or double meaning. English is very condensed and exact (which is why I love it), but these very qualities make possible sentences that can be read in two different ways, according to whether you insert or omit a comma.[2]

She wrote *We the Living* during her transition from Russian to English, which most likely explains why there were so many changes in punctuation later. Of the over 900 punctuation changes, the majority involve commas: by my count, she inserted over 500 commas and deleted about 100. For example, she added a comma to the following sentence:

> When the train pulled out<,> she was seen sitting on her bundles (14/28),

and deleted a comma from this one:

> She answered[,] and her voice had the intensity of a maniac's (544/444).[3]

These examples are typical.

There were nearly 300 other punctuation changes, usually involving the change of one kind of punctuation mark into another. For example,

> Irina studied Art. She devoted her time to solemn research . . . (76)

became:

> Irina studied Art; she devoted her time to solemn research . . . (76).

This line change also provides us with an example of a typical change in capitalization. Most of the approximately 150 changes in capitalization accompanied changes in punctuation. Other changes in capitalization involved titles. For example, in the line:

It's a present from mother (363),

"mother" is capitalized in the 1959 edition (300). Here's another example, from the scene with Andrei and Captain Karsavin:

The Captain said:
"Your gun" (123).

This is revised to:

The captain said: "Your gun" (112).

Note the change in paragraphing as well. Rand made changes in paragraphing nearly 800 times as she revised *We the Living*. (In only three of these cases did she *add* paragraphing.)

The changes in punctuation are explained by her having become—in the over twenty years between versions—more comfortable with, and knowledgeable of, the nuances of English, a language which she claims is more affected by punctuation than is Russian. The changes in capitalization (not linked to punctuation revisions) and the changes in paragraphing might reflect changes in literary conventions.[4]

CHANGES IN WORDING

Typographical Errors

Of the more than three thousand changes Ayn Rand made, I found only fifteen that were corrections of typographical errors: "our" was changed to "your" (21/33); "its" was changed to "it's" (47/53); "Sachs'" was changed to "Sachs" (47/53); "some one" was changed to "someone" (62/65; cf. 190/222); "slubbering" was changed to "slobbering" (70/71); "flopping" was changed to "flapping" (100/94); "the" was inserted before "dictatorship of the proletariat" (103/97); the period after "anemic girl" was changed to a comma (177/155); "wardhobe" was changed to "wardrobe" (210/180); "Swans' Lake" was changed to "Swan Lake" (220/189); "Misha" was changed to "Mishka" (232/198); "preying" was changed to "prying" (233/199); "stranger" was changed to "stronger" (315/261); "Galine" was changed to "Galina" (549/447); "mowing" was changed to "moving" (561/457).

Factual Errors

A few corrections were not of typographical, but of factual, errors. For example, the many instances of "pulpit" in the first edition were corrected to "lectern" in the revised one (e.g., 374/308). In one passage, she writes that Mitya Vessiolkin "tried to jump off a moving tramway, and he fell under, but he was lucky: just one wrist cut off" (176). A wrist can be cut, but not cut off; so the line was changed to "just one hand cut off" (154). One last example: Vasili Dunaev had a prosperous fur business that had provided—according to the original—"the chinchillas that embraced many shoulders white as marble" (23). But chinchillas come from South America, whereas Vasili was a fur trapper in Siberia; so, "chinchillas" was changed to "sables" (34).

Spelling

There were dozens of changes in spelling that were not the correction of typos. A number involved hyphenation: for example, dry goods/dry-goods (114/106). Others involved the spelling of Russian words and names: roubles/rubles (66/68), Trotzky/Trotsky (225/192). And still others involved changes to verbs in the past tense with a -t ending: smelt/smelled (49/54), sunburnt/sunburned (3/19; 324/268).

There were also dozens of changes involving contractions—usually, the removal of the contraction, son's/son is (79/78), didn't/did not (107/101).

Grammar

Although Ayn Rand writes, in describing her revision of *We the Living*, that "the chief inadequacy of my literary means was grammatical," there were not all that many blatant grammatical errors (considering the short period in which she had been writing in English). Here's one example:

> The library was like all the other rooms in the 'House of the Peasant,' except that it had more posters and [less] <fewer> books (240/205).

This is pretty obvious. In another case, Rand simply removes the dangling modifier:

> The girl in the leather jacket [from Kira's office] was chairman of the Club (240/205).

In another, Rand rewrites the sentence to remove the improper double negative:

It's better if no one—not a soul—nowhere—knows, but you and I (278).
It's better if no one—not a soul anywhere—knows this, but you and I (234).

One grammatical error that Rand commits about fifty times is the use of "as" where "like" is necessary.[5] For example:

Galina Petrovna whispered confidentially, [as] <like> a conspirator (52/57).

Here is a description of melting snow:

gray with city dust [as] <like> dirty cotton, brittle and shining [as] <like> wet sugar (164/144);

and of a sunrise:

A band of pink, pale and young, [as] <like> the breath of a color, [as] <like> the birth of a color (569/463).

Similarly, though not as grammatically incorrect, Rand often (in the '36 edition) used a single "as" where two would be better. For example:

He was sixty years old; his backbone had been <as> straight as his gun; his spirit—<as> straight as his backbone (23/35).

In scores of places, Ayn Rand changed the tense of verbs, to achieve more grammatical precision. For example:

The only hero she had known was a Viking whose story she <had> read as a child (41/49).

Other instances involve such changes as: having climbed/climbing (124/113); came/had come (151/134); was looking/looked (364/300).

What I find surprising is not that the young Ayn Rand committed a number of grammatical errors—she was in her twenties, and had been in the United States for less than a decade when she wrote *We the Living*—but that her copyeditors at Macmillan failed to catch so many errors. This may say something about the attention and commitment Macmillan gave to *We the Living*.

Word Order

There were a few changes in word order (by which I mean the order of the words was changed, but the words themselves were not changed nor were other words omitted or added). In most cases, the change is not sig-

nificant, merely adding precision or making the passage smoother. For
example:

> Galina Petrovna sat straight up (25)

became:

> Galina Petrovna sat up straight (37).

In another case, Rand wrote:

> She stood silently looking into his eyes (57)

which was changed to:

> She stood looking silently into his eyes (61).

There is a subtle difference, in that the "silently" is meant not to modify Kira's
standing, but her looking into Leo's eyes.

Word Replacement

There are cases in which Ayn Rand simply exchanged one word for
another (with no other omissions or additions). Often, the new word is simply better. For example:

> And the golden spire of the Admiralty held defiantly a [disappeared] <van-
> ished> sun high over the dark city (106/100).

We don't normally use "disappeared" as an adjective in that way; "vanished"
is more elegant and standard.

In dozens of cases, Rand traded one preposition for another, more appropriate, one. For example:

> Maria Petrovna was talking [in] <with> a nervous, fluttering hurry (23/35);
> Lydia . . . had a suspicion [of] <about> the reason of her popularity at all the
> rare parties (177/155);
> little shadows of raindrops rolled slowly [on] <down> the wall (377/311).

In each case, what is achieved—beyond grammatical correctness—is a bit
more precision.

There are cases in which Rand replaced one word with another a number
of times. For example, "look" and related words is replaced by "glance" and

words related to it over ten times. In this example, Syerov is looking at Leo and Kira:

> He turned once to [look] <glance> back at them (105/99).

In the 1936 edition, she used "look," which, after all, is what Syerov is doing. But it's a very broad word. Glance has a narrower meaning—"look quickly or briefly," according to one dictionary—and suggests a more directed look. Such changes lend more precision and clarity to the scenes in which she uses these words.

She also replaced the word "immobile" a half dozen times, but more for accuracy than for connotation. Here are three:

> She stood straight, [immobile] <motionless>, with the graceful indifference of a traveler on a luxurious ocean liner (3/19);
> the notes rose, trembling, repeating themselves, too rapt to be held [immobile] <still>, like arms raised . . . waving . . . in the sweep of banners (74/74);
> When Kira and Leo spoke to each other, their words were [short] <brief>, [precise] <impersonal>, their indifference exaggerated, their [immobile] <expressionless> faces guarding a secret they both remembered (155/137).

In each of these cases, the problem is that "immobile" means (or can mean) "incapable of moving or being moved." But that's not what she wants to say. For instance, in the first example, the point is not that Kira stood incapable of motion, but that she—though capable—was not moving. It's a subtle difference, but the change is worth making.

In at least four cases, Ayn Rand changed the name of a country or person. In one case, "Saint Russia" is replaced by "Holy Russia" (176/154), probably because Rand—who I assume simply translated the Russian in the first edition—later discovered that "Holy Russia" was the convention in English. In another case, "British" replaces "English" (as in "British Trade Unions") making the usage a bit more accurate (233/200). Another example of Rand making such a change for the sake of accuracy occurs in the scene in which Andrei forces Pavel Syerov, through threat of exposing his illegal scam, to release Leo from prison. The original line reads:

> "All right, King Arthur or whatever it's called," he [Syerov] said. "King Arthur of the blackmail sword" (511/416).

Rand properly replaces "King Arthur" with "Sir Galahad," who is a better representative of chivalrous behavior toward females.

The most interesting name change comes in the passage wherein Rand describes the young Leo. One line in the original reads:

When his young friends related, in whispers, the latest French stories, Leo quoted Kant and Nietzsche (156).

In the '59 edition, "Kant" is changed to "Spinoza" (138). Rand had a mild respect for Spinoza's egoism; more important, however, in her mature philosophical writings, she makes it clear that she regards Kant as the most evil philosopher in history, a view she apparently did not hold in Russia or when she first got to the United States. (Later in the novel, when Leo is arrested, the '36 edition has him uttering an arguably Kantian line to Andrei: "A tendency for transcendental thinking is apt to obscure our perception of reality" [487/397]. Rand cut this line.)

In a few cases, a word was changed because its connotation does not fit the character it describes. For example, Ayn Rand a few times in presenting Kira replaces "funny" with "strange." Here's one:

> the soldier noticed . . . that the [funny] <strange> girl in the child's stocking-cap had [funny] <strange> eyes (17/30).

This change was no doubt made because Rand wants to convey that her heroine, though unusual, is in no way silly. On the other side of the spectrum of characters, she changed a word in the following line about Victor:

> Victor came in, shuffling [leisurely] <lazily> in bedroom slippers (158/139).

"Lazily" better fits Victor in general, and this scene in particular.

In a number of places, the word-change makes the passage more accurate or precise. For example, in the scene depicting the university student elections, describing the student speakers from the Communist faction, Ayn Rand writes:

> Its speakers bellowed [loudly] <belligerently> about the Dictatorship of the Proletariat (71/71).

The first time Leo comes to Kira's home, Lydia asks him where he comes from. The response:

> "From jail," Leo answered with a [charming] <courteous> smile" (146/130).

Leo may have been coolly polite, but there is nothing particularly charming about his behavior toward Kira's family that evening, so the change to "courteous" better fits the scene. Similarly, when Andrei explains to Kira why he likes listening to music with her, he says:

> Because you have a very [cruel] <stern> mouth—and I like that—but when you listen to that music, your mouth is gay, as if it were listening, too (335/277).

"Cruel" is too harsh, and might seem to clash with "gay," so Rand made the appropriate change.

Here's another example of a change made for the sake of greater accuracy:

> She made a raft of tree branches and . . . [rode] <sailed> down the river (38/46).

Similar changes are made involving "table" and "desk" (72/72), "pictures" and "photographs" (122/112), and a number of times, "purging" and "purge" (e.g., 246/209).

One word-exchange was made to avoid a possible misunderstanding and some unintended humor during a very serious scene from Andrei's past:

> "Brothers," he cried, "I have no [arms] <weapons>. I am not here to shoot" (118/108).

Some words were replaced, I suspect, because of a change in usage over time (and perhaps in location as well, reflecting California versus New York usage). In the '36 edition, Irina is described as "a young lady of eighteen" (22); in the '59 edition, she is "a young girl of eighteen" (34). In the first edition, Comrade Sonia predicts that she and Kira are "going to be great pals" (68); in the revised edition, her prediction—equally inaccurate—is that they will be "great friends" (69). Two more examples: "pupils" is replaced with "students" (e.g., 41/48); and "store" becomes "shop" (e.g., 18/31).

In a discussion of connotation, in *The Art of Nonfiction*, Ayn Rand states: "Watch out for philosophical implications, too. For example, if someone writes, 'He had an instinct for courage,' he may only want to convey, 'He is brave.' But the actual, and improper, implication is that courage is an instinct."[6] Ayn Rand replaced some words in *We the Living* to avoid improper philosophical implications. Here are six examples.

(1) The *ABC of Communism* was "a book whose study was compulsory in every school [of the Republic] <in the country>" (241/205).

To leave this passage unchanged could leave the impression that Rand considered the Soviet Union a Republic, like the United States or France, which she did not.

(2) Vasili Dunaev says that in the old days, "they had culture, and [faith] <moral values>, and . . . and integrity" (253/214).

Although these are the words of Vasili, and thus do not necessarily represent the views of Ayn Rand, he is sufficiently a positive character that she would want to eliminate the implication that faith was in any way a positive value from "the old days." Changing it to "moral values" avoids this implication, while at the same time leaving open what someone like Vasili would have considered moral values.

(3) "When a reduction of staffs came to the 'House of the Peasant' and she saw her name among those [fired] <dismissed> as 'anti-social element,' she was not surprised" (267/225).

I initially thought that this must be a significant change, on the grounds that "fired" is usually used in the context of a free (or semifree) market, where employers have the right and the power to get rid of a person they no longer wish to employ, whereas in the Soviet Union, who got and kept what job depended largely on party membership and/or political pull. One could argue that "fired" gives too much dignity to Kira's job at the House of the Peasant, and thus "dismissed" is the better word. There may be something to this, though Rand must have regarded this as a minor difference; for she does use "fired" in the revised edition of *We the Living* (137, 153, 167, 192, 290, 327, 447)—in fact, more often than she uses "dismissed" (225, 272, 274, 325).

(4) Galina Petrovna describing Victor: "Now there's nothing [mystical] <sentimental> about him. He has his eyes open to [our] modern reality" (330/274).

Not only is "mystical" simply less accurate and appropriate than "sentimental," further, its use here might imply that Rand accepts the notion that ideals (as opposed to what's "practical") are inherently irrational.

(5) "what reason could possibly keep her from her work, her life work, her only [dream] <desire>" (394/324).

"Dream" *might* suggest, however subtly, that what Kira desires is impossible—something to be dreamed of but never obtained.[7] Now it's certainly true that what she desired *was* impossible in the Soviet Union—that's why she tried to escape. But it was not a mere dream in her mind. This may be why Rand changed "dream" to "desire."

(6) Fairly late in the novel, Rand writes that Leo "would leave in the morning, smiling and cheerful and brisk with [activity] <energy>" (396/325).

To have Leo leave in the morning "brisk with activity" suggests a certain level of purposefulness—a level which, alas, he does not possess. His sole function in the food scam he's involved in is to be a fall-guy; if the authorities discover the illegal business he and his partners are in, Leo, not Syerov or Morozov, will be held responsible. Leo gets up in the morning with no real purpose, only some options: stay home and read, see Tonia, get drunk, empty the store's cash-register, etc. One can do this with more or less energy, but this is not genuine activity.

Additions

Some additions were quite minor, the words being added to make a passage smoother or a bit clearer. For example:

Some letters had dried with long<, thin> steaks of red (16/29)

A more important clarification is to the following line, on Kira's thoughts about Leo in the weeks after she first met him:

> She had never had any thought of him beyond the one that he existed. <But she found it hard to remember the existence of anything else.> (64/67).

On its own, the first line could be read to mean that Kira is aware of Leo's existence, but beyond that he is of no importance to her. The addition clarifies what is meant: that Leo's existence was constantly on Kira's mind—that he was of supreme importance to her.

Here's an example of an addition of words to avoid an unintended philosophical implication. Speaking of the lines of a soldier's face, Rand writes:

> there was an <air of> innate temerity (17/30).

As stated in the original, the line implies that temerity is an innate characteristic. Adding "air of" removes or softens that implication.

Finally, consider this exchange between Andrei and Kira:

> "We're crumbling, like a wall, one by one. Kira, I've never been afraid. I'm afraid, now. It's a strange feeling. I'm afraid to think. <Because . . . because I think, at times, that perhaps our ideals could have had no other result.>"
> "<That's true! The fault was not in men, but in the nature of your ideals.>
> . . . I wish I could help you. But of all people, I'm the one who can help you least. You know it" (408/334).

In the original, we are not told why or of what Andrei is afraid to think. The addition makes it clear that this is an ideological issue. Andrei's life is not crumbling under the stress of work or of Kira's refusal to live with or marry him; he is afraid, it is now made explicit, because it is beginning to dawn on him that that ideology for which he has been willing to die and for which he has killed may itself be the cause of the destruction he sees around him. Of course, having made that clear, Rand could not let Kira remain silent. Hence the rest of the addition.

Deletions

There were many more deletions than additions. Some were quite minor: "[Sister] Lydia" (5/2); "A [darn] fool peasant woman" (14/28); "At the Institute, she listened to [many] lectures, but spoke to few people" (49/55); "We had [very] red banners" (455/371).

Ayn Rand tells us in her foreword to the '59 edition that some passages

were cut to eliminate repetition. In some cases, such passages, though repetitious, could nevertheless be well written and quite interesting. Here are two
that qualify.

In the first, Kira is waiting for Leo to come home from one of his "dates"
with Tonia. The 1936 edition describes the following activity while Kira
waited:

> She picked up her book, but she did not want to read; the book told the story
> of a dam built by heroic Red workers in spite of the nefarious machinations of
> villainous Whites who tried to destroy it (405/332).

This brief paragraph is well written, and illustrates Kira's lack of options for
enjoyable activities while at home, as well as the ubiquity of Soviet propaganda. The problem is that the passage is repetitious and unnecessary:
unnecessary, because the scene does not require it; repetitious, because Ayn
Rand had already indicated the nature of Red literature, when she described
the kind of foreign novels that Leo was allowed to translate into Russian.

> They were novels . . . in which a poor, honest worker was always sent to jail for
> stealing a loaf of bread to feed the starving mother of his pretty, young wife
> who had been raped by a capitalist and committed suicide thereafter, for which
> the all-powerful capitalist fired her husband from the factory, so that their child
> had to beg on the streets and was run over by the capitalist's limousine with
> sparkling fenders and a chauffer in uniform (136–37).

Thus the entire paragraph with "the nefarious machinations of villainous
Whites" was omitted.

In another scene, Ayn Rand cuts a long sentence from a paragraph
describing women at the European roof garden:

> Women moved among the tables, with an awkward, embarrassed insolence. A
> head of soft, golden waves nodded unsteadily under a light, wide eyes in deep
> blue rings, a young mouth [open] in a vicious, sneering smile. [At a table, a blue-
> veined hand raised a glass with a liquid transparent as water; through the liquid,
> a heavy diamond dog-collar sparkled on a pale, thin throat; at the rim of the
> glass a painted mouth smiled gaily; and over the glass two dark eyes were
> motionless, as those of a Madonna looking into the heart of an eternal sorrow.]
> In the middle of the room, a gaunt, dark woman with knobs on her shoulders,
> holes under her collar-bones and a skin the color of muddy coffee[,] was laugh-
> ing too loudly, opening painted lips [as] <like> a gash over strong white teeth
> and very red gums (451/368).

I'm not sure why Rand cut this passage. She probably found it repetitious,
and perhaps she concluded that the image of a Madonna clashed with the
diamond-studded dog collar.

Some passages were cut because they did not fit the character who uttered the line or who is being described. In an early conversation, Kira says to Andrei: "If your cause can succeed, Comrade Taganov, I hope you'll see its success" (95/91). Now however much Kira likes Andrei (despite his ideas), it was not like her to wish him success in establishing a Soviet state; yet she sounds as if she were doing just that, so the line was cut. In another scene, Tonia tells Kira that she should wear lipstick. In the first edition, Kira responds: "I appreciate your interest" (321). It's possible that this was intended as sarcasm, but that isn't clear. And taken straight, the response gives Tonia too much importance in Kira's mind, and makes Kira sound too conventional. So in the revised version, Kira does not reply at all, which better fits her character (266). Later, after seeing the wedding present Leo bought for Victor—an extremely expensive vase—Kira says: "Leo, we can't give it to them. Not that I mind the price, but we can't let them see that we can afford it" (360). But it is clear that Kira *does* mind the price—in the sense that the vase was a waste of money that she preferred to save for their future, as well as the fact that such an ostentatious display could get them in trouble. So "Not that I mind the price" was cut (297).

Finally, Andrei says to Kira: "When one can stand any suffering[,] one can also see others suffer. [Perhaps one wants to see them suffer.] This is martial law" (221/189). Andrei is a communist, and he can be cruel and implacable; but to have him wanting to see people suffer goes too far, since Andrei is a communist that Ayn Rand wants us to sympathize with to some degree (at least to the degree Kira does). The deleted line makes that more difficult.

Some words or passages were omitted primarily because of their unpleasant or odd connotations. For example, here is an early passage from the description of the life of the young Vasili:

> He had started as a trapper in the wilderness of Siberia, with a gun, a pair of boots, and two arms that could lift an ox. [He ate blubber.] He wore the scar of a bear's teeth on his thigh (22/34).

Eating blubber, whether or not a typical activity of fur trappers, might come across as funny or odd, especially given the non-serious use of "blubber" as a term for excessive fat in humans. Further, to make the passage clearer, it would help if Rand specified the animals from which the blubber came. But the line isn't worth the trouble. Since it doesn't add much to the passage, it was cut.

Here is a more striking example. After Leo has informed Kira that he is going to become Tonia's gigolo, he says: "She's an old bitch [and her underwear stinks]" (541/441). But it's enough that Leo acknowledges that he's leaving Kira for "an old bitch"; the rest is simply gross and thus distracting—and in fact may imply that he has a more intimate knowledge of Tonia than Rand wanted to convey.

Some passages were cut to avoid dubious philosophical implications. For example, pleading to a commissar to sign Leo into a State sanitarium, Kira says:

> Don't you see why he can't die? I love him. We all have to suffer. We all have things we want<, which are> taken away from us. It's all right. But—because we are living [creatures] <beings>—there's something in each of us, something like the very heart of life condensed—and that should not be touched. [It's something very sacred and we should not even name or mention it] (269/227).

But it is no part of Ayn Rand's philosophy that our highest and most sacred values ought not to be named or mentioned; that has a mystical ring to it, and so the line was removed.

In another passage, Sasha says to Kira and Irina:

> There are some outward circumstances which an autocratic power can control. There are some [intrinsic] values it can never reach or subjugate (306/254).

By 1959, Ayn Rand had identified the crucially important difference between the concepts of objective value and intrinsic value. So the improper word was removed. And there was no need to replace it with another word ("objective" or "absolute"), because it is clear from the sentence itself that Sasha does not regard values as subjective.

Finally, a minor (but interesting) deletion. Kira says to Andrei: "And who—in this damned[, endless] universe—who can tell me why I should live for anything but for that which I want?" (496/404). Ayn Rand probably removed "endless" because it was repetitious—"universe" is extensive enough on its own. But it is also possible that she deleted the word because—at least by 1959—she maintained that the universe is finite.

Rewording

Many phrases, sentences, and in some cases paragraphs, were reworded. Often, Ayn Rand's editing simply improved the language. For example:

> In that bundle were . . . /That bundle held . . . (5/21).
> a light sudden as an explosion slashed the car . . . /a ray of light swept across the car . . . (10/26).
> The bare plaster walls of the station rose before Kira . . . /Kira looked at the words on the bare plaster walls of the station . . . (16/29).

Other such changes increased the accuracy of the passage. Here's one example, from Kira's description of engineering:

It's the only profession . . . for which I don't have to learn one single lie. Steel is steel. Every other science is someone's guess, and someone's wish, and many people's lies (32).

This was changed to:

It's the only profession . . . for which I don't have to learn any lies. Steel is steel. Most of the other sciences are someone's guess, and someone's wish, and many people's lies (42).

It is not the case that most professions besides engineering require lies, though this may have been close to the truth in the Soviet Union. But Rand changes "Every other science" to "Most of the other sciences" when she says they are someone's guess, because it is simply inaccurate to say that—even in the Soviet Union—*every* science but engineering is based on guesswork.

Sometimes Ayn Rand changed the language because its connotation didn't fit the context. For example, speaking of the anticommunist students towards the beginning of the novel, she says: "students had always had a good nose for tyranny" (71). But that's slang; it lacks both the precision and the dignity of her revision: "students had always known how to fight tyranny" (71). Describing Kira seeing Leo for the first time after his return from the Crimea, Rand originally wrote: "her mouth sank into his hand and held it as a leech" (313), but she changed this to: "she pressed her mouth to his hand and held it" (260)—no doubt to avoid the negative connotations of the word "leech" and the image the word evokes.

Some passages were reworded because they did not fit a character (and, in this first example, because they were as distracting as Tonia's underwear). In the first edition, when Stepan Timoshenko is explaining the nature of revolution to Morozov, he says:

Do you know what a revolution is? I'll tell you. We took officers on our ship and we tore their epaulets off. We tore them off and we cut new ones, red ones, on their shoulders. On their skins. We cut bellies open and we pulled guts out, by the fistful, and their fingers still moved, like that, opening and closing, like a baby's. We stuck them into the boilers, alive, head first. Ever smelt human flesh burning? There was one—he couldn't have been more than twenty. He made the sign of the cross . . . (455).

Timoshenko is pretty vulgar for a mixed or semi-heroic Ayn Rand character; but this passage goes too far—there's a sadistic side to it that I don't think she wanted to attribute to Timoshenko. Further, the passage's level of detail is unnecessary and distracting. So it was reworded as follows:

Do you know what a revolution is? I'll tell you. We killed. We killed men in the streets, and in the cellars, and aboard our ships. . . . Aboard our ships . . . I remember . . . There was one boy—an officer—he couldn't have been more than twenty. He made the sign of the cross . . . (371).

Here's a passage from the scene of the climactic arrest of Leo Kovalensky, as found in the 1936 edition:

> Leo walked leisurely to the mirror, adjusted his tie, straightened his hair, with the meticulous precision of a man of the world dressing for an important social engagement. He pressed a few drops of toilet water on his handkerchief and folded it neatly in his breast pocket (490).

The toilet water had to go. An Ayn Rand hero does not splash on cologne or toilet water as a prelude to the firing squad, which is what Leo had every reason to expect. Here is the revised passage:

> Leo walked to the mirror and adjusted his tie, his coat, his hair, with the meticulous precision of a man dressing for an important social engagement. His fingers were not trembling any longer. He folded his handkerchief neatly and slipped it into his breast pocket (399).

Finally, given what we have seen so far, we should not be surprised to learn that some passages were reworded to avoid improper philosophical implications. Some could be quite minor. For example, Kira spoke the following line to Leo, expressing her concern that Soviet reality might be causing him to give up on life: "It can't do that to you" (445). Ayn Rand changed this to: "I won't let it do that to you" (364). At first glance, this may not seem like a significant change, but the original line, taken literally, implies that it is impossible for Leo to lose his battle against the Soviet state; and yet we know it is possible, because he does lose. Kira may turn out to be wrong when she says she "won't let it do that" to him, but she is no longer stating that it's impossible. Further, Rand is shifting the emphasis from Leo—who is increasingly passive with respect to his own survival—to Kira, who is a fierce fighter to the end.

As noted earlier, in her *Art of Nonfiction*, Ayn Rand warns us not to use "he had an instinct for courage" when all we want to say is "he is brave." She made just this sort of change in *We the Living*:

> And because she had a deep instinct against all things weighty and solemn, Kira had a solemn reverence for those songs of defiant gaiety (44),

became

> And because she felt a profound rebellion against the weighty, the tragic, the solemn, Kira had a solemn reverence for those songs of defiant gaiety (50).

In the scene describing Kira's Viking, the original has:

> a Viking who walked through life bringing destruction and reaping victories, who walked through ruins while the sun made a crown over his head (41).

This need not, but might, suggest that the Viking's purpose is destruction itself—that he fights simply to destroy. Thus the line needed to be changed. Note that Rand had no intention of softening the line to make the Viking's actions less destructive—the reference to walking through ruins, which she does not cut, makes that evident—but in the revision, she clarifies the purpose of the destruction:

> a Viking who walked through life, *breaking barriers* and reaping victories, who walked through ruins while the sun made a crown over his head (49, emphasis added).

In the 1936 version, we read that Kira, during her attempt to get Leo into a sanitarium for his tuberculosis, "learned firmly as a prayer that if one had consumption one had to be a member of a Trade Union" (262). But this implies that Kira (and Ayn Rand) believe that prayers are in fact "firm," that is, absolutely certain. Actually, Rand believed (in 1936 as well as in 1959) that prayers were irrational and unconnected to reality—and thus in no way "firm." Moreover, even to religious people, prayer doesn't convey absolute certainty. She therefore changed the line so that Kira now "learned, as firmly as if it were some mystical absolute, that if one had consumption one had to be a member of a Trade Union" (223). The change is very effective. First, "mystical absolute" subsumes prayer, but also includes divine commands and other religious notions, thus making the line even stronger and more precise. Second, the "as if" construction makes it clear that Kira (and Ayn Rand) do not regard mystical absolutes as real, which further conveys how out of reach a state sanitarium was for Leo (given the irrational nature of the ban). He didn't have a prayer.

SEX, CAPITALISM, AND NIETZSCHE

I have so far provided examples of all the different kinds of revisions Ayn Rand made to the original version of *We the Living*. I turn now to three areas in which she made some especially interesting, substantial, and in some cases controversial, changes.

Sex Changes

Ayn Rand made numerous changes to a number of love scenes, and they are worth considering in greater detail.

The first type of change under this heading involves revisions to scenes involving kissing, in which a change is made to bring the kissing in *We the Living* more in line with Ayn Rand's later (or more consciously developed) conception of male-female relationships. In every case, in the original, the two parties are equal or the woman is in control; whereas in the revised version, the man does the kissing. These are subtle, but interesting, changes.

> When houses rose close over the mast, [they kissed] <he kissed her>. (140/126)
> he bent [for a kiss] <to kiss her>. (255/216)
> Irina was standing by the window in Sasha's arms, [her lips on his] <his lips on hers>. (379/312)

Such changes, though slight, bring *We the Living* more in line with Rand's handling of romantic relationships in *The Fountainhead* and *Atlas Shrugged*.[8]

The second type of change under this heading is the cutting of details in love scenes. Some time between 1936 and 1959, Ayn Rand changed her mind about how much detail was necessary in describing love scenes. (Note that there is not a single such scene in which she embellished what was in the 1936 edition.)

I begin at the bottom, with Comrade Sonia and Pavel. The 1959 edition has:

> Comrade Sonia had pulled a chair close to Syerov's, and he sprawled, his head on her lap, while she stroked his hair. (353)

The original has pretty much the same, but adds: "His hand wandered slowly up her tunic" (292).

The five remaining examples all involve Leo and (with one exception) Kira. I start with Leo's first sexual encounter.

(1) He spent his first night in a woman's bed at the age of sixteen[; the bed had white, perfumed sheets, white and fragrant as the body of the woman who moaned, her arms crushing him imperiously, possessively] (156–57/138).
(2) she knew that his hand was on her breast [and his hand was hungrier than his lips] (107/101).
(3) Then they were on the bed, her whole weight on his hand spread wide between her naked shoulder blades. [Of her whole world there was only Leo, and of Leo there was only his hand, the other hand that moved slowly down pulling off one of her stockings, then returning to where the stocking had been, and higher, very slowly. His fingers were bruising, furrowing the skin under them, crawling up reluctantly,

digging into the flesh as if it could stop them. She did not move. Then
he got up and stood looking down at her. She lay very still as he had
left her, her one foot touching the floor.] Then he blew out the lantern.
She heard his sweater falling to the floor (136/123).

(4) She heard nothing in the silence [but her skin under his hands and the
bed trembling.] <but the sound of his breath.> She crushed her body
against his[; she did not know how hungry her thighs, and her hips,
and her stomach could be] (155/137).

(5) There was a contemptuous tenderness in his movement, and a command, and hunger; he was not a lover, but a slave owner[; she could
feel a whip in his fingers. She wanted to be crushed; she wished she
were lying still under a real whip in his hands] (398/326–27).

Why did Ayn Rand make these sorts of revisions? To return to her foreword to the 1959 edition, she said that she "cut out some sentences and a
few paragraphs that were repetitious or so confusing in their implications
that to clarify them would have necessitated lengthy additions" (xvi). None
of these is confusing in its implications. So she no doubt made these cuts
because she regarded them as, however well-written, repetitious or unnecessary. In each case, she wants to convey that the two parties are making love;
the details—the concretes—are unnecessary.[9]

Capitalism

A couple of passages in *We the Living* were changed in such a way that
they *might* be taken as evidence that Ayn Rand's conception of capitalism
changed between 1936 and 1959. The first is part of a long speech, made by
a communist who "had a little black beard, and wore a pince-nez" (374/308).
I quote the original at length, employing italics to indicate the interesting
revisions.

Comrades! A grave new danger has been growing among us in this last year. I
call it the danger of over-idealism. We've all heard the accusations of its deluded
victims. They cry that Communism has failed, that we've surrendered our principles, that since the introduction of NEP—our New Economic Policy—the Communist Party has been retreating, fleeing before a new form of *victorious
capitalism* which now rules our country. They claim that we're holding the
power for the sake of the power alone and have forgotten all ideals of Communism. Such is the whining of weaklings and cowards who cannot face practical
reality. It is true that we've had to abandon the policy of Military Communism
of the civil war years. It is true that we've had to make concessions to private
traders *and foreign capitalists*. Well, what of it? A retreat is not a defeat. A temporary compromise is not a surrender. *We are a lonely oasis in a world ruled
by capitalism.* We were betrayed by the spineless, weak-kneed, anemic social-

ists of foreign countries who sold out their working masses to their bourgeois masters. The World Revolution which was to make a pure world Communism possible, has been delayed. We, therefore, have had to compromise for the time being. *What if we do have private stores and private profit? What if we are learning capitalistic methods of production?* What if we do have inequality of wages? What if some foul speculators in our midst do make exorbitant profits in spite of our implacable struggle against them? Our time is a transitory period of proletarian state building. (374–75/308–9)

Rand made four significant changes:

(1) In the line "the Communist Party has been retreating, fleeing before a new form of victorious capitalism which now rules our country," "victorious capitalism" is replaced by "private profiteering."
(2) In the line "It is true that we've had to make concessions to private traders and foreign capitalists," she cut "and foreign capitalists."
(3) She cut the line "We are a lonely oasis in a world ruled by capitalism."
(4) She cut the lines "What if we do have private stores and private profit? What if we are learning capitalistic methods of production?"

There are likely two related reasons for these changes. First, she may have concluded that the speech in the original version was too pro-capitalist for a communist—even one as pragmatic and compromising as the man who delivered this speech. Second, she probably wanted to eliminate any chance that one might take this passage to imply that she believed (a) that outside Soviet Russia is a world ruled by capitalism, and (b) that the "concessions" the Soviets made to stay afloat were actual concessions to capitalism—that the private profiteering (best represented in the novel by Morozov) had anything in common with genuine capitalism.

Another passage involving capitalism is somewhat more difficult to explain. Describing the failure of Alexander Argounov's first business venture under communism (contrasting his failure with the successes of speculators), Ayn Rand writes (in the first edition): "the dreaded word 'speculator' gave him a cold shiver; and he was not born a business man" (97). This line is objectionable in that it suggests (1) that those who succeed at business are born with their talent; (2) that speculators and businessmen are the same; and (3) that the man behind the Argounov textile factory was *not* a businessman. Therefore, Rand changed the second part of the line to: "he lacked the talents of a racketeer" (92).

Does the original line suggest that in 1936 Ayn Rand had a lower view of businessmen? This is unlikely, especially given her portrayals of Vasili Dunaev and Alexander Argounov in *We the Living*, and her admiration for her father (a successful businessman—he owned a pharmacy) in real life. That having been said, I do not know what she intended in writing that Alexander Argounov "was not born a business man." In any case, by 1959, she was more aware of or sensitive to the false implications of such a line, and thus changed it.

The "Nietzschean" Passages[10]

I begin with three passages that might imply that Ayn Rand held the Nietzschean view that we are born to be the kind of people we are—to have the characters we have.

(1) In the passage just discussed, Ayn Rand writes that Alexander Argounov "was not born a business man" (97). She changed this to "he lacked the talents of a racketeer" (92).

(2) The following passage was not changed: "The revolution . . . found Leo Kovalensky with a slow, contemptuous smile, and a swift gait, and in his hand a lost whip he had been born to carry" (157/139).

(3) In the following passage, Rand left in—in a revised form—"born without the conception of bending," but removed "born to rule" and "born to live":

> He moved as if his whole body were a living will, straight, arrogant, commanding, a will and a body that could never bend because both had been born without the [conception] <capacity to conceive> of bending[, born to rule as they had been born to live].
>
> She stood [motionless] <still>, afraid to approach him, afraid to shatter one of the rare moments when he looked what he could have been, what he was [born] <intended> to be. (397–98/326)

Ayn Rand uses such "born with" or "born to be" language in *Anthem, Night of January 16th* and *The Fountainhead* as well. For example, Equality 7-2521 was "born with a curse" and "born with a head which is too quick"; Bjorn Faulkner was "born with life singing in his veins"; Gail Wynand was not "born to be a second-hander."[11]

We should not conclude too quickly that these passages are strong evidence of an earlier Nietzschean phase in Ayn Rand's development, because such language can be strictly metaphorical (even if the result of an early interest in Nietzsche). For example, one can call someone a born loser—or as Ayn Rand describes Ellsworth Toohey in her notes for *The Fountainhead*, "a born enemy of everything heroic"[12]—without that necessitating any kind of determinism. However, because it *could* be taken as deterministic, Rand removed most of this language from *We the Living*. Philosophically, at *most* these passages suggest that when she wrote *We the Living*, she was not entirely clear about the nature of human volition. For example, she may not have seen fully the contradiction between human volition—which is obviously embodied in the actions of the characters in *We the Living*—and the existence of innate characteristics.[13]

Before I turn to the more substantive and problematic passages, I want to look at a 1965 letter that Ayn Rand wrote to a high school student. The student had asked her a series of questions concerning problems he had with certain passages in her fiction, and she answered them. For example:

> You quote Karen Andre's line in *Night of January 16th*: "I am capable of murder—for Faulkner's sake," and ask: "Isn't murder a violation of the Objectivist Ethics? Doesn't this statement make Karen Andre an Attila?" The answer is: Yes, murder is a violation of the Objectivist ethics. No, this statement does not make Karen Andre an Attila. It is not to be taken literally, it is merely her deliberate challenge to the moral philosophy propounded by Mr. Flint [the District Attorney] and an expression of the intensity of her love for Bjorn Faulkner. . . .

Rand then gives this fan the following advice, which I suggest we keep in mind when investigating the so-called Nietzschean passages from the first edition of *We the Living*:

> Now that I have answered your specific questions, let me give you an important suggestion: do not read any statement out of context, particularly when you read fiction. In analyzing the philosophical ideas presented in fiction, you must identify the total meaning of the story, of its plot, its main events and its characters. You must never judge any incident out of context, and this applies particularly to the dialogue. In real life and in fiction, people do not speak in terms of precise, legalistic philosophical definitions. This does not mean that people contradict philosophical principles, but it means that one must learn to distinguish when a particular statement does represent a precise definition and when it is a verbal part of a wider whole. In reading literature, one must learn how to analyze its parts, but one must never forget to put them together again, that is, one must know how to analyze and how to integrate.[14]

Interestingly, Ayn Rand was herself, in real life, capable of fitting the dialogue to the situation. For example, following a lecture she gave in 1974, she was asked the following unsympathetic question: "In the event that you rewrote your novels, would you liberate your heroines, and change the way they subject themselves to passive behavior in romance?" She responded: "Dagny is very passive: In *Atlas Shrugged*, she's nearly raped three times, by the three men in her life. Dominique, the heroine of *The Fountainhead, is* raped. If this is passivity, make the most of it."[15] I submit that this is Rand's "deliberate challenge" to this questioner—that it is her way of being defiant, of making it clear to the questioner (and the audience generally) that if he expects her in any way to retreat from or feel awkward about her conception of men and women, and the love scenes that express it, he should think twice. Because as stated, this answer does *not* represent her actual view of

the "rape" scene in *The Fountainhead*. I again quote from that same letter
to a fan:

> You say you were asked whether "the rape of Dominique Francon by Howard
> Roark was a violation of Dominique's freedom, an act of force that was contrary
> to the Objectivist Ethics?" The answer is: of course not. It was not an actual rape,
> but a symbolic action which Dominique all but invited. This was the action she
> wanted and Howard Roark knew it.[16]

I suggest that in evaluating the following "Nietzschean" passages, we keep
in mind that Kira was a lot like her creator, and that in her first ideological
confrontation with Andrei, she perhaps spoke in an exaggerated way. She
certainly exaggerated the differences between them the first time they
learned each others' names:

> "Are you going home, *Comrade Argounova?*" he asked.
> "Yes, *Comrade Taganov.*"
> "Would you mind if you're compromised by being seen with a very red Com-
> munist?"
> "Not at all—if your reputation won't be tarnished by being seen with a very
> white lady." (88)

Kira (like Rand) did not really regard herself as a "white" (to use the language of the Russian Civil War), which generally stood for God and country—Holy Mother Russia. But in this exchange, Kira purposely underscores
the contrast between Andrei and herself.[17]

The importance of the above points is that we should not make too much
of the ideological content of the "Nietzschean" passages. As will be seen,
their content is misleading—which is why they were changed. It could be
that in what follows, all that these revisions represent is the removal of what
is misleading, and not any change in Ayn Rand's actual convictions.

I present and analyze these pairs of passages—(a) the original and (b) the
revision—in the order in which they appear in the novel.

(1) Kira to Victor:

> (a) It is an eternal, unpleasant necessity that the masses should exist and make
> their existence felt. This is a time when they make it felt particularly unpleas-
> antly. (53)
> (b) It is an old and ugly fact that the masses exist and make their existence felt.
> This is a time when they make it felt with particular ugliness. (58)[18]

Passage (1), unlike the others, does not involve Andrei. This is significant,
in that an important part of understanding the other passages is that Andrei

sets the context and the terms of the discussion. But in passage (1), Kira is speaking to Victor (and other relatives), which may suggest that the line expresses her (and perhaps Rand's) own view. Rand may have believed, in her early years, that what she saw everywhere around her in Soviet Russia— the masses existing and claiming the right to sacrifice the best people—was not simply an ugly Soviet aberration, but was something metaphysical, that is, built into the nature of human existence. Passage (1a) lends some support to this possibility. The best evidence, however, that (1a) was not a mere slip but represents an actual conviction of Ayn Rand's (however ambiguously held) are her 1928 notes to a novel she was planning to write but later abandoned, entitled "The Little Street" (which I can merely refer to here).[19]

But even if she did hold such a view, she did not hold it for long. For example, by the time *The Fountainhead* was published (in 1943), she had a radically different view of the American worker (exemplified by the character Mike Donnigan), who she regarded as independent and proud. In 1947, she wrote that "America is the land of the *uncommon man*. . . . No self-respecting man in America is or thinks of himself as 'little,' no matter how poor he might be. That is precisely the difference between an American working man and a European serf."[20]

What remains untouched in passage (1) is her loathing for the *Soviet* masses. She makes it clear in *We the Living* that she regards them as partly responsible for the Communists being in power—that the Soviet masses were complicit in the Communists' sacrifice of the best people. Consider, for example, what Ayn Rand wrote, before *We the Living* was published, about Ivan Ivanov, Kira's killer:

> After the reader has seen Kira Argounova, has learned what a rare, precious, irreplaceable human being she was—I give him the picture of the man who killed Kira Argounova, of the life that took her life. That soldier is a symbol, a typical representative of the average, the dull, the useless, the commonplace, the masses—that killed the best there is on this earth. I believe I made this obvious when I concluded his biography by saying—quoting from the book: "Citizen Ivan Ivanov was guarding the border of the Union of Socialist Soviet Republics." Citizen Ivan Ivanov *is* the Union of Socialist Soviet Republics. And that Union killed Kira Argounova. Kira Argounova against citizen Ivan Ivanov— that is the whole book in a few pages.[21]

The remaining passages all appear in conversations between Kira and Andrei, and four of them (2–5) occur in a relatively brief section of one chapter (92–94/89–90). This is extremely important, because (i) these passages represent a *very* small percentage of the novel, and in their original versions they seem to conflict with the rest of the novel, and (ii) in these passages, Andrei sets the terms of the discussion, and Kira reacts to him (which perhaps suggests that in the first edition, when Kira discusses politics with

Andrei, her views are warped by Andrei's own language, ideas, and choice of topics).

(2) Kira to Andrei:

> (a) Haven't you ever wanted a thing for no reason of right or wrong, for no reason at all, save one: that *you* wanted it? (92)
>
> (b) Haven't you ever wanted a thing for no reason save one: that *you* wanted it? (89)

Passage (2a) is unproblematic. At a superficial glance it may sound as if Kira condones action done without regard for what is right and wrong— "beyond good and evil"; but such an interpretation does not hold up. (2a) almost certainly refers to *Andrei's* discussion of right and wrong, or *his* standards, in which case Kira is asking if he ever thinks of his own happiness apart from what the party considers right and wrong. But (2a) does not clearly state this, which is why Rand revised it.

(3) Andrei (speaking first) and Kira:

> (a) "I know what you're going to say. You're going to say, as so many of our enemies do, that you admire our ideals, but loathe our methods."
>
> "I loathe your ideals. I admire your methods. If one believes one's right, one shouldn't wait to convince millions of fools, one might just as well force them. Except that I don't know, however, whether I'd include blood in my methods."
>
> "Why not? Anyone can sacrifice his own life for an idea. How many know the devotion that makes you capable of sacrificing other lives? Horrible, isn't it?"
>
> "Admirable. If you're right. But—are you right?"
>
> "Why do you loathe our ideals?"
>
> "For one reason, mainly, chiefly and eternally, no matter how much your Party promises to accomplish, no matter what paradise it plans to bring mankind. Whatever your other claims may be, there's one you can't avoid, one that will rise to the surface as a deadly poison to turn your paradise into the most unspeakable of all hells: your claim that man must live for the state." (92–93)
>
> (b) "I know what you're going to say. You're going to say, as so many of our enemies do, that you admire our ideals, but loathe our methods."
>
> "I loathe your ideals."
>
> "Why?" (89)[22]

Passage (3a) certainly sounds Nietzschean and amoral; and I think it's clear that when Ayn Rand wrote this passage she had not yet identified (fully) the evil of the initiation of force. But note that even here, Kira is reluctant to advocate bloodshed: "I don't know . . . whether I'd include blood in my methods." Kira is ambivalent (or ambiguous) here: she seems to advocate force, but not bloodshed.

I think there are two ways of taking this exchange between Kira and Andrei: (i) Kira could be saying that if a group of people think they are right, they are free to try to force others to follow them (and even enslave and kill if necessary); or (ii) she could be saying that if a group of people *are* right, even if they are a minority, they can establish a proper form of government against the wishes of the majority. Ayn Rand was never a defender of democracy, in any strict sense of the term. For example, if the Founding Fathers had been a minority (the majority being royalists), it would have been perfectly moral for them to use their army to impose "by force" a constitution on the country—one that guaranteed individual rights. They would not be obliged to wait for the rest of the people to come to see that a constitutional form of government is superior to monarchy. (This is only an example; I'm not suggesting that Ayn Rand had the Founding Fathers in mind when she wrote this passage.) Of course, it isn't clear that (ii) is the proper interpretation of (3a); and (i) is the more natural way to take the passage, especially given Kira's statement "If one believes one's right." In fact, I think the most likely explanation is not that either (i) or (ii) is correct, but that when Rand first wrote the passage, she did not fully or clearly see the difference between (i) and (ii)—between Andrei and the communists forcing their ideas on Russia, and the American Founding Fathers, say, "forcing" their views on royalist Americans. Because of this confusion or error, the passage was changed.

Moving on, what is the implication of Kira saying: "Admirable"? What does she find admirable? She clearly does not admire Andrei's *ideals*. So, she must be referring to his willingness to fight for what he thinks is right (which is a possible way of reading this) and/or his willingness to sacrifice others. If it is his willingness to sacrifice others that Kira admires (and that's the most natural way to take this line) in what sense does she mean it? The next line is: "If you're right. But—are you right?" Kira is probably saying that Andrei's willingness to sacrifice others is admirable, *if* he is right about communism being the proper social system; but he is not right.

So, there is nothing about passage (3a) that forces us to conclude that Ayn Rand at one time defended some kind of Nietzschean amoralism. What we can say, however, is that the philosophical implications of passage (3a) are dubious and confused, and hence it had to be rewritten.

The most important part of passage (3)—basically the same in both versions—is Kira's statement about why she loathes Andrei's ideals: "the claim that man must live for the state." Kira's disagreement with Andrei here contains the essence of her political philosophy in *We the Living*—in '36 as well as in '59—and it is pure Ayn Rand, *not* Friedrich Nietzsche.

(4) Kira to Andrei:

> (a) Don't you know that we live only for ourselves, the best of us do, those who are worth leaving alive? (93)

(b) Don't you know that we live only for ourselves, the best of us do, those who are worthy of it? (89)

The context of passage (4) is a discussion about sacrificing lives for what is right. The important part of the line—the part Rand changed—is "those who are worth leaving alive." This certainly could be taken to mean that whether or not someone is left alive should be up to the best people in society. However, the passage is unclear, because "those who are worth leaving alive" could simply refer to those who deserve life—i.e., those who have not betrayed it, who have not declared war against those who truly know it. But the passage as written is unfortunate in its implications—it is more naturally read in the first sense—and so it was changed.

(5) Kira to Andrei, on sacrificing millions for the sake of the few:

> (a) You can! You must. When those few are the best. Deny the best its right to the top—and you have no best left. What *are* your masses but mud to be ground under foot, fuel to be burned for those who deserve it? What is the people but millions of puny, shriveled, helpless souls that have no thoughts of their own, no dreams of their own, no will of their own, who eat and sleep and chew helplessly the words others put into their mildewed brains? And for those you would sacrifice the few who know life, who *are* life? I loathe your ideals because I know no worse injustice than justice for all. Because men are not born equal and I don't see why one should want to make them equal. And because I loathe most of them. (93–94)
>
> (b) Can you sacrifice the few? When those few are the best? Deny the best its right to the top—and you have no best left. What are your masses but millions of dull, shriveled, stagnant souls that have no thoughts of their own, no dreams of their own, no will of their own, who eat and sleep and chew helplessly the words others put into their brains? And for those you would sacrifice the few who know life, who *are* life? I loathe your ideals because I know no worse injustice than the giving of the undeserved. Because men are not equal in ability and one can't treat them as if they were. And because I loathe most of them. (90)

Passage (5a) contains two elements, each of which can be taken in more than one way. First, Kira's remarks about sacrificing the worst for the few best could mean: (i) we must sacrifice the best in society for the sake of the worst, or the worst for the sake of the best, and the latter is obviously the best choice; or (ii) in the Soviet Union, there is a war between the best in society and the worst, and the best should win. Rand certainly believed (ii), but in 1936 she may have accepted (i) as well—or failed to see the difference between (i) and (ii). But it is also possible that (iii) Kira is saying that although we need not in fact choose between sacrificing the best and sacrificing the worst, *if* that were the choice (as Andrei suggests it is) then we should not sacrifice the best. Hank Rearden will later say as much in *Atlas Shrugged*:

> If it were true that men could achieve their good by means of turning some men into sacrificial animals, and I were asked to immolate myself for the sake of creatures who wanted to survive at the price of my blood, if I were asked to serve the interests of society apart from, above and against my own, I would refuse. I would reject it as the most contemptible evil, I would fight it with every power I possess, I would fight the whole of mankind, if one minute were all I could last before I were murdered, I would fight in the full confidence of the justice of my battle and of a living being's right to exist. Let there be no misunderstanding about me. If it is now the belief of my fellow men, who call themselves the public, that their good requires victims, then I say: The public good be damned, I will have no part of it![23]

In *Atlas Shrugged*, it clear that Ayn Rand did not believe the "public good" required victims. In any case, since the passage is unclear, and by 1959 she certainly rejected (i), this part of (5a) was revised accordingly.

Second, Kira's remarks on equality could be taken to mean: (i) political equality is wrong—the best and the worst should not be treated the same (which includes their not having the same rights); or (ii) egalitarianism (the idea that the best should not rise above the lowest) is wrong. Rand always believed (ii) and there's little evidence she ever believed (i)—though at the time she wrote *We the Living*, she may not have seen clearly the difference between them. Since the remarks in the original are unclear, she made the revision.[24]

(6) Kira to Andrei:

> (a) You have a right to kill, as all fighters have. But no one before you has ever thought of forbidding life to those still living. (211)
> (b) You may claim the right to kill, as all fighters do. But no one before you has ever thought of forbidding life to those still living. (189)

In light of what we have seen—and considering the context of the entire novel—there is no reason to think that when passage (6a) was written, Kira (or Rand) actually believed that if a person thought he was right, then he was justified in killing others. It's more likely that this line was simply imprecisely written, and so was revised in 1959.

The original versions of the above six passages might seem to contain the following Nietzschean ideas—all of which Rand rejected in her later, mature philosophy:[25]

I. The existence of the masses—an ugly, low, worthless herd of people—is a necessary fact; they simply (but unfortunately) do exist.

II. Either the masses sacrifice the best for the sake of the masses, or the
best sacrifice the masses for the sake of the best. There is no other
option.

III. Each of the best people should live only for himself, a fact which justifies actions that are beyond good and evil, for example, the use of
force and even killing.

IV. One should not strive for *any* kind of equality, including political
equality.

The confusing implications of the "Nietzschean" passages in *We the Living*
are at most a residue of Ayn Rand's early exposure to Nietzsche (though they
do not add up to some full-blown Nietzschean "phase"). We are told that
Leo sometimes quotes Nietzsche (156/138); and, early in her life, Ayn Rand
admired (what she took to be) the philosophy of Nietzsche. But which of
these four Nietzschean views, if any, did she ever actually hold? She probably accepted View I for a time in the twenties and thirties; and, she *may* have
believed View II at some level and for some period. But there's little evidence that she ever held Views III or IV (and beyond the above "confused"
passages, there is no evidence at all).

The "Nietzschean" passages—especially when interpreted unsympathet-
ically—contradict the spirit of the novel. For outside of these passages,
Kira—the heroine—is not Nietzschean but Objectivist: she is against sacrifice
of all kinds; she wants political freedom—freedom from the rule of the
masses and from any other tyrant; she values the lives of others, and she acts
not beyond good and evil, but with a heroic moral stature. In both the original and revised versions, *We the Living* is about the importance of the individual and of political freedom, and what happens to an individual when
political freedom is denied (as it was in Soviet Russia). The Nietzschean ideas
outlined above conflict with the novel's theme.

Whatever Nietzschean influence—or rather, Nietzschean flavor—there
might be evidence for in a few passages in the first edition of *We the Living*,
Ayn Rand later made explicit her complete rejection of Nietzsche's philosophy. For example, here is what she said about him, in a 1965 interview:

Nietzsche has certain very attractive, very wise quotations purported to uphold
individualism with which one could agree out of context. But excepting his general "feeling for" individualism, I would not consider Nietzsche an individualist;
and above all, he is certainly not an upholder of reason. . . . In all fundamentals—particularly metaphysics, epistemology and ethics—Objectivism not only
differs from Nietzsche but is his opposite. Therefore, I don't want to be confused
with Nietzsche in any respect.[26]

CONCLUSION

Ayn Rand's foreword to the 1959 edition of *We the Living* opens: "I had not reread this novel as a whole, since the time of its first publication in 1936, until a few months ago. I had not expected to be as proud of it as I am" (xiii). In her revision, she improved the novel without changing its essence. Whatever grammatical or stylistic problems and philosophical confusions existed in the original, "The novel remains what and as it was" (xvii).[27] It had the same plot, the same characters, the same theme. She was right to be proud of it.[28]

APPENDIX: THE BRITISH EDITION

A few months after the American first edition of *We the Living* appeared, a British edition was published by Cassell & Co., Ltd. It sold much better than the American edition (at least in part because Macmillan destroyed the type, limiting the American first edition to 3,000 copies), going into at least seven printings, and remaining in print until the mid-1940s.

This British edition was not identical to the American, however, and it is worth indicating the nature of the differences. (Note that I have not made an exhaustive study of this edition.)

Most are minor differences in spelling. Here is a sample (giving the American word first): toward (7), towards (5); theater (7), theatre (5); Traveled (14, Travelled (11); labor (30), labour (26); honor (51), honour (47); esthetic (53), æsthetic (49); jail (55), gaol (51); today (107), to-day (101); gray (374), grey (362); sniveling (376), snivelling (363); color (569), colour (552).

Some American words were replaced by their British equivalents, though there were not as many cases of this as I expected (e.g., "elevator" was not replaced with "lift," nor "line" with "queue").[29] For example, "truck" in the American version (e.g., 58 and 117) is replaced with "lorry" in the British (e.g., 49 and 123). In the American first edition, the young Ivan Ivanov was "beaten with leather suspenders" (563); in the British, he is "beaten with a leather belt" (546). The American word "cookies" appears three times in *We the Living*. In the first case—"a tray of home-made cookies" (132)—the British edition replaces "cookies" with "sweets" (125); in the second, "potato skin cookies" (180) becomes "potato skin cakes" (172); in the third, there is oddly no change in the British edition: "And here's the tea. And some cookies" (308/298).

Some word changes involved more than merely differences between British and American usage. For example, in the American edition, Timoshenko tells Leo: "Make your little whore keep quiet" (139); the British edition replaced "whore" with "trollop" (132). The "Because" scene, which ends with "Leo Kovalensky was sentenced to die," includes: "On a sack of flour in the basement, a man tore a woman's pants off" (270). In the British edition, the second clause is changed to "a man tore a woman's dress off" (259). Finally, whereas in the American edition, Marisha has an abortion (216), in the British, she has a miscarriage (207).

I encountered a couple of other minor differences. First, song titles are in quotes in the American edition, and italicized in the British: e.g., "John Gray" and "Song of Broken Glass" (244–45), *John Gray* and *Song of Broken Glass* (234–35). An interesting typo in the British edition, involving the title of an operetta, seems to combine these two approaches, making use of italics and *one* quotation mark: "*Bajadere* (234). Second, in at least one case, there is a difference in punctuation and capitalization:

"Congratulations, pal," someone slapped Pavel Syerov's shoulder. (376)
"Congratulations, pal." Someone slapped Pavel Syerov's shoulder. (364)

In the body of the chapter, I describe typographical and grammatical errors that Ayn Rand corrected for the 1959 edition. So far as I can tell, the British edition does not contain corrections of any of the grammatical errors, though it does correct *some* of the typos. For example: the British edition has "Sachs" (43) instead of "Sachs'" (47), "wardrobe" (200) instead of "warhobe" (210), "Galina" (533) instead of "Galine" (549), and "your" (18) instead of "our" (21). In the following two examples, however, the British edition contains the same typo as the American: "Swans' Lake" instead of "Swan Lake" (211/220), and "mowing" instead of "moving" (545/561).

There are more significant differences in two of the love scenes. In both cases, the British edition cuts parts that were considered inappropriate. Ayn Rand approved of these changes (which is not to say she was pleased with them—more on that shortly). In a June 3, 1936, letter to the Managing Director of Cassell, Sir Newman Flower, she writes:

I am perfectly willing to make the changes suggested, for I consider the somewhat too frank love passages as the least important ones in the book and I certainly would not want to let them handicap the novel as a whole or detract any possible buyers from it. I do approve of the changes made and I have marked them on each galley with my initials.[30]

Here are the two scenes, as found in both editions. I begin with the briefest:

(1) (a) *American*.[31]
She crushed her body against his; [she did not know how hungry her thighs, and her hips, and her stomach could be]. (155/137)

(b) *British*.
She crushed her body against his; she did not know how hungry it could be.
(147)

(2) (a) *American*.
     She rose slowly, obediently, looking up at him. She stood still as if his eyes
were holding her on a leash.
     He said:
     "Take your clothes off."
     She said nothing and did not take her eyes off of his, and obeyed.
     [It was difficult to unfasten the hooks of her skirt, for she could not look
down at her hands, she could not blink, her eyes in his.]
     He stood watching her. She did not think of the thoughts of the world she
had left. But that world came back once, for an instant, when she saw her skirt
on the floor. Then she regretted that her underwear was not silk, but only heavy
[Soviet] cotton.
     She unbuttoned the shirt strap on her shoulder and let it fall under her breast.
She was going to unbutton the other strap, but he tore her off the ground, and
then she was arched limply in the air, [her legs hanging between his,] her hair
hanging over his arm, her breast at his mouth.
     Then they were on the bed, her whole weight on his hand spread wide
between her naked shoulder blades. [Of her whole world there was only Leo,
and of Leo there was only his hand, the other hand that moved slowly down
pulling off one of her stockings, then returning to where the stocking had been,
and higher, very slowly. His fingers were bruising, furrowing the skin under
them, crawling up reluctantly, digging into the flesh as if it could stop them. She
did not move. Then he got up and stood looking down at her. She lay very still
as he had left her, her one foot touching the floor.]
     Then he blew out the lantern. She heard his sweater falling to the floor.
     Then she felt his legs like a warm liquid against hers. Her hair fell over the
edge of the bed. His lips parted in a snarl. (136/123)

(b) *British*.
     She rose slowly, obediently, looking up at him. She stood still as if his eyes
were holding her on a leash.
     He said:
     "Take your clothes off."
     She said nothing and did not take her eyes off of his, and obeyed. (129)

Of passage (2), Rand wrote in her letter to Flower:

On galley 39, in the most objectionable scene of the book, I cut out the entire
ending of the scene. I think you will agree with me that it is better to do so. The
only importance of the scene is the psychology of Kira's surrender in a cold,
tense, matter-of-fact manner, without the usual sentimental love-making. I have
kept enough of the scene to suggest this. The rest—the description of physical
details—is not really important. Particularly if the strongest lines are cut out of

the last paragraphs, the remaining lines have very little meaning, since they do not even create a definite mood. So I think it is best to omit these last paragraphs entirely. It will be safer and the story as such will not suffer from the omission.[32]

In a letter to Leonard Read, Ayn Rand wrote of the 1937 British edition: "It's the same as the American edition, except that my love scenes have been slightly censored, unfortunately."[33] So, she was "perfectly willing to make the changes," since they were not important enough "to let them handicap the novel;" but she was nevertheless displeased at having to make them. This must in part explain why, in the 1959 edition, she included more of love scene (2) than is found in the 1937 British edition, though she did leave out the most explicit of the "somewhat too frank love passages."

NOTES

1. See Richard E. Ralston, "Publishing *We the Living*," in the present volume for more on the publication history of *We the Living*.

2. Ayn Rand, *The Art of Nonfiction: A Guide for Writers and Readers*, Robert Mayhew, ed. (New York: Plume, 2001), 102–3.

3. Whenever two numbers are given in this way, the first refers to the page number in the 1936 edition, the second in the 1996 paperback edition. With rare (and obvious) exceptions, square brackets [ ] indicate a deletion, pointed brackets <> an addition.

4. On the issue of paragraphing, a brief survey of some American novels published in the thirties was inconclusive: the manner in which Rand used paragraphing in dialogue (in 1936) was neither standard nor unique.

5. Shoshana Milgram pointed out to me that the Russian word for both "as" and "like" is the same: *kak*.

6. Rand, *Art of Nonfiction*, 119.

7. In the early seventies, commenting on McGovern's campaign for the presidency, Rand quotes this line from a McGovern speech—"Come home to the affirmation that we have a dream"—and comments: "'Dream,' like 'imagination,' is a very dubious kind of attribute or compliment. Its value or disvalue depends on its relation to reality." From "A Preview," Part III, *The Ayn Rand Letter* 1, no. 24 (August 28, 1972).

8. A word-search for "kiss" and its cognates in *The Fountainhead* and *Atlas Shrugged* supplies ample evidence for this.

9. That she did regard these details as unnecessary to the love scenes, see the Appendix on the 1937 British Edition, pp. 215–17.

The love scenes in *The Fountainhead* and *Atlas Shrugged* tend to be more elaborate than those in *We the Living* (both editions)—especially concerning the meaning of the scenes and what the lovers are feeling—while being less detailed about concretes than the 1936 edition. See, for example, *The Fountainhead* (New York: Bobbs-Merrill, 1947; Signet fiftieth anniversary paperback edition, 1993), 216–19, 273–74,

282–85, 483–84, and *Atlas Shrugged* (New York: Random House, 1953; Signet thirty-fifth anniversary paperback edition, 1992), 106–7, 239–41, 255–56, 600, 887–88.

10. What is needed to understand fully the sources and nature of these "Nietz-schean" passages is a detailed and scholarly account of Ayn Rand's early intellectual development, which cannot be undertaken here. Given limitations of space, I merely provide brief comments that offer some suggestions on how best to understand these passages.

11. Ayn Rand, *Anthem*, fiftieth anniversary edition (New York: Signet, 1995), 18, 20, 21; Ayn Rand, *Night of January 16th*, final revised edition (New York: Plume, 1987), 118; Rand, *The Fountainhead*, 609, 664.

12. David Harriman, ed., *Journals of Ayn Rand* (New York: Plume, 1997), 89.

13. See Harriman, *Journals*, 21.

14. Michael S. Berliner, ed., *Letters of Ayn Rand* (New York: Dutton, 1995), 631–32.

15. Q&A period following Ayn Rand's 1974 Boston Ford Hall Forum lecture, "Egalitarianism and Inflation."

16. Berliner, *Letters*, 631.

17. Compare this description of Leo's attitude toward the Reds and Whites:

Resenting the portrait of the Czar in his father's study and the Admiral's unflinching, unreasoning loyalty, Leo attended a secret meeting of young revolutionists. But when an unshaved young man made a speech about men's brotherhood and called him "comrade," Leo whistled "God Save the Czar," and went home. (138)

18. Compare the following line, which Andrei speaks to Kira: "no matter what human wreckage [I have to see] <I see around me>, I still have you" (408/335).

19. Harriman, *Journals*, 20–48.

20. Ayn Rand, "Screen Guide for Americans," in Harriman, *Journals*, 362. (See the entire section entitled "Don't Deify 'The Common Man.'") Cf. the passage from her essay "Altruism as Appeasement" (1966), in *The Voice of Reason: Essays in Objectivist Thought*, Leonard Peikoff, ed. (New York: New American Library, 1988), in which she makes clear her rejection of what she calls the "elitist" premise, i.e., "the dogmatic, unshakeable belief that 'the masses don't think,' that men are impervious to reason, that thinking is the exclusive prerogative of a small, 'chosen' minority" (36).

21. Berliner, *Letters*, 18. See also Ayn Rand's description of Ivan Ivanov in *We the Living* (458–60).

22. Kira responds as in (3a).

23. Rand, *Atlas Shrugged*, 452.

24. In a 1950 letter, Ayn Rand writes that Kira's statement about knowing of no worse injustice than justice for all "is a bad sentence when taken out of context." Berliner, *Letters*, 463.

25. I cannot go into interpretive questions about whether or to what extent Nietzsche did hold these ideas. I think he did, and I follow the standard outlook in so thinking; but there are scholarly debates on these issues. The important point here is that in certain passages, Rand *seems* to accept some of these views, although they are not part of her own philosophy.

26. The Ayn Rand Program, WKCR radio, 1965. See also Harry Binswanger, ed.,

The Ayn Rand Lexicon: Objectivism from A to Z (New York: New American Library, 1986), s.v. Nietzsche.

27. There is no contradiction in saying that the novel was, in essence, unchanged, though parts of the novel were changed (which is basically what Rand says in her foreword). To think otherwise is to commit what in logic is called the Fallacy of Division: what is true of the whole must be true of all of the parts (i.e., it is to maintain that ' *We the Living* as a whole remains the novel it was in 1936' implies 'every part of *We the Living* remains what it was in 1936').

28. I wish to thank Shoshana Milgram and Tore Boeckmann for their comments on earlier versions of this chapter, and Harry Binswanger for his comments on the last section. Finally, thanks are due Allan Gotthelf, who, in the mid-1980s, first brought to my attention the question of a possible Nietzschean influence on the 1936 edition of *We the Living*.

29. In a letter to William H. Steer, of Cassell's editorial department (September 2, 1936), she thanks "the editor [apparently someone other than Steer] for his splendid work in replacing some of the American words I used by their English counterparts."

30. Letter from Ayn Rand to Newman Flower, June 3, 1936, Ayn Rand Archives.

31. Square brackets indicate sections omitted in the 1959 edition. I indicate no other differences.

32. Letter from Rand to Flower, June 3, 1936.

33. Letter from Ayn Rand to Leonard Read, November 30, 1945 (Ayn Rand Archives).

II

WE THE LIVING AS LITERATURE AND AS PHILOSOPHY

10

We the Living and Victor Hugo: Ayn Rand's First Novel and the Novelist She Ranked First

Shoshana Milgram

Ayn Rand loved the novels of Victor Hugo. She loved his work when she discovered it in her childhood; she loved it when she reread his novels throughout her life; she loved it when she paid her highest tribute to his genius, calling him "the greatest novelist in world literature."[1] She said: "I love the work of Victor Hugo, in a deeper sense than admiration for his superlative literary genius, and I find many similarities between his sense of life and mine, although I disagree with virtually all of his explicit philosophy."[2] Her love not only went far beyond the respect of one artist for another, but also outweighed her disagreement with his explicit ideas.

A full account of her love for Hugo would take into account her public commentary on his work: her analysis of his prose style in her lectures on fiction-writing, her introductions to editions of Hugo's *Ninety-Three* (*Quatre-vingt-Treize*) and *The Man Who Laughs* (*L'Homme qui rit*), her remarks in numerous lectures and essays (some reprinted in *The Romantic Manifesto*). Her unpublished commentary, also extensive, includes more than twenty pages of notes on *Ninety-Three* and more than thirty pages of a translation of the opening of *The Man Who Laughs*.

Even in nonliterary contexts, she quotes him more than she quotes any artist other than herself. In her preface to the 1968 edition of *The Fountainhead*, for example, she quotes from a letter he wrote about the public neglect of *The Man Who Laughs*: "If a writer wrote merely for his time, I would have to break my pen and throw it away."[3] The title image of "The Comprachicos"

(1970)—an indictment of the spiritual torture of children at the hands of contemporary educators—is drawn from the second chapter of the same novel (in which the torture and deformity are literal).[4] In "From the Horse's Mouth" (1975), she quotes from book 5, chapter 2 of Hugo's *Notre Dame of Paris* ("This will kill that") to describe the relationship between two works: an 1898 book by Friedrich Paulsen praising Kant and the play *Cyrano de Bergerac* of the previous year.[5] She quotes Hugo in the conclusion to her 1972 article ("The Stimulus and the Response") on B. F. Skinner's *Beyond Freedom and Dignity.*

> In *Les Misérables*, describing the development of an independent young man, Victor Hugo wrote: ". . . and he blesses God for having given him these two riches which many of the rich are lacking: work, which gives him freedom, and thought, which gives him dignity."
>
> I doubt that B. F. Skinner ever did or could read Victor Hugo—he wouldn't know what it's all about—but it is not a mere coincidence that made him choose the title of his book. Victor Hugo knew the two essentials that man's life requires. B. F. Skinner knows the two essentials that have to be destroyed if man qua man is to be destroyed.[6]

The current chapter is far from a full account of Ayn Rand's artistic response to Hugo: it is not the last word on the subject, but rather the first (of any length) by anyone other than herself. My purpose here is to examine several important features of *We the Living*, her first novel, in the light of the analogous features in Hugo's novels and to consider, when available, her commentary on those features of his novels. What will emerge, I hope, is evidence not only of her admiration for Hugo and her affinity with his approach to life and art, but also of her originality, highlighted by her differences from him. *We the Living*, as we shall see, has parallels with the work of Hugo—but it is never imitative. Instead, the near-parallels themselves show her distinctive style and story.

GRANDEUR AND HEROIC SCALE AGAINST A HISTORICAL BACKGROUND

What Ayn Rand loved about Victor Hugo, when she discovered him in her early teens, was that he made "everything important and he feature[d] that which is dramatic and important," that she found in him "the grandeur of man and the focus on man," that his drama was "magnificent." She felt, she said, that *Les Misérables* was so "grand scale that I became almost possessive about that book" and thought of "anything from *Les Misérables*, whether the name Jean Valjean or Gavroche or any of the lesser characters [as] the souvenirs of my loved ones. Everything was holy to me in that sense."[7]

In later years, she was to point repeatedly to the nobility of his estimate of man: as a writer, he was the "nearest to creating the kind of people and events I would like to observe or live with."[8] In spite of the differences between his concretes and convictions and hers (differences she recognized implicitly from the beginning), she thought of his universe, his sense of life, as fundamentally "my world." That world—the artistic universe of Victor Hugo and Ayn Rand—is one of larger-than-life characters engaged in life-or-death conflicts about issues of world-scale significance.

This is true, moreover, even in *We the Living*, which is superficially an exception in that it appears to be of more limited scope and has, as one of its purposes, the goal of publicizing specific circumstances regarding life in Soviet Russia. Indeed, in a note to her publisher, she had written: "I have been asked why I wrote this novel. I think the answer is obvious. I have seen Soviet life as few writers outside Russia have seen it." The implications of this "obvious" answer—that is, the reason behind her intention to describe Russian life under communism—are contained in the following paragraph of the same statement:

> Also, if one takes even the swiftest look at the world today, one cannot help but see the greatest, most urgent conflict of our times: the individual against the collective. That problem interests me above all others in my writing. No country on earth offers such a startling and revealing view of that conflict as Soviet Russia. Hence—*We the Living*.[9]

Her subject, in other words, was not merely the conditions in one country, but a significant, large-scale conflict.

In her foreword to the 1959 edition of the novel, Ayn Rand makes this point explicitly, and repeatedly:

> *We the Living* is *not* a novel "about Soviet Russia." It is a novel about Man against the State. Its basic theme is the sanctity of human life—using the word "sanctity" not in a mystical sense, but in the sense of "supreme value." (xiii)

> *We the Living* is not a story about Soviet Russia in 1925. It is a story about Dictatorship, any dictatorship, anywhere, at any time, whether it be Soviet Russia, Nazi Germany, or—which this novel might do its share in helping to prevent—a socialist America. What the rule of brute force does to men and how it destroys the best, will be the same in 1925, in 1955, or in 1975. . . . (xv)

Although the novel addresses the specific collectivism of Soviet Russia, its scope is not limited to that target.

Her point about the theme of her first novel is the same as one she makes about Hugo's *Ninety-Three* (set at the time of the Vendée revolt of 1793):

The fact is that *Ninety-Three* is *not* a novel about the French Revolution.
To a Romanticist, a background is a background, not a theme. His vision is always focused on man—on the fundamentals of man's nature, on those problems and those aspects of his character which apply to any age and any country. The theme of *Ninety-Three . . .* is: *man's loyalty to values.*

To dramatize that theme, to isolate that aspect of man's soul and show it in its purest form, to put it to the test under the pressure of deadly conflicts, a revolution is an appropriate background to select. Hugo's story is not devised as a means of presenting the French Revolution: the French Revolution is used as a means of presenting his story.[10]

Hugo himself points to the large-scale significance of his fiction in several places, notably *Les Misérables*:

Le livre que le lecteur a sous les yeux en ce moment, c'est, d'un bout à l'autre, dans son ensemble et dans ses détails, quelles que soient les intermittences, les exceptions ou les défaillances, la marche du mal au bien, de l'injuste au juste, du faux au vrai, de la nuit au jour, de l'appétit à la conscience, de la pourriture à la vie, de la bestialité au devoir, de l'enfer au ciel, du néant à Dieu. Point de départ: la matière, point d'arrivée: l'âme. L'hydre au commencement, l'ange à la fin.

[The book the reader has now before his eyes—from one end to the other, in its whole and in its details, whatever the omissions, the exceptions, or the faults—is the march from evil to good, from injustice to justice, from the false to the true, from night to day, from appetite to conscience, from rottenness to life, from brutality to duty, from Hell to Heaven, from nothingness to God. Starting point: matter; goal: the soul. Hydra at the beginning, angel at the end.] (part 5, book 1, chapter 20)[11]

Ayn Rand's first novel is like Hugo's novels in having an abstract theme concerned with the projection of human greatness. Her first novel—more than any of her later novels—is also like his in dramatizing that theme against a historical background with clear political implications.

The historical background in *We the Living* appears in several ways, all of which are reminiscent of Hugo. One is the use of mini-essays on cultural phenomena such as the Primus stove (134) and the song "John Gray" (155–56), which are analogous to Hugo's mini-essays on the Notre Dame Cathedral (*Notre Dame of Paris*, book 3, chapter 1) or street slang (*Les Misérables*, part 4, book 7). Another is the presentation of vignettes and images involving characters other than the principals; we see, for example, posters proclaiming the country's new name (USSR) and children marching and singing (162). Analogies in Hugo include the description of the Paris Convention in part 2, book 3 of *Ninety-Three* and the description of aristocratic decadence in *The Man Who Laughs* (part 2, book 1, chapter 4). A third means of conveying the historical background is a mini-essay that takes a long historical view and presents the setting symbolically, i.e., the extended description of Petrograd that opens part 2 of *We the Living* and that is analogous to Hugo's portrait of Paris in *Notre Dame of Paris* (book 3, chapter 2).

But Ayn Rand's historical background is not Hugo's. Even in these passages, Ayn Rand is more purposeful, in a specifically literary sense, than Hugo. She integrates the background more closely with the narrative and the theme. Hugo often appears to be offering the reader information simply because he himself is interested, regardless of the purpose at hand. When Jean Valjean and Cosette take refuge in a convent, Hugo seizes the opportunity to inform us about the conditions in convents, including the nuns' dental history (*Les Misérables*, part 2, book 6). The description of Parisian politics in *Ninety-Three* is detailed and fascinating. It could stand alone as an analysis of political movements—and, in fact, it should. When Ayn Rand offers similar information, she uses it to help us grasp something significant about the characters and their story. If she tells us about the history of the Primus, we see Kira struggling to use it, and we recognize how a stove can be a tool of spiritual suffocation. The posters announcing the country's new name greet Leo and Kira when they return from a weekend in the country—by which we understand that the respite they experienced was temporary, illusory. The "No" sequence, as originally designed, followed the same pattern of using background material to make vivid the story line of the main characters.[12]

The description of Petrograd, by Ayn Rand's own account, was written in the style of Hugo—and is the weaker for it, in being overemphatic. The positive portrait of Petrograd, moreover, is not integrated with the story line and action in the way that other features of the background are. The novel, to be sure, begins with Kira's return to Petrograd and her belief that it is a place where "so much is possible." One might say that it is presented as a "best case": if even Petrograd is airtight, then there is no hope for a better life anywhere in Russia. But Ayn Rand's description of Petrograd is indeed more like one of Hugo's descriptions of a city than like one of her own (e.g., Dominique's view of New York from the Staten Island ferry, in *The Fountainhead*[13]). It stands alone better than it fits in. The point of view is external to the characters.

And yet even here, where Ayn Rand is most like Hugo, she also takes a step toward her own style of writing. Peter the Great, founder of the city, was a dictator, and the city's history includes his exercise of force: "No willing hands came to build the new capital" (238). Without either endorsing or condemning his use of force, the novel underlines the purposefulness of his goal, his persistence in achieving it, his refusal to submit. "An implacable emperor commanded into being the city and the ground under the city" (238). Petrograd was "the city raised by man against the will of nature" (239). Ayn Rand stresses the contrast between the man-made and the natural:

> Cities grow like forests, like weeds. Petrograd did not grow. It was born fin-
> ished and complete. Petrograd is not acquainted with nature. It was the work of
> man.
>   Nature makes mistakes and takes chances; it mixes its colors and knows little
> of straight lines. But Petrograd is the work of man who knows what he wants.
> (241)

Peter's character and his founding of the city are integrated with the novel's theme and characterizations, if not with the plot line. The adjective
"implacable" links Peter with Andrei Taganov (386) and, implicitly, with the
"steady and irrevocable" step of Kira's Viking[14] and with the "calm, severe"
Leo Kovalenky (61). The city was raised by the "will of a man" (238); in personal allegiance to that sort of purposeful creation, Kira frequently watches
the process of construction, "red bricks and oaken beams and steel panels
growing under the will of man" (47). The contrast between the man-made
and the natural (a contrast that is to the advantage of the man-made) is
explicit in an exchange between Lydia and Kira:

> "How beautiful!" said Lydia, looking at a stage setting. "It's almost real."
> "How beautiful!" said Kira, looking at a landscape. "It's almost artificial." (48)

And, most powerfully, the description of the city as "the work of man who
knows what he wants" is integrated with Kira's impassioned declaration to
Andrei:

> I was born and I knew I was alive and I knew what I wanted. What do you
> think is alive in me? Why do you think I'm alive? Because I have a stomach and
> eat and digest the food? Because I breathe and work and produce more food to
> digest? Or because I know what I want, and that something which knows how
> to want—isn't that life itself? And who—in this damned universe—who can tell
> me why I should live for anything but for that which I want? (404)

The city described as "the work of man who knows what he wants" is thus
linked with the heroine who declares that knowing what she wants is the
spirit of life itself. Although Ayn Rand criticized the description of Petrograd
as written too much by Hugo's method rather than by her own (a subject I
will discuss shortly), she integrated it more effectively into her novel than
Hugo did in similar artistic situations.

The mature Ayn Rand, to be sure, had a stronger conceptual grasp of the
meaning of life, of the morality of life, and would not have had a heroine
maintain, without qualification, that it is right to live for what one wants (a
formulation that does not distinguish between rational self-interest and sub-
jectivism). Her philosophical understanding of her theme grew in the years
after her first novel, as she explains in her foreword to the 1959 edition. The

"essence of my theme" appears in Irina's thoughts about the sanctity of life, the "sacred treasure" of life:

> Now it's over, and it doesn't make any difference to anyone, and it isn't that they are indifferent, it's just that they don't know, they don't know what it means, that treasure of mine, and there's something about it that they should understand. I don't understand it myself, but there's something that should be understood by all of us. Only what is it? What? (xiii)

While writing *We the Living*, Ayn Rand says, "I knew a little more about this question than did Irina, but not much more. . . . It was not until *Atlas Shrugged* that I reached the full answer to Irina's question" (xiii–xiv).

Victor Hugo, whom Ayn Rand described as a sense-of-life writer, did not make similar intellectual progress. "He never translated his sense of life into conceptual terms, he did not ask himself what ideas, premises or psychological conditions were necessary to enable men to achieve the spiritual stature of his heroes."[15] Asking those questions—identifying the ideas, premises, or psychological conditions required for the heroic human ideal—became part of Ayn Rand's life work as a philosopher-novelist. In her first novel, we see her projecting human greatness and dramatizing—against a historical background—a large-scale, abstract theme, as did Victor Hugo. She has surpassed him regarding the integration of the background into the rest of the novel, and, by her focus on the individual, she has identified a deeper theme than Hugo ever did. She was to make further advances in both of these, as she was to do regarding human greatness as well, specifically by creating her own kind of heroic figures.

HEROIC PROTAGONISTS—AND ANTAGONISTS

Ayn Rand loved Victor Hugo's vision of man, of the human capacity for greatness. She did not, however, admire most of the men he created. "I was enormously impressed, . . . yet I was very aware that there isn't a character in all of his writing that is what I would want a man to be."[16] Regarding the characters of *Les Misérables*, she commented: "No character like Jean Valjean could appeal to me—not anybody who, no matter how grandly presented, was really intended to be an average man. And Marius I resented very much. . . . He was a stuffed shirt. He was just a meaningless, sentimental young man. I, incidentally, resented sensitive young men in fiction enormously."[17] The romance of Marius and Cosette was "mush."[18] In *We the Living*, Ayn Rand conveys that resentment through Kira: "She had the same feeling for eating soup without salt, and for discovering a snail slithering up her bare leg, and for young men who pleaded, broken-hearted, their eyes humid, their lips soft" (47). Victor Dunaev, for example, may well have reminded

Kira of a snail: at night in the Summer Garden, he told her "he had always been unhappy and lonely, searching for his ideal, that he could understand her, that her sensitive soul was bound by conventions, unawakened to life— and love" (59). (Kira is indeed sensitive—but not in ways Victor understands.) Sensitive young men are especially distasteful in the role of suitors. The "eminent young poet" in *The Fountainhead* who offers Dominique a ride back from a party to her country house has "a soft, sensitive mouth, and eyes hurt by the whole universe. . . . As they drove through the twilight she saw him leaning hesitantly closer to her. She heard his voice whispering the pleading, incoherent things she had heard from many men."[19] Another snail, another instance of Marius-like mush.

Within the same novel, though, was a character Ayn Rand admired, "the only one that had a personal sense of life meaning for me."[20] That character was Enjolras, leader of the young revolutionaries, "a man of exclusive, devoted purpose."[21] Hugo emphasizes his serenity, his austerity, and his integrity. Although *We the Living* does not satisfy the goal of Ayn Rand's writing—that is, does not project an ideal man—all three of her principal characters display significant resemblances to her favorite Hugo character.

Kira Argounova, to begin with, is described as having the signature quality of Enjolras: heroic devotion to a purpose. When she announces that she intends to study building at the Institute, even those who disapprove do not expect to stop her. "You can't argue with her," says her mother; "She always gets her way," says her sister (42). She never notices what she eats (36) or what she wears (39). She decided to be an engineer "with her first thought about the vague thing called future" (50). When she walks through the snow with Leo to the ship by which they intend to escape, she moves continually forward, fighting the wind, fully aware that life "began beyond the snow" and that only going forward will take her there (121). She maintains her hold on her values: when she stands in the line for bread ("She thought that somewhere beyond all these many things which did not count, was her life and Leo,"199), when she attends a lecture ("For a short hour, even though her stomach throbbed with hunger, she could remember that she was to be a builder who would build aluminum bridges and towers of steel and glass; and that there was a future," [202]), when she struggles to retain her awareness of her important values and her hope that she will achieve them, telling herself often: "Well, it's war. It's war. You don't give up, do you, Kira? It's not dangerous so long as you don't give up. And the harder it gets, the happier you should be that you can stand it. That's it. The harder—the happier. It's war. You're a good soldier, Kira Argounova" (207).

Her Enjolras-like one-track purposefulness is in the tone of her voice, which has "the intensity of a maniac's" when she says the word "Abroad" (444). It is present when she sits on a train feeling "as if her body were only an image of her will and her will—only an arrow, tense and hard, pointing at a border that had to be crossed" (453), when she walks through the snow (as she did before, with Leo) and tells herself, over and over, that she has to "get out," when she reminds herself, "You're a good soldier, Kira Argounova, you're a good soldier and now's the time to prove it" (461). She dies, as does Enjolras, as a good soldier, and with a smile of spiritual triumph. The events of Kira's life are not parallel to the actions of Enjolras; she makes no public speeches, leads no men to die on barricades, and disclaims any concern with politics or revolution. But in portraying Kira's attitude to her own life, Ayn Rand stresses the dedicated, one-track purposefulness she admired in Enjolras.

In the case of Leo Kovalensky, the contrast between him and Enjolras is, at first, more vivid than the comparison. When Kira meets him, he is dedicated to no purpose; Soviet Russia has drained his capacity for dedication, and his love for Kira does not restore it. Nonetheless, the physical image of Leo suggests Enjolras: "His mouth, calm, severe, contemptuous, was that of an ancient chieftain who could order men to die, and his eyes were such as could watch it" (61). Enjolras was described as "sévère" and his lower lip as "dédaigneuse" [disdainful] (part 3, book 4, chapter 1)[22]; he too is able to order men to die, and to watch their deaths. Ayn Rand, moreover, originally intended to associate Leo directly with Kira's Viking. In the first draft, Kira is said to recognize, coming down the street, the face of her Viking, the hero of her favorite childhood book, a man who is indefatigable and uncrushable (i.e., like Enjolras).

The face and body of Leo, then, link him to Enjolras, a connection suggested repeatedly. The young Leo is associated with the marble statue of Apollo: "The tutors, and the servants, and the guests looked at Leo as they looked at the statue of Apollo in the Admiral's studio, with the same reverent hopelessness they felt for the white marble of a distant age" (138).[23] Kira too associates his body with marble and a god: "His body was white as marble and as hard and straight; the body of a god, she thought, that should climb a mountainside at dawn, young grass under his feet, a morning mist on his muscles in a breath of homage" (186). Later, his face is "white as marble" (307). Enjolras is introduced in terms of marble: "C'était l'amoureux de marbre de la Liberté" [He was the marble lover of liberty] (part 3, book 4, chapter 1).[24] Enjolras has the "immobilité de marbre" [marble immobility] (part 4, book 12, chapter 8).[25] When he is about to kill an enemy, there is a tear on his "joue de marbre" [marble cheek] (part 5, book 1, chapter 8).[26] And Enjolras, like Leo, is associated with Apollo: "C'était de lui peut-être que parlait le témoin qui disait plus tard devant le conseil de guerre: 'Il y avait un insurgé que j'ai entendu nommer Apollon'" [Perhaps it was of him that the witness spoke who said afterward before the court-martial, "There was one insurgent whom I heard called Apollo"] (part 5, book 1, chapter 23).[27]

Kira, who loves Leo at first sight and forever, sees in him "what he could have been, what he was intended to be" (326). That Leo in action is not more like Enjolras than he is, is the direct result of the poisonous world in which he lives and of the ideas that poison it. And *We the Living*, in a sequence of passages, underscores the significance—in the context of that world—of a man's having a face and body that suggest an Enjolras.

When Hugo introduces Enjolras, he describes his face and form, and comments that he would attract female attention, but that a woman who tried to attract his attention in return would be disappointed. If any grisette—intrigued and charmed by his youthful figure, unruly curls, and fresh lips—"eût eu appétit de toute cette aurore" [felt a desire to taste all this dawn], Enjolras would have brusquely rejected any such advances (part 3, book 4 chapter 1).[28] This sort of rebuff has a counterpart in *We the Living*. Compare it to Ayn Rand's description of Leo, seeking work, standing in a line of defeated men.

> He stood among them, tall, straight, young, a god's form with lips that were still proud.
> A streetwalker passed by and stopped; and looked, startled, at that man among the others; and winked an invitation. He did not move, only turned his head away. (172)

The first draft of this scene even includes the words "dawn on his forehead,"[29] which is similar to "toute cette aurore" [all this dawn]. Leo looks like Enjolras, and evokes a similar response, to which he responds similarly.

This scene, however, has a sequel later in the novel. A customer in Leo's store "stopped involuntarily, for a brief, startled moment, looking at the young man who had entered. . . . She . . . knew that she could not have many occasions to see that kind of young man on the streets of Petrograd" (293). She "looked straight at him, softly, defiantly." This time, Leo's response is different: "He answered with a glance that was an invitation, and a mocking insult, and almost a promise" (293–94). When he leaves the shop, he sees her waiting for him. "He hesitated for a second; then smiled and turned away" (294). The transition from the first scene to the second traces the decline of the Leo who should have been Kira's mate, that is, who should have been Enjolras.

This pair of scenes, in the first draft, had another matching scene, in connection with Andrei. When Kira and Andrei are dining at the Garden:

> A woman with a very red mouth and a slow, very graceful walk, her hips and stomach thrown forward, her shoulders slouched back, passed by their table and stopped for a brief second to look at the scar on the forehead of a man whose likes she did not see there often. She shrugged and walked on, but she threw a glance back at the child in the red dress, who had conquered the unconquerable.[30]

In all three scenes, a woman who appreciates men, a woman we otherwise do not know, observes that a man is distinctive. The scene with Andrei, which Ayn Rand decided to omit, makes one point that is significantly different from the scenes with Leo: here, the emphasis is on the observer's respect for Kira, who has attracted a man hitherto romantically indifferent. Leo, by contrast, has considerable experience with women, although he truly loves no one but Kira. But Andrei, before Kira, has had no such experience. Comrade Sonia describes him as "the kind of saint that sleeps with red flags" (95). He has marched, in the uniform of the Red Army, "as a man walks to his wedding" (107). Enjolras is similar in having loved his cause as other men might love women. The name of Enjolras's mistress is "Patria"; he has no other sweetheart (part 5, book 1, chapter 14).[31]

In this respect, Andrei is more like Enjolras than is Leo. And even when Andrei is attracted to Kira, he initially retains his outward austerity: "The grim lines of his tanned face were like an effigy of a medieval saint; from the age of the Crusades he had inherited the ruthlessness, the devotion, and also the austere chastity" (150).

Andrei Taganov is in fact like Enjolras in a number of important respects. Consider the description of Enjolras as soldier of the revolution: "Il n'avait qu'une passion, le droit, qu'une pensée, renverser l'obstacle. . ." [He had one passion only, justice: one thought only, to overcome all obstacles] (part 3, book 4, chapter 1).[32] Enjolras is described as one for whom will and action are one: he " avait cette qualité d'un chef, de toujours faire ce qu'il disait" [had this quality of a leader, always to do as he said] (part 5, book 1, chapter 2).[33]

For Andrei, as for Enjolras, his life has been his dedication to his cause, without compromise, hesitation, or doubt. As he says to Kira: "If you know that a thing is right, you want to do it. If you don't want to do it—it isn't right. If it's right and you don't want to do it—you don't know what right is and you're not a man" (89). He is as devoted, and as implacable, as Enjolras, even after he has grown to love Kira and to experience through her a personal joy in life. He asks Kira not to talk with him about the case against Leo: "I'm expecting the highest integrity from the men I'm going to face. Don't make me face them with less than that on my part" (386). When Kira nonetheless asks him to drop the case, he turns to her with "the implacable face of Comrade Taganov of the G.P.U., a face that could have watched secret executions in dark, secret cellars" (386).

The execution performed by Enjolras is not secret, but he acts with equally stern resolution and with the strictest adherence to principle. When Enjolras sees Le Cabuc, ostensibly one of his men, kill an old doorkeeper without reason, he immediately announces that Le Cabuc must prepare to die. Enjolras's profile is "implacable" and "grec" [Greek], his gaze "convaincu et sévère" [determined and severe], his serenity "redoutable" [fearful], and his purpose clear: "nous sommes sous le regard de la révolution; nous sommes les prêtres de la république, nous sommes les hosties du devoir, et il ne faut pas qu'on puisse calomnier notre combat" [we are under the eyes of the Revolution, we are the priests of the Republic, we are the sacramental host of duty, and no one can defame our combat] (part 4, book 12, chapter 8).[34] In their pride in their purity, and in the purity of their pride, Enjolras and Andrei speak a similar language.

In describing Enjolras, Hugo invokes Antinoûs, a Greek page who became the last of the Roman gods (part 3, book 4, chapter 1) and Themis, a Greek god of justice and human rights (part 4, book 12, chapter 8). In describing Andrei, Ayn Rand refers to Romans and crusaders:

> A street lamp beyond the tall window threw a blue square of light, checkered into panes, on the wall by the staircase; little shadows of raindrops rolled slowly down the wall. Andrei walked down, his body slender, erect, unhurried, steady, the kind of body that in centuries past had worn the armor of a Roman, the mail of a crusader; it wore a leather jacket now.
>
> Its tall, black shadow moved slowly, across the blue square of light and raindrops on the wall. (311)

Ayn Rand mentioned this passage as one that she considered especially effective.[35]

An incident with Enjolras, finally, is in part parallel with a striking episode in Andrei's personal history. Enjolras—with sorrow but without hesitation—is responsible for the death of a man he respects, an artillery gunner who has killed two of Enjolras's men, and wounded three. The gunner is described as very young, blond, handsome, with an intelligent air. Combeferre, Enjolras's comrade in arms, says: "Figure-toi que c'est un charmant jeune homme, il est intrépide, on voit qu'il pense . . . il a un père, une mère, une famille, il aime probablement, il a tout au plus vingt-cinq ans, il pourrrait être ton frère" [Just think that he's a charming young man; he's intrepid; you can see that he's a thinker . . . he has a father, a mother, a family; he's in love, probably; he's twenty-five at most; he might be your brother]. Enjolas responds: "Il l'est" [He is].

But when Combeferre asks that they not kill him, Enjolras responds: "Laisse-moi. Il faut ce qu'il faut" [Leave me alone. We must do what we must]. Then, he acts.

> Et une larme coula lentement sur la joue de marbre d'Enjolras.
> En même temps il pressa la détente de sa carabine
> [And a tear rolled slowly down Enjolras's marble cheek.
> At the same time he pressed the trigger of his carbine.] (part 5, book 1, chapter 8)[36]

Perhaps the most dramatic aspect of this scene is the simultaneity of his actions: he shoots and weeps at the same time.

An analogous episode in Andrei's life occurs after the battle of Perekop. Andrei walks for many miles with a White soldier, whom he eventually discovers to be Captain Karsavin, "one of the last names to fear in the White Army" (110), a leader with buckets of Red blood on his hands. As the two, both wounded, walk together struggling to reach any sort of camp, they develop a respect for each other's tenacity. Andrei physically supports his enemy, almost carrying him, even though doing so makes the walk harder for him. As they approach a camp that turns out to belong the Reds, Andrei recognizes the "young, indomitable face." Karsavin, who looks white in the light of dawn, speaks of his childhood; he is the son of a mother who would not let him see the sunrise because she worried about his health. Karsavin asks Andrei to shoot him, which Andrei cannot do. What he does instead, at Karsavin's request, is to give him a gun, and to walk on, hearing in the background Karsavin's shot.

Whereas the other parallels with Enjolras simply show that Ayn Rand dramatized in Andrei some of the features Hugo attributes to his hero, this instance shows how she improved upon Hugo. The notion that one's enemy in war may be in some respect a brother in spirit is a commonplace of war literature; Hugo makes the scene more dramatic by having his hero show an emotion incongruous for him (a tear on his marble face). Ayn Rand makes the scene even more dramatic by having the hero "show" emotion by keeping the memory to himself—he is said not to like to talk about how he got the scar he received in this battle. Hugo uses dialogue between Enjolras and his companion to dramatize the victim's family ties and the bond the hero feels between himself and the man he kills. Ayn Rand makes the family ties more dramatic by having the victim himself refer to them—not generally, but concretely, with a memory of his mother and his mornings. Ayn Rand makes the bond between Andrei and Karsavin more dramatic by showing how they earned each other's respect in action, whereas Hugo stresses instead the contrast between Combeferre's impulse to be merciful and Enjolras's commitment to his battle. Most significantly, Ayn Rand concludes the scene not with the conventional (one soldier shoots his enemy) but with two principled choices (Andrei will not betray his own code by shooting a soldier who ought to be treated as a prisoner, but he will not withhold from a man he admires an escape from intolerable capture and torture) that achieve the same result.

The Karsavin episode, moreover, is the first of two suicides that matter to Andrei (the second is that of Stepan Timoshenko) and that precede his own. For Andrei is not privileged to die the heroic death of Enjolras (Ayn Rand's favorite scene[37]). He is not entitled to die Enjolras's death, in the context of *We the Living*, because not only is he not the novel's hero, but he is actually one of its villains.

His ideal—in his explicit statements, in his conscious convictions, and in his actions as an agent of the G.P.U.—is an evil ideal, the ideal of collectivism. That his love for Kira—and for the individualist, life-loving spirit she embodies—contradicts his chosen ideal creates a conflict for him, one that ends in tragedy. This sort of contradiction is dramatized in Hugo's fiction, in two characters who are officially villains, but whom Hugo treats with dignity and dramatic color. Andrei, in other words, has qualities in common not only with Enjolras, but with Claude Frollo in *Notre Dame of Paris* and Inspector Javert in *Les Misérables*.

Andrei, like Frollo, is austere, implacable, and chaste—until he becomes passionately obsessed with a woman who represents the opposite of the ideal that has governed his life. Ayn Rand has analyzed in detail a speech in which Frollo avows his love for Esmeralda; she pays tribute to Hugo's style and contrasts it with her own. Later in the present article, I will discuss her style and his, and at that point will also contrast Andrei's love for Kira with the priest's love for the gypsy.

Here, I want to consider Ayn Rand's comments on Javert, some of which are pertinent to her characterization of Andrei. When she first read the novel, she "considered him very much the villain" and "was very much out of sympathy with him throughout." His regard for the law, which stood for "society or tradition or the status quo," was, in her view, a highly unworthy motivation, of which she strongly disapproved. She approved, however, of his letting Jean Valjean go, and of his suicide: "he acquired stature for me" when "he broke [the law] and [underwent] that struggle in his soul. . . . I took that incident to be [that] the right wins. And that he atoned nobly for his errors."[38]

As described by Hugo, Javert is the epitome of the implacable. He sounds, in fact, significantly like Enjolras: "Il était stoïque, sérieux, austère. . . . Son regard était une vrille. Cela était froid et cela perçait" [He was stoical, serious, austere. . . . His stare was cold and piercing as a gimlet] (part 1, book 5, chapter 5).[39] He has "la sérénité intrépide de l'homme qui n'a jamais menti" [the intrepid severity of the man who has never lied] (part 4, book 12, chapter 7).[40] He is, like Enjolras, a man of marble. "C'était le devoir implacable, la police comprise comme les Spartiates comprenaient Sparte, un guet impitoyable, une honnêteté farouche, un mouchard marmoréen" [It was implacable duty; the police as central to him as Sparta to the Spartans; a pitiless detective, fiercely honest, a marble-hearted informer] (part 1, book 5, chapter 5).[41]

In the long chapter "Javert Déraillé" [Javert Off the Track] (part 5, book 4, chapter 1), Hugo depicts, at length, Javert's bewilderment at two actions: that Jean Valjean, the convict, has spared Javert's life, and that Javert, the man of the law, has released the man he has spent his life pursuing. Hugo writes that Javert could not understand himself, that his "code n'était plus qu'un tronçon dans sa main" [code was no longer anything but a stump in his hand].[42] He thinks: "Cela ne pouvait durer ainsi" [This could not go on].[43] He writes a note, his last. He goes to a parapet overlooking the whirlpool of the Seine. He stands calmly.

Tout à coup, il ôta son chapeau et le posa sur le rebord du quai. Un moment après, une figure haute et noire, que de loin quelque passant attardé eût pu prendre pour un fantôme, apparut debout sur le parapet, se courba vers la Seine, puis se redressa, et tomba droite dans les ténèbres; il y eut un clapotement sourd; et l'ombre seule fut dans le secret des convulsions de cette forme obscure disparue sous l'eau.

[Suddenly he took off his hat and laid it on the edge of the quay. A moment later, a tall, black form, which from the distance some belated pedestrian might have taken for a phantom, appeared standing on the parapet, bent toward the Seine, then sprang up, and fell straight into the darkness: there was a dull splash; and the night alone was admitted to the secret convulsions of that obscure form which had disappeared under the water.][44]

Andrei too acted against the ideal he had served, atoned for his actions, and took his own life instead of either continuing or altering its course. His disillusionment with the ideal of collectivism has been ongoing. Whereas Hugo spends ten pages describing Javert's thoughts on a single night, Ayn Rand has shown Andrei progressively seeing, stating, and disowning his errors—in conversations with Kira about the nature and purpose of life, in saving Leo by blackmailing Syerov, in calling the Party Committee to account for the evil goals of collectivism. By contrast with Hugo's depiction of Javert's spiritual "derailment," Ayn Rand's analysis of Andrei's transformation is not only more philosophical, but more tightly integrated with the rest of the novel.

The suicide itself has the calm deliberateness of Javert's, and is a similarly private act. He piles up his books, burns the relics of his romance with Kira, and writes a note, his last. "There was only one shot, and because the frozen marble stairway was long and dark and led to a garden buried in deep snow, no one came up to investigate" (428). In evaluating her artistic success in *We the Living*, Ayn Rand singled out this sequence as one in which, through understatement, she achieved what she attempted.[45] And we see that although Andrei does not die the heroic, smiling death of Enjolras, he has some qualities of Enjolras (as did Kira and Leo), and his death has the tranquil dignity of the death of Javert, and more.

TIGHT PLOTTING

When Ayn Rand looked back on her first reading of Hugo, she recalled being impressed by his "plot inventiveness";[46] she mentioned the episode of the bishop's candlesticks in *Les Misérables*, but did not dwell on or analyze the plot of that novel or any of the others. In her lectures on fiction writing and in her published essays on Hugo, however, she pays a great deal of attention

to his plots and plot-theme integration. She considered plot "*the* crucial attribute of the novel,"[47] and she worked hard at constructing her own plots,
including the novel at hand, which she considered her most tightly plotted
novel.[48] What she said about Hugo's plots and her own is pertinent to our
subject: the connections between Hugo and *We the Living*.

Speaking of Hugo's *Ninety-Three* (and, by implication, of all his novels),
she commented that the excellence of his plotting derives from integration:
"Hugo's inexhaustible imagination is at its virtuoso best in an extremely difficult aspect of a novelist's task: the integration of an abstract theme to the
plot of a story."[49] The events in the narrative all feature the theme, and these
events, logically connected, compose a plot. In her analysis of *Ninety-Three*,
she emphasizes the way all episodes and all characters dramatize the theme,
and she shows how the climax resolves the plot line.

In her lectures on fiction writing, she provides a similarly detailed analysis
of the plotting of *Notre Dame of Paris*. Starting "from scratch," she shows
how the plot-theme of the novel could be developed, step by step, from a
"germ" of an idea (a priest in the Middle Ages), by identifying and intensify-
ing a conflict—and then she comments that Hugo himself would not have
needed to develop his plot-theme step by step: "The inexhaustible ingenuity
for plot shown in his plays indicates that writing and conflict were nearly
synonymous to him. He had such a grasp of the nature of conflict that its
projection became automatic."[50] Every event in the plot supports the plot-
theme. The structure is unified: "Every incident of *Notre-Dame de Paris* is
ruled by the same principle: make it as hard as possible for the characters,
and tie the lesser characters' tragedies to the main line of events."[51] And the
climax, which she analyzes at length, is "a resolution in action of their [Qua-
simodo's and Frollo's] conflict of values."[52]

In her comments on *We the Living*, she points to the same virtues, in this
context, that she praised in Hugo. The novel's plot depends on conflicts of
values among individuals; the progression of its events is designed for maxi-
mum conflict; its climax derives from, and resolves, the key conflict. Of the
nature of the plot, she states:

> By contrast [with *Anthem*, which has no plot], *We the Living*, my most tightly
> plotted story, has not only a social message, the evil of a collective society, but
> also a conflict among specific persons. The story is not "Kira [the heroine]
> against the state"; the villain is actually Andrei, along with such lesser represen-
> tatives of the communist system as Syerov, Sonia, and Victor. Had it been "Kira
> against the state," the story would have been plotless.[53]

Regarding the maximizing of conflict, she points out that the specific plot-
theme of *We the Living* is a more dramatic version of the "trite plot-theme:
the woman who sells herself to a man she does not love for the sake of the

man whom she does love." Such a conflict, as in the opera *Tosca*, is, according to Ayn Rand, "good, but simple, one-line"—and hence inadequate for her purposes:

Now ask yourself how one can make it harder for the characters. Suppose the woman sells herself, not to a villain who forces her into it, but to a man who really loves her, whom she respects and whose love she takes seriously. He does not want to buy her, and she must hide from him that it is a sale—but she has to sell herself to save the man she really loves, a man who happens to be the particular person the buyer hates most. This is a much more dramatic conflict—and it is the plot-theme of *We the Living*.[54]

The climax of *We the Living* is the scene in which Andrei discovers, while arresting Leo, that Kira is Leo's mistress; this sequence includes the scene in which Kira throws in Andrei's face her pride in what she has done, and the scene in which he proclaims to the Party Committee the life-centered values he has learned from Kira. The climax thus resolves, at once, the conflicts of individuals and the conflicts of ideas.

A full analysis of the plot structure of *We the Living* is beyond the scope of the present chapter. Such an analysis would show how the novel builds suspense by postponing the revelation of the truth about the romantic triangle, how it heightens dramatic conflict by making Andrei in some respects nobler than Leo, how it emphasizes the specific agony of Kira's unbearable position by comparing it with Irina's as she faces what amounts to a death sentence ("Well, kid, I don't know which of us needs more courage to face the future," 350), and how it provides numerous opportunities for additional comparisons and contrasts, involving characters both major and minor.

Consider, as a small example, the novel's three pregnancies: Marisha Lavrova aborts an unwanted pregnancy; Comrade Sonia Presniakova seeks pregnancy to blackmail Pavel Syerov into marriage; Vava Milovskaia accedes to pregnancy as part of her general surrender to lethargic despair. Or consider, as a larger example, three variations on prostitution. Leo tries to buy Kira; Kira later sells herself to Andrei; Leo ultimately sells himself to Antonina Platoshkina. Contrasts between major and minor characters—for example, the battle of Melitopol, at which Andrei takes a big risk and Syerov makes a big speech—are significant, as are the points of contrast (the multiple versions of "If I'm still alive, and if I don't forget") and continuity within characters: addressing the Party Committee, Andrei's voice "rose, ringing, as it had risen in a dark valley over the White trenches many years ago" (409; cf. 109). Nothing in this novel is accidental or irrelevant.

TRAGIC ENDINGS

Although Ayn Rand's later novels had tragic elements (e.g., Wynand's self-betrayal in *The Fountainhead*, and the death in *Atlas Shrugged* of Tony, the

"Wet Nurse"), *We the Living* is the only one of her novels to have a tragic ending. She commented on tragic endings in Hugo and in her own first novel, emphasizing the similarity in the approaches to tragedy:

> The justification for presenting tragic endings in literature is to show, as in *We the Living,* that the human spirit can survive even the worst of circumstances—that the worst that the chance events of nature or the evil of other people can do will not defeat the proper human spirit. To quote from Galt's speech in *Atlas Shrugged:* "Suffering as such is not a value; only man's fight against suffering, is" . . . .
>
> In *We the Living,* all the good people are defeated. The philosophical justification of the tragedy is the fact that the story denounces the collectivist state and shows, metaphysically, that man cannot be destroyed by it; he can be killed, but not changed or negated. The heroine dies radiantly endorsing life, feeling happiness in her last moment because she has known what life properly should be. . . .
>
> Victor Hugo, who usually has unhappy endings, always presents his characters' suffering somewhat in the way that I do in *We the Living.* Even if a particular character meets with disaster, the tragedy and pain are never complete; they are not, metaphysically, the final word on man.[55]

Tragic endings show that nothing, not even death, can conquer the spirit of life, that disaster and suffering are tests over which the soul can triumph. Why, though, were tragic endings characteristic of Victor Hugo and atypical for Ayn Rand? She states:

> Most of his novels have tragic endings—as if he were unable to concretize the form in which his heroes could triumph on earth, and he could only let them die in battle, with an unbroken integrity of spirit as the only assertion of their loyalty to life; as if, to him, it was the earth, not heaven, that represented an object of longing, which he could never fully reach or win.[56]

This description applies well to many of the deaths in Hugo's novels, including that of Enjolras (who dies in physical battle, and with a smile on his face). Jean Valjean says he is dying happy; his deathbed is attended by the spirit of the bishop who instigated Valjean's spiritual redemption. Dea and Gwynplaine in *The Man Who Laughs* seek paradise regained not "ici-bas" [below], but "là-haut" [on high] (part 2, conclusion, chapters 3 and 4).[57] Gauvain in *Ninety-Three*—"debout, superbe, tranquille" [erect, proud, tranquil]—has on his bright face "joie pensive" [pensive joy] (part 3, book 7, chapter 6);[58] his departing soul mingles with that of Cimourdain, who dies at the same moment.

Enjolras and Gauvain have prophesied a glorious future on earth, and Hugo suggests that they will find glory in heaven. As novelist, however, he conveys neither of these states of glory. Instead he implies that the heroes' lives are such that they have already experienced what they will see in heaven and what others will eventually see on earth. Ayn Rand's equivalent might be the statement: "Anyone who fights for the future, lives in it today."[59] In her fiction, though, she typically shows the achievement of values, and the continuing fight for them. Why, then, does *We the Living* have an ending closer to that of a Hugo novel? Because Soviet Russia, in this novel, is analogous to the earth in a novel by Hugo. As Hugo believed that no triumph was possible on earth, so Ayn Rand knew that no triumph was possible in Soviet Russia.

Hugo imagined a mystical "beyond" where heroes would receive their due and would be reunited with those they love, and some of his tragic deaths imply that the characters had in their sight this other realm. For Ayn Rand, who is no mystic, the relevant other realm is a real place, "Abroad," and Kira, as she dies, imagines she is going there, to see again the man she loves.[60] *We the Living*, to be sure, does not imply that Kira will reach this place or that the person she expects to see is actually there. Ayn Rand removes the mystical implications of Hugo's ending while retaining his power and his point: It is worth living while one is alive, even though death is always the end and often too soon.

> She was calling him, the Leo that could have been, that would have been, had he lived there, where she was going, across the border. He was awaiting her there, and she had to go on. She had to walk. There, in that world, across the border, a life was waiting for her to which she had been faithful her every living hour, her only banner that had never been lowered, that she had held high and straight, a life she could not betray, she would not betray now by stopping while she was still living, a life she could still serve, by walking, by walking forward a little longer, just a little longer. (463)

Kira, the good soldier, dies at dawn. In the draft of the novel, Ayn Rand associated that death with the triumph of the Viking who had been Kira's lifelong inspiration.

> A Viking had lived, who had laughed at Kings, who had laughed at Priests, who had laughed at Men, who had held, sacred and inviolable, high over all temples, over all to which men knew how to kneel, his one banner—the sanctity of life. He had known and she knew. He had fought and she was fighting. He had shown her the way. To the banner of life, all could be given, even life itself.[61]

Kira's thoughts at the time of her death were, Ayn Rand said, "in a way" the thoughts that she herself had had when she and her family were held up by bandits on their journey to the Crimea. As Kira reflected on her life, on her song, on her love, Ayn Rand held in her mind the death of Enjolras, smiling, serene, unbroken: "Now if they are going to shoot, I want to die as well as he did . . . that's what I want to be thinking of last—not of Russia nor the horrors."[62]

STYLE

Ayn Rand, by her own account, labored over the use of language in her first novel, and was not entirely satisfied with the result—not only because she was not able, at first, to devote full time to writing, not only because she was still gaining control over English, and not only because she was not certain how much she needed to write in order to be clear to the reader, but also because, at times, she was writing too much in the style of the writer she most admired. A full analysis of the style of *We the Living* would include detailed reports regarding such aspects as syntax, diction, metaphor, and rhythm—in the multiple versions of the text[63]—as well as comparisons and contrasts with Ayn Rand's later writing (and, if relevant, the prose of other authors). The present chapter will be limited to the following: some specific features of Hugo's style that have counterparts in *We the Living*, the passage in *We the Living* that Ayn Rand considered to be too much like Hugo, a passage in *Notre Dame of Paris* that she analyzed and contrasted with her own writing, and the nearest equivalent in *We the Living* to the artistic function of the episode Ayn Rand cited as one of her favorites in *Les Misérables*.

Hugo, to begin with, frequently described characters as if they were combinations of individuals, sometimes contradictory in nature. In *Les Misérables*, for example, he writes:

> Cette Thénardier était comme le produit de la greffe d'une donzelle sur une poissarde. Quand on l'entendait parler, on disait: C'est un gendarme; quand on la regardait boire, on disait: C'est un charretier; quand on la voyait manier Cosette, on disait: C'est le bourreau.

> [This Thénardiess was a cross between a whore and a fishwife. To hear her speak, you would say this was a policeman; to see her drink, you would say this was a cartman; if you saw her handle Cosette, you would say this was the hangman.] (part 2, book 3, chapter 2)[64]

Her husband "avait le regard d'une fouine et la mine d'un homme de lettres" [had the look of a weasel and the air of a man of letters] (part 2, book 3, chapter 2).[65] In *The Man Who Laughs*, the doctor on the *Matutina* hooker is said to have "le sourcil d'un trabucaire modifié par le regard d'un archevêque" [the brow of an incendiary tempered by the eyes of an archbishop] (part 1, book 2, chapter 2).[66] One parallel passage would be the description of Kira as alternately "a Valkyrie with lance and winged helmet in the sweep of battle" and "an imp perched on top of a toadstool, laughing in the faces

of daisies" (44). Another would be Kira dressed for Victor's wedding—
"severe as a nun, graceful as a Marquise of two centuries past"; Leo, in effect,
adds two more characters: he "took her hand, as if she were a lady at a Court
reception, and kissed her palm, as if she were a courtesan" (297).
Hugo frequently commented on the relationship (harmonious or contrasting) of body and soul. In *Notre Dame of Paris*, for example, it is observed of
Frollo and Quasimodo that the soul of one is like the body of the other (book
4, chapter 6); Josiane, in *The Man Who Laughs*, similarly asserts, with pride,
that she is a moral monster and that Gwynplaine is a physical monster (part
2, book 7, chapter 4). The child Gwynplaine was one "qui, pygmée par la
stature, avait été colosse par l'âme" [who, a pigmy in stature, had been a
colossus in soul] (part 2, book 5, chapter 5).[67] Of Kira, we are told that it
"seemed that the words she said were ruled by the will of her body and that
her sharp movements were the unconscious reflection of a dancing, laughing soul" (44). Of Uncle Vasili, we learn that "his backbone had been as
straight as his gun: his spirit as straight as his backbone" (35).
   Hugo's sentences and paragraphs cover the extremes of terseness and
length. On the one hand, he has one-sentence paragraphs and rapid-fire
question-and-answer dialogue. Examples include the episode of the ship-
wrecked comprachicos in *The Man Who Laughs* (part 1, book 2), the conversation between Lantenac and Halmalo in *Ninety-Three* (part 1, book 3,
chapter 1) and that between Cimourdain and Imânus later in the novel (part
3, book 4, chapter 8). Parallels in *We the Living* would be the first meeting
of Leo and Kira (part 1, chapter 4), parts of the death scene of Maria Petrovna
(part 1, chapter 14), and Andrei's meeting with the executive of the Economic Section of the G.P.U. (part 2, chapter 12).
   On the other hand, Hugo also has—for times of great emotion—long, private speeches of appeal and even longer public speeches of inspiration or
rebuke. Examples of the private speeches include those of the recluse in
Notre Dame of Paris (Book 11, chapter 1) and Michelle Fléchard in *Ninety-
Three* (part 3, book 5, chapter 1). Examples of public speeches include those
of Enjolras in *Les Misérables* (part 5, book 1, chapter 5) and Gwynplaine in
The Man Who Laughs (part 2, book 8, chapter 7). A parallel private speech
is Kira's appeal to the Commissar (part 1, chapter 16); a parallel public
speech is Andrei's address to the Party Committee (part 2, chapter 13).
   Another of Hugo's devices is a contrast built on syntactic parallelism. An
example from *Ninety-Three* is Lantenac's statement to Halmalo, the brother
of the sailor who carelessly released a cannon, then bravely stopped it. Lantenac, after awarding the sailor a high rank, had ordered him shot. "'Ton frère
avait été courageux, je l'ai récompensé; it avait été coupable; je l'ai puni. Il
avait manqué à son devoir, je n'ai pas manqué au mien" [Your brother was
courageous; I recompensed that. He was culpable; I punished that. He had
failed in his duty; I did not fail in mine] (part 1, book 3, chapter 1).[68] In this

instance, as is frequently the case with Hugo, the style dramatizes the contrast.

One example from *We the Living* is the death of Andrei's mother: "Some said it was the wooden trough that had killed her, for it had always been too full; and some said it was the kitchen cupboard, for it had always been too empty" (105). An example from the dialogue is Andrei's explanation to Kira and Leo: "Syerov has powerful friends. That saved him. But he's not very brave. That saved you" (420).

Although the stylistic features mentioned here are not unique to Hugo, they are characteristic of him, and he was the writer Ayn Rand most read and admired (although not uncritically). Looking back, she commented, as follows, on the process of influence:

> My mind would work in those literary forms which had most impressed me. Because I could not yet have any of my own, not on a first novel. And the first novel took care of that influence. . . . And I was very aware, even epistemologically, that my mind seem[ed] to follow at times his kind of pattern, because the field of expressing myself [was] totally new to me. And what I [was] learning in the process [was] how to form my own methods of expression. And only at times would it run into those methods which had impressed me so much in his case . . . .

Such an approach, she thought, was "almost necessary" for a beginner: "this is the way you would think of expressing yourself, because that's the most forceful way you had ever seen and you have not yet developed your own methods."[69]

By way of contrasting his method with her own, she commented:

> If you compare *We the Living* to *The Fountainhead*, you'll see the difference. A certain kind of over-assertive, over-editorial, and slightly over-dramatic turn of sentences, particularly the description of Petrograd in *We the Living*. I think it is as near as I came to being influenced by Hugo. That description is very much his influence on me; that is not the way I would write today.[70]

She criticizes Hugo for "wild or broad assertions," for "wild or inexact figures of speech."[71] She also points to her changing evaluation of the passage in question:

> I thought by the time I was finishing it that the description of Petrograd was well done. But today [1960] I don't particularly like it, or rather, I can objectively say, yes, it's fairly well done for what it is. But it's the one passage that shows Hugo's influence. So the style is not mine; it's not the method natural to me.[72]

Hugo's influence is evident not only in the matter of content—the five pages she spends describing the history and appearance of a city—but in what she terms the "over-assertive, over-editorial, and slightly over-dramatic turn of sentences."

Earlier in this chapter, in the context of the novel's historical background, I tried to show that Ayn Rand's use of history in this passage, while unusual for her, was more closely integrated with the novel as a whole than was typically the case for parallel passages in Hugo. Even when she is somewhat like Hugo, she is also unlike him, and more like herself. The same is true in this context. She does not commit all of the stylistic excesses she criticizes in Hugo. Although I do not know what she would have considered "wild," I myself would consider "wild" such assertions as "Un éléphant que hait une fourmi est en danger" [An elephant hated by a worm is in danger] (*Man Who Laughs*, part 2, book 1, chapter 9)[73] or "Qui a soif de flatterie revomit le réel, bu par surprise" [he who thirsts for flattery vomits the real, when he has happened to drink it by mistake] (*Man Who Laughs*, part 2, book 9, chapter 2)[74] and such figures of speech as "Figurez-vous l'abîme, et au milieu de l'abîme une oasis de clarté, et dans cette oasis ces deux êtres hors de la vie, s'éblouissant" [Imagine to yourself an abyss, and in its centre an oasis of light, and in this oasis two creatures shut out of life, dazzling each other] (*Man Who Laughs*, part 2, book 2, chapter 5).[75] A reader can appreciate the color of such sentences, but no reader would expect to find such sentences in Ayn Rand—even in *We the Living*.

We do, however, see sentences such as "The palace looks like a barracks; the theater looks like a palace" (239). Hugo specializes in such incongruity: "On l'avait d'avance fiancé à une plaie guérissante. On l'avait prédestiné à être consolé par une affliction. La tenaille de bourreau s'était doucement faite main de femme" [They had affianced him beforehand to a healing wound. They had predestined him for consolation by an affliction. The pincers of the executioner had softly changed into the delicately molded hand of a girl] (*Man Who Laughs*, part 2, book 2, chapter 4).[76] The mature Ayn Rand would convey incongruity with more subtlety, for example, "The Top and the Bottom" in *Atlas Shrugged* (part 1, chapter 3): a penthouse restaurant has the physical and moral darkness of a cave, while a basement cafeteria is its opposite in every sense.

The Petrograd passage describes four black statues of men with horses: in the first, the horse threatens to crush the man; by the last, the "beast is tamed" (239). The statues together "may be the spirit of Petrograd, the city raised by man against the will of nature." Hugo specializes in attribution of symbolic meaning to physical objects, such as the stone monument, a monstrous Egyptian elephant, based on an idea of Napoleon's (*Les Misérables*, part 4, book 6, chapter 2). For her own literary purposes, the mature Ayn Rand would not comment on existing statues or buildings, but would invent appropriate objects, such as the Stoddard Temple in *The Fountainhead*.

She comments, in general, that her style, contrasted with Hugo's, is "much more calculated, much more conscious, much more intellectual, and more economical."⁷⁷ She makes similar observations in a specific context: her analysis of Frollo's avowal of love to Esmeralda in *Notre Dame of Paris* (book 8, chapter 4). This analysis, accompanied by Ayn Rand's own translation of Frollo's speech, is worth reading in full.⁷⁸ To summarize: she praises Hugo's exact concretization of Frollo's pain and the essence of his conflict (as a priest in love with a pagan gypsy): his awareness that what he desires is impossible, combined with his decision to try to win her anyway because he cannot fight his passion. Along with praising Hugo's virtues, Ayn Rand also indicates his deficiencies: the repetitions, the interference of the narrator's commentary, and the fact that the character would not be capable of the literary speech Hugo places in his mouth. Hugo is, she says, "much freer" in his presentation than she is in that "he does not strive for minute precision or tight economy of intellectual content" as she does.⁷⁹

When she lectured on this material, she was asked about a possible parallel between Claude Frollo's speech here and Hank Rearden's to Dagny at Ellis Wyatt's house, and she agreed that there was a resemblance.⁸⁰ In both, an austere man confesses to a passion he has tried to suppress, a passion that contradicts his explicit convictions; she had earlier mentioned that, when she first read *Notre Dame*, her attitude about Frollo's passion for Esmeralda "would be, in effect, [her] attitude toward Rearden."⁸¹ But before Rearden, there was Andrei. In examining his avowal to Kira in the light of Frollo's speech to Esmeralda, we will see that Ayn Rand gave him some of the qualities not only of Enjolras and Javert (as discussed earlier), but also of Frollo— and she did so, as we would expect, not in imitation, but in her own way.

Andrei is like Frollo in several respects. As Frollo's religious code forbids any relationships with women, Andrei's dedication to his cause has precluded any romantic involvements. Both of them, however, have developed violent passions, and the objects of their obsessions are distinctly unsuitable. The least appropriate choice for Frollo is a pagan gypsy; the least appropriate choice for Andrei is a woman who defies (or at least denies) his cause, a woman who "is everything [he] always expected to hate" (232). And these choices are impossible for an additional reason: the men have reason to expect rejection. Frollo knows that Esmeralda loves a soldier, and he sees the "squalid cassock of a priest," with all that it represents, as an inadequate substitute. Andrei feels that he has nothing to offer Kira because his life "represents twenty-eight years of that for which [she feels] contempt" (232).

We the Living sums up the situation of Andrei's avowal as follows: "It was not an admission of love, it was the confession of a crime" (231). The sentence applies equally well to Frollo's avowal. Frollo, moreover, tries first to kidnap Esmeralda, and then to have her arrested, so that he can possess her; Andrei has a similar thought: he thinks of having Kira arrested for the same purpose. Frollo pleads "Have pity, young girl";⁸² Andrei imagines Kira "crying for pity as [he had] been crying to [her] so many months" (232).

And Ayn Rand does, literally, what she praises Hugo for doing: she conveys the "intense passion and conflict" by means of concretes. Whereas Hugo has Frollo imagine the girl's feet dancing on his prayer book, Ayn Rand has Andrei say:

> To see you, and laugh with you, and talk of the future of humanity—and think only of when your hand would touch mine, of your feet in the sand, the little shadow on your throat, your skirt blowing in the wind. To discuss the meaning of life—and wonder if I could see the line of your breast in your open collar!
> (231)

But Ayn Rand eliminates the flaws she observes in Hugo. Andrei, unlike Frollo, is not over-literary or over-articulate. He speaks with the directness of the austere soldier that he is, and with the slight awkwardness of a man unaccustomed to the subject he speaks of here for the first time: "I'd take you—and I wouldn't care if it were the floor, and if those men stood looking" (232). Her style is more economical, avoiding repetition, whereas for Hugo less was never more: Andrei's confession is less than one-third the length of Frollo's.

Another contrast lies in the difference between Ayn Rand's conscious control of her craft and intention and Victor Hugo's uneven control. The characterization of Andrei—the villain who is also noble—was part of the design of *We the Living*: he was intended to represent the best supporter of a corrupt ideal. Hugo, by contrast, apparently created a sympathetic villain in spite of himself.

> Although the priest does terrible things in the novel, one is never convinced that he is a total villain. Hugo obviously *intended* him as a villain, but, psychologically and philosophically, he was not sold on the idea. This conflict between Hugo's conscious convictions and his deepest, subconscious view of life shows in his style.
> If Hugo's full conviction had been that the priest's passion is evil, the priest's way of speaking of his passion would have been much less attractive.[83]

The contrast between these parallel scenes in *Notre Dame of Paris* and *We the Living* shows how Ayn Rand, in depicting a situation similar to one dramatized by Hugo, derived emotional power from concretes, as did he, while avoiding his flaws and applying the scene to a more coherent characterization.

A final aspect of Hugo's style that is relevant to *We the Living* is the recurrent object or motif, introduced early and recalled continually at key points. Two examples are the bishop's candlesticks in *Les Misérables* and the message in the flask in *The Man Who Laughs*. Although Ayn Rand does not analyze the recurrent use of these devices, she mentioned being impressed by the way Hugo introduced both of them.[84] Regarding the scene in which the flask remains on the surface of the sea, after the comprachicos drown, she writes: "To appreciate the full meaning of that scene, one has to read the rest of *The Man Who Laughs* and discover the nature, as well as the enormous consequences, of the message in that flask."[85]

The motif or object can be an aid to integration. Hugo wants the reader to remember that the bishop gave Jean Valjean the candlesticks in order to "buy" his soul, and to notice that the candlesticks are consistently associated with the hero's best self. Indeed, it is a moral turning point when Jean Valjean almost destroys the candlesticks, and realizes what he would be destroying if he did so. The hero ultimately dies with the light of the candlesticks on his face.

The corresponding devices in *We the Living* are the story of the Viking and the "Song of Broken Glass." Whereas the candlesticks were a gift from a bishop, who assigned them their meaning, Kira's story and song are chosen values, whose meaning she herself assigns. In editing the novel, Ayn Rand shortened the story of the Viking and removed the literal references that were originally designed to appear later (when Kira first glimpsed Leo's face and when she died). But she retained all references and allusions to the song.

The song is introduced as part of Kira's background, as the symbol of something she expects of life, something other than the work of being an engineer. "The other thing which she expected, she did not know, for it had no name, but it had been promised to her, promised in a memory of her childhood" (50). That memory, we learn, is one of the songs she heard from a casino below as she sat on a cliff, songs that "had a significance for Kira that no one else ever attached to them" because she heard in them "a profound joy of life" (50). There follows a description of the song she "selected . . . as her, Kira's, own" (51), "sharp blows," "quick, fine notes," "slow notes," and "the leap into the explosion of laughter." The song is the promise. "A lonely little girl on a slippery rock listened to her own hymn and smiled at what it promised her." The "hymn" is also a military march (a term Andrei will later use to describe Kira herself): "Kira Argounova entered [life] with the sword of a Viking pointing the way and an operetta tune for a battle march" (51).

She hears the song again on the night she meets Leo, in the red-light district. "It was the song of a nameless hope that frightened her, for it promised so much, and she could not tell what it promised; she could not even say that it was a promise; it was an emotion, almost of pain, that went through her whole body" (60). In the first draft, Ayn Rand wrote, then crossed out, the following line: "As a soldier at the sound of his anthem, Kira stood at attention, smiling up at the window."[86] The references to the "soldier" and the "anthem" associate the song with Kira's ongoing battle for life. Then, as in the novel, Kira looks at the sky and sees in the clouds the splinters of broken glass, as if her song, her personal universe, has become the actual physical universe. The song ends not with the laughter characteristic of the song, but with "someone's loud laughter," that is, with laughter characteristic of the red-light district. Kira, recognizing where she really is, tries to escape. "And then she stopped" (60). In the first draft, Ayn Rand wrote, then crossed out, the following line: "For coming down the street she saw a face. And it was the face of the Viking."[87] The song was intended to be associated both with the Viking and with what Kira sees when she looks at Leo.

Kira refers to her song as she and Leo walk through the snow to the ship in which they hope to escape from Russia. They mention concretes, including lipstick, champagne—and the "Song of Broken Glass." The song is associated with everything they expect to find in their life abroad.

The song returns to Kira, subtly, on the morning after her first night with Leo. They are caught trying to escape, and he is in the hands of the G.P.U., but she still hears her song. "She should be terrified, she thought, and she was: but under the terror there was something without name or words, a hymn without sound, something that laughed, even though Leo was locked in a cell on Gorokhovaia 2. Her body still felt as if it were holding him close to her" (126–27). Although Ayn Rand does not mention the specific song, the word "hymn" has been used for Kira's song, and the laughter, too, is part of the "Song of Broken Glass." Even the fact that the "something" is "without name" is characteristic of the song ("nameless hope," 60) and the promise it represents ("it had no name," 50).

Kira thinks of her song when she dances with Leo at Vava's party; Lydia plays "John Gray" and Leo speaks of how they would dance together, abroad. "She closed her eyes, and the strong body that led her expertly, imperiously, seemed to carry her to that other world she had seen long ago, by a dark river that murmured the 'Song of Broken Glass' " (156). Her song is again associated with Leo and with the hope for a human life, abroad.

Another reference to the song is the comparison with a song in Kálmán's *Die Bajadere*, which Kira and Leo see together. The operetta song has the quality of the promise: "a music that laughed defiantly, panting, gasping, hitting one's ears and throat and breath, an impudent, drunken music, like the challenge of a triumphant gaiety, like the 'Song of Broken Glass,' a promise that existed somewhere, that was, that could be" (208). And although this song in *Bajadere* has the quality of laughter associated with the "Song of Broken Glass," Kira sobs.

The song itself is heard again in the European roof garden. Kira sits there with Andrei, their first meeting in two weeks. Kira has not been free to see Andrei because Leo has returned from the Crimea. The orchestra is playing *Bajadere*, the operetta Kira had attended with Leo. When she comments on the music, it is likely that Leo is not far from her mind. Andrei, without context, asks her if Leo is in love with her, and tells her he does not trust Leo

and hopes she doesn't see him often. Perhaps the operetta music makes him
think of Leo, or perhaps it is the way Kira looks when she hears the music.
Kira then asks Andrei to ask the orchestra to play the "Song of Broken
Glass." When the orchestra plays Kira's song, she looks sad (much in the
way that she sobbed at the performance of *Bajadere*), and explains her reaction in terms of disappointment:

> It's something I liked . . . long ago . . . when I was a child . . . . Andrei, did you
> ever feel as if something had been promised to you in your childhood, and you
> look at yourself and you think, "I didn't know, then, that this is what would
> happen to me"—and it's strange, and funny, and a little sad? (277)

It's much more than "a little sad." Lying to both of the men who love her,
forbidden to pursue the work she intended to make hers, Kira grieves at the
chasm between the promise and the fulfillment, between what she wants
and what she has. And because she does not know how to fight her battle,
she hears in her song—her hymn, her anthem, her march—a lament for the
hope that is slipping from her grasp.

But in the novel's final scene, even as she dies, she hears her song, "as a
last battle march" (463), and she does not grieve. The "Song of Broken
Glass," as always, has notes that "laughed, laughed with a full, uncondi-
tional, consummate human joy." And the music, as before, is associated with
the promise: "But the music had been a promise; a promise at the dawn of
her life. That which had been promised her then, could not be denied to her
now."

In the penultimate paragraph, Kira realizes that the promise of the song is
and has always been the spirit of life. "She had known something which no
human words could ever tell and she knew it now" (464). That is the "something without name," the thing that "had no words." "She had been awaiting
it and she felt it, as if it had been, as if she had lived it." What she expected,
what she was promised, has come to pass—in her spirit if not in a full span
of years.

"Life had been, if only because she had known it could be, and she felt it
now as a hymn without sound. . . ." The "hymn without sound" is the phrase
used to convey Kira's feeling when Leo was at Gorokhovaia 2; it is the
"something that laughed"; it is her "Song of Broken Glass," the song she first
heard when she sat on a cliff over a "silent river," when a star seemed to
drop into that river, as "the summer sun sank behind the hills" (50). She
hears it now as a snowy plain stretches into the sunrise, which looks like
"the faint, fading ghost of a lake in a summer sun."

Ayn Rand, as I have noted, intended to include the Viking as well in this
scene. Although she removed the paragraph and the explicit reference, she
retained the reference to Kira's "banner"—"her only banner that had never

been lowered, that she had held high and straight, a life she could not betray" (463)—which is associated with the Viking. The Viking in her story had refused the banners offered by the King and the Priest; instead, "on the tall mast, lashing the wind, was his own banner, that had never been lowered."[88] Like Kira's.

As the bishop's candlesticks are with Jean Valjean through every stage of his moral regeneration, so Kira's symbols—the song and the story that encapsulates the promise of life—are with her throughout.

AFTER *WE THE LIVING*

Ayn Rand did not learn from Victor Hugo the fundamental premises of her art. By her own account, she had already formed in her mind "the idea that a story had to present its theme in terms of action" and "that a story had to have some important theme apart from just action." But he was the supreme exemplar of those fundamentals: "He was the first and the best illustration of that technique—on the grandest scale."[89] Because she loved his novels and wanted to be able to do what he did, she used some of his methods in her first novel, as she was developing her own. *We the Living* "took care of that influence." But she still had Hugo in mind when she thought about what she had written.

While planning *The Fountainhead,* she reread and outlined *Les Misérables,* to see how Hugo had structured and focused a long narrative.[90] When, years later, she spoke about Enjolras, she commented that a scene of his was "actually the Wynand-Roark in spirit."[91] She was referring, I believe, to his death scene (her personal highlight, as I've noted) and specifically to the fact that Grantaire, after sleeping through most of the action on the barricades, awakens to see Enjolras facing the firing squad and promptly asks permission to be shot along with him. Hugo had introduced Grantaire as an unlikely friend for the idealistic Enjolras. "Le scepticisme, cette carie sèche de l'intelligence, ne lui avait pas laissé une idée entière dans l'esprit" [Skepticism, that dry rot of the intellect, had not left one entire idea in his mind] (part 3, book 4, chapter 1).[92] And yet:

Grantaire admirait, aimait, et vénérait Enjolras. . . . Sans qu'il se rendît clairement compte et sans qu'il songeât à se l'expliquer à lui-même, cette nature chaste, saine, ferme, droite, dure, candide, le charmait. . . . Ses idées molles, fléchissantes, disloquées, malades, difformes, se rattachaient à Enjolras comme à une épine dorsale. Son rachis moral s'appuyait à cette fermeté. Grantaire, près d'Enjolras, redevenait quelqu'un.

[Grantaire admired, loved, and venerated Enjolras. . . . Without understanding it clearly, and without trying to explain it to himself, that chaste, healthy, firm, direct, hard, honest nature charmed him. . . . His soft, wavering, disjointed, diseased, deformed ideas hitched onto Enjolras as to a backbone. His moral spine leaned on that firmness. Beside Enjolras, Grantaire became somebody again.] (part 3, book 4, chapter 1)[93]

When he rises from his drunken stupor to see Enjolras facing the firing squad as if "l'autorité de son regard tranquille . . . contraignît cette cohue sinistre à le tuer avec respect" [the authority of his tranquil eye . . . compelled that sinister mob to kill him respectfully] (part 5, book 1, chapter 23),[94] Grantaire wants to share that authority and that respect. He wants literally to be beside Enjolras, even now. Recognizing that to die with Enjolras would be an honor and a privilege, he asks permission, which Enjolras graciously grants. Smiling, Enjolras extends his hand.

The "Wynand-Roark in spirit" is the transfusion of values from a great man to one who has not lived up to his own potential for greatness. The love the lesser man feels for the greater one carries with it the hope that it is not too late for the two to join hands and minds.

And perhaps there was also a place in *The Fountainhead* for some elements of the physical image of Enjolras, he of the "dédaigneuse" [disdainful] mouth (part 3, book 4, chapter 1),[95] with "cette chevelure tumultueuse au vent" [his hair flying in the wind] (part 3, book 4, chapter 1),[96] a "grave jeune homme, bourreau et prêtre, de lumière comme le cristal, et de roche aussi" [severe young man, executioner and priest, luminous like the crystal and rock also] (part 4, book 11, chapter 8).[97] In the opening pages of *The Fountainhead*, Ayn Rand introduces her hero, her ideal man, Howard Roark. He is standing on a rock, on stone that "glowed, wet with sunrays," as the "wind waved his hair against the sky"; his face has "a contemptuous mouth, shut tight, the mouth of an executioner or a saint."[98]

She commented, in 1958, on the influence Hugo had had on her. When (as discussed earlier) she was asked about a parallel between Claude Frollo's avowal of love to Esmeralda in *Notre Dame of Paris* and Rearden's morning-after speech to Dagny, she replied that she, too, had noticed the parallel, but not at the time she wrote *Atlas Shrugged*.

> Now I had read this novel originally between the ages of fourteen and sixteen somewhere. I had looked at it once in Hollywood, after the Rearden scene was written. I had not thought of this speech in relation to Rearden's speech until I was translating it [for the lecture], and yet the influence is tremendous. It's tremendous. It's directly Hugo's influence.
>
> But do you see in what sense I was not copying him? There is no single sentence that you would say is taking his concretes, but the essence of the drama was there. . . . Wouldn't I have thought of the drama of Rearden's speech even without ever reading this book? Possibly. But that is not the point. The point is that I was very aware at the time I read *this* in my teens, [that] this is a tremen-

dously important scene that I liked, that the conflict of a man torn between a love which in fact is proper because of wrong premises—which is how I interpreted him, even at that age. The drama of that remained with me as a very strong impression. Therefore by the time I needed the scene, like Rearden and Dagny, that value literarily was already in my mind. I would be attracted emotionally, literarily, to that kind of scene. You see, that's the way an influence works.[99]

In this chapter, I have tried to show how the influence may have worked, as Ayn Rand, in her own first novel, created her own form of some of the literary values she loved in the novelist she ranked first.

NOTES

1. Ayn Rand, "What is Romanticism?" in *The Romantic Manifesto: A Philosophy of Literature*, revised edition (New York: Signet, 1975), 119, and "Introduction to *Ninety-Three*," in *Romantic Manifesto*, 154.

2. Ayn Rand, "Art and Sense of Life," in *Romantic Manifesto*, 43.

3. Ayn Rand, "[1968] Introduction," *The Fountainhead* (New York: Signet fiftieth anniversary paperback edition, 1993), v.

4. Ayn Rand, "The Comprachicos," in *Return of the Primitive: The Anti-Industrial Revolution*, Peter Schwartz, ed. (New York: Meridian, 1999).

5. Ayn Rand, "From the Horse's Mouth," in *Philosophy: Who Needs It* (New York: Bobbs-Merrill, 1982; Signet paperback edition, 1984).

6. Ayn Rand, "The Stimulus and the Response," in *Philosophy: Who Needs It*, 151. The passage appears in part 3, book 5, chapter 3: ". . . et il bénit Dieu de lui avoir donné ces deux richesses qui manquent à bien des riches: le travail qui le fait libre et la pensée qui le fait digne" (*Les Misérables*, ed. Marius-François Guyard, 2 vols. [Paris: Garnier, 1966], I, 817).

7. Biographical interviews (Ayn Rand Archives).

8. Ayn Rand, *The Art of Fiction: A Guide for Writers and Readers*, Tore Boeckmann, ed. (New York: Plume, 2000), 176.

9. David Harriman, ed. *Journals of Ayn Rand* (New York: Dutton, 1997), 65.

10. Rand, "What is Romanticism?" in *Romantic Manifesto*, 121, and "Introduction to *Ninety-Three*," in *Romantic Manifesto*, 156.

11. Guyard, II, 489–90; Victor Hugo, *Les Misérables*, translated by Lee Fahnestock and Norman MacAfee, based on the translation by C. E. Wilbour (New York: Signet, 1987), 1242. Quotations from Hugo will appear first in French, the language in which Ayn Rand read him, and then in English; the references, too, will be first to the French edition, then to the English.

12. Leonard Peikoff, ed. *The Early Ayn Rand: A Selection from Her Unpublished Fiction* (New York: New American Library, 1984; Signet paperback edition, 1986), 195–200.

13. Rand, *The Fountainhead*, 309–10.

14. Peikoff, *Early Ayn Rand*, 201.

15. Ayn Rand, "Introduction to *Ninety-Three*," *Romantic Manifesto*, 158.
16. Biographical interviews (Ayn Rand Archives).
17. Biographical interviews (Ayn Rand Archives).
18. Biographical interviews (Ayn Rand Archives).
19. Rand, *The Fountainhead*, 209.
20. Biographical interviews (Ayn Rand Archives).
21. Biographical interviews (Ayn Rand Archives).
22. Guyard I, 773; Fahnestock, MacAfee, Wilbour, 648.
23. The sixtieth anniversary edition of *We the Living* contains a typo here: "from" instead of "for."
24. Guyard I, 773; Fahnestock, MacAfee, Wilbour, 649.
25. Guyard II, 347; Fahnestock, MacAfee, Wilbour, 1116.
26. Guyard II, 442; Fahnestock, MacAfee, Wilbour, 1200.
27. Guyard II, 499; Fahnestock, MacAfee, Wilbour, 1251.
28. Guyard I, 774; Fahnestock, MacAfee, Wilbour, 649.
29. First draft, 351 of pagination that begins with chapter 4 (Ayn Rand Archives).
30. First draft, 105 of pagination that begins with part 2 (Ayn Rand Archives).
31. Guyard II, 457; Fahnestock, MacAfee, Wilbour, 1213.
32. Guyard I, 773; Fahnestock, MacAfee, Wilbour, 648.
33. Guyard II, 417; Fahnestock, MacAfee, Wilbour, 1178.
34. Guyard II, 346–47; Fahnestock, MacAfee, Wilbour, 1115–16.
35. Biographical interviews (Ayn Rand Archives).
36. Guyard II, 442; Fahnestock, MacAfee, Wilbour, 1200.
37. Biographical interviews (Ayn Rand Archives).
38. Biographical interviews (Ayn Rand Archives).
39. Guyard I, 214; Fahnestock, MacAfee, Wilbour, 171.
40. Guyard II, 343; Fahnestock, MacAfee, Wilbour, 1112.
41. Guyard I, 214; Fahnestock, MacAfee, Wilbour, 171–72.
42. Guyard II, 581; Fahnestock, MacAfee, Wilbour, 1323.
43. Guyard II, 581; Fahnestock, MacAfee, Wilbour, 1322.
44. Guyard II, 590; Fahnestock, MacAfee, Wilbour, 1330.
45. Biographical interviews (Ayn Rand Archives).
46. Biographical interviews (Ayn Rand Archives).
47. Ayn Rand, "Basic Principles of Literature," in *Romantic Manifesto*, 82.
48. Rand, *Art of Fiction*, 37.
49. Ayn Rand, "Introduction to *Ninety-Three*," in *Romantic Manifesto*, 157.
50. Rand, *Art of Fiction*, 35.
51. Rand, *Art of Fiction*, 39.
52. Rand, *Art of Fiction*, 40.
53. Rand, *Art of Fiction*, 37.
54. Rand, *Art of Fiction*, 38.
55. Rand, *Art of Fiction*, 174–75.
56. Rand, "The Esthetic Vacuum of Our Age," in *Romantic Manifesto*, 125, and "Introduction to *Ninety-Three*," in *Romantic Manifesto*, 160.
57. Victor Hugo, *L'Homme qui rit*. 2 vols. (Paris: Nelson, 1960), II, 419, 427; *The Man Who Laughs*, translated by Joseph L. Blamire (Cresskill, N.J.: Paper Tiger, 2001), 564, 569.

58. Victor Hugo, *Quatrevingt-Treize*, ed. Jean Boudout (Paris: Garnier, 1963), 489–90; *Ninety-Three*, translated by Frank Lee Benedict (New York: Carroll and Graf, 1988), 388–89.

59. Rand, "Introduction," *Romantic Manifesto*, viii.

60. In "The 'Inexplicable Personal Alchemy' " (1969), reprinted in *Return of the Primitive: The Anti-Industrial Revolution*, Ayn Rand discusses the meaning of the word "abroad" for Soviet citizens: "if you project what you would feel for a combination of Atlantis, the Promised Land and the most glorious civilization on another planet, as imagined by a benevolent kind of science fiction, you will have a pale approximation" (125).

61. Peikoff, *Early Ayn Rand*, 204.

62. Biographical interviews (Ayn Rand Archives).

63. See Shoshana Milgram, "From *Airtight* to *We the Living*: The Drafts of Ayn Rand's First Novel," and Robert Mayhew, " *We the Living*: '36 & '59," in the present volume.

64. Guyard I, 456; Fahnestock, MacAfee, Wilbour, 378.

65. Guyard I, 457; Fahnestock, MacAfee, Wilbour, 378.

66. *L'Homme qui rit*, I, 114; Blamire, 77.

67. *L'Homme qui rit*, II, 191; Blamire, 411.

68. Boudout, 72; Benedict, 56.

69. Biographical interviews (Ayn Rand Archives).

70. Biographical interviews (Ayn Rand Archives).

71. Biographical interviews (Ayn Rand Archives).

72. Biographical interviews (Ayn Rand Archives).

73. *L'Homme qui rit*, I, 323; Blamire, 219.

74. *L'Homme qui rit*, II, 389; Blamire, 545.

75. *L'Homme qui rit*, I, 377–78; Blamire, 255.

76. *L'Homme qui rit*, I, 374; Blamire, 252.

77. Biographical interviews (Ayn Rand Archives).

78. Rand, *Art of Fiction*, 98–104.

79. Rand, *Art of Fiction*, 104.

80. The source here is Ayn Rand, *Fiction Writing: A Thirteen Lecture Course*, taped in 1958 (Second Renaissance Books, 1994), Lecture 8.

81. Biographical interviews (Ayn Rand Archives).

82. Rand, *Art of Fiction*, 99.

83. Rand, *Art of Fiction*, 101.

84. Biographical interviews (Ayn Rand Archives).

85. Ayn Rand, "Introductory Note to 'The Man Who Laughs,' " *The Objectivist* 6 (December 1967).

86. First draft, 23 in pagination that begins with part 1, chapter 4 (Ayn Rand Archives).

87. First draft, 23 in pagination that begins with part 1, chapter 4 (Ayn Rand Archives).

88. Peikoff, *Early Ayn Rand*, 203.

89. Biographical interviews (Ayn Rand Archives).

90. Biographical interviews (Ayn Rand Archives).

91. Biographical interviews (Ayn Rand Archives).

92. Guyard I, 784; Fahnestock, MacAfee, Wilbour, 657.
93. Guyard I, 784; Fahnestock, MacAfee, Wilbour, 658.
94. Guyard II, 499; Fahnestock, MacAfee, Wilbour, 1250–51.
95. Guyard I, 773; Fahnestock, MacAfee, Wilbour, 648.
96. Guyard I, 774; Fahnestock, MacAfee, Wilbour, 649.
97. Guyard II, 348; Fahnestock, MacAfee, Wilbour, 1116.
98. Rand, *The Fountainhead*, 15–16.
99. Rand, *Fiction Writing: A Thirteen Lecture Course*, Lecture 8.

11

Red Pawn: Ayn Rand's Other Story of Soviet Russia

Jena Trammell

While working at RKO and writing *We the Living* in 1931, Ayn Rand drafted a movie originally titled *Red Pawn*, which she sold to Universal Pictures in 1932. The filming of *Red Pawn* was delayed repeatedly in a series of studio decisions, and by the mid-1930s it is unlikely that *Red Pawn*'s anticollectivist themes would have appealed to many directors or studios during Hollywood's Red Decade. Like Rand's struggle to publish *We the Living*, the troubled production history of *Red Pawn* illustrates the degree to which Marxist ideology was embraced by American intellectuals and much of Hollywood's elite during the early decades of the twentieth century. Though never made into a film or novel, *Red Pawn*—Ayn Rand's only other work of fiction set in Soviet Russia—marks a critical point in her professional career and in her developing aesthetics of fiction.

THE HISTORY OF *RED PAWN*

In *We the Living*, Kira and Leo watch an American motion picture entitled *The Golden Octopus*, directed by Reginald Moore, censored by Comrade M. Zavadkov (174). In Russia's early postrevolutionary years, the Soviet censoring of American films consisted typically of cutting and inserting anticapitalist propaganda into subtitles, though sometimes the Russian film editors went as far as to add entirely new scenes featuring characters who spoke out in tirades against the rich.[1] As Kira and Leo watch *The Golden Octopus*, its newly altered storyline clashes with its scenes of attractive, well-dressed American men and women, radiant with good health and happiness. The subtitles identify the characters as "our American brothers under the capitalistic yoke." The new storyline adds that a capitalist has stolen documents of great value to the Soviet Union. The original ending of the film has been cut, and is replaced with Russian titles that explain that the savage American capitalist was killed by striking laborers and that the young working-class hero will devote his life to the revolutionary cause. "Hell," remarks Leo, "do they also make pictures like that in America?" (175).

Despite the obvious and ludicrous incongruity of such Soviet changes to American films, this example of censorship in *We the Living* draws attention to the seriousness with which Soviet propagandists regarded Vladimir Lenin's declaration that "of all the arts, the most important one is the cinema."[2] And to answer Leo's question: Yes; for many years, beginning in the 1920s, the American film industry released dozens of motion pictures with anticapitalist messages—for example, *Success at Any Price* and *The President's Mystery*—although U.S. films were usually subtler and more sophisticated in their propagandistic efforts.

Such themes in American movies would have been especially contemptible to Rand, who early in her life was deeply influenced by American films that conveyed to her a joyous, benevolent sense of the universe. She later credited them with helping to preserve her life and mind during her difficult years growing up in a society hostile to her deepest and most fundamental beliefs. Before leaving the Soviet Union in January 1926, Rand studied for one year at the State Institute for Cinematography in Leningrad, where she intended to learn screen writing as an entry into her career as a novelist. By late 1926, she was living and working in Hollywood, first as a film extra and then as a junior screenwriter for director Cecil B. DeMille, until the close of his studio in 1928.[3]

After Rand married Frank O'Connor in April 1929, she began work as a filing clerk in the wardrobe department at RKO. In 1930, while still at RKO, she took her first steps toward writing *We the Living*, a novel that would give Americans an accurate picture of the oppressive conditions of life in Soviet Russia. She planned an outline for the entire book and began drafting. Her progress on *We the Living* was slow, the opening paragraph alone requiring many days. She was still mastering the English language, and she frequently worked overtime at her job in the wardrobe department, often six days a week and nine to ten hours per day. After approximately a year of writing on weekends and during her one-week vacation, she was exhausted and merely two chapters into *We the Living* when she decided to postpone the novel's composition to attempt to write and sell a movie original. Her goal was to earn enough money to be able to write full-time.

Ayn Rand developed two screen originals in late 1931, *Red Pawn* and

Treason, both set in Soviet Russia. She wrote both synopses in less than a week. She decided to try to sell *Red Pawn* first, since she believed it to be the more interesting piece for its suspenseful plot of a courageously independent heroine who enters a Soviet prison as the mistress of its Communist commander in order to save her anticommunist husband. Selling the story required hiring an agent, a process that could take months for a beginning writer. While waiting, Rand showed *Red Pawn* to a young woman at RKO who was assistant to the studio head and believed to have influence in the story department. The woman dismissed *Red Pawn*'s story as improbable. She particularly disliked the ending and told Rand that the story would never sell. Ignoring the advice of this woman—who later provided Rand with inspiration for the parasitical character of Peter Keating in *The Fountainhead*—Rand found an agent, Nick Carter. She thought Carter was honorable in working hard even for the beginning writers he signed. He began submitting *Red Pawn* to the major studios. For months, however, he received only rejections without explanations.[4] One Hollywood insider reported that when Carter offered *Red Pawn* for sale to Paramount at this time, actress Marlene Dietrich read the story and liked it, though her director Josef von Sternberg did not.[5]

In late summer 1932, Nick Carter called Ayn Rand unexpectedly to say that Universal Pictures wished to purchase *Red Pawn*. Universal's business manager had been hospitalized, and they would have to meet him bedside. She went with Carter to the hospital, and there they settled the terms of *Red Pawn*'s sale. She was to receive $700 for the story itself and $800 for her work on a treatment and screenplay. Rand immediately left her job at RKO and went to work on an eight-week contract at Universal. *The Hollywood Reporter* announced that she completed her screenplay for *Red Pawn* in mid-November 1932, and that Universal planned the film's production as a vehicle for its new star, Viennese actress Tala Birell.[6] Rand had written *Red Pawn* with Marlene Dietrich in mind for the lead, and the studio seemed to agree with her choice, because Tala Birell was Universal's hope for a new Marlene Dietrich or Greta Garbo, the leading stars of the era. Birell had served as understudy to Dietrich in a 1927 Berlin theatrical production, and Universal had signed Birell in 1931 to a long-term contract. Birell starred in two films for Universal: *Doomed Battalion* in June 1932 and *Nagana* in early 1933.[7] These pictures failed at the box office, and Universal released her from her contract. At the same time, the studio's plans to produce *Red Pawn* were shelved.[8]

On June 19, 1934, Paramount Pictures secured the rights to *Red Pawn* from Universal in exchange for a property Paramount had paid $20,000 for, British mystery writer E. Phillips Oppenheim's *The Great Impersonation*.[9] Ayn Rand was immediately called in to work at Paramount on a new *Red Pawn* screenplay. At Paramount, she was told that studio executives liked her story and wanted it for Marlene Dietrich's next picture, to be directed by Josef von Sternberg. Press releases in *Variety* and *The Los Angeles Examiner* that week announced that *Red Pawn* would be the next Dietrich–von Sternberg film.[10] Dietrich and von Sternberg had previously collaborated on six films for Paramount, two of which were very profitable for the studio. *Morocco* had earned Paramount $2 million in profits in 1930, at the beginning of the Depression. *Shanghai Express* earned a $3 million profit in 1932, when the company had been on the verge of bankruptcy.[11] Dietrich and von Sternberg's more recent motion pictures, however, had been financial failures. *Blonde Venus* in 1932 and *The Scarlet Empress* in 1934 were panned by critics at the time and failed at the box office.[12] In *The Scarlet Empress*, an epic portrait of Catherine the Great of Russia, von Sternberg had minimized dialogue, preferring to advance the story by images, silent film titles, and a dramatic musical score, resulting in a film described as episodic and nondramatic. Even Paramount executives were said to have hated the film.[13]

Paramount was again on the brink of bankruptcy, making story choice critical for its next motion picture. Dietrich's and von Sternberg's two successful films at Paramount had been studio selections. Afterward, von Sternberg's renewed contract awarded him final control over script selection, and his own picks had increasingly threatened the company's stability. Nevertheless, though *Blonde Venus* and *The Scarlet Empress* were disastrous for Paramount, the studio was forced to honor its contract and allow von Sternberg to choose and direct one more motion picture. Ernst Lubitsch, Paramount's leading director, detested von Sternberg's style of filmmaking, and began negotiating with Dietrich for a new contract without von Sternberg.[14] It is likely that Lubitsch, who creatively ruled the studio, chose *Red Pawn* to pitch to von Sternberg as Paramount's choice for his final picture.

Meanwhile, Ayn Rand sat in the Paramount studios for four weeks at $100 per week waiting to see if von Sternberg would select *Red Pawn*, because her contract required her to work with the director alone on the final screenplay. The head of the scenario department told Rand they were all trying to sell von Sternberg on *Red Pawn* as the right story for Dietrich. But von Sternberg, who was more interested in background than plot, ultimately decided against it, because he did not want another Russian story—a view Rand found ridiculous in light of *Red Pawn*'s modern Soviet setting and dramatic plotting.[15] Von Sternberg's last film at Paramount, *The Devil Is a Woman*, was chosen for its Spanish setting. Released in 1935, *The Devil Is a Woman* was von Sternberg's greatest box office failure, reviled by studio executives like Lubitsch, film critics, and audiences. Afterward, von Sternberg's career continued to decline. Ironically, in 1944, it was Ayn Rand who purchased his home, which had been designed for von Sternberg in the 1930s by architect Richard Neutra.[16]

At the same time von Sternberg was having trouble in Hollywood, the efforts of the American Communist Party to win the support of liberals, intellectuals, and Hollywood's elite had been underway for a number of years. The 1920 Soviet congress known as the Third International, or Comintern, had passed a resolution to overthrow the bourgeois governments of all European and American nations and replace them with communist administrations in order to create a global Soviet Socialist Republic. For many citizens of the United States, the Depression, the rise of Hitler and Nazism, and the Soviets' own propaganda obscured the communists' totalitarian principles. Record levels of unemployment in the United States contrasted painfully with Soviet Russia's claims of productivity and full employment. Hitler's destruction of any existing liberty in Germany seemed to be at odds with Soviet Russia's professed commitment to peace and equality.[17] The Soviets believed their opportunity with Americans was at hand. Although the U.S. Communist Party had originated in 1919, just two years after the Bolshevik coup, it had never succeeded in attracting more than about 30,000 members, and the party's following had dropped to fewer than 10,000 by 1929.[18] In the mid-1930s, American Communists decided to take advantage of the social climate by infiltrating and persuading the rich and often politically naive of Hollywood to promote Soviet objectives.

Like Lenin, Stalin saw the enormous possibilities of cinema as a tool for propaganda and the indoctrination of people worldwide. Stalin, who himself enjoyed American movies, reportedly once said that with the power of the American film industry he could conquer all the world's nations for communism. Even in the worst years of the Depression, Hollywood was filling theaters throughout the United States and in many other countries and was taking in unprecedented earnings.[19] In 1935, the Communist Party organized over 300 Hollywood writers in the Screen Writers' Guild in exchange for a pledge of party loyalty.[20] As Adolf Hitler's power increased, the Communists organized more movie industry workers into its Hollywood Anti-Nazi League, a Communist Party front that quickly drew more than 4,000 members and brought lavish new financial contributions into party hands. *The Daily Worker*, the newspaper of the American Communist Party, reported the rapidly increasing support of the movie capital, from meetings and protests to star-studded fund-raising benefits and dinners. It is estimated that from 1936 to 1939 the Hollywood left donated over $2 million to the communist cause.[21] After Hitler and Stalin signed the Nazi-Soviet pact of August 1939, many in Hollywood began to withdraw their support.[22]

For Ayn Rand, the opportunity to see *Red Pawn* produced as a film may have appeared too remote to pursue in the years when Hollywood communism was at its height. Though the nation's entertainment industry was generally opposed to motion pictures with expressly political messages, writers for the Hollywood Anti-Nazi League ensured that many movies carried anti-capitalist themes that played into the ambitions of their communist sympathies. For example, John Howard Lawson, who served as the first president of the Screen Writers' Guild and also wrote proletarian novels, scripted *Success at Any Price*, released by RKO in 1934. Starring Douglas Fairbanks Jr., the film celebrates a young worker almost driven to suicide before exposing the financial corruption of the American firm that employs him. Lawson is remembered as one of the Hollywood Ten, subpoenaed to testify at the hearings of the House Un-American Activities Committee in 1947. Lester Cole, another of the Hollywood Ten, was one of the screenwriters of *The President's Mystery*, produced by Republic Pictures in 1936 (and based on an idea by F. D. R.), about an attorney who aids Depression-era capitalists in exploiting the working classes.

In July 1934, while Rand awaited von Sternberg's decision on *Red Pawn* at Paramount, she wrote to Cecil B. DeMille, for whom she first worked in Hollywood and who now produced and directed pictures at Paramount. She enclosed a synopsis of *Red Pawn* and expressed her desire for him to read the story and grant her an appointment to discuss it with him.[23] There is no evidence, however, that DeMille read *Red Pawn* or met with her concerning it. After von Sternberg's rejection of the script, Rand wrote to her agent for *We the Living*, Jean Wick, on August 20, 1934, suggesting the sale of *Red Pawn* in novelette form.[24] In her contract with Paramount, Rand retained the right to publish *Red Pawn* both serially and as a book. At the moment, however, *We the Living* was running into resistance with American publishers for being anti-Soviet, and in frustration Rand lamented to Wick:

> The American reader has no knowledge of [life under dictatorship]. He has not the slightest suspicion of it. If he had—we would not have the appalling number of parlor Bolsheviks and idealistic sympathizers with the Soviet regime, liberals who would scream with horror if they knew the truth of Soviet existence.[25]

In the interval since *Red Pawn*'s original sale to Universal Pictures in 1932, Rand had completed a drama entitled *Penthouse Legend* in 1933. When the Hollywood Playhouse contracted to produce *Penthouse Legend* with the title *Woman on Trial* in the fall of 1934, her plans to publish *Red Pawn* as a novel were apparently placed on hold. The following year, she moved to New York City, where *Penthouse Legend* began its Broadway run as *Night of January 16th*, and she began making notes for her next novel, *The Fountainhead*.

In subsequent years, Ayn Rand occasionally returned to the idea of seeing *Red Pawn* produced as a film or revised for publication as a novella. She brought the *Red Pawn* script to director Hal Wallis's attention when she worked for him as a screenwriter for three years (beginning in 1944). Wallis liked the story and noted the resemblance in dramatic situation between his acclaimed film *Casablanca* and *Red Pawn*, which had been written earlier than *Casablanca.* But he seemed reluctant to make a decision about *Red Pawn,* owing to its Soviet setting. Eventually, Rand dropped the issue.[26] As Kenneth Billingsley reports in *Hollywood Party,* communism in Hollywood remained pervasive. In the 1940s, the party's greatest success in Hollywood was not so much propaganda, but the suppression of films with anti-Soviet themes. In the studios, Communist story analysts rejected movie scripts with anticommunist themes, and Communist agents undermined their own anti-Communist clients' careers. The party initiated boycotts and smear campaigns against anticommunist films and actors. Billingsley points out that Wallis claimed in these years that it was foolish to even consider an anticommunist movie in view of threats from the Communist Party.[27]

Ayn Rand persisted, however, and in a 1946 letter to her friend Barbara Stanwyck, she urged the actress to consider *Red Pawn* for her next film role. Rand recounted Wallis's praise of *Red Pawn* to Stanwyck and stated that it was the best script she had ever written. Further, Rand thought Stanwyck was perfect for the female lead, and hoped the actress would help her to convince Wallis to produce it.[28] Stanwyck had already experienced the censure of the Communists in 1945 when she was blacklisted with fifty-one other performers who crossed the picket lines of striking workers for the Communist-controlled Conference of Studio Unions.[29] After reviewing *Red Pawn* with her manager, Stanwyck telegrammed Rand to decline the offer, stating simply that the story was not right for her.[30]

Many years later, after Rand completed *Atlas Shrugged* (in 1957), she once more turned to *Red Pawn.* In June 1963, though busy writing nonfiction, she contacted Paramount and the New York publisher New American Library, hoping to sell them on *Red Pawn.*[31] Paramount still retained the film rights, as well as rights to any alterations in the story, if Rand were to revise and publish it in serialized or novel form. Initial replies to her inquiries were disappointing. Victor Weybright at New American thought *Red Pawn* unworthy of publishing, given Rand's later fiction.[32] Alvin Manuel at Paramount responded that the studio was interested, having commissioned a new treatment of *Red Pawn* only a year before. But studio executives, who desired a story "neither pro- nor anti-Russian," decided not to ask Rand to work on a new script, aware she would not agree to the major changes they sought.[33] Rand was soon discussing with Paramount and Bennett Cerf of Random House the possibility of her writing an entirely new novel and screenplay based on *Red Pawn.* If Paramount refused to purchase the new screenplay, Rand wanted to be free to sell her story elsewhere.[34] Negotiations over *Red Pawn* continued for about eight months, but an agreement was never reached.[35] Ultimately, no motion picture of *Red Pawn* was ever produced.[36] The screen story was published posthumously, in 1984, in *The Early Ayn Rand.*[37]

CECIL B. DEMILLE, *RED PAWN*, AND AYN
RAND'S LITERARY AESTHETICS

Ayn Rand's letters to film producer Kenneth MacGowan and to Cecil B. DeMille on her method of plot construction in *Red Pawn* convey her earliest written perspectives on key elements in her literary aesthetics: the central importance of plot in a work of fiction and the necessary integration of plot and theme. In both fiction and film, Rand detested plotless works as well as action stories unrelated to philosophical meaning. She recognized that philosophical values consciously and subconsciously motivate human choices and actions, and that purposeful living requires conscious thought and goal-directed action. Dramatized action in fiction, she would later write, provides the proper inspirational model for conscious, purposeful living: "One cannot preserve that vision or achieve it without some knowledge of what is greatness and some image to concretize it."[38] Rand's experiences as a moviegoer and her work in the film industry strengthened her developing conviction of the fundamental importance in fictional art of expressing the values that motivate human actions within a dramatic and suspenseful progression of events. The plot development of *Red Pawn*, Rand's first completed work of fiction and her first professional sale, evidences a young writer who in her mid-twenties was already skillfully applying the principles that would later become cornerstones in her unique philosophy of literary composition.

Rand discerned her preference for goal-oriented plot action in literature as a child. At age nine, she was captivated by an exotic adventure story for children called *The Mysterious Valley*, by Maurice Champagne. The main character, Cyrus Paltons, a British captain in India, forever fixed in her mind an image of the heroic human ideal. Cyrus was strong, intelligent, courageous, and motivated by firm values into unflinching action, whether thwarting an enemy or punishing a traitor.[39] At thirteen, Rand began reading the novels of Victor Hugo, whom she always regarded as the greatest novelist in world literature.[40] Hugo provided her with the Romantic model for realism in fiction. Against contemporary literary theory, Rand argued that realism makes plot structure fundamental to fiction. "The method of romantic realism," she wrote, "is to make life more beautiful and interesting than it actually is, yet give it all the reality, and even a more convincing reality than that of our everyday existence. Life, not as it is, but as it could be and should be."[41] This principle of inspiration in aesthetics, derived from Aristotle, is the most important value in literary art, according to Rand.[42] And since inspirational art must recreate reality, dramatization is essential in fiction. As she states in "Basic Principles of Literature," "Life is a process of action. The entire content of man's consciousness—thought, knowledge, ideas, values—has only one ultimate form of expression: in his actions; and only one ultimate purpose: to guide his actions."[43] Therefore, a sequence of dramatized human action, or plot, is the most critical element in a work of literary fiction, and Hugo's masterful integration of plot structure and theme in works like *Les Misérables* and *Ninety-Three* was especially admired by Rand.

Prior to *Red Pawn*, in Rand's early career in Hollywood as a scenarist for DeMille's studio, even the notes she wrote to herself on plot development and plot-theme integration are consistent with the literary principles in her later aesthetic writings. For example, she wrote in her screenwriting notebook in 1927, "A concrete story is built in such a way as to express the idea, the universal traits, in the most colorful way" and "The plot [should] express and unite everything, all the concretes. The plot flows from the essence of the theme; one constructs the plot after analyzing the theme, the epoch."[44] Her early silent film scenarios for movies like *The Skyscraper* are structured on sequences of dramatized events that build upon a central storyline. For *Red Pawn*, Rand's method of plot construction was directly influenced by DeMille's own method of plotting stories, as she stated in a letter to him in 1934, enclosing a copy of *Red Pawn*'s synopsis: "I am very anxious to show you what I have accomplished, particularly since it is accomplished in accordance with your ideas as to story construction and situations."[45] Indeed, strong similarities exist between DeMille's perspectives on plot and dramatic development and Ayn Rand's principles of literary aesthetics.

From the 1920s to the 1950s, states Robert Birchard, DeMille's box-office record in Hollywood was unmatched.[46] No other director in movie history has ever earned so great a popular success for so many decades as DeMille. Nevertheless, film critics to the present have traditionally disparaged and even ignored his work. Birchard argues that opposition to DeMille is owed to a preference among critics for "realism in the arts" in contrast with DeMille's preference for dramatic storytelling centered upon moral conflict. "DeMille placed a heavy emphasis on story," says Birchard, "and often employed intricate plot devices and narrative complications."[47] To intensify his films' conflicts, DeMille avoided the cliché of virtuous protagonists fighting villainous antagonists. Instead, his major characters were often married couples, brothers, or friends in dispute over moral issues: "In films like *Why Change Your Wife?* and *Don't Change Your Husband,* DeMille dared to suggest that husbands and wives could drift apart without the necessity of painting him as a cad or her as a whore. In *Saturday Night*, he introduced two couples who are very much in love—but love is not enough to keep them together."[48] DeMille's upbringing contributed to his appreciation for such drama. His father, Henry DeMille, was a successful playwright of the domestic drama who told his son: "The dramatist is a camera, and his photography of life must be true if he would reach men's hearts."[49] Truth in drama, as Cecil DeMille later explained, resides in the proper motivation of the characters' actions.[50] DeMille also wrote in his autobiography that his favorite memories of his father were evenings spent together reading classic stories of moral conflict from the Bible and authors like Victor Hugo.[51]

Cecil B. DeMille's ideas for story building were legend among those who worked for him in Hollywood. Actor Henry Wilcoxon wrote in his memoirs that DeMille never wavered in his view that the most important element in any film was the basic plot and that a successful film required an intricate conflict. DeMille ordered his writers to supply him only with storylines that could be used in a diversity of settings: "Tell me a story about people, a very basic story, which could be dropped into a fish cannery, a studio, or a circus. First I want the plumbing in this house and a strong foundation."⁵² Though DeMille indulged his love of spectacle in many films, often to the derision of critics, he consistently maintained the dramatic focus in each film on a story of personal dimensions, of personal hopes and fears, with which his viewers might identify. Of his art, DeMille wrote: "I like spectacle. I like to paint on a big canvas. I like it when the critics say I do it well. But I spend much more time working on dramatic construction than I do planning spectacular effects. The audience does not analyze these elements in a picture, but I must or the audience will not come to see my pictures. And they do come."⁵³

In *The Art of Fiction*, Ayn Rand recounts a valuable lesson in plot construction learned from DeMille. During her first year working for him in Hollywood, she could identify a well-plotted story, but she could not explain the qualities that made it so. DeMille advised her that good stories depend upon a "complicated conflict" that can be summarized in a single sentence. Once the conflict is established, a writer can then devise the events leading to the establishment of the conflict, as well as the consequences, in order to achieve a "dramatically constructed progression." DeMille told Rand that he purchased the story for his film *Manslaughter* based on just such a summary of its central conflict: "A righteous young district attorney has to prosecute the woman he loves, a spoiled heiress, for killing a policeman in an automobile accident."⁵⁴ *Manslaughter*, produced and directed by DeMille for Paramount in 1922, earned the studio profits in excess of $800,000.⁵⁵ One reviewer for the *Motion Picture News* praised "the newest DeMille achievement," stating that "we must give him credit for building the most direct action which has graced the screen in many a day. It is direct storytelling. . . . It moves and by moving holds your attention through a chain of events dramatic, perhaps impossible, but which points to a moral notwithstanding."⁵⁶ To the end of his career, DeMille would insist upon dramatic action and moral conflict as the foundation of successful filmmaking.⁵⁷

As influential as DeMille's techniques of story construction were for Ayn Rand, her letters on *Red Pawn*'s plot-theme development, written a few years after its composition, already convey a deeper understanding of the abstract principles involved in successful story writing than DeMille was to express. Rand wrote to Kenneth MacGowan in May 1934 regarding *Red Pawn* and her new theory of motion picture development, and she sent a similar description of her theory with a synopsis of *Red Pawn* in a letter to

DeMille in July 1934. MacGowan was a story editor and producer at RKO in the early 1930s, who went on to make such classic films as *Tin Pan Alley* and *Lifeboat*. Rand writes that she purposefully constructed the story in *Red Pawn* to express multiple "tiers or layers of depth" in meaning in order to appeal to all levels of moviegoers. Rarely do motion pictures present any intellectual interest, she pointed out, and the ones that try are most often plotless and tedious and unsuccessful commercially. "There is only one common denominator," she states, "which can be understood and enjoyed by all men, from the dullest to the most intelligent, and that is plot. Everyone goes into a theatre to enjoy primarily *what* they are going to see and not *how* it is going to be presented to them. If they are not interested in what they see, they do not care how it is shown."[58]

In her letters on *Red Pawn*, Ayn Rand explains her new theory of building stories in such a way that higher levels of meaning arise naturally and convincingly from within the conflict and dramatic action of the basic plot. Such stories would satisfy the interests of those who care only for intrigue and suspense in their entertainment, and also those who appreciate more intellectual matter as well. *Red Pawn* is a story built on three tiers. [59]

(1) On the foundational level of plot, it is the story of a woman who enters a prison and becomes the commander's mistress in order to help her husband escape an unjust life sentence for political "crimes." The plot focuses also on the growing love for the woman by the commander, who originally sought only her sexual services. These situations, says Rand, are developed into an integrated pattern of dramatic action, each action motivated clearly by reasons and emotions that all viewers will readily comprehend and sympathize with. The mystery of the woman's identity, her deepening conflict, and the final resolution together build a progressive, suspenseful plot to engage every attention level.

(2) For viewers who desire more than merely suspenseful action, Rand says, the second tier or layer of meaning in *Red Pawn* arises directly from the events of the plot and features the "unusual emotional crisis" of the three major characters. At issue are the matters of the woman's potentially divided love and the jealousies of the husband and commander. In addition, viewers of *Red Pawn* will gain a realistic sense of the oppressive and inhuman conditions of life under dictatorship, conditions most Americans know little about.

(3) Finally, on the highest tier of the story's meaning, *Red Pawn* conveys the philosophical struggle between the woman's belief in the moral supremacy of joy and personal happiness and the commander's belief in the moral supremacy of duty and sacrifice to the state. Plot structure is essential for dramatizing spiritual values, since philosophical themes cannot be produced credibly by adding philosophical dialogue to an unrelated storyline. Rand emphasizes that the philosophical dimensions of the story are integrated completely and develop necessarily from its dramatic chain of events. All the

layers of abstract meaning in *Red Pawn* are inseparably linked to and develop from within the story's plot actions. Expressing confidence in her original new theory of story building, Rand states, "It is, in a way, the same principle as that of an airplane carried by three motors. If two of them fail, the third one is still enough to carry the plane safely. But how much safer the plane is, starting out with the three! As a matter of fact, in the example in question, I am more than sure that neither of the three motors would fail."[60]

The letters on *Red Pawn*'s composition were Rand's first attempt to explain her unique new method of story construction based on her original conception of structural and thematic unity in literature. In her later "Basic Principles of Literature," she adds theoretical support for her process of plot development, a process beginning with "plot-theme."

> The link between the theme and the events of a novel is an element which I call the *plot-theme*. It is the first step of the translation of an abstract theme into a story, without which the construction of a plot would be impossible. A "plot-theme" is the central conflict or "situation" of a story—a conflict in terms of action, corresponding to the theme and complex enough to create a purposeful progression of events.[61]

Consistent with Rand's philosophical rejection of the mind-body dichotomy, "plot-theme" is what she asserted to be "a cardinal principle of good fiction: *the theme and the plot of a novel must be integrated*—as thoroughly integrated as mind and body or thought and action in a rational view of man."[62] Since all human action is purposeful and undertaken to gain or preserve values, Rand states, a plot must also be centered upon conflict, or opposition, in order to dramatize human action. Proper character development depends upon the convincing presentation of value premises that inform each character's actions, that is, the motivation behind individual choices and behavior. A well-constructed plot therefore dramatizes the struggle between abstract values and relevant concrete goals in a series of integrated, motivated actions building to a climax and resolution.[63]

In his autobiography, Cecil B. DeMille wrote: "The dramatic construction of the story is the steel framework that holds up the building. Everything else—spectacle, stars, special effects, costume, music, and all the rest—are essentially trimmings."[64] Rand expanded the same metaphor in "Basic Principles of Literature":

> The plot of the novel serves the same function as the steel skeleton of a skyscraper: it determines the use, placement and distribution of all the other elements. Matters such as number of characters, background, descriptions, conversations, introspective passages, etc. have to be determined by what the plot can carry, i.e., have to be integrated with the events and contribute to the progression of the story. Just as one cannot pile extraneous weight or ornamen-

tation on a building without regard for the strength of its skeleton, so one cannot burden a novel with irrelevancies without regard for its plot. The penalty, in both cases, is the same: the collapse of the structure.[65]

After *Red Pawn*, the principles of plot-theme integration shaped the distinctively unified structures of Rand's three major novels: *We the Living, The Fountainhead,* and *Atlas Shrugged*.[66] Several decades afterward, she composed her groundbreaking work in aesthetics, illuminating man's metaphysical need for art and the relationship of philosophy to artistic creation. She redefined Romantic art, not as emotionally centered but as based on the premise of volition, and established the critical principles for plot and thematic integration.[67] Perhaps the most extraordinary facet of Rand's thought is its consistency in the course of her life and work. Even as a young writer starting out in Hollywood, her mind rejected any breach of theory and action, many years before she was to articulate the principles of an objective aesthetics and systematic philosophy that support her multiple tiers of meaning in *Red Pawn*.

WE THE LIVING AND *RED PAWN*: AYN RAND'S HEROINES

The theme of both *We the Living* and *Red Pawn* is the individual against the state. Ayn Rand wrote both stories to convey the evil of dictatorship, particularly as it crushes individual minds and spirits, making human life and happiness impossible. The basic plot situation of each story is the same: a woman must choose between two men—one whom she loves, and one who can help her save the man she loves. The conventional pattern of the romantic triangle may have been inspired by works like Giacomo Puccini's opera *Tosca* or even the domestic dramas of Cecil B. DeMille.[68] In *We the Living* and *Red Pawn*, however, the love triangles are unconventionally adapted to new and unique purposes. By portraying the principal male figures as essentially good, for example, Rand crucially alters the romantic triangles to heighten the suspense of the plots and to intensify the heroines' conflicts. In addition, the men represent varying philosophical premises that contrast with the ideal union of moral values and action exemplified in the heroines. Rand wrote in her personal papers in 1934: "I believe . . . that the worst curse on mankind is the ability to consider ideals as something quite abstract and detached from one's everyday life."[69] The heroines Kira Argounova in *We the Living* and Joan Harding in *Red Pawn* are the earliest fictional representatives of the integrated human ideal that would find its most complete expression in Rand's later fiction in the characters of Howard Roark and John Galt.

Between the years of *We the Living*'s first printing in 1936 and its revised publication in 1959, Rand published her novels *The Fountainhead* and *Atlas Shrugged*. In them, she accomplished her primary ambition in fiction: a vision of the moral ideal in man.[70] Howard Roark in *The Fountainhead* and John Galt in *Atlas Shrugged* are Rand's great heroic models of independence and integrity, men who think rationally and act consistently on their moral premises to achieve their values in reality. In *We the Living*, Kira is the feminine counterpart to Roark and Galt. Like them, her character is at the center of the novel's story, and she displays both rational independence and moral virtue. And like Kira, Joan in *Red Pawn* is her story's model of moral and practical integration.

In her notes for *We the Living*, Rand sketched Kira's individuality, idealism, and proud, unbreakable spirit. Kira is "the only one in the book—who, as a person, is not in the least affected by the new conditions. . . . She fights them—externally; and the fight is the more tragic because, internally, she is left absolutely untouched and unaffected."[71] The key to Kira's character is moral integrity, her allegiance in practice to rational principles. She thinks and judges for herself, worships only the highest human qualities, and pursues her values with unfaltering dedication. She exemplifies moral perfection, defined by Rand as "an *unbreached rationality*—not the degree of your intelligence, but the full and relentless use of your mind, not the extent of your knowledge, but the acceptance of reason as an absolute."[72]

The complete union of Kira's mind and body, values and action, is revealed in every word and gesture: "It seemed that the words she said were ruled by the will of her body and that her sharp movements were the unconscious reflection of a dancing, laughing soul. So that her spirit seemed physical and her body spiritual" (44). True to herself, and against family members' objections, Kira chooses engineering for her profession and begins study at the Technological Institute in Leningrad. "It's the only profession for which I don't have to learn any lies. Steel is steel. Most of the other sciences are someone's guess, and someone's wish, and many people's lies" (41). When Kira meets Leo Kovalensky, she immediately perceives his freethinking individualism and idealism, and she is attracted at once. His deep sense of pessimism, however, runs counter to Kira's optimism and to her determination to fight for her values. "Fight what?" asks Leo. "Sure, you can muster the most heroic in you to fight lions. But to whip your soul to a sacred white heat to fight lice . . . ! No, that's not good construction, comrade engineer" (83).

In *Red Pawn*, Joan Harding displays a corresponding unity of rationality and action that constitutes moral perfection. Joan consents to become the mistress of a Communist prison commander to help her husband Michael escape from an isolated Soviet prison. In the original *Red Pawn* story and in Rand's first screen treatment for Universal in 1932, Joan's character was a Russian aristocrat named Tania Sokolova, whose real identity was Princess Alexandra Karsavina. In Rand's edited version for her later synopsis of *Red*

Pawn, Tania became Joan Harding, whose real identity is Frances Volkont-
zeva, the American wife of a Russian engineer. Her husband, Michael Vol-
kontzev, was originally a Russian nobleman, Prince Victor Karsavin, and his
fellow convicts in the Soviet prison were revised from aristocrats into middle-class characters as well.[73] The change from a Russian to American heroine suggests that Rand hoped American audiences would find greater
interest in the film, as she hoped for *We the Living,* which she was writing
"from the viewpoint of and for the American public."[74] In both works, Rand
wished to depict middle-class men and women and the tragic reality of their
lives concealed beneath the Communist propaganda. No one, she believed,
had yet shown in novel or film the devastating conditions of life in Russia.
Of *We the Living,* she stated in a letter to her agent Jean Wick: "It is not a
story of glamorous grand dukes and brutal Bolsheviks—or vice versa—as
most of the novels of the Russian Revolution have been; it is the story of the
middle class, the vast majority of Russian citizens, about whom little has
been said in fiction."[75]

The nobility of Joan and Kira is thus attributed to proper thinking and values, not social class. They are united in mind and spirit. In Rand's first screen
treatment for *Red Pawn,* her notes include the following description of Tania's (later Joan's) character:

> Joan of Arc on battlefield of love instead of war. A woman of fire under the
> mask of a cold, superior calm. An iron will in frame of most thoroughly femi-
> nine, almost fragile charm. Profoundly loyal in her affection and ruthless in fol-
> lowing her duty. An aristocrat to her fingertips. A woman who represents to the
> men in the story all the beauty and joy of living they have missed.[76]

Clearly it seems when Tania's character was renamed Joan, Rand was
inspired by the historical Joan of Arc, whom she described over thirty years
later in a 1968 essay as "the most heroic woman and the most tragic symbol
in history."[77]

Joan of Arc was tragic, Rand stated, not only because she was executed
for saving her nation, but because she was spiritually isolated among both
men and women in possessing the strength of mind and dedication necessary to wage war for her ideals without discouragement or compromise.
Rand seems to have identified in this sense with Joan's tragedy, and she
referred to Joan of Arc as an inspirational figure in her published and unpublished writings throughout her lifetime. In *We the Living* and *Red Pawn,* the
influence of the historical Joan is alluded to in the frequent war imagery
associated with the heroines. Every Rand heroine, from Joan Harding and
Kira to Dominique Francon and Dagny Taggart, displays an affinity with Joan
of Arc's spiritual isolation and unrelenting devotion to ideals. Yet, in *We the
Living* and *Red Pawn,* the parallels with Joan of Arc's tragedy are most perva-
sively developed.

In her 1968 essay "About a Woman President," Ayn Rand addressed the question of women in authority and asserted the greatest spiritual disaster for Joan of Arc to be the absence of any heroic men that she might admire and be protected by. Psychologically, states Rand, femininity longs to experience reverence for a male: "Intellectually and morally, that is, as a human being, she has to be his equal; then the object of her worship is specifically his *masculinity*, not any human virtue she might lack."[78] Like Joan of Arc, Kira and Joan Harding share this spiritual tragedy, for they are spiritually elevated above their men and ultimately must carry their responsibilities with little or no help from them.

When Joan Harding arrives at Strastnoy Island in *Red Pawn*, she challenges Commandant Kareyev's personal devotion to the ethics of self-sacrifice as she tours the former monastery. "The only sin is to miss the things you want most in life," she tells him. "If they're taken from you, you have to reclaim them—at any price."[79] When she asks whether Kareyev is happy on the island, he responds by declaring his unquestioned devotion to duty: "When it's duty, you don't ask why and to whom. When you come up against a thing about which you can't ask any questions—then you know you're facing your duty."[80] True to his convictions, Kareyev is lifeless and soulless: "His glance held no menace, no anger. It held no meaning at all. His eyes never held any human meaning. The convicts had seen him reward some guard for distinguished service or order a prisoner to be flogged to death—with the same expression."[81] Joan faces an unusual battle in *Red Pawn*: to win over Kareyev's affection and trust while reassuring her husband Michael she is loyal to him.

Michael, like Leo, suffers when he perceives the woman he loves in a debased position. The idea of Kira in a dirty apron, hunched over a Primus, or wearing another's discarded stockings at first angers Leo. Long before he learns Kira is Andrei Taganov's mistress, Leo is defeated spiritually in spite of her efforts to preserve their life together. After Leo is banned from the university and forced into harsh labor, he never lifts himself from the despair he sinks into. Instead of hurting him, his knowledge of Kira's infidelity is merely his justification to leave her. Michael, on the other hand, is spiritually unbroken. Of the Strastnoy convicts, he is especially disliked by Kareyev for his spirited pride and fearlessness of the prison's authorities. Michael often expresses his contempt for Kareyev's collectivist ideals, speaking out "when it would have been far safer to remain quiet; he would risk his life drawing caricatures of Commandant Kareyev on the wall of his cell. . . ."[82] Kareyev complains of Michael: "I've broken many a hard one here, but he's steel—so far."[83] Because Michael deeply loves his wife Joan, seeing her with Kareyev is the greatest pain he must face.

Joan has spent two years and all her money trying to get Michael out of Strastnoy Island, but he hesitates also for the reason of Joan's honor. "She spoke proudly, solemnly, her head high, her voice tense, ringing, throwing each word straight into his face: 'I have a shield that my honor will carry high through any battle: I love you . . . .'" She asks him to accept the responsibility of fighting for their future by accepting the way she has chosen to fight for it—though his role will be harder: "It's not for your sake only, Michael. It's our life. It's the years awaiting us, and all that is still left to us, still possible—if we fight for it."[84] So while Michael is understandably jealous, he is willing to trust Joan and agrees to her plan.

In contrast with Michael and Leo are the two men faithful to their collectivist ideals and disciplined in duty. Commandant Kareyev in *Red Pawn* and Andrei Taganov in *We the Living* display devotion to their principles at the expense of personal happiness. In Rand's first Universal screen treatment for *Red Pawn*, she describes Kareyev as "saint, pagan, tiger" with the "cruelty of a beast of prey in his slow, deliberate movements. Steel nerves and tense, high-pitched energy. A man who for the sake of his ideal could send others to burn at the stake or be the one to burn—with the same inexorable calm." She adds that in Kareyev "the austere spirituality of a martyr blends with the cold cruelty of the new Russian rulers into one fearful, tragic being."[85] Like Andrei, he has become an unthinking, unfeeling machine of the state, his own life void of human fulfillment or pleasure. Indeed, Kareyev is known by convicts and staff at the prison as "the Beast."

Even such a "beast" as Kareyev cannot long resist the attraction to personal joy that Joan brings to his awareness as she wages war on his ideals. Joan personifies joy as a self-sufficient woman who lives for her own values; she is no inhuman pawn whose life is to be used by others. Just as Rand described her heroine Dagny Taggart, Joan's life expresses

> the conviction that joy, exaltation, beauty, greatness, heroism, all the supreme, uplifting values of man's existence on earth, are the meaning of *life* . . . that happiness matters, but suffering does not—that no matter how much pain one may have to endure, it is never to be taken seriously, that is: never to be taken as the essence and meaning of life—that the essence of life is the achievement of joy, *not* the escape from pain.[86]

Joan conveys her joyous sense of life to the men of Strastnoy Island first through the operetta music she plays in the prison's library: "It was a challenge, it was an insulting burst of laughter right into the grim face of Strastnoy Island. It was like a ray of light split by a mirror, its sparkling bits sent flying, dancing over the dark painted walls. It was the halting, drifting, irregular raving of music drunk on its own gaiety."[87]

Joan's "Song of Dancing Lights," like Kira's "Song of Broken Glass," furnishes emotional inspiration as her "battle march."[88] It also wins Joan numerous converts to her values and sense of life among the men of the island.

Through the years Kareyev has suppressed an attraction to life beneath "his cold ascetic strength," Rand writes in her screen treatment.[89] In just three months, Joan and her joyful music bring Kareyev's sense of life to the surface, and soon he is shown searching for *their* "Song of Dancing Lights" on the old prison radio. Increasingly captivated by her joyous spirit and values, he confesses to her: "It's strange, Joan. I've never really known what it was to want to live. I've never thought of tomorrow. I didn't care what bullet ended me—or when. But now, for the first time, I want to be spared."[90] In the same way, Kira awakens the desire for life in Andrei, who says to her, "And so my own existence was only the fight and the future. You taught me the present" (278). Like Andrei, Kareyev achieves a special sense of heroism in the story. Both men have strived to live faithfully by their false collectivist ideals, unlike hypocritical characters such as Victor Dunaev and Pavel Syerov in *We the Living*. And Andrei and Kareyev each possesses the elevated moral stature that enables them to comprehend and embrace the truth they find in Kira and Joan.

Just when Joan seems to have won Kareyev's devotion and trust, her plan is complicated by Michael's growing distrust. She entreats: "We can't weaken now. We can't retreat. It's our last battle."[91] She persuades Michael to escape the following day, but in a passionate rage he exposes the plot and reveals Joan's identity to Kareyev, at the risk of execution to both Joan and himself. With Joan caught between two jealous men, the outcome depends on her clear-minded reasoning.

In *We the Living* and *Red Pawn*, the endings for Kira and Joan are dramatically opposed. After losing Leo, Kira accepts the impossibility of achieving her values in Soviet Russia, and she attempts escape across the border. Alone and disoriented at night, she persists through the snowy darkness, whispering to herself, "You're a good soldier, Kira Argounova, you're a good soldier . . ." (458). When shot by a Soviet guard, she lies slowly dying. As she perishes in the dawn, her mind is filled with the values she lived for, with images of Leo and the life they might have shared, and with sounds of the music she loved:

> There, in that world, across the border, a life was waiting for her to which she had been faithful her every living hour, her only banner that had never been lowered, that she had held high and straight, a life she could not betray, she would not betray now by stopping while she was still living, a life she could still serve, by walking, by walking forward a little longer, just a little longer. Then she heard a song, a tune not loud enough to be a human sound, a song as a last battle march. And it was not a funeral dirge, it was not a hymn, it was not a prayer. It was a tune from an old operetta, the "Song of Broken Glass." (463)

We the Living's theme of the evil of totalitarianism is presented in its tightly integrated pattern of actions: every good character in the novel is destroyed, true to the nature of the collectivist state. The story's development of a full presentation of life under communism requires the heroine's death as an issue of the novel's total thematic integration: to show in detail how the nature of communism eliminates individual happiness, fulfillment, and ultimately life itself, even for the best like Kira, who fights most strongly against its self-sacrificial ethics. On the metaphysical level, as Rand pointed out, Kira's portrayal emphasizes "that man cannot be destroyed by [collectivism]; he can be killed, but not changed or negated. The heroine dies radiantly endorsing life, feeling happiness in her last moment because she has known what life properly should be."[92] Though defeated in externals, Kira exemplifies moral virtue in resisting evil and by refusing to compromise her commitment to rational truth. As Kira dies, she smiles, knowing that within herself "life, undefeated, existed and could exist" (464).

In *Red Pawn*, Joan's outcome is happier, an ending suited to the plot-theme of prison escape and to *Red Pawn's* genre as an original film story. When Michael discloses Joan's escape plan to Kareyev, she calmly and rapidly devises a new strategy. She assures Kareyev she loves him and persuades him to take her from the island, with Michael along to free her from guilt. Michael, who still loves her and is still angry, agrees to the scheme, and now both men are confused regarding Joan's true feelings. In the course of *Red Pawn's* dramatic escape sequences, the greater suspense builds over which man Joan loves. At one point they demand that she state her choice. Joan refuses: "She stood straight, facing them. She raised her head high. Her eyes and her voice were clear. It was not her apology. It was the proud, defiant verdict of her sublime right. 'I love—one of you. No matter what I've done, don't you understand that there is a love beyond all justice?' "[93]

Joan's success in *Red Pawn* lies ultimately in Kareyev's hands, who alone has the power to free her and Michael when they are captured by the Soviets. In an act of surpassing heroism, Kareyev affirms Joan's values and his own devotion to them.

As in *We the Living*, the final scene of *Red Pawn* takes place at dawn. The rising sun, scattering rays "like arms outstretched in a solemn blessing," fills the forest with dazzling rainbow-colored light. Ayn Rand stated in her notes for *We the Living* that the beauty of dawn symbolizes the beauty of an idea: the idea of life's undefeated promise.[94] The beauty of the idea is larger than social or political circumstances; it is the integrity of the human mind and its allegiance to reality. Dawn, like life, is lost to those who betray themselves when they betray the mind's reason. As John Galt states, such traitors exist in "a self-made night, in a desperate quest for a nameless fire, moved by some fading vision of a dawn you had seen and lost."[95] Dawn's promise is what unites Kira and Joan, a promise each makes to herself and to life.[96]

NOTES

1. "Russia Girl Jeers at U.S. For Depression Complaint," *Oakland Tribune*, September 1932. In this brief article, written when *Red Pawn* was sold to Universal, Ayn Rand cited economic realities of the Soviet Union and the Russian censorship of film: "American motion pictures are cut and propaganda against the rich is inserted before the pictures are shown. The Russians even shoot additional scenes with people who do not resemble the leads in the pictures, who launch into diatribes against the rich."

2. Quoted in *We the Living*, 366.

3. Ayn Rand, *Russian Writings on Hollywood*, Michael S. Berliner, ed. (Marina del Rey, Calif.: The Ayn Rand Institute Press, 1999), 9–10.

4. Biographical interviews (Ayn Rand Archives).

5. "Russian Girl Finds End of Rainbow in Hollywood," *Chicago Daily Times*, September 26, 1932.

6. "Ayn Rand Assigned a Spot on Universal's Writing Staff," *The Hollywood Reporter*, November 18, 1932.

7. Michael G. Fitzgerald, *Universal Pictures: A Panoramic History* (Westport, Conn.: Arlington House, 1977), 257.

8. Biographical interviews (Ayn Rand Archives).

9. "Paramount Gets *Red Pawn*, Maybe for Dietrich," *The Hollywood Reporter*, June 20, 1934.

10. "Preps for Marlene," *Variety*, June 25, 1934; "Gossips Wrong Again! Von Sternberg Will Direct Marlene's Next Picture," *Los Angeles Examiner*, June 26, 1934.

11. Steven Bach, *Marlene Dietrich: Life and Legend* (New York: W. Morrow, 1992), 146, 154.

12. Maria Riva, *Marlene Dietrich* (New York: Ballantine, 1994), 152, 320.

13. Bach, *Marlene Dietrich*, 178–81.

14. Scott Eyman, *Ernest Lubitsch: Laughter in Paradise* (Baltimore: Johns Hopkins University Press, 1993), 228, 230, 232.

15. Biographical interviews (Ayn Rand Archives).

16. Josef von Sternberg, *Fun in a Chinese Laundry* (New York: Macmillan, 1965), 272.

17. Richard Pipes, *Communism: A History* (New York: Modern Library, 2001), 91–98.

18. Harvey Klehr, *The Heyday of American Communism: The Depression Decade* (New York: Basic Books, 1984), 3–5.

19. Kenneth Lloyd Billingsley, *Hollywood Party: How Communism Seduced the American Film Industry in the 1930s and 1940s* (Rocklin, Calif.: Forum, 1998), 20–21.

20. Eugene Lyons, *The Red Decade: The Stalinist Penetration of America* (New York: Bobbs-Merrill, 1941), 286.

21. Billingsley, *Hollywood Party*, 52.

22. Lyons, *Red Decade*, 294.

23. Michael S. Berliner, *Letters of Ayn Rand* (New York: Dutton, 1995), 11.

24. Berliner, *Letters*, 14–15.

25. Berliner, *Letters*, 17–18.

26. Berliner, *Letters*, 318.

27. Billingsley, *Hollywood Party*, 93.
28. Berliner, *Letters*, 317–18.
29. Billingsley, *Hollywood Party*, 121.
30. Berliner, *Letters*, 318.
31. Letter to Victor Weybright, June 24, 1963, Ayn Rand Archives.
32. Letter from Victor Weybright, July 2, 1963, Ayn Rand Archives.
33. Letter from Victor Weybright, July 9, 1963, Ayn Rand Archives.
34. Berliner, *Letters*, 610–11; Letter from Bennett Cerf, July 30, 1963, Ayn Rand Archives.
35. Letter from Bennett Cerf, August 28, 1963, Ayn Rand Archives.
36. Letters from Al Ramrus, January–February 1964, Ayn Rand Archives.
37. Leonard Peikoff, ed., *The Early Ayn Rand: A Selection from Her Unpublished Fiction* (New York: New American Library, 1984; Signet paperback edition, 1986), 123–92.
38. Ayn Rand, "Ninety-Three," *Los Angeles Times*, September 16, 1962; reprinted in Peter Schwartz, ed., *The Ayn Rand Column* (New Milford, Conn.: Second Renaissance, 1991), 41–43.
39. Harry Binswanger, Introduction, Maurice Champagne, *The Mysterious Valley*, translated by Bill Bucko (Lafayette, Colo.: Atlantean Press, 1994), xi–xiv.
40. Ayn Rand, "Introduction to *Ninety-Three*," *The Romantic Manifesto: A Philosophy of Literature*, revised edition (New York: Signet, 1975), 160.
41. Berliner, *Letters*, 243.
42. Ayn Rand, "Basic Principles of Literature," *Romantic Manifesto*, 80.
43. Rand, "Basic Principles of Literature," 81–82.
44. David Harriman, ed., *Journals of Ayn Rand* (New York: Dutton, 1999), 15-16.
45. Berliner, *Letters*, 11.
46. Robert S. Birchard, "Cecil B. DeMille vs. The Critics," in *L'Eredita DeMille* (Pordenone: Edizione, 1991), 284.
47. Birchard, "Cecil B. DeMille," 288.
48. Birchard, "Cecil B. DeMille," 287.
49. Cecil B. DeMille, *The Autobiography of Cecil B. DeMille*, Donald Hayne, ed. (Englewood Cliffs, N.J.: Prentice-Hall, 1959), 31.
50. Henry Wilcoxon, "The Biggest Man I've Ever Known," *DeMille: The Man and His Pictures*, ed. Gabe Essoe (New York: A.S. Barnes, 1970), 271.
51. DeMille, *Autobiography*, 31.
52. Wilcoxon, "The Biggest Man," 270.
53. DeMille, *Autobiography*, 170.
54. Ayn Rand, *The Art of Fiction*, Tore Boeckmann, ed. (New York: Plume, 2000), 57.
55. Phil A. Koury, *Yes, Mr. DeMille* (New York: Putnam, 1959), 81.
56. Laurence Reid, "Review of *Manslaughter*," *The Motion Picture News*, September 30, 1922. Reprinted in Gene Ringgold and DeWitt Bodeen, *The Films of Cecil B. DeMille* (New York: Citadel Press, 1969), 209.
57. Cecil B. DeMille, "DeMille's Bible," Essoe, ed., *DeMille: The Man and His Pictures*, 13.
58. Berliner, *Letters*, 6–7.
59. Berliner, *Letters*, 8.

60. Berliner, *Letters*, 8.
61. Rand, "Basic Principles," 85.
62. Rand, "Basic Principles," 85.
63. Rand, "Basic Principles," 93.
64. DeMille, *Autobiography*, 170.
65. Rand, "Basic Principles," 84.
66. See Rand's notes for plot construction in her novels in Harriman, *Journals*.
67. Ayn Rand, "What is Romanticism?" *Romantic Manifesto*, 99–122.
68. Rand refers to *Tosca* in *Art of Fiction*, 38.
69. Harriman, *Journals*, 66.
70. Ayn Rand, "The Goal of My Writing," *Romantic Manifesto*, 162.
71. Harriman, *Journals*, 50.
72. Ayn Rand, *Atlas Shrugged* (New York: Random House, 1957; Signet thirty-fifth anniversary paperback edition, 1992), 1059.
73. Ayn Rand, *Red Pawn* Treatment, September 27, 1932.
74. Berliner, *Letters*, 5 (emphasis in the original).
75. Berliner, *Letters*, 5.
76. Rand, *Red Pawn* Treatment, September 27, 1932.
77. Ayn Rand, "An Answer to Readers (About a Woman President)," in *The Voice of Reason: Essays in Objectivist Thought*, Leonard Peikoff, ed. (New York: New American Library, 1989; Meridian paperback edition, 1989), 267–70.
78. Rand, "About a Woman President," 268.
79. Ayn Rand, *Red Pawn*, in Peikoff, *Early Ayn Rand*, 134.
80. Rand, *Red Pawn*, 138.
81. Rand, *Red Pawn*, 129.
82. Rand, *Red Pawn*, 132.
83. Rand, *Red Pawn*, 146.
84. Rand, *Red Pawn*, 148.
85. Rand, *Red Pawn* Treatment. (Ayn Rand Archives.)
86. Berliner, *Letters*, 584.
87. Rand, *Red Pawn*, 155.
88. Rand, *We the Living*, 42.
89. Rand, *Red Pawn* Treatment.
90. Rand, *Red Pawn*, 161.
91. Rand, *Red Pawn*, 164.
92. Rand, *The Art of Fiction*, 174.
93. Rand, *Red Pawn*, 188.
94. Harriman, *Journals*, 65.
95. Rand, *Atlas Shrugged*, 973.
96. I wish to thank Shoshana Milgram and Tore Boeckmann for their comments on earlier versions of this chapter.

12

The Integration of Plot and Theme in *We the Living*

Andrew Bernstein

The plot of *We the Living* involves an original and superb twist on the love triangle motif. Ayn Rand herself stated that *We the Living* had the best plot of all of her novels.[1] But the book is much more than that, for it also effectively dramatizes a theme of profound moral significance.

Literary analysis too often proceeds on a "touchy-feely," subjectivist basis, lacking intellectual precision. One purpose of this chapter is to present the rudiments of a more rigorous method of analysis. The other is to apply it to *We the Living* in order to better understand the intimate relationship between its plot and its theme.

In *The Romantic Manifesto*, Ayn Rand argues that the fundamental distinction between Romantic and Naturalist literature involves differing answers to the philosophical issue of free will versus determinism. Romantics believe, explicitly or implicitly, that men control their own destinies—that their choices possess causal efficacy shaping the outcomes of their lives. Consequently, Romantics depict characters choosing and pursuing goals, that is, their lives are quests to reach some end or value precious to them. This is why protagonists of Romantic stories are heroes.[2]

Naturalists, on the other hand, believe that man the individual is the molded plaything of external agencies—in modern literature, most often of society—and depict characters helplessly buffeted by powerful forces. The protagonists of their stories are anti-heroes.

A great work of Romantic fiction shows the conflict that results when a character pursuing some goal is opposed by an antagonist(s). The first question a critical reader needs to ask is: Who is the main character of *We the*

Living? A Romantic work's main character can be defined as: the one principally responsible for advancing the action. The main character, in pursuing a goal, clashes with whatever forces oppose that goal. It is his value-quest that initiates, sustains, and carries to climax the story's central conflict.

The main character of *We the Living* is Kira Argounova. Her value-quest and actions drive the story. She seeks to study engineering—despite her family's objection that the profession is inappropriate to a woman—because *she* aspires to build. She is determined to succeed in her chosen field although the communist dictatorship opposes her bourgeois background and, especially, her individualistic principles. It is she who loves, lives with, and seeks to save the life of an aristocrat despised by the state. It is she who, when all other values are denied her, seeks to escape from the communist dictatorship. She has her own ideas and values. She refuses either to compromise with her family or to capitulate to the state. It is her actions that initiate and sustain the conflict.

Logically, the second question is: What does she want? In the main action of *We the Living,* Kira seeks to save the life—both physically and spiritually—of the man she loves. Some professors of literature forget that novels, dramas, and short stories deal with specifics. It is true that great literature presents concretes that embody universal themes, but their plots deal with particulars. It is too general and too vague to say in this context that Kira wants to live on her own terms in a totalitarian state until it collapses or until she can escape. Novels present particular characters pursuing particular goals who are opposed by particular antagonists.

The next question is: Who or what stands in her way? Clearly, it is the Soviet state, exemplified by Andrei Taganov, Pavel Syerov, Victor Dunaev, and Comrade Sonia. The communists forcibly prevent Leo and Kira from emigrating; they expel them from school because of their bourgeois backgrounds and beliefs; they deny the aristocratic Leo access to a sanitarium. The collectivist rulers persistently deny their individual rights.

When the specific antagonists have been identified it can then be asked: What is the book about in essential terms, that is, what is its central conflict? The answer: the struggle of a woman to save the man she loves from the crushing power of a totalitarian state.

This is the essence of the book's conflict—but is it its sum? Is the story simply about Kira's quest to save Leo from the Communists—or is there another significant element? Once a story's essential conflict has been identified, it is important to ask whether the total conflict is simple or complex. In *We the Living,* there is another central element.

Andrei Taganov of the G.P.U., the Soviet secret police, loves Kira. He is a man unfailingly dedicated to moral principles, but the principles are those of Communism. Andrei loves Kira in the teeth of everything he has ever stood, fought and bled for. A man of principle—though his principles are catastrophically mistaken—he recognizes and responds to Kira's unbending integrity, as well as to her physical beauty. And Kira, with no other options open to her, uses Andrei's love to save Leo's life. The author presents a bourgeois woman in love with an aristocrat, who, because every other door is slammed in her face, uses the love of a Communist, *and of a secret police officer,* to save her lover's life. This novel tells the startlingly original story of G.P.U. money used in a Communist dictatorship to save the life of an aristocrat.

When the full range of a story's conflict has been identified, it is then possible to derive what Ayn Rand terms a novel's plot-theme—the essence, not of a story's abstract meaning, but of its events or story line.[3] In discussing methods to improve the commonly used plot device of a woman selling herself to a villain as the means of saving the man she loves, Ayn Rand states:

> Suppose the woman sells herself, not to a villain who forces her into it, but to a man who really loves her, whom she respects and whose love she takes seriously. He does not want to buy her, and she must hide from him that it is a sale—but she has to sell herself to save the man she really loves, a man who happens to be the particular person the buyer hates most. This is a much more dramatic conflict—and it is the plot-theme of *We the Living.*[4]

The plot-theme of *We the Living* is: *The struggle of a young woman in a Communist dictatorship to use the love of a Communist to save the life of the aristocrat she loves.*

A plot-theme functions in literature much like a definition does in epistemology. If a reader is thoroughly familiar with the concretes presented in the book's universe, then the plot-theme serves as a unifying thread. If one is not familiar with the book, then the plot-theme alone is an empty abstraction. Similarly, a definition does a man little good if he is ignorant of a concept's units. For example, if he had no experience with automobiles, their (rough) definition as a "form of motorized ground transportation specifically designed for a small number of passengers" would not be helpful. But if he is well acquainted with the concept's units, then the definition is a valuable tool of essentialization, not an empty abstraction. Like a definition, a plot-theme is a tool of unit-condensation, reducing a vast amount of data to a single highly essentialized principle.

The plot-theme tells us the "what" of a novel—what happens. When someone asks what the book is about, this would be the answer. But in serious literature the reader still must ask the "so what?" What does it mean? What's important about it? What is the author trying to show his audience? The theme, the core of the book's abstract meaning, must be identified.

A method of identifying the theme is necessary. Such a method requires the serious reader to shuttle back from the highly essentialized plot-theme to the core events and central conflict portrayed in the author's universe. A theme must be *induced* from the observable similarities of a story's events, just as a concept is induced from the existents in the world that are observably similar. A theme in literature, much like a concept in epistemology, is a mental integration identifying similar characteristics possessed by a broad range of concretes.

What are the main actions of *We the Living* that form the core concretes of the novel's universe? Kira wants to be a builder—but is prevented by the state. She wants to save Leo's physical life—and succeeds only by selling her body after her desperate struggle against the Communist state fails. She wants to save his soul—but cannot, because the crushing weight of the totalitarian system is brought to bear even more fully against the nobility of his character than against that of his birth, leaving him no way to achieve the exalted life appropriate to him. Leo wants to be a philosopher, a scholar, and to write books—but is prevented by the state. Andrei wants to love a woman of the bourgeois class, a woman exquisitely principled—but is not permitted by the state. Irina, Kira's cousin, wants to paint beautiful, stylized human figures—but is prevented by the state. Irina and Sasha want to have a life together—but are not permitted by the state. Irina and Sasha want at least to die together—but the Communists won't even permit that.

Here is the book's main conflict at an abstract level: there are goals that the main characters seek to reach versus some force that prevents them. The ends that an individual strives to achieve, those things that are important and fill his life with meaning are: his values. And the force in the universe of *We the Living* that prevents these individuals from achieving theirs is: the Soviet state—communism—or more abstractly: collectivism. The observably similar characteristics that unite the core events of the story are the quest for personal values opposed and thwarted by the collectivist state. This insight provides the theme of *We the Living*. It is: *values versus collectivism*. The book is about man's quest to live and love versus the totalitarianism that prevents him. In *The Art of Fiction,* Ayn Rand states:

> The theme of *We the Living* is: the individual against the state [a similar formulation] and, more specifically, the evil of statism. . . . Incidentally, if one names only the most general meaning of *We the Living*—the individual against the state—one does not indicate on whose side the author is. It could be a communist story showing the evil of the individual; but then the plot would be different. . . . The theme, however, would still be the individual against the state.[5]

It is helpful to identify the author's own evaluation of his theme. Where does the author stand? In terms of this general theme: Does the author support individualism? Collectivism? Or does she, a la Shakespeare, "hold up a mirror to life," relating important events but taking no sides in the moral struggle? We can call the writer's assessment of his own theme the work's *meaning*.

Regarding *We the Living*, the answer is obvious. Its meaning is: *the evil of collectivism.* As an example from outside of Rand's fiction, consider Jerome Lawrence and Robert E. Lee's superb play *Inherit the Wind*, which depicts the struggle between evolution and creationism. The theme is: science versus religion—or reason versus faith. What is the authors' estimate of this intellectual struggle? The play's meaning is: The superiority of reason as a means of gaining knowledge, and the need of man's mind to be free. Or take Dostoevsky's *The Brothers Karamazov.* The novel's theme is: Religion versus irreligion; its meaning is: The need of God in man's life, and the resulting horrors when men repudiate religion.

Ayn Rand's assessment of her own theme necessitates the death of all three of the main characters. There are two reasons for this in Ayn Rand's thinking. One is that collectivism embodies a moral code of self-sacrifice, requiring individuals to subordinate personal desires and goals to the state. When the state's needs come first, the individual is construed not as a sovereign, self-determining being, but as a mere cog in a larger machine, an ant serving his colony; his specific hopes, goals, and values are of no consequence. Under collectivism—whether of the National Socialist or Communist versions—it is considered morally and legally permissible for the state to coercively bend individuals to its will, indeed to imprison, even enslave and/or exterminate them by the millions.

The second point is that life requires the achievement of values. Plants must gain the sunlight, water, and chemical nutrients that their lives depend on. Similarly, animals must find the food and shelter from the elements without which they will perish. Human beings must employ their rational faculties to grow food, build homes, cure diseases, and create the other values on which man's life depends.

Values must be attained; never sacrificed, surrendered, or renounced. Man's life depends on this. In totalitarian states, where individuals are denied the right to pursue values, there is no possibility to achieve flourishing, healthy lives. The forcible prevention of individuals gaining values necessitates their deaths. This is a fundamental reason that collectivist dictatorships lead inevitably and universally to mass slaughter—whether by starvation, extermination, or military aggression.

Ayn Rand, seeking to dramatize the unvarnished truth regarding collectivism, must show that its self-sacrificial code leads necessarily to an inability to freely pursue life-giving values and, consequently, to death. Collectivism permits only four possibilities: extermination, escape, suicide, or spiritual decay—two versions of bodily demise, one of spiritual, and a tenuous glimmer of hope that one may resuscitate life by gaining freedom. In *We the Living*, Irina and Sasha are exterminated, Kira is murdered trying to escape, Andrei commits suicide, and Leo—the collectivist state's especial target—is spiritually crushed by the ubiquitous life-stifling policies of collectivism: he loses his reverence for moral principles and becomes a cynical gigolo.

Before her successful escape from the Soviet Union, Ayn Rand received a request from an acquaintance: "Tell them [in America] that Russia is a huge cemetery and that we are all dying slowly."[6] She promised that she would. Ayn Rand understood, as fully as any thinker of the twentieth century, that collectivism is a moral disease, similar in virulence to the plague or Ebola, and that its contraction by a society meant certain death for millions. The heroes of *We The Living* die because their world permits no possibility of survival. Ayn Rand's theme and meaning necessitate this plot outcome. This is the deepest reason for the superb integration of plot and theme in this story.

NOTES

1. In the question period to Lecture 11 of Leonard Peikoff's 1976 course, "Philosophy of Objectivism."

2. On the differences between Romanticism and Naturalism, see Ayn Rand, *The Romantic Manifesto: A Philosophy of Literature*, revised edition (New York: Signet, 1975) (and especially chapter 6, "What is Romanticism?") and Ayn Rand, *The Art of Fiction: A Guide for Writers and Readers*, Tore Boeckmann, ed. (New York: Plume, 2000).

3. On the conception of a novel's plot-theme, see Ayn Rand, "Basic Principles of Literature," *Romantic Manifesto*, 85–87, and *Art of Fiction*, chapter 4.

4. Rand, *Art of Fiction*, 38.

5. Rand, *Art of Fiction*, 17. In her foreword to the revised edition of *We the Living*, Ayn Rand writes that *We the Living*'s "basic theme is the sanctity of human life" (xiii).

6. See Leonard Peikoff's introduction to the sixtieth anniversary edition of *We the Living* (v).

13

Kira's Family

John Lewis

We the Living is not a novel that creates false hopes. The people with the highest love for life—characters such as Kira, Leo, and Andrei—are smothered under the totalitarian state, while ruthless mediocrities rise to prominence. But the society of *We the Living* does not consist solely of magnificent heroes and consciously heinous villains. Countless people of less exalted status spend their lives trying to cope with inhuman circumstances, struggling to achieve the physical and psychological values needed for a truly human existence. Characters such as Galina, Alexander, Lydia, and Vasili illustrate the deep impact of collectivism on millions of heretofore unacknowledged victims. *We the Living* is their story, too.

This chapter will consider the place of certain minor characters—in particular, Galina in comparison to Lydia, and Alexander in comparison to Vasili—in the society of *We the Living*. In re-creating the stifling effects of that society on those characters, the novel presents a consistent point of view about the need for freedom by human beings, and the obsessive aim of tyrants to squelch any semblance of freedom wherever it appears. This allows us to consider the economic, intellectual, and moral aspects of the conflict between collectivism and human life. *We the Living* is focused on a political theme—the individual versus the state—but in developing that theme the novel never loses sight of the effects of collectivist conditions on real people. Nor does it ever let us forget that those effects are universal, applicable to all men, everywhere.

As complete persons, Ayn Rand's characters are embodied with a full range of thoughts, values, and emotions. But each character is motivated by certain basic premises, the specific ideas and values that lie at the core of his soul and that he has accepted over years. These ideas unite each character into a comprehensive whole, dictating why he speaks and acts as he does. As Ayn Rand taught in her fiction writing seminars, "Good characterization is not a matter of giving a character a single attribute or making him monotonous. It is a matter of integrating his every particular aspect to the total, the focus of integration being his basic premises."[1] We know what makes a character tick when we understand the premises that motivate his actions.

In turn, we know what makes a society tick when we understand the dominant premises accepted by the individuals that constitute it. Ayn Rand's concern to comprehensively re-create totalitarian social conditions places important demands on how she draws those individuals. As each character is tightly integrated by the fundamental ideas he accepts and practices, so the society is integrated by the dominant ideas that are practiced in it. Ayn Rand's portrayal of that society is comprehensive precisely because she creates characters that exhaust the possibilities of thought and action open to people in that society. A reader who ignores the minor characters in *We the Living* will fail to grasp the nature of the individual's struggle to attain the values he needs to live, the depths of the collectivist attack on those values, and the richness of the author's systematic dissection of the totalitarian universe.

At the opening of the novel Kira and her immediate family—her mother Galina, her father Alexander, and her sister Lydia—are returning to Petrograd from the Crimea. They anticipate seeing Kira's aunt Maria, uncle Vasili, and cousins Victor, Irina, and Acia. Although these characters are part of the backdrop against which the tragedy of Kira, Leo, and Andrei takes place, each is also a distinct person whom the reader can isolate from the background and consider as an individual. This characterization is achieved through precisely formulated dialogue and tightly controlled action that reveal the fine nuances differentiating the fundamental premises held by the characters.

How do the members of Kira's family reveal these premises? Kira, Galina, Alexander, and Lydia offer unique perspectives on events. They often see the same things from the same vantage point, whether riding in the same rail car, standing on the same street corner or living in the same apartment. Yet they react differently to what they experience, often not even focusing on the same aspects of the scene. When the characters are placed side by side, a reader can clearly comprehend how each is motivated to think and act as he does.

Consider the first glimpses of Kira's family, as they set off by train from the Crimea:

> When they were in the train and the wheels screeched and tore forward for the first time, in that first jerk towards Petrograd, they looked at one another, but said nothing. Galina Petrovna was thinking of their mansion on Kamenostrov-

sky and whether they could get it back; Lydia was thinking of the old church where she had knelt every Easter of her childhood, and that she would visit it on her first day in Petrograd; Alexander Dimitrievitch was not thinking; Kira remembered suddenly that when she went to the theatre, her favorite moment was the one when the lights went out and the curtain shivered before rising; and she wondered why she was thinking of that moment. (23)

These inner states reveal what each character thinks is important about his return to Petrograd. Galina Petrovna's concern for their material things, Lydia's desire to pray, Alexander Dimitrievitch's lack of thought about anything, and Kira's anticipation of the rising theater curtain imply fundamental differences in their approaches to the world.

It is important to stress that Ayn Rand's characters are not always aware of their own basic ideas and thought processes. Like many real people, a character may be a type who goes through life on autopilot, without examining the fundamental ideas that he has accepted and that shape his life. The premises that motivate a person's *conscious* thoughts and actions are often held only *subconsciously*. "Subconsciously" here means that the ideas are not in conscious focus and have not been explicitly evaluated, but are rather stored in the mind in an implicit form. Uncritical acceptance and practice have allowed these unexamined ideas to become automatic in the character's thinking. This is not determinism, but rather the recognition that fundamental ideas are important to a person's mental functioning. For example, Lydia's first thoughts are of prayer and the church. She has deeply accepted traditional religious teachings, and they dominate her thinking. These are the ideas she uses to evaluate the world. As the crisis around her deepens, she strengthens her own dependence upon these ideas without ever questioning what they really mean.

In the scene above, none of the characters knows why this particular thought happens to come to mind. It simply rises up into conscious awareness. Only Kira is aware of this issue; only she "wondered why she was thinking of that moment." She is aware of her own thoughts and that there is a reason why she thinks as she does, even though she does not follow through on her own question. Likewise a reader who wishes to understand these characters must follow Kira's lead and ask continually: "What motivated the character to think, speak, or act as he did?"

The crisp dialogue between Kira and her family as they arrive in Petrograd is further evidence for the basic premises motivating them:

> "Well," said Alexander Dimitrievitch, "we're back."
> "Isn't it wonderful!" said Kira.
> "Mud, as ever," said Lydia.
> "We'll have to take a cab. Such an expense!" said Galina Petrovna. (31)

Other conversations underscore the motivations that lie behind such responses. For instance, as Kira and her family stand on a street corner in Petrograd, Lydia wonders about what the years have done to their relatives the Dunaevs. Galina worries about their fortune. Alexander says it makes no difference. Kira watches the streets (32–33).

Such dialogue is neither arbitrary nor unimportant. Each character is revealing a consistent approach to the scene before him. In essence, Alexander expresses no interest in the present and no expectations for the future; he is simply here, a hapless victim of the Communists. Lydia sees only the mud and trials in this world and awaits the solace of kneeling in the church. Galina remains concerned with her past and present wealth. Kira is enraptured with the wonders in the city spread before her. Each character exposes his deep-seated evaluations of the world, and each will follow a direction set by those evaluations in order to cope with what is to come.

Further analysis of these characters may begin with Kira. In contrast to her mother and sister, Kira is not the kind of person who puts her mind into the service of the mundane. Her vision is not of kerosene stoves and stale bread, but of big cities, epic stories, and lavish artistic productions. She pays no attention to the revolution. She notices neither what she eats nor what she wears. She wishes to learn engineering in order to build great bridges, not to serve society. When her aunt Maria tells her that she should become a typist in order to get lard, sugar, and a chance at high office, her uncle Vasili perceptively replies: "Hell, you can't make a drayhorse out of a racing steed" (36, 39, 41, 135). Kira is a racing steed not only because of her unwillingness to compromise her exalted view of life in order to obtain a bag of sugar, but because she wants to make her values real through hard, honest work. Engineering is the only profession "for which I don't have to learn any lies" (41–42).

Kira's approach to routine tasks reflects her basic joy in being alive. She has blisters from carrying packages into their new apartment, but her sense of the gaiety of life shines in contrast with Lydia's pain:

> skipping briskly over the steps, sliding down the banister, she met Lydia, climbing up slowly, heavily, clutching the bundles to her breast, panting and sighing bitterly, steam blowing from her mouth with every word: "Our Lord in Heaven! . . . Saint Mother of God!" (52–53)

Kira, of course, is the major foil to her family, as she is to everyone else in the book. On the train to Petrograd a series of conversations by unidentified passengers about matters of immediate survival—dried fish, sunflower seed oil, acorns, and coffee grounds—leads to this exchange between Kira, Lydia, and Galina:

"Citizens," Lydia asked boldly, "do they have ice-cream in Petrograd? I haven't tasted it in five years. Real ice-cream, cold, so cold it takes your breath away. . . ."

"Yes," said Kira, "so cold it takes your breath away, but then you can walk faster, and there are lights, a long line of lights, moving you as you walk."

"What are you talking about?" asked Lydia.

"Why, about Petrograd." Kira looked at her, surprised. "I thought you were talking about Petrograd, and how cold it was there, weren't you?"

"We were not. You were off—as usual."

"I was thinking about the streets. The streets of a big city, where so much is possible and so many things can happen to you."

Galina Petrovna remarked dryly: "You're saying that quite happily, aren't you? I should think we'd all be quite tired of 'things happening,' by now. Haven't you had enough happen to you with the revolution, and all?"

"Oh, yes," said Kira indifferently, "the revolution." (24–25)

Kira and her family exhibit diametrically opposite approaches to reality. Like most people in the novel, Kira's family remains anchored to the commonplace, short-range concerns of life. But Kira is literally unable to force herself to remain oriented to the prosaic; her family has to remind her to do routine tasks like getting bread. She maintains a life-saving contempt for the immediate actions needed to survive and a profound love for the highest values possible to her. She carries in her both "the conviction that labor and effort were ignoble" and a desire for "a future of the hardest work and most demanding effort" (49–50). She is able to ignore the revolution when it is not of immediate concern to her, but she faces it head-on when it affects her values. For instance, on a physical level she understands immediately the consequences of Leo's food speculations (283). Intellectually, she also understands and rejects the ideals of the revolution in her first discussion with Andrei (88–91). Her proper place is not looking down at soup on a stove but rather up at a construction site—or at a hero, like Leo. Kira's rapture toward the sublime is a central issue that makes compromise between her and the people around her impossible.

But this distinction between Kira and everyone else is not sufficient to explain the motivations of the others. The members of her family are individuals, and they have accepted subtly different ideas and ways of thinking. To grasp the nuances of difference between the other members of Kira's family, the reader must understand the different layers of characterization provided by the author.

On the surface, Galina Petrovna and her daughter Lydia often express similar values. During their trip back to Petrograd they both make the sign of the cross when they find a place in a boxcar (28). Both react passionately to Chopin (93). They remain united in their opposition to declining standards of morality, specifically against "Pagans" and Kira's living with Leo (115,

132). Lydia, like the masses crowding the churches, prayed for Russia and for the fear in her heart, and Galina also hoped that God would forgive and lead them (146–47). Clearly the two women share strong moral, religious, and aesthetic values that are expressed in terms of standards taken from a dying old world.[2]

However, important differences between them are evident. Galina is concerned primarily with practical material issues, while Lydia is rather more taken with matters of the "spirit." Once Lydia understands that material prosperity is gone forever, her early attempts to show off her wealth and social position give way to a stronger commitment to religious idealism. Lydia's view of morality is more solidly anchored in orthodox religion than is her mother's; she accepts the mystical tradition that Holy Mother Russia will be saved by divine intervention:

> . . . spiritual consolation. I know. It has been revealed to me. There are secrets beyond our mortal minds. Holy Russia's salvation will come from faith. It has been predicted. Through patience and long suffering we shall redeem our sins. . . . (272–73)

Lydia's premise of salvation through faith provides her with consolation, a sense of moral rightness and hope for the future. As time passes the power of this idea intensifies in her soul, and becomes her dominant means of dealing with life.

In contrast, Galina will turn from the promise of the church to the promises of the Communist revolution. The seeds of her attitude toward the Communists began to sprout at the first family get-together at the Dunaev apartment: Galina was aghast at the suggestion that Alexander should take a Soviet job, but she smiled in admiration at Victor's claim to be turning the situation to his own benefit (38). She sees Victor as practical, like herself, and amenable to the "new realities" of the day. The next time she sees Victor she speaks to him positively of the New Economic Policy reforms (57). She also shows an early willingness to accept revolutionary bromides, if they seem to serve her advantage. In her first meeting with Andrei she blurts out that she was glad her daughter will get to hear "a real proletarian opera in one of our grand Red theatres" (96). She later protects herself by assimilating into the Soviet system. She teaches sewing to children while mouthing slogans that preach the value of work in creating a new future (163).

At first Galina repeats these slogans without any implication that she believes them, as a pragmatic means to self-protection but also to express her concern for material wealth. Repetition and practice eventually strengthen these slogans in her mind; she begins to use them automatically as means to cope with the world. She eventually changes her mind about Alexander's working for the Soviets, pressuring him to take a state job and belittling him when his job is not as important as her own (272). The earlier implication that she does not think he is "practical" has become full-fledged contempt for his inability to advance in the world of the Soviets; in accepting the ideals of revolution she rejects her own husband and the values they once shared. By dint of repetition she replaces the ineffectual traditional and religious symbols in her mind with bromides that can rise up in her with genuine fervor when she needs them.

Lydia avoids a turn to communism by continually reinforcing her religious ideas and practices, specifically her prayers and her focus on icons. But Galina openly invites the proletarian revolution into her mind. Eventually she will blame Kira's supposed unhappiness on Kira's inability to appreciate what the Communists have done for her. Ayn Rand again places Kira's family side by side, and their responses reveal their core premises:

"Still thinking of your engineering, aren't you?" asked Lydia.
"Sometimes . . ." Kira whispered.
"I can't understand what's wrong with you, Kira," Galina Petrovna boomed. "You're never satisfied. You have a perfectly good job, easy and well-paid, and you mope over some childish idea of yours. Excursion guides, like pedagogues, are considered no less important than engineers, these days. It is quite an honorary and responsible position, and contributes a great deal to social construction—and isn't it more fascinating to build with living minds and ideologies rather than with bricks and steel?"
"It's your own fault, Kira," said Lydia. "You'll always be unhappy since you refuse the consolation of faith."
"What's the use, Kira?" said Alexander Dimitrievitch.
"Who said anything about being unhappy?" Kira asked loudly . . .
"Kira has always been unmanageable," said Galina Petrovna, "but one would think that these are the times to make one come down to earth." (273)

The contrast between Lydia's faith in traditional religion and Galina's faith in working for the state is heightened by the claims each makes to attain the "consolation of faith" and to "come down to earth." What follows is an elaboration of these premises: Lydia relates an omen that includes a vision of a tree that appears as a white chalice, while Galina speaks glowingly of her Communist nephew Victor's "practical" abilities in "modern reality."

Galina's slogans and Lydia's prayers reach their logical ends in the final scenes between Kira, Lydia, and Galina. In preparation for a play her Club is putting on, Galina speaks feverishly by telephone to a comrade, "Now when we present Lord Chamberlain crushing the British Proletariat . . ." (446). The concern in her soul to be "practical" and "accommodating" has reduced her life to impassioned espousal of party propaganda and feverish running between meetings and club events. Her physical actions now center on party activities as her thoughts center on revolutionary bromides. Given her private chiding of Kira, it has become apparent that she sincerely believes that working for the party can bring some measure of prosperity and happiness: "There is a chance for everyone in this new country of ours" (448). In contrast, Lydia tells Kira that she has been to see a holy man who will redeem Russia through suffering and patience (445–47). On the face of it, Galina has rejected the spiritual in favor of the material; Lydia has deserted the material for the spiritual. Each woman moves toward the world of her ideals.

Galina's pragmatic materialism may seem to differ fundamentally from Lydia's religious idealism. But at a deeper level the motivations of Galina and Lydia are closely related. This similarity is in one sense implied by their common rejection of Kira's values. But also, despite Communism's materialism and atheism, the ease with which the tradition-minded Galina accepted Communist ideals suggests that the differences between the two women are not fundamental. At age fifteen Lydia had fallen in love with St. Francis of Assisi, a medieval ascetic who "talked to the birds and helped the poor, and she dreamed of entering a convent" (49). He pursued poverty now with the promise of heaven later. Lydia accepts that impoverished work on behalf of the poor is necessary to complete the promise of redemption. Failure is due to self-interested sinners. Galina has rather come to believe that communism's promises can be fulfilled by slavish work in service to poverty in Russia, and that failure is due to self-interested anti-revolutionary speculators. Lydia accepts that virtue is found in the poor; Galina claims it by serving the proletariat. Lydia glorifies ascetic holy men; Galina glorifies poor farmers. Lydia's faith is in impending salvation from God; Galina awaits it from the proletarian revolution.

Ultimately Lydia and Galina embody the same basic premises. Service to the proletariat and service to paupers are both, after all, service to the poor; hatred of self-interested speculators and hatred of self-interested sinners are both hatred of self-interest; and faith in the proletarian revolution and faith in God are both faith. That communism promises prosperity on earth for the grandchildren of the poor while religion promises other-worldly heaven for today's needy is a difference in degree, not in kind. Christianity promised that the meek shall inherit the earth; the *Internationale* says that those who were nothing shall be all (73), as Andrei told starving Kira that "every little figure will grow" (189). Orthodox religion and Marxism share complementary views of material wealth, human action, and the future. In *We the Living*, the alleged conflict between religion and communism is shown to be a shadow war between allies who share the same fundamental ideals and are united against the same enemies.

We the Living's views of communism and religion, as presented in Galina and Lydia, can be understood characterologically in terms of a hierarchy of premises. On a superficial level, the two women agree that the present world is deeply flawed; they are conservatives who oppose today's decadence in the name of traditional morals. Consequently they reject Kira and her "Pagan" values. On a deeper level, they disagree about what to do about that decadence; Marxism and religion demand different slogans and see different sources of redemption. They disagree about what Kira should give up her values *for*. However, on an even deeper level, Marxism and religion share the same basic premises: faith (the Marxists' claim to being scientific notwithstanding), virtue through unending poverty and toil, and hatred of success. It is no accident that both women disagree with Kira's approach to life and her values.

The rituals and incantations of communism and religion also serve similar purposes in each woman's mind. Like everyone, Galina and Lydia need some way to understand their world, and to guide their own actions in that world. Their slogans provide points of focus that serve the function of ethical principles. Each claims that loyalty to these slogans is the only path to the salvation that the people of *We the Living* desperately need but cannot attain. These promises are projections into the future, purported to be attained through faith and sacrifice today. And as Galina and Lydia repetitiously chant these slogans they deepen the impact of these ideas on their minds. This ensures that the ideals of the Party or the Church will come to mind when either woman needs guidance.

It is clear that material misery is only the first level of impact that the totalitarian system has on its victims. There are ethical and cognitive consequences as well. Ethically, both Galina and Lydia accept that salvation can only come by valuing a good that is greater than themselves; cognitively, each has come to believe that only the ideology she has accepted is valid. *We the Living's* real message pertains not to particular economic or political flaws in communist practice, but rather to the nature of collectivism's attack on the spirit and the mind of an independent man. These attacks have deadly consequences. The victims of tyranny are forced to shrink the range of their aspirations and their thinking, renouncing hopes of personal long-range achievement in order to focus on the immediate, tedious needs of survival. Ethically they must abandon every value that exists apart from attaining a meal today and serving the party tonight. Cognitively, they must abandon every thought that exists apart from the content of today's meal and tonight's speech.

This has pronounced effects on men like Kira's father, Alexander Dimitrievitch, and her uncle, Vasili Ivanovitch Dunaev. Vasili is a fur trader of tremendous energy; "His muscles and the long hours of the Siberian nights had paid for every hair of every fur that passed through his hands" (34). Alexander is a textile manufacturer of similar energy and achievement. Each man has seen his self-made accomplishments taken by the Soviets. Each refuses to work for them, although Alexander eventually relents. Each is forced to look downwards from thoughts of long-range success onto mere physical survival for the immediate moment. Neither can quite grasp that his down-cast eyes mark the success of the revolution.

Alexander's reaction to Communist Petrograd is profound resignation; "What's the use?" is his unchanging motto from start to finish. He renounces all hope for the future and consigns himself to mere survival in the present. He acknowledges that his situation is futile not because of any conscious refusal to face reality, but rather because of his justified conclusion that thought and action are pointless in the society of the communists. When Kira and her family arrive at their new apartment, Galina says that a little work will fix it and Lydia calls out the Lord's name. But Alexander's sigh encapsulates his view that nothing can restore their prosperity.

Alexander is entirely cut off from any values; he can work, but can attain nothing from that work beyond bare survival. He tries to live in the only way he can: by starting one small-scale business after another, turning to a low-level Soviet job only under pressure from his wife and the threat of starvation. Neither the church nor the state made his success possible; he knows that neither the church nor the party will save him and his family. In the present world he has no chance of success; that world belongs to the so-called "Nepmen" like Karp Karpovitch Morozov, dishonest speculators who get rich under Lenin's New Economic Policy. Such men were beyond his comprehension; "Alexander wondered dully about their secrets. But the dreaded word 'speculator' gave him a cold shudder; he lacked the talents of a racketeer" (92). As events progress his estrangement from the world grows deeper; his "feeble shadow of a smile" may have indicated happiness at a visit from Kira, "had it not been for a dull haze grown between him and the life around him" (163).

Separated from his values, in a world not of his making, with every thought frustrated by threat of expropriation and every effort crushed by hostile social conditions, he is trapped between the energy of his own spirit and the decrees of the Communists. His motivations to give up are conscious in the sense that he knows he will never be allowed to succeed; he does not pretend that he can. Yet he is also motivated subconsciously by a profound virtue that he has cultivated for years, has never named, and now must stifle: his productive ability. His desire to live and to act thwarts his attempts to give up. Unable to act in any meaningful way, but also unable to remain idle, he is torn on a rack between his own virtue and the tyrants over him. By the time Galina takes a job, the best energy he can muster is to concoct imitation milk for a cat he found in a gutter (163). In the end the only values he has left are a pair of galoshes, which he wipes off carefully after using them, and a jealously guarded collection of matchbox labels that he attaches to a wooden frame (445). It is his inalienable need for values that motivates him to guard these particular things as he does.

Alexander, like every character, illustrates the importance of politics. He is a productive entrepreneur who is doomed to extinction in a culture of cannibals. In America he would have created a business empire. In Soviet Russia he can produce nothing, feel nothing, think nothing. In contrast to Alexander, Kira's uncle Vasili Ilyitch Dunaev clings tenaciously to his vision of the future. He consciously renounces his most sacred values by disavowing the past: "Take one advice from an old man, Kira. Don't ever look back. The past is dead. But there is always a future. There is always a future" (78). Yet, denials notwithstanding, he continues to hold a profound respect for the values of the past. After selling a priceless clock he had given to his wife for her birthday, he gives a million rubles to a disabled Imperial Army veteran: "Keep it. And I'll still be your debtor" (87). Grasping at the values of the past, he is unable to see that everything once dear to him is now worthless. The clock he sold was once so valuable that its sale required an Imperial order; it is now worth a few pounds of bread. The same is true for illegal Czarist money, which he hoards. He intends to use it to pay a foreign debt, as well as to regain his possessions. His honor demands that the debt be paid, and he looks forward with a sense of achievement to paying it off (78). Although both his debt and his possessions are from the past, he is actually projecting his need for achievement into an otherwise barren future. He is looking *forward* to these achievements. But the implications of the Czarist money are clear to Kira as well as to the reader: the values of the past are worthless in the world of the Communists, to hold onto them in the present is a capital crime, and the future he desires—a return to a pre-Soviet era of decency and values—will not come to be. Despite his conscious protestations to the contrary, Vasili clings to those values at the risk of his life. And, like all such values, they must remain hidden, as Galina had taken pains to hide the French novel she read on the train from the Crimea (21).

Yet Vasili's hopes are not centered primarily on material values. Like Galina and Lydia, his past has moral import; he reads Chekhov, and when he hears of a new production of *La Traviata* he says, "Yes . . . old classics are still the best. In those days they had culture, and moral values, and . . . integrity" (214). Doubtless Czarist culture was not the nirvana that he remembers, but his very need for an alternative to the crushing staleness around him strengthens the effects of those memories on him.

Trapped in a miserable present that is cut off from the past, he places all his hopes on a future that he can conceive of only in terms of the values of the past. Unable to think that the values he craves have been exterminated everywhere, he projects them onto nations abroad, imagining a world where people live as human beings and not as animals. In response to what he thinks is a benevolent action from abroad, he says to his family:

> But that's Europe for you. That's abroad. That's what a human life does to a human being. I think it's hard for us to understand kindness and what used to

be called ethics. We're all turning into beasts in a beastly struggle. But we'll be saved. We'll be saved before it gets us all. (257)

But his wife had long ceased hearing this; Vasili had predicted salvation from abroad for five years (77). But there is no indication that such a failure was lessening his faith in the intervention of nations from abroad.

His faith in the future is also drawn from his hopes for his children, a faith that is also not lessened by failures. Early on, when Kira meets him in the market, he says:

> "You know, this is not a cheerful place. I feel so sorry for all the people here, selling the last of their possessions, with nothing to expect of life. For me it's different. I don't mind. What's a few knick-knacks more or less? I'll have time to buy plenty of new ones. But I have something I can't sell and can't lose and it can't be nationalized. I have a future. A living future. My children. You know, Irina—she's the smartest child. She was always first in school; had she graduated in the old days she would have received a gold medal. And Victor?" The old shoulders straightened vigorously like those of a soldier at attention. "Victor is an unusual young man. Victor's the brightest boy I've ever seen. Sure, we disagree a little sometimes, but that's because he's young, he doesn't quite understand. You mark my word: Victor will be a great man someday."
>
> "And Irina will be a famous artist, Uncle Vasili."
>
> "And Kira, did you read the papers this morning? Just watch England. Within the next month or two. . . ." (85–86)

These claims for the future suffer a serious blow when Irina is expelled from school. But the deadly threat to Vasili is rather that Victor has not been expelled from school, and has joined the Communist Party. Galina thinks that Victor is smart and adaptable, but Vasili knows that he is losing his son (214). He cannot foresee that his future will be demolished by Victor's betrayal and Irina's sentence to Siberia, but he recognizes early the implications of Victor's sell-out to the Communist Party. Consequently, when Irina is condemned, Vasili has no uncertainty about Victor's complicity in her arrest. Her protestations notwithstanding, in this issue it is Vasili who is "practical" and Galina who is an "idealist." Victor and Irina illustrate two possible ways that a father can lose his children: physical death by rejecting the party and spiritual death by joining it. Victor and Irina embody, in a microcosm, the basic alternative facing many of the minor characters in *We the Living*.

In his final goodbye to Kira, standing on the street, Vasili grasps onto all that is left of his future, his child Acia:

> "It's such a joy to watch her growing, day by day. She's getting better at school, too. I help her with her lessons. I don't mind standing here all day,

because then I go home, and there she is. Everything isn't lost, yet. I still have Acia's future before me. Acia is a bright child. She'll go far."

"Yes, Uncle Vasili."

"I read the papers, too, when I have time. There's a lot going on in the world. One can wait, if one has faith and patience." (450–51)

Vasili is torn by internal as well as external conflicts. From the outset he is aware of the consequences of consorting with the Communists, and he steadfastly refuses to work for them. This is evidence for his integrity, his refusal to act in any way contrary to what he knows to be right. Alexander had vowed, with sudden strength, "Not as long as I live" when Maria suggested that he take a Soviet job (37), but he did not keep this vow. Vasili, however, did hold true to this commitment, making the same statement much later to Victor: "I will not work for your government so long as I live" (312). But Vasili also must realize that Irina and Victor are gone, that his wife has died, that Acia is absorbing pure propaganda at school (and that she is a brat), and that the outside world is little interested in Russia. Yet he continues to claim that the future will improve. The conclusion is unavoidable: he is consciously evading the nature of his situation. He is refusing to admit that there is no hope for the future. His is a faith in the future that is immune to the facts.

At each step Kira is aware that her uncle's hopes are impossible, yet she treats him gently; she does not dispute that Victor and Irina will succeed, and she later agrees that Acia has a bright future. Vasili deserves this gentle treatment. He stands on the edge of a chasm that he cannot traverse. The present is misery. Like Alexander's, his material values have been reduced to pittances, and have become actual dangers to his life. He too is trapped between his own unacknowledged virtues and the demands of the collectivist state. The moral values he craves are out of reach. He is an achievement-oriented man who is unable to pursue any goals and yet unable to give up. He creates a future because he must; without a future he will have to admit that no values are possible and that he cannot live. Vasili's faith in Acia (and in England) has been created for the same reason as Galina's faith in communism and Lydia's faith in religion—and it is just as hopeless. Although Vasili's error emerges from a more steadfast devotion to the values necessary for human life, his demise is inevitable once Acia follows either Irina or Victor to her logical end. But he is simply unable to abandon his grasp on life by giving up on his one remaining child and the world outside Russia.

To be cut off from all values is to be cut off from all goals. No thinking and no plans are possible if one's values can be destroyed at any time. Vasili knows this from the first. When Alexander says, early in the novel, that he will open a store, Vasili disagrees with Victor over what this means:

"New enterprises, Uncle Alexander, have a great future in this new age," said Victor.

"Until the government squashes them under its heel," Vasili Ivanovitch said gloomily.

"Nothing to fear, Father. The days of confiscations are past. The Soviet government has a most progressive policy outlined."

"Outlined in blood," said Vasili Ivanovitch. (38–39)

Ayn Rand is systematic when presenting the basic ways that the victims grasp at the values needed for life. Lydia oscillates between her worship of religious icons and the classical composers she plays violently at the piano. Alexander has narrowed his vision to small-scale, particular things; he feeds his cat, wipes his galoshes, and guards his matchbox labels jealously. Galina, embracing the new ideology, screams party propaganda to get a pound of millet. Vasili holds onto hopes for his daughter's future. Kira, always trying to protect her highest value, does whatever is necessary to save Leo's life. Like every member of every overflow audience at every foreign film in *We the Living*, Kira and her family act desperately to hold on to the values that make life as a human being possible. Each is trapped between the selfish needs of life and the sacrificial demands of the party. And in each, the desire to live is facing a relentless onslaught. Only Kira is strong enough to withstand the attack on her spirit. It takes a bullet to bring her down.

Ayn Rand is also systematic when she shows how Kira's family members move psychologically and physically toward inevitable destruction. Alexander gives up all expectations of improvement and simply exists, without hope or promise. Galina turns to a feverish faith in the revolution. Lydia strengthens her faith in God. Vasili affirms his faith in his children and the outside world. Irina, beginning to understand, disappears in prison. Maria dies from disease, crying out her desire to live. Victor sells his soul to the party by betraying a family member. Kira dies trying to escape. Through such systematic characterizations, Ayn Rand creates the society in which Kira, Andrei, and Leo play out their passionate tragedy, each coming to the end that he must.

There are deeper implications to the tragedies in *We the Living*. These implications reach far beyond the events of the book, to include the nature of tyranny and its foundations in the moral nature of a collectivist society. The portrayal of collectivist social conditions is one of Ayn Rand's central concerns. She wrote in her *Journals* that "The Picture" in *We the Living* is "a terrific machinery crushing the whole country and smothering every bit of action, life and air." This picture is created through (1) "Economic Conditions" of "terrific poverty," including hunger, cold, disease, lice; (2) "Mental Conditions" with "everything centered around one idea—one propaganda—and that idea fed to the people until they suffocate"; and (3) "Moral Conditions" where "men turn into cornered animals."[3] There are powerful economic, mental, and moral implications of the thoughts and actions of Kira's family, and of the conditions under which they live.

The characters of Galina, Alexander, Lydia, and Vasili are vital to creating these social conditions and to showing their consequences. As members of the educated classes, and with a high degree of material well-being, they stand apart from the party insiders and the dirt-poor peasants in the country-side. As formerly successful businessmen and their families, they illustrate how the well-to-do are the targets of special economic vituperation by the party and the masses it claims to represent. Kira's family members also illustrate the effects of revolutionary propaganda on the minds of people who have some degree of education. The moral conditions that result are precisely those of cornered animals, most vividly illustrated by Victor's betrayal of Irina.

In *We the Living*, any attempt to pursue life-affirming values becomes a potential death sentence. On the physical level, any implication that a person or a member of his family has ever attained material wealth is reason for expulsion from school, dismissal from employment, an arbitrary tax levy, and brute physical labor. Kira and her family are made special targets of party animosity precisely because of the ambitious achievements of Vasili and Alexander. The moratorium on ambition elevates unscrupulous speculators into positions of unearned wealth while pushing productive individuals down into mindless physical labor.

But the hatred of success by tyrants is an old story that serves a special purpose. Aristotle, a philosopher much admired by Ayn Rand, understood the special antipathy of tyrants toward any men of ability. He wrote that "tyrants have mostly begun as demagogues, being trusted because they abused the well-to-do." But the well-to-do are also a source of special danger for the tyrant, and a tyrant must control them most of all. To keep men from plotting, Aristotle continues, "It is in the interest of the tyrant to keep his subjects poor, so that the tyrant may be able to afford the cost of a body-guard, while the people are so occupied with their daily tasks that they have no time for plotting." Aristotle observes that public monuments such as the pyramids of Egypt were intended to siphon the energy of the population away from independent activities.[4]

Likewise, in *We the Living* the activities of the party are not intended to attain prosperity through a "proletarian victory," but rather to ensure that such a victory does not occur. It is a matter of self-protection for the party to require that everyone be absorbed in a daily struggle to survive. Prosperity is not possible under such conditions, since the basic requirement of prosperity—thinking—is precisely what is proscribed. But if material abundance did somehow fall out of the sky (or an international aid truck) the party would have to end it. Prosperity in any terms would provide people with the free time needed to think, the greatest enemy of the dictator. This must be avoided at all costs. The destruction of Kira's family does not represent the failure of the communist plan, but rather its success. Among the symbols of that success are the treacherous Victor mounting the speaker's platform to assume his place at the top—while Kira bends over a stinking kerosene stove, cooking moldy cabbage, soon to die in the snow.

But physical activity is only the first level of the totalitarian attack. The party's destruction of human life goes far deeper than proscribing certain actions or confiscating property. A corollary to these miserable economic conditions is the airtight mental conditions. To hold its power the party must make it impossible for anyone to develop a long-range, *conceptual* plan of action apart from party ideology. The rulers want to destroy every man's ability to *act* beyond the range of the moment by making it impossible to *think* meaningfully into the future. This attack is cognitive. The target is the conceptual mind. To control human action, the party must control human thoughts. To understand how the party does this, it is necessary to understand the relationship between perceptual awareness and conceptual understanding in Ayn Rand's later philosophy.

According to her theory, human consciousness operates on several levels. It begins on the level of immediate perception, which is seeing that which is immediately in front of our eyes. Human beings share this ability with higher animals, such as cows, who also perceive what is before them, such as grass (although they have no concepts such as "grass," "food," etc.). A cow, if hungry, can move forward to eat the grass, but he cannot plan this action or consider its implications.

But man has a higher level of awareness: he has a conceptual faculty that allows him to understand abstract issues, to think about his physical and psychological values, and to undertake long-range actions to achieve those values. He knows not only grass but also organic chemistry. He builds food-processing plants and operates computer-controlled distribution systems. Man's conceptual ability alone allows him to think into the future, to aspire and to imagine, and to create an industrial civilization. It also allows him to understand, and evaluate, his political systems, and to act against them if they contradict his values.

Such thinking is dangerous to tyrants. Thinking minds are free minds, and free minds think for themselves, forming difficult questions that require subversive answers. To counter this threat, the Soviets need to create a new man, a being who functions not with a rational capacity for abstract thought, but rather with the immediate perception of an animal. As long as a person is forced to focus on the next meal, the way a cow looks for grass, he will be unable to plot against the brutes that have turned his country into a slaughterhouse. To the extent that Kira must think about cooking food for Leo, she cannot think about engineering formulas, soaring bridges, or shivering theatre curtains. As long as Alexander has to struggle to obtain his ration of bread, he will not be able to think about establishing an independent business. As long as Vasili can take no meaningful action beyond selling family possessions, his thoughts cannot rise above simple faith in his children. Collectivism destroys the men of independent spirit and independent wealth, on every level of intellectual achievement, by striving to reduce the range of their minds to a daily struggle for life, focused on that which is immediately before their eyes.

If the totalitarians could do so, they would empty every person's mind and turn him into a materialistic robot. But man cannot function in this way. He must have some central focus, some means to connect disparate thoughts into a conceptual system and some means to guide his actions by principles. Nature abhors a vacuum, in physical reality and in the mind. So the leaders must create an ideology to replace what was once in their victim's minds, so that each person never turns his thoughts away from this ideology. As there must be no empty spaces in the physical activities of daily life, so there must be no room for thinking in the minds of the people.

We the Living demonstrates that such propaganda is dangerous to those who are not actively aware of it. Galina is a perfect example of a woman who allows this propaganda to take over her soul, and Acia is the young person who is placed into a situation where there is no alternative to this propaganda. There is an ominous portent of Alexander's changing state of mind; when Galina propagandizes about this being "a transitional period of . . ." Alexander yells out "State construction!" He then weakly speaks of his new Soviet job, as if defending himself from an accusation (273). His weakness contrasts with his earlier strength in denying that he will ever work for the Soviets.

Irina understands the intentions of this propaganda, telling Kira:

> "Kira, I . . . I'm so afraid . . . I don't know why, it's only at times, but I'm so afraid . . . You know, we're all trying so hard no to think at all, not to think beyond the next day, and sometimes even not beyond the next hour . . . Do you know what I believe? I believe *they're* doing it deliberately. *They* don't want us to think. That's why we have to work as we do." (327)

That's why, Irina comes to understand, they have to memorize the names of innumerable people's oil wells, recite mountains of newspaper articles, and give endless speeches to political clubs. As the party cannot demand that the people *do* nothing, so the party cannot demand that their minds remain completely empty. In both the physical and intellectual aspects of human life, the party must provide a substitute that commands a person's primary attention and that accepts no competitors for that attention. Ultimately, it is because man is a conceptual being that the party must provide propaganda for his mind to focus on. Similarly, it is because man is a being with material values that the party must force him to struggle for immediate survival, without thought of long-range achievement.

Ayn Rand understood that life in a truly human sense is a progression of purposeful activity toward the achievement of life-affirming values. "Happiness is that state of consciousness which proceeds from the achievement of one's values."[5] To destroy a person's ability to choose and achieve values is to leave him nothing to act *for*, no reason to strive, no chance to be happy. It is to divorce his actions from results and to demand that he act without purpose. The collectivist tyranny in *We the Living* is a vicious attack on any attempt to achieve any personal values. Every member of Kira's family has to deal with the realization that no individual achievement is possible, and that struggle without requite is to be their lot. The terms by which Kira's family are murdered can be found in the severance of individual thought and action from the achievement of values.

The political and social system of *We the Living* is important to Kira's family; it demands their misery. Kira's family constitutes an aspect of the society that the party must dominate. The tyrants maintain their power not only through their overt supporters like Victor and Galina, but also through people such as Lydia, who accept the fundamentals of the tyrant's ideals even if they differ outwardly with the practice. For the present misery Lydia blames the sins of Russia, and Galina blames private speculators. In either case, the remedy is to blot out all selfish claims to flourishing, and to accept as virtuous an impoverished slavery that everyone secretly fears is its own end. Both sides reject Kira, the woman who demands the right to live for her own sake. Similarly, religious conservatives and Marxist liberals today reject Ayn Rand with equal vehemence, because they reject any claim that a man has a moral right to live selfishly, for his own sake. But affirmation of that right is the central value that Kira, Alexander, Galina, and Lydia cry out for, as Kira's dying aunt Maria cried "I want to live!"

NOTES

1. Ayn Rand, *The Art of Fiction: A Guide for Writers and Readers*, Tore Boeckmann, ed. (New York: Plume, 2000), 67.

2. In her journals Ayn Rand described Vasili, Lydia, and Alexander in terms of "the dying old world" or "the old world." See David Harriman, ed., *Journals of Ayn Rand* (New York: Dutton, 1997), 59–60.

3. Harriman, *Journals*, 56–57.

4. Aristotle, *Politics*, 5.11.

5. Ayn Rand, *Atlas Shrugged* (New York: Random House, 1957; Signet thirty-fifth anniversary paperback edition, 1992), 940.

14

Kira Argounova Laughed: Humor and Joy in *We the Living*

Robert Mayhew

Most people familiar with Ayn Rand's fiction came to it through her two most popular novels, *The Fountainhead* and *Atlas Shrugged*. Evident in both is what Rand calls the benevolent universe premise—the conviction that we live in a world in which people can prosper and achieve their values, and where evil is ultimately impotent.[1] Both novels are serious in tone, and both have tragic characters; but neither is a tragedy. Thus, some readers are surprised when they turn to *We the Living*, Rand's first novel and sole tragedy.[2] For instance, in the mid-seventies, Rand was asked: "If the universe is benevolent, why does Kira die at the end of *We the Living*, just as she's about to escape?"[3] (I give her answer later.)

So, why would an author who maintains that the universe is benevolent write a tragedy? Is there evidence of this benevolent universe outlook in *We the Living*? And on a connected point, what role does the humor in *We the Living* play?

HUMOR IN *WE THE LIVING*

"Humor," Ayn Rand says, "is the denial of metaphysical importance to that which you laugh at."[4] It is the denial of that which contradicts what she calls one's "metaphysical value-judgments"—one's appraisal of reality and man's relationship to it.[5] Laughter comes (at least in part) from the awareness of that which does not fit your view of reality. If one is rational and moral, she

303

argues, one will laugh at what is evil, absurd, or inconsequential; if one is irrational or immoral, one will laugh at what is good and rational.[6]

According to Rand, humor should not be a major issue or play a major role in a person's life. It is, she says, like sports and good food: they are enjoyable—"they are the spice"—but they should not be a person's primary concern. One's own life—and particularly one's career—should be one's primary concern. There is something wrong, in her view, with a person who hates his job, lacks ambition, and so lives for eating good food or watching football on Sundays or telling jokes around the water cooler.[7]

Ayn Rand maintains that just as humor should not play a major role in life, so it does not play such a role in her novels or in the lives of the heroes in them. The tone of her novels is serious.[8] To be sure, there are humorous touches in all of her novels (and especially in *The Fountainhead*), but consistent with her account of humor, most of them are directed at the evil, the incompetent, and/or the inconsequential. Nevertheless, why include humor in a *tragedy?*

To better understand the purpose of the humorous touches in *We the Living*, let's consider some representative samples of humor involving Comrade Sonia, Communist clichés, and Red art.

Comrade Sonia is arguably the most evil character in *We the Living*. (In notes for the novel, Ayn Rand describes her as "'the new woman,' mob womanhood at its most dangerous."[9]) Sonia is presented as evil and dangerous, but she is also presented humorously. For example, she is first described as follows:

> The young woman had broad shoulders and a masculine leather jacket; short, husky legs and flat, masculine oxfords; a red kerchief tied carelessly over short, straight hair; eyes wide apart in a round, freckled face; thin lips drawn together with so obvious and fierce a determination that they seemed weak; dandruff on the black leather of her shoulders. (69)

Later, she is said to waddle (95). Touches such as this and the dandruff are humorous and undercutting.

At one point, she says to Kira: "Well, bye-bye. Have to run. Have three meetings at four o'clock—and promised to attend them all!" (88). In a particularly comic scene, Sonia (who is pregnant) and Pavel Syerov discuss what to name their child. She suggests 'Ninel,' if it's a boy. "What the hell's that?" asks Syerov. Sonia replies: "Ninel is our great leader Lenin's name—reversed. . . . Or we could call him Vil—that's for our great leader's initials—Vladimir Ilyitch Lenin. See?" She suggests, in the case of a girl, Octiabrina (after the October Revolution), Marxina, Communara, Tribuna, Barricada, or Universiteta. She then asks: "What do you want it to be, Pavel, a boy or a girl?" "I don't care," he replies, "so long as it isn't twins" (410–11).[10]

Soviet citizens were free to choose the names of their children, but not the ideas they mouthed or were expected to hold. They had a number of communist clichés stuffed down their throats, providing them with all the ideas they needed to "survive." Kira's cousin Victor is full of them. Early in the novel, his visits to the Argounov family are strewn with clichés. To Lydia, he says: "short skirts are the height of feminine elegance and feminine elegance is the highest of the Arts" (39). He tells Kira: "A typewriter's keys are the stepping stones to any high office" (41); and, "Society . . . is a stupendous whole" (42). To Galina Petrovna, he says: "A man of culture . . . has to be, above all, a man attuned to his century" (56). Later in the novel, he tells Lydia (who has heard this on several occasions, she tells us): "Diplomacy is the highest of the Arts" (115). At Vava's party, he rattles off a number of clichés, for example: "My career is my duty to society" (154, see also 152).

Victor is not the only one who utters such clichés. The government official filling out Kira's Soviet passport says: "The trade unions are the steel girders of our great state building, as said . . . well, one of our great leaders said" (49). And we are told that Comrade Bituik *constantly* reminded the people who worked under her (including Kira) that the House of the Peasant was "the heart of a gigantic net whose veins poured the beneficial light of the new Proletarian Culture into the darkest corners of our farthest villages" (194).

Later, after Kira's mother (Galina Petrovna) has warmed to the new political system, she speaks of the Soviet Union enthusiastically:

"It's not like in the dying, decadent cities of Europe where people slave all their lives for measly wages and a pitiful little existence. Here—each one of us has an opportunity to be a useful, creative member of a stupendous whole. Here— one's work is not merely a wasted effort to satisfy one's petty hunger, but a contribution to the gigantic building of humanity's future."
"Mother," Kira asked, "who wrote all that down for you?" (270)

Galina goes on to praise the Soviet system of education, at which point her other daughter "Lydia's head drooped listlessly; she had heard it all many times." Galina has only one complaint:

"Of course, our distribution of commodities has not as yet reached a level of perfection and, really, the sunflower-seed oil I got last week was so rancid we couldn't use it . . . but then, this is a transitional period of . . ."
". . . State Construction!" Alexander Dimitrievitch [Kira's father] yelled suddenly, hastily, as a well-memorized lesson. (271)

Like the other examples involving communist clichés, this scene is meant to be a little humorous (however pathetic).

In *We the Living,* Ayn Rand regularly subjects Red art to a comic critique. Here is her parody of anticapitalist propaganda novels:

> They were novels . . . in which a poor, honest worker was always sent to jail for stealing a loaf of bread to feed the starving mother of his pretty, young wife who had been raped by a capitalist and committed suicide thereafter, for which the all-powerful capitalist fired her husband from the factory, so that their child had to beg on the streets and was run over by the capitalist's limousine with sparking fenders and a chauffer in uniform. (136–37)[11]

The odd structure of this passage captures the relentless, droning-on, anticapitalist tone of the propaganda, as well as the episodic (and thus inept) structure of these works—and it enables Rand to convey this economically.

Later, Rand gives us a glimpse of some of the other forms of art Leo and Kira encountered.

Magazine stories:

> Masha looked at him coldly. "I fear that our ideologies are too far apart. We are born into different social classes. The bourgeois prejudices are too deep-rooted in your consciousness. I am a daughter of the toiling masses. Individual love is a bourgeois prejudice." "Is this the end, Masha?" he asked hoarsely, a deathly pallor spreading on his handsome, but bourgeois face. (174)

Poetry:

> "My heart is a tractor raking the soil,
> My soul is smoke from the factory oil . . ." (174)[12]

Movies: *The Golden Octopus,* directed by Reginald Moore, censored by Comrade M. Zavadkov. This foreign movie is cut to pieces, and different foreign titles and even some scenes are inserted. For example: "On the screen, a man was bending over the hand of a delicate lady, pressing it slowly to his lips, while she looked at him sadly, and gently stroked his hair." The accompanying title reads: "I hate you. You are a bloodsucking capitalistic exploiter. Get out of my room!" (174–75). The film—the end of which was cut— concludes abruptly with this title: "Six months later the bloodthirsty capitalist met his death at the hands of striking workers. Our hero renounced the joys of a selfish love into which the bourgeois siren had tried to lure him, and he dedicated his life to the cause of the World Revolution" (175).

Finally, toward the end of the novel, Leo takes Tonia to a Red ballet: "On the glittering stage a chorus of fragile ballerinas in short, flame-red tulle skirts fluttered, waving thin, powered arms with gilded chains of papier-mâché, in a 'Dance of the Toilers' " (387).

Soviet art has all the originality and seriousness of Sonia's baby-names and

Galina's political philosophy. As such, it makes excellent grist for the humor mill. What do these humorous touches add to *We the Living*—which is, after all, a tragedy? Obviously, they contribute to the critique of communism contained in the novel, by ridiculing it. But this cannot be the sole reason for their presence. After all, *We the Living* is much more effective as a critique of statism when its content and tone are serious. Ayn Rand did not believe that in tragedy or other serious fiction an author needed to provide comic relief—to give the reader a break, as it were.[13] So why the humor?

One way to discover why Rand sometimes employed humor in *We the Living* is to examine her discussion of how *not* to use humor to criticize communism. At one point during her 1969 nonfiction writing course, she was asked: "You say that it is inappropriate to treat evil humorously, if one knows that it is an actual evil. In this connection, what is your view of the film *Ninotchka?*" She responded:

Ninotchka is an excellent movie. It is brilliantly done, and yet, when I saw it for the first time, although I could admire it technically, it depressed me enormously. The reason was that the subject is not funny. If you remember the details, when Ninotchka returns to Russia [from Paris] and talks about her beautiful hat, her roommate asks, "Why didn't you bring it?" and she says "I'd be ashamed to wear it here." The roomate replies: "It was as beautiful as that?" Now the audience chuckles, but this is not funny. It is very eloquent, and typical of the Russian atmosphere. It is a good, realistic line, and for that very reason it is not the subject for humor. Moreover, I assume the author was anti-communist, because ideologically the film is anti-communist. Yet observe: by the mere fact of treating [communism] humorously, he leaves you with a certain element of sympathy—with the idea that the evil is unreal. . . . It makes you feel: "Oh, well, yes, Russia; that's *Ninotchka*"—a kind of good-natured disapproval. It makes you feel that these Russians are naughty, when in fact they are evil. In that sense, *Ninotchka* is an inappropriate film—morally inappropriate. Artistically, it was very well done. But in order to enjoy it, you really have to evade (at least for the duration of the film) the nature of the background. The same would be true if you transposed *Ninotchka* to Nazi Germany. . . .[14]

Rand holds that it is okay to laugh at what is evil, "provided you take it seriously, but occasionally permit yourself to laugh at it."[15] *Ninotchka* does not take the evil of communism seriously, and then laugh at it—on the side, as it were. Rather, it treats communism humorously only—which undercuts or vitiates the film's critique of communism.

In *We the Living*, Rand launches a *serious* attack on communism—or rather, on statism and collectivism generally—and from time to time permits herself to laugh at it. I suggest that the humor in *We the Living* aimed at evil (at the villains, and the Soviet state generally) serves as a reminder of Rand's conviction that the universe is benevolent, and that in the end, the evil does not matter. Clearly, she believes we must take certain kinds of evil—here, statism—dead seriously. Not to do so creates the problems she identifies in *Ninotchka*. But we must not forget, even when fighting in earnest against the worst kinds of evil, that it is impotent: for example, that Comrade Sonia, however evil, is also ridiculous and ultimately insignificant; that Red art, however ubiquitous and propagandistic, cannot ultimately defeat the good.

JOYFUL LAUGHTER IN *WE THE LIVING*

Armed with the benevolent universe premise, one can use laughter to combat evil in two ways: one is negative—laughter directed at the evil (while taking it seriously), as was just examined; another is positive—laughter as a celebration of the good. According to Ayn Rand, humor—even the best, most benevolent humor—always involves a negation. When we laugh in response to the humorous, we are considering or focusing on the evil or the unimportant at least long enough to dismiss it with laughter. But there is a special kind of laughter, which transcends humor: laughter in response to a benevolent universe.

In *We the Living*, this benevolent sort of laughter is associated most of all with two young women. One is a minor character, the other is the novel's heroine. And though each meets a tragic end, both evoke and concretize this joyful laughter, which is virtually impossible to find outside of Ayn Rand's novels.

Irina Dunaeva

In her notes for *We the Living*, Ayn Rand describes Irina simply as "an average girl, caught by events."[16] But this does not do justice to the kind of "average" girl Irina is—Rand was clearly fond of her—or the horrific way in which she is "caught by events."

Irina is first described in the novel as "a young girl of eighteen with the eyes of twenty-eight and the laughter of eight" (34). She loved to draw, and we hear of her drawings early in the story:

> She sketched cartoons whenever she was supposed to, and at any other time. A drawing board on her lap, throwing her head and hair back once in a while for a swift glance at Acia through the smoke, she was sketching her little sister. On the paper, Acia was transformed into a goblin with huge ears and stomach, riding on the back of a snail. (76)

Acia wasn't the only relative Irina sketched pictures of: "Lydia disliked her cousin ever since Irina, following her custom of expressing her character judgments in sketches, had drawn Lydia in the shape of a mackerel" (115).

Later, we learn Irina has fallen in love with Sasha, a student with revolutionary, anticommunist ideas, and that he loves her. She tells Kira: "Sasha is studying history . . . , that is, he was. He's been thrown out of the University for trying to think in a country of free thought" (254). Eventually, Irina and Sasha are arrested: Sasha for counterrevolutionary activities, Irina for hiding him. They get married in prison, but are nonetheless assigned to different labor camps. The last we see of them is in a train bound for Siberia. Sasha is dejected and miserable; Irina is a rock. She lifts Sasha's spirits, and remains beautifully benevolent in the face of horrible tragedy.

> Sasha sat up, erect, his face the color of brass, darker than his hair, and said, his voice changed, firm: "If they let us write to each other, Irina, will you . . . every day?"
> "Of course," she answered gaily.
> "Will you . . . draw things in your letters, too?"
> "With pleasure . . . Here," she picked a small splinter of coal from the window ledge, "here, I'll draw something for you, right now."
> With a few strokes, swift and sure as a surgeon's scalpel she sketched a face on the back of her seat, an imp's face that grinned at them with a wide, crescent mouth, with eyebrows flung up, with one eye winking mischievously, a silly, infectious, irresistible grin that one could not face without grinning in answer.
> "Here," said Irina, "he'll keep you company after . . . after the station . . . ."
> Sasha smiled, answering the imp's smile. (352–53)

A bit later, they are forced to separate, as Irina must take another train to her camp.

> The guard tore her away from him and pushed her out through the door. She leaned back for a second, for a last look at Sasha. She grinned at him, the homely, silly grin of her imp, her nose wrinkled, one eye winking mischievously. Then the door closed. The two trains started moving at once. Pressed tightly to the glass pane, Sasha could see the black outline of Irina's head in the yellow square of a window in the car on the next track. . . .
> Sasha lost sight of the window; but he could still see a string of yellow spots that still looked square, and above them something black moving against the sky, that looked like car roofs. Then there was only a string of yellow beads, dropping into a black well. Then, there was only the dusty glass pane with patent leather pasted behind it, and he was not sure whether he still saw a string of sparks somewhere or whether it was something burned into his unblinking, dilated eyes.
> Then there was only the imp left, on the back of the empty seat before him, grinning with a wide, crescent mouth, one eye winking. (353–54, ellipses added)

Irina's benevolence underscores the tragedy. This is not Ayn Rand's joyful laughter in the face of tragedy—rather, it is her way of saying (in a most heart-rending manner) that the capacity for joy that Irina represents is precisely what a dictatorship destroys. Nevertheless, as Rand gives the imp the last word (or look), this ending to the story of Irina and Sasha is also an affirmation of the benevolent universe premise in the face of grotesque cruelty, injustice, and tragedy.

Kira Argounova

In "What is Romanticism?" Ayn Rand writes the following of O. Henry, one of her favorite writers:

> O. Henry['s] . . . unique characteristic is the pyrotechnical virtuosity of an inexhaustible imagination projecting the gaiety of a benevolent, almost childlike sense of life. More than any other writer, O. Henry represents the spirit of youth—specifically, the cardinal element of youth: the expectation of finding something wonderfully unexpected around all of life's corners.[17]

This is an excellent description of Kira, when she arrives in St. Petersburg at the beginning of *We the Living*.

> She had a calm mouth and slightly widened eyes with the defiant, enraptured, solemnly and fearfully expectant look of a warrior who is entering a strange city and is not quite sure whether he is entering it as a conqueror or a captive (19).
> Kira . . . looked straight into [the young soldier's] eyes and smiled. She thought that he understood her, that he guessed the great adventure beginning for her. (30)
> "Well," said Alexander Dimitrievitch, "we're back." "Isn't it wonderful!" said Kira. "Mud, as ever," said Lydia. "We'll have to take a cab. Such an expense!" said Galina Petrovna (31, paragraphing omitted).
> During the lectures, she smiled suddenly, once in a while, at no one in particular; smiled at a dim, wordless thought of her own. She felt as if her ended childhood had been a cold shower, gay, hard and invigorating, and now she was entering her morning, with her work before her, with so much to be done. (55)

We are told early on that "because she worshipped joy, Kira seldom laughed" (50). But this must be relative to other people in Russia at the time, because often when Ayn Rand describes Kira or her actions, laughing and smiling have a special place.[18]

> It seemed that the words she said were ruled by the will of her body and that her sharp movements were the unconscious reflection of a dancing, laughing soul (44).
> Kira's mouth was thin, long. When silent, it was cold, indomitable, and men thought of a Valkyrie with lance and winged helmet in the sweep of battle. But

a slight movement made a wrinkle in the corners of her lips—and men thought of an imp perched on top of a toadstool, laughing in the faces of daisies (44).[19]
She ran, sliding along the frozen sidewalks, laughing at strangers . . . (136).
She smiled happily and kicked an icicle in a puddle, splashing water at the passersby, laughing (148).
She laughed, that strange laughter of hers which was too joyous to be gay, a laughter that held a challenge, and triumph, and ecstasy. (162)

Of course, Kira is living in Soviet Russia. To present her as utterly unaffected by her surroundings would have been unrealistic and inconsistent with the novel's theme, and would perhaps have sent the wrong message—namely, that a hero is in no way bothered or affected by his or her evil, irrational surroundings. This in part explains Kira's reaction to the operetta *Die Bajedere*:

> They [Leo and Kira] saved the money for many months and on a Sunday evening they bought two tickets to see "Bajadere," advertised as the "latest sensation of Vienna, Berlin and Paris."
>
> They sat, solemn, erect, reverent as at a church service, Kira a little paler than usual in her gray silk dress, Leo trying not to cough, and they listened to the wantonest operetta from over there, from *abroad.*
>
> It was very gay nonsense. . . . There were women in shimmering satin from a place where fashions existed, and people dancing a funny foreign dance called "Shimmy," and a woman who did not sing, but barked words out, spitting them contemptuously at the audience, in a flat, hoarse voice that trailed suddenly into a husky moan—and a music that laughed defiantly, panting, gasping, hitting one's ears and throat and breath, an impudent, drunken music, like the challenge of a triumphant gaiety, like the "Song of Broken Glass," a promise that existed somewhere, that was, that could be.
>
> The public laughed, and applauded, and laughed. When the lights went on after the final curtain, in the procession of cheerful grins down the aisles many noticed with astonishment a girl in a gray silk dress, who sat in an emptying row, bent over, her face in her hands, sobbing. (208)[20]

The music laughs, the audience laughs, but Kira cries. Why? Unlike most people in the audience, Kira had a greater capacity to see the gaiety in *Bajadere*, to see that this wasn't a pleasant momentary diversion, but that such was possible in life—life outside the USSR. She could see more clearly than others the contrast between what was possible to man in a human society, and what was the Soviet reality. That is why she cries.[21]

Aside from this scene, Kira is often presented as laughing and full of joy. Or more accurately, she is presented that way in part 1.

By my count, Kira is described as laughing or smiling (in a benevolent, joyful way) twenty times. Of these twenty, seventeen are in part 1; of the three in part 2, two are toward the beginning, the other is in the novel's last scene. What explains this distribution? During much of the novel, but especially from about the time Leo returns from the Crimea (near the beginning of part 2), Kira is fighting a losing battle. We get an indication of this battle in part 1:

> [Leo's] eyes looked at her, wide and dark, and he answered a thought they had not spoken: "Kira, think what we have against us."
> She bent her head a little to one shoulder, her eyes round, her lips soft, her face serene and confident as a child's; she looked at the window where, in the slanting mist of snow, men stood in line, motionless, hopeless, broken. She shook her head.
> "We'll fight it, Leo. Together. We'll fight all of it. The country. The century. The millions. We can stand it. We can do it."
> He said without hope: "We'll try." (133)

Toward the end of the novel, after Leo discovers Kira's affair with Andrei, we know her battle is lost.

> She was packing a suitcase, her back turned to him, when he asked suddenly: "Aren't you going to say anything? Have you nothing to say?"
> She turned and looked at him calmly, and answered: "Only this, Leo: it was I against a hundred and fifty million people. I lost." (443)

In losing the battle, did she also lose her benevolent view of the universe and life? No. She had little cause for laughter in the second part of the novel, because—and in one sense, this is the theme of *We the Living*—the benevolent universe outlook is incompatible with statism. In a dictatorship, one can hold on to this outlook for a time (as Irina did, even as her train took her away from Sasha and to Siberia) and hope to realize such an existence elsewhere; but one cannot *live* it. Yet we discover—even as we find out (against hope) that this *is* ultimately a tragedy—that Kira's failure to achieve her goals does not destroy her sense of life.

Attempting to escape from the Soviet Union, Kira is shot by an utter mediocrity—a border guard named Ivan Ivanov.[22] *We the Living* ends:

> She smiled. She knew she was dying. But it did not matter any longer. She had known something which no human words could ever tell and she knew it now. She had been awaiting it and she felt it, as if it had been, as if she had lived it. Life had been, if only because she had known it could be, and she felt it now as a hymn without sound, deep under the little hole that dripped red drops into the snow, deeper than that from which the red drops came. A moment or an eternity—did it matter? Life, undefeated, existed and could exist.
> She smiled, her last smile, to so much that had been possible. (464)

CONCLUSION

A girl like Irina Dunaeva *could* end up in a prison camp in Siberia; a creature like Ivan Ivanov *could* kill a woman like Kira Argounova. But this does not mean that we are doomed, that the universe is malevolent; it means only that we are doomed—that human life is worth nothing—in the kind of existence created by Soviet Russia (or any other dictatorship). Ayn Rand affirms the benevolent universe premise even in the face of tragedy. And given her spirit, it was inevitable that some of her heroes would not only laugh in the spirit of Kira, they would succeed in the world as well—that the "so much that had been possible" for Kira would be realized on earth. Thus *The Fountainhead* begins with "Howard Roark laughed," and ends with Roark triumphant, standing atop a skyscraper; and *Atlas Shrugged* contains Rand's fullest characterizations of the benevolent universe premise: Francisco D'Anconia, Dagny Taggart, and John Galt.

Still, why *write* a tragedy, if one maintains that the universe is benevolent? I return to the question asked at the outset, and this time provide Ayn Rand's answer:

> Question: If the universe is benevolent, why does Kira die at the end of *We the Living*, just as she's about to escape?
> Rand: I did not sit there and decide arbitrarily to let Kira die. A novel isn't written that way. If you want to know about anything in a novel, ask what its theme is. The theme of *We the Living* is the individual against the state. I present the evil of dictatorship, and what it does to its best individuals. If I let Kira escape, I leave the reader with the conclusion that statism is bad, but there's hope because you can always escape. But that isn't the theme of *We the Living*. In Russia, a citizen cannot count on leaving or escaping. Someone who does escape is an exception, because no borders can be totally closed. People do escape, but we'll never know the number of people who died trying. To let Kira escape would have been pointless. Given the theme of *We the Living*, she had to die.[23]

Kira's death is not a reflection of Rand's view of reality and man's life; rather, it is necessitated by Rand's desire to write a novel portraying the fate of the individual—and especially the best, most heroic sort of individual—under a dictatorship. But even in selecting and presenting such a theme—one that is as important today as it was in the 1930s—Rand wanted to affirm the benevolent universe outlook at the very moment her heroine meets a tragic end. She gets the last word:

> The justification for presenting tragic endings in literature is to show, as in *We the Living*, that the human spirit can survive even the worst of circumstances—that the worst that the chance events of nature or the evil of other peo-

ple can do will not defeat the proper human spirit. To quote from Galt's speech in *Atlas Shrugged:* "Suffering as such is not a value; only man's fight against suffering, is." . . .

In *We the Living,* all the good people are defeated. The philosophical justification of the tragedy is the fact that the story denounces the collectivist state and shows, metaphysically, that man cannot be destroyed by it; he can be killed, but not changed or negated. The heroine dies radiantly endorsing life, feeling happiness in her last moment because she has known what life properly should be.[24]

NOTES

1. On the benevolent universe premise, see Leonard Peikoff, *Objectivism: The Philosophy of Ayn Rand* (New York: Dutton, 1991), 342–43.

2. I am referring to her novels. Her short story "The Husband I Bought" and her play *Ideal* are arguably tragedies. Both were first published in Leonard Peikoff, ed., *The Early Ayn Rand* (New York: New American Library, 1984; Signet paperback edition, 1986).

3. From the question period (in which Rand took part) following lecture 8 of Leonard Peikoff's 1976 "Philosophy of Objectivism" course.

4. In a question period following lecture 11 of Leonard Peikoff's "Philosophy of Objectivism" course, Ayn Rand answers, at length, a question on humor. The description of humor quoted here comes from this source, which is referred to throughout as the Q&A on humor. Similar statements can be found in Ayn Rand, *The Art of Fiction: A Guide for Writers and Readers,* ed. Tore Boeckmann (New York: Plume, 2000), 165, and in Ayn Rand, *The Art of Nonfiction: A Guide for Writers and Readers,* ed. Robert Mayhew (New York: Plume, 2001), 126.

For the brief presentation of Rand's conception of humor that follows, I draw on my article, "Ayn Rand Laughed: Ayn Rand on the Role of Humor in Literature and Life," *The Intellectual Activist* 16, no.1 (January 2002).

5. See Harry Binswanger, ed., *The Ayn Rand Lexicon: Objectivism from A to Z* (New York: New American Library, 1986; Meridian paperback edition, 1988), s.v. Metaphysical Value-Judgments.

6. Rand does not believe it is appropriate to laugh at *all* evil. See *Art of Nonfiction,* 126–27.

7. See the Q&A on humor. There she notes an exception: humor might be central to one's profession. Humor *can* properly be a primary value for a comedian, just as sports can properly be a primary value for a professional tennis player, and good food for a chef.

8. See the Q&A on humor. I should mention, however, that the tone of some of her early short stories—especially "Good Copy," "Escort," and "Her Second Career"—*is* light and humorous. These were all first published in Peikoff, ed., *Early Ayn Rand.*

9. David Harriman, ed., *Journals of Ayn Rand* (New York: Dutton, 1997), 59.

10. Such names were not some joke invented by Rand. See Sheila Fitzpatrick,

Everyday Stalinism: Ordinary Life in Extraordinary Times: Soviet Russia in the 1930s (New York: Oxford University Press, 1999), 83–84.

11. Cf. the description of a Red novel in the 1936 edition of *We the Living*, which Ayn Rand omitted from the revised edition: "She [Kira] picked up her book, but she did not want to read; the book told the story of a dam built by heroic Red workers in spite of the nefarious machinations of villainous Whites who tried to destroy it" (405).

12. Tonia, in the presence of Leo and Kira, tries to remember a line from a poem of Valentina Sirkina: "my heart is asbestos that remains cool over the blast-furnace of my emotions—or something like that" (264).

13. On humor in fiction, see Rand, *Art of Fiction*, 165–68.

14. The transcripts of Ayn Rand's 1969 nonfiction writing course was edited and published as *The Art of Nonfiction*, but there were several passages not on nonfiction—including this one on Ninotchka—excluded from the book. For more of Rand's praise of *Ninotchka*, see *Art of Fiction*, 168.

15. The Q&A on humor.

16. Harriman, *Journals*, 60.

17. Ayn Rand, "What is Romanticism?," *The Romantic Manifesto: A Philosophy of Literature*, revised edition (New York: Signet, 1975), 110.

18. On the dearth of smiles in Russia when Rand lived there, see her testimony before the House Un-American Activities Committee, in Harriman, *Journals*, 373, 380–81, and Robert Mayhew, "Russian Smiles: The Leftist Response to Ayn Rand's HUAC Testimony," *The Intellectual Activist* 16, no. 2 (February 2002).

19. Cf. Leo's smile, *We the Living*, 83.

20. On Kálmán's operetta *Die Bajadere*, see Michael S. Berliner, "The Music of *We the Living*," in the present volume, p. 119–21.

21. In an earlier draft of the *Bajadere* passage, Ayn Rand wrote that this was the first time Kira ever cried. I am grateful to Shoshana Milgram for bringing this to my attention, and for a better understanding of this passage.

22. For Rand's account of the importance of the character Ivan Ivanov, see Michael S. Berliner, ed., *Letters of Ayn Rand* (New York: Dutton, 1995), 18.

23. From the question period following lecture 8 of Leonard Peikoff's 1976 "Philosophy of Objectivism" course.

24. Rand, *Art of Fiction*, 174. I wish to thank Shoshana Milgram and Tore Boeckmann for their comments on an earlier version of this chapter.

15

Forbidding Life to Those Still Living

Tara Smith

"Andrei, why doesn't your Party believe in the right to live while one is not killed? . . . You may claim the right to kill, as all fighters do. But no one before you has ever thought of forbidding life to those still living."

—Kira in *We the Living* (189)

Collectivism kills. With bullets and clubs. Through its material deprivations: poverty, hunger, primitive medical care, abysmal living conditions. And—what I focus on in this chapter—by crushing people's spirits. *We the Living* eloquently portrays the way in which collectivism destroys human life not only physically, but spiritually. Collectivism's impact penetrates far beyond its severe material damage, and its toll on the human psyche, I believe, is what makes *We the Living* an especially poignant story.

In her writings on aesthetics, Ayn Rand expressly rejected the idea that the purpose of any work of art should be the moral education or political conversion of its audience.[1] Accordingly, my purpose here is not to *prove* (or to argue that *We the Living* proves) the evils of collectivism. I wish simply to show how the spiritual expense of collectivism is displayed in the novel and, through intermittent references to the historical practice of collectivist principles, indicate how true to the nature of collectivism Ayn Rand's portrait is.

I shall speak of collectivism rather than communism because communism is merely one manifestation of the more fundamental (and more widespread) collectivist thesis that the individual should be subordinated to the group. An individual possesses no rights, according to collectivism, but is a tool to be used for the good of the whole. The individual's interests should be sacrificed to the collective's.[2]

The material destruction of collectivism should need no lengthy documentation here. Reams of empirical data testify to collectivism's assault on human lives, whether through outright annihilation or its strangulation of creativity and production and the consequent debasement of living conditions. *The Black Book of Communism*, a recent collection of essays by European-based scholars cataloguing the impact of communism in different parts of the globe, estimates the victims of communism worldwide to stand between 85 and 100 million.[3] In quantifying collectivism's damage to humanity, one should not forget that Nazism, whose collectivist nature is usually neglected, claimed approximately 25 million victims.[4] For some perspective on these figures, consider that more people died in Stalin's war against the peasants in the early 1930s alone than the total number killed in World War I.[5]

Collectivism's economic record is also a disaster. In the final decade of the Soviet Union, only a third of households had hot running water.[6] As late as 1989, meat and sugar were still rationed—in peacetime. After sixty years of socialism, an average welfare mother in the United States received more income in a month than the average Soviet worker earned in a year.[7] To this day, people suffer the aftereffects of decades of collectivist policies. In contemporary Russia, per capita gross domestic product is $1,800. In the United States, it is $36,500.[8]

Collectivism's material toll is certainly on display in *We the Living*. The novel opens with an overdue, overloaded train disgorging unwashed hordes into a Petrograd smelling of carbolic acid. Throughout, we see that the most taken-for-granted incidentals of daily life—getting warm, getting food—pose a continual struggle for Soviet citizens. When they can obtain provisions, rations for one or two often feed entire families, who face the monotony of eating the same few unappetizing things—millet, lentils, onions, often spoiled—day after day. Residents stand in interminable lines to buy matches that do not light, kerchiefs that tear the first time worn, shoes with cardboard soles (193). Out of desperation to get something that they *might* be able to put to some use, people buy things they don't want (54). At home, space and privacy are steadily eroded, as apartments are divided among ever-increasing numbers of strangers.

Should one suspect that Ayn Rand is indulging in the exaggerations of poetic license, historian Sheila Fitzpatrick's recent book on everyday life in 1930s Russia testifies to the exact conditions that Ayn Rand depicts. Fitzpatrick reports, for instance, that people would sometimes start lining up for goods in the middle of the night and that access to goods was so unreliable that people would join queues before they knew what they were for. People developed the habit of carrying around "just in case" bags, on the chance that they would be unexpectedly able to acquire some needed items.[9] Once obtained, quality was every bit as shoddy as described in the novel. It was not uncommon to find clothes with missing sleeves, handles that fell off pots, matches that refused to strike, or foreign objects baked into bread.[10] Slavenka Drakulic, a contemporary journalist who was raised in communist Yugoslavia, observes that people reared under communism to this day tend to buy junk, so deeply engrained is the expectation that quality will never be available.[11] Another recent book details the conditions in communal apartments. When its author, Ilya Utekhin, was born in St. Petersburg in the late 1960s, thirty-five people shared the apartment he was raised in. In the 1920s, his grandfather had been one of fifty-six in the apartment. (Even today, Utekhin reports, many people in downtown St. Petersburg continue to inhabit such apartments.)[12]

Quite simply, Fitzpatrick summarizes, "For the greater part of the urban population, life revolved around the endless struggle to get the basics necessary for survival—food, clothing, shelter."[13]

For all of collectivism's material destruction, however, what *We the Living* depicts especially powerfully is the usually overlooked spiritual impact of collectivism—its effects on people's attitudes, outlooks, sense of themselves, and sense of life. Following Ayn Rand's usage, by "spiritual" I do not mean mystical or religious, but those aspects of our experience that pertain primarily to consciousness—such as beliefs, hopes, feelings.[14] A human being is a union of mind and body. The experience of our minds is a vital dimension of what matters to us. The spiritual *matters* both in physically sustaining us (the actions necessary to support our existence rely on rational thought) and in psychologically sustaining us (by providing the convictions, satisfactions, and hopes that fire the will to live and that motivate life's requisite actions).[15]

Ayn Rand has said that the theme of *We the Living* is the individual against the masses.[16] To consider collectivism's spiritual repercussions, I will first consider the masses—the novel's portrait of the kind of people and the kind of social relations engendered by collectivism—and then turn to the three central individuals.

LIFE AMONG THE COMRADES

The living conditions created by collectivist economic policies are naturally demoralizing. Material hardships are not necessarily discouraging; when people understand and endorse the reason for such strains, as during the struggle for a cause they believe in, they can accept temporary suffering for the sake of their goal. Under Soviet rule, however, people had little reason to expect conditions to improve. Wrenched from their privacy, property, and previous occupations, reduced to manufacturing soap in their kitchens, selling cherished family heirlooms, and speaking for causes they didn't believe in, this *was* the "better" world in which the collective good was served. Such abject conditions would naturally deflate a person's dreams, constricting his beliefs about what is attainable in life. If hard work leads, at best, to this, life is apparently not the open-ended wonder that it might have seemed in childhood. The relentless deprivations and indignities erode a person's hope, over time, and diminish his ambitions. Drakulic tells of people in collectivist societies hoarding all sorts of unlikely goods (stockings, shoeboxes, jars) for any conceivable use to be made of them in the future and interprets this as indicative of their loss of hope that the future would be better. What people stockpiled in their cupboards was a better sign of morale than anything they might have written, she observes.[17]

Accordingly, we see most of *We the Living*'s characters resigning themselves to a drastically circumscribed idea of life's possibilities. This is best (and to me, most startlingly) captured when Kira is about to make her final attempt to escape. Arguing that she shouldn't go, Kira's mother asks: "what's wrong with this country?" (448).

Collectivism corrupts not only a person's view of life and its possibilities; it also poisons a person's view of humanity. A principal means of effecting this is by criminalizing the entire population. Under collectivism, survival requires lawbreaking. People must lie, cheat, and bribe in order to secure bread, medicine, a job, a room, or simply to stay out of trouble. Fitzpatrick discusses "pull" or "*blat*" as an essential tool for navigating everyday Russian life. Having the right connections (enabling a person to get around the law) was not a convenience for securing the occasional luxury, but an indispensable survival mechanism.[18] Accordingly, we see Kira's family, and later Kira, bribing the building superintendent to try to keep rooms (52, 178). We see Leo denied a job because he cannot offer a bribe (170–71). Vava's family is rich only because her father performs illegal surgery (158). Kira, the most obvious victim, is forced to prostitute herself as a desperate means of obtaining the money for Leo's medical treatment.

Soviet authorities created so many restrictions that people could not help but run afoul of some of them.[19] And collectivism's strictures on production and trade brought shortages that necessitated extralegal activities in order to make ends meet.

Compounding the effect of unavoidably committing legal crimes, collectivism demands the moral crime of denying one's personal convictions. Kira's marching in the parade for a cause she detests, and delivering a lecture entitled "Marxism and Leninism" (200, 205) are but two examples of collectivism compelling people to espouse the party line regardless of their actual evaluation of it and to hide, apologize for, if not denounce those things that they truly value—be it one's political views, moral convictions, or the people one loves.[20] The cost of being made to regularly engage in "criminal" activity (legal or moral) and of seeing one's fellows doing the same is a soiled image of human nature. It is difficult to develop a respect for mankind when you routinely observe people in compromised positions. A given person might realize that it is the system that is unjust, rather than the coerced subjects.

Actions that are coerced are not truly immoral. Such clarity and self-posses-
sion as Kira displays, however, is a rare exception, particularly difficult in a
society that pounds its message in from all sides, doing its damnedest to stifle
even the germination of anticollectivist points of view. And regardless of a
person's reserves of self-esteem and independent judgment, it is demeaning
to have to adopt the devious, sordid methods of criminals, to act even under
the suggestion of moral depravity.

Collectivism is a menace not only to a person's image of humanity and to
his self-esteem; it also injures the self itself. It penalizes independence and
makes the achievement of a truly *personal* identity all but impossible.

The basic thesis of collectivism, recall, is that the group takes precedence
over the individual. We see the practical implementation of this principle
concretized throughout *We the Living*. The standard mode of address in collectivist Russia, "comrade Argounova," "citizen Kovalensky," introduces a
person first, primarily, as a member of the group. The implicit message? *You
exist insofar as you are a part of this larger body.* When Leo is asked to offer
language lessons three nights a week, his desire for a personal life is dismissed as irrelevant (166). He is viewed not as a sovereign individual entitled
to his own life, but as a tool whose sole function is to serve the collective
good. Andrei's appeal to his "personal affairs" in an exchange with a G.P.U.
executive is brusquely interrupted: "Your *what kind* of affairs, Comrade
Taganov?" (344, emphasis in original). The individual simply does not count.

Kira encounters the collectivist attitude as her pleas to officials for Leo's
medical care meet with cold indifference. As the Comrade Commissar asks:
"Why—in the face of the Union of Socialist Soviet Republics—can't one aristocrat die?" (228). Another Soviet official explains, when chastising her for
not being a union member: "What's a citizen? Only a brick and of no use
unless cemented to other bricks just like it" (49). Much later in the story,
when Kira is looking wistfully at a building under construction, a militia man
inquires what she wants. "I was just looking," Kira answers. His response
reflects perfectly the collectivist contempt for the self: "You have no business
looking" (324).

Independence is the virtue of forming and acting according to one's own
judgments. Independence does not preclude learning from other people, but
it does demand that a person understand and evaluate ideas by using his
own reasoning. A person's ends and decisions about how to achieve those
ends should be rational, but in order to be rational, they must be his own.
At its core, independence is a matter of orienting oneself around the facts of
reality rather than around other people's beliefs or wishes.[21] An independent
posture for dealing with the world is systematically beaten down by collectivism, however. Citizens are made to obey, to conform, to serve. Collectivism does not want a person to think for himself. Comrade Sonia repeatedly
admonishes Andrei at any hint of his independent thinking. "Why do you

think you are entitled to your own thoughts?" she asks accusingly (311). Pliability is the trait most conducive to the collectivist agenda.

Under collectivism, survival (economic, social, literal) is completely politicized.[22] Goods, position, and security are obtained not by rationality, virtue, hard work, or productiveness, but by trading favors; you must get on with the right people. This reign of pull *asks* for the soulless, groveling parasitism of Victor. (In the lexicon of *The Fountainhead*, it asks for second-handedness and propagates Peter Keatings.)[23] A person is rewarded in direct proportion to his obedience—that is, his following the dictates of others rather than forming and following judgments of his own. Victor is the natural result of collectivist rule, a person who purges any remnant of a distinct self and eagerly complies with the perceived wishes of those in power. (Even Victor's obsequiousness does not win him security, however. Since "the collective good" is an elastic ideal arbitrarily invoked to justify any action against any individual, a person has no way to truly safeguard himself, however self-sacrificially he may aim to please.)[24]

Collectivism breeds puppets.[25] Because it compels people to follow its rulers' script, collectivism cripples the exercise of independent judgment. Not only does it discourage people from thinking for themselves, however; it also stunts people's capacity to want for themselves, to develop their own ends. Collectivism renders personal desire pointless (since such desires must be subordinated to the professed good of the whole) and thereby strangles the entire realm of the personal. Having a self—*your* convictions, your ambitions, your values—becomes nearly impossible, as the freedom necessary to exert that self is obliterated.

A self is not simply a body and a passport number. Kira understands the centrality of desire to simply *being* a self.

> I was born and I knew I was alive and I knew what I wanted. What do you think is alive in me? Why do you think I'm alive? Because I have a stomach and eat and digest the food? Because I breathe and work and produce more food to digest? Or because I know what I want, and that something which knows how to want—isn't that life itself? (404)

One reflection of the diminished selves that are possible under collectivism is the diluted emotional experience of those who have adapted to collectivist ways. The marchers at Andrei's funeral are utterly indifferent to the loss of this comrade's life (432–34). Sonia's attitude toward having a baby—usually a joyful prospect—is completely impersonal (316–17). No respect, let alone affection, marks Sonia's marriage. Victor forgets to kiss his wife Marisha as he leaves for his assignment on Lake Volkhov, just pages after the painfully exquisite parting of the trains carrying Sasha and Irina to their separate exiles (353–55). The ache of their parting is a result of the intensity of their love—which is made possible by their each being selfish individuals—which is precisely what collectivism does its utmost to quash. Ayn Rand is showing us not simply people of different political opinions. She is showing us how collectivism produces a different kind of people.

What remains, in collectivist society, are shells of human beings, quivering before Party officials, sweatily anxious to please and appease. Far from "a new humanity" or "men of granite," as Timoshenko concludes, collectivism creates "little puny things that wiggle. Little things that can bend both ways, little double-jointed spirits" (372–73).

Alongside its damage to a person's self, self-image, and image of humanity, collectivism also poisons relations between people. Social relations are basically hostile, marked by wariness, resentment, and betrayal. At their best, most "comrades" are indifferent to one another's experience.

What is Pavel's reaction when told that people have been waiting in his office for three hours? "Tell them to go to hell" (288). The hospital refuses to treat Kira's aunt Maria because she does not belong to a trade union (187). Leo cannot obtain medical treatment (for a life-threatening illness) because of his father's former social status and his political views.[26]

One of the reasons for this pervasive callousness is, no doubt, the fact that relations between people are forced. *You* cannot choose whom to associate with, but are made to sacrifice for others, whether you like the relevant others and choose to or not.

Further, collectivist control of the economy causes material scarcity, which pits individuals against one another. By denying the freedom that fuels production and by centralizing distribution, collectivism shackles economic growth and forces people to fight for access to a shrunken pool of goods doled out by the authorities. The arrival of ever more strangers in one's home, for instance, would hardly encourage communal attitudes, as Fitzpatrick observes. "Envy and covetousness flourished."[27] Since another person's needs typically demand a greater sacrifice from you (for the sake of the collective), wariness and resentment are understandable. Collectivism *creates* a "dog eat dog" universe.

According to Fitzpatrick, collectivist duty as well as shrewd calculation required a person to be "endlessly suspicious" of his fellow citizens. Denouncing someone could be a means either of improving one's own image as a loyal Party servant or of gaining more immediate advantages, such as having that person ejected from your apartment.[28] Collectivism encourages people to continually search for what they can "get" on another person. Treachery is instilled as a way of life. You succeed by turning comrades in.[29]

In this environment, personal relationships are reduced from enduring values of potentially great significance to disposable, tactical alliances. Sonia warns Pavel (her *husband*) that she is keeping an eye on his activities (366).

Victor obtains a room for Marisha in Leo and Kira's apartment so that he can meet Marisha's friends in the Party (176–82). To preclude any damage to his party standing should his sister marry the counterrevolutionary Sasha, Victor turns both of them in to the authorities, resulting in their ten-year sentences to Siberian prisons. And he refuses to try to help his sister at least be with Sasha in exile, thus betraying his pleading father, as well (339, 347–48).

It is worth noting that as a devout collectivist, Victor does not only betray friends and family. He also betrays himself. By marrying Marisha rather than his longtime romantic interest Vava, whose family wealth was politically incorrect, Victor surrenders his own desires. He abdicates his happiness to satisfy the party's decree of how to promote the good of the whole. Where the collective good is enforced as the paramount value, political calculation replaces affection as the basis for social relations. Personal preferences are a luxury that a person cannot afford.

Overall, we observe little brotherhood or warm fellow feeling among the comrades. The only respect or kindness in evidence is offered by those who disdain the collective and who retain the ability to value specific individuals: Kira, giving bread she had waited hours to obtain to her hungry family, and Vasili, giving money to the amputee newspaper vendor who had fought against the Communists years before (146–47, 87). Andrei, a collectivist in name who gradually realizes his truer individualism, also shows respect for his fellows when he allows Captain Karsavin to take his own life (112–13).

ANDREI

If this much describes collectivism's spiritual ramifications for people at large, let us now focus more specifically on the novel's three principal figures. Of these, Andrei undergoes the greatest transformation. Collectivism destroys him not as one of its enemies, but despite his being among its staunchest advocates. Unlike Leo and Kira, Andrei accepts collectivist ideology, but ultimately finds that it crushes *him*. Introduced as a steely Communist hero, in the end, Andrei publicly renounces the party and takes his own life.

What enables this transformation is the fact that from the start, Andrei is self-possessed. Whereas the Party loyalty of Victor, Sonia, Pavel, and their ilk consists of "playing the game" to stay on the higher-ups' good side, Andrei's allegiance stems from philosophical conviction. He fought in the revolution, before the outcome was assured and the party gained power, because he sincerely believed in its ideals. Collectivism would improve people's lives, he thought, and Andrei valued human life. It is only when he comes to see that collectivism does not actually value life that he abandons that philosophy.

The contrast between Andrei and the Party groupies could not be clearer. His values and his identity led him to embrace the party; their amorphous identities are *supplied* by the party. While the Victors and Sonias are playthings of the authorities, tapping to whatever tempo party leaders dictate, Andrei is his own man. He embraced collectivism because he thought it was based on noble ideals; he rejects it when he judges it to be evil.

Kira is attracted to Andrei's integrity. She senses that his is a colossal, but honest, intellectual error. His honesty is evident in the fact that he pursues the truth about the party and about Leo and Kira, knowing the pain and punishment that might result. What binds Kira and Andrei is their basic root: their belief in life, as Kira describes it (117). Like Kira, Andrei is independent, as anyone who truly loves his own life must be. "I joined the Party because I knew I was right. I love you, because I know I'm right" (278). He thinks for himself. And increasingly, he *wants* things for himself—for his pleasure in seeing Kira wear certain clothes, for instance. Andrei eventually accepts the idea, foreign in a collectivist society, that things' loveliness *to him* is reason enough to pursue them (357).

Over the course of his relationship with Kira, Andrei becomes more of an egoist. More precisely, the egoism muffled by his commitment to collectivism emerges more explicitly, as he gradually recognizes its propriety. At the roof garden of the European Hotel with Kira, Andrei speaks of discovering what it's like to have "no purpose but myself" and "how sacred a purpose that can be . . ." He realizes that "a life is possible whose only justification is my own joy" (277). It is largely *through* loving Kira that Andrei discovers the value of his own life. Observing his reactions to her reveals to him the entire realm of truly personal values. Originally, he admits, he thought of going to the stylish bar as a sacrifice for Kira's sake. "And now I like it" (277).

Andrei's love for Kira is at once intense and tender. He relishes her reading a book whose hero shares his name (247). Sometimes, he tells her, "I want just a look at you . . . the same day you've been here . . . sometimes even a minute after you've left" (247). The fact that she means so much to him is a sign of his strong self-love. Kira could not mean so much to Andrei unless *his* happiness meant so much.

As Ayn Rand has explained elsewhere, love is not a causeless emotion. The emotional force of love results from a person's underlying evaluation of the object loved—and of how it affects his happiness. Without an unequivocal commitment to his own happiness, however, a person would not have the foundation necessary for a definite, strong valuing of any particular person. "Only a rationally selfish man, a man of *self-esteem*, is capable of love—because he is the only man capable of holding firm, consistent, uncompromising, unbetrayed values."[30] The more developed a person's own identity and knowledge of his values and the more deeply a person values himself, the more he can appreciate another person's genuine value to him—and correspondingly, feel profound love for that person. As the hero of *The Fountainhead* says, "To say 'I love you' one must first know how to say the 'I.' "[31]

Andrei's virtue—his independence, his honesty, his integrity, his egoism—leads him to pursue the evidence he is encountering, to face its profound implications, and to take appropriate action. He pursues the case against Leo despite Kira's begging him not to because *he* needs to establish whether the party has integrity (385–86). Once he reaches his conclusions, he addresses his critique directly to the party, bravely attacking its most central creeds, declaring that "No one can tell men what they must live for." Every honest man, Andrei proclaims in his speech, lives for himself. "The one who does not, does not truly live" (408).

Collectivism does not permit a man to live for himself. Thus, Andrei realizes, collectivism does not permit life.

Andrei's integrity is equally great in the personal sphere. When Andrei learns that Kira had actually loved Leo all along, he is pained largely because of the pain that he has caused her. Since he cherishes Kira, the thought that he had been a source of pain to her is piercing. And consider his response after Kira's tirade explaining the reasons for her relationship with Andrei: he would have done the same thing (405). This is a man of a large and honest soul.

Andrei takes his own life, yet it is collectivism that destroys him. At one level, he is disillusioned by its lies and corruption. While most party members cynically accept the double standards and disdain for those not well-connected, Andrei's commitment had been earnest. This was the basis for his distinguished career in collectivism's service. By the story's end, the entire worldview to which Andrei had ardently devoted himself has been kicked out from under him. The problem cannot be solved by cleansing the Party of a few bad apples. Andrei realizes that collectivism requires hypocrisy; a person *couldn't* faithfully follow its dictates. He sees how collectivism has shattered his personal life, forcing Kira to fake a love for him in order to save another man. The greatest value that Andrei had ever enjoyed, his love affair with Kira, is thus revealed to be a sham.[32]

Still more devastating than his discovery of Kira's true motivations, which Andrei understands, is what Andrei discovers about what *he* has done. Andrei realizes that he had been a traitor to himself all these years (358)—and that that is what collectivist principles demand. It was only to the extent that he had deviated from the collectivist course that he found himself, enjoyed himself, and truly lived.

Collectivism teaches you to kill yourself *while* living. This is what Kira realizes, in the passage cited as my preface, long before Andrei. In a sense, then, ending his life physically was only the completion of the extended suicide he had committed through his years of dutiful self-abnegation for the collective.

Andrei is spiritually crushed, in the end, by the realization that he had erected two altars, as Kira puts it: on one stood a harlot, and on the other, the immoral speculator citizen Morozov (404). This was the "life" that collectivism had given him.

KIRA

I cannot describe the spiritual destruction of Kira because no such destruction takes place. She is the exception. While she is gunned down physically by the collectivist state, Kira remains spiritually unconquered, her soul intact.

Kira's spirit survives because of the unusual depth of her egoism. She exerts heroic independence against the most extraordinary obstacles. Kira refuses to acquiesce to the reigning political dogma or to seek a "safer" existence, recognizing that no security worth having could result from surrendering her own judgment.

Frequently, Kira seems oblivious to the burdens of Soviet living conditions. She does not notice what she is eating, whether she is hungry, or the dimness of the reading light (36, 55). She certainly suffers the deprivations as much as any—the food, the cold, the cramped living quarters. Indeed, she is expelled from school and thus denied the pursuit of her passion, engineering. Yet these blows remain, at core, peripheral. She does not allow her experience to be defined by external events. Witness her attitude toward politics, as she tells Andrei: "I don't want to fight for the people, I don't want to fight against the people, I don't want to hear of the people. I want to be left alone—to live" (90).

Kira is wholly selfish. She feels reverence for her own life, and wants "the best, the greatest, the highest possible, here, now, for [my] very own" (117). Kira thinks continually of the future, of life abroad, of her values. On arriving in St. Petersburg, she relishes "the streets of a big city where so much is possible" (25). Getting to know Leo, she tells him not about her present but about all that she will construct in the future (83). On lines for rations, "she thought that somewhere beyond all these many things which did not count, was her life with Leo" (199).[33] At school, thoughts of the future bring her solace (202). Even late in the story, she looks longingly at a construction site, telling herself "Perhaps . . . some day . . . abroad . . ." (324).

The future was consecrated, for Kira, "because it was *her* future" (50, emphasis in original). Kira is not in denial. She is not a naïve schoolgirl and this is not evasive escapism. It is devotion to her own positive values that drives Kira to action—to everything from secretly sewing a dress in order to look attractive to Leo to sleeping with Andrei in order to save Leo. Ultimately, Kira's self-love leads her to try to cross the border and escape altogether collectivism's stranglehold. While Kira may not gripe about collectivism's daily assaults as much as her neighbors, she fights collectivism far more profoundly—physically, by attempting escape; spiritually, by never surrendering her soul.

To the end, Kira is living—acting, trying, aiming at a selfish purpose. Her attitude toward life is not fundamentally altered by the carnage around her or by her own suffering. Kira holds fast to herself—to her judgment, her values, and the goal of her own happiness. "I'll be afraid only on a day that will never come," she tells Irina. "The day when I give up" (350).

Yet it is precisely Kira's unshakeable commitment to herself that dooms her under collectivism. Her drive to make the most of her life is what collectivism emphatically opposes. The doctrine demanding individual submission before group supremacy will not abide a woman pursuing her own well-being. It greets any attempt to break free with bullets.

Human life, by its nature, is individual. Only individual human beings breathe and think and feel. Insofar as collectivism denounces the individual as subordinate to the group, collectivism sets itself against life itself, permitting only the living death we witness among the prisoners of St. Petersburg: begging for favors, food, jobs, pumping the primus and coughing through greasy soup, memorizing propaganda, with bribery and betrayal the only means of eking out a precarious subsistence. Anyone who is truly living—anyone like Kira, cultivating personal values and pursuing a selfish purpose—is exterminated. Our heroine remains smiling in the end; yet, for the glory of the collective good, she is also bleeding to death.

LEO

Unlike Kira and Andrei, Leo is not killed—yet he is hardly better off. His protracted spiritual death may actually be a more cruel fate.

Leo is largely defeated from the outset—from his first encounters with Kira. He admits to having no desires other than to desire something (83). It is safer not to aspire, he says; he struggles to muster the will to fight lice (83). And he advises Kira not to look too closely at people (62).

Leo does manage some resistance, early on. His attempt to flee to Germany with Kira is fueled by hope for a better life abroad. Once that effort fails, however, we see a steady, ever more encompassing descent. Leo becomes a gambler and drinker, reckless in both word and action. He defies the rules of the state, spends irresponsibly the money he makes at illegal speculation, and flaunts his wealth in ways that could only invite official scrutiny. Leo is maddeningly indifferent to significant positive events: his return to Kira in good health after lengthy treatment at the Crimean sanatorium, his release after being arrested (261, 417–19). It is as if normal human reactions have been drained out of him. We would expect excitement, or at least relief, on these occasions, some enthusiasm for new opportunities. Collectivism, however, permits a man no opportunities.

In Leo, we observe most completely the spiritual devastation of collectivism. (Andrei retains the will to take his own life; in Leo, even that is destroyed.) On Leo's return from the Crimea, Kira "noticed something in his eyes that had not been cured; something that, perhaps, had grown beyond cure" (261). Leo is utterly without hope. Collectivism has shredded Leo's will to live.

Fairly early in his downward spiral, when Kira objects to his drinking and urges him to take care of himself, Leo's response is simply: "for what?" (213). When she asks him why he drinks, he replies: "why shouldn't I?" (216). His attitude is at best one of resignation. While Kira struggles to obtain medical care for his incipient tuberculosis, "she made Leo do his share of inquiries. He obeyed without arguing, without complaining," but also "without hope" (222).

On returning from the treatment, Kira asks if he is completely well and free to live again. "I am well—yes. As to living again . . . " (261). Asked his plans for the winter by Kira's father, Leo admits to having none. "Nor for any winter to come" (274). When Kira pleads with him not to be a front in the speculative venture with Morozov, warning that he would be risking his life, Leo counters that it is not much to risk (284). Finally, when Kira proposes another attempt to flee the country, his reaction epitomizes his broken spirit: "Why bother?" (363).

Reading the novel, it is easy to be exasperated by Leo's behavior. Yet he illustrates perfectly the psychological ravages inflicted by collectivism. As Ayn Rand observed, it is the background that creates these characters' tragedy.[34] In a free society, background would be only that: background. But collectivism's obliteration of individual freedom asphyxiates its subjects. Any anger at Leo presupposes a context in which rational action is possible and can be efficacious. That is what collectivism prevents.

By denying freedom, Leo understands, collectivism kills the future. Slavenka Drakulic, the Yugoslav writer, describes this as a particularly corrosive legacy of collectivist ideology.

> What communism instilled in us was precisely this immobility, this absence of a future, the absence of a dream, of the possibility of imagining our lives differently. There was hardly a way to say to yourself: This is just temporary, it will pass, it must. On the contrary, we learned to think: This will go on forever, no matter what we do. We can't change it. It looked as if the omnipotent system had mastered time itself.[35]

In her later book, written several years after the relevant collectivist governments had dissolved, Drakulic observes East Europeans' continuing image of the future as "distant and blurred and not yet to be trusted."[36]

This corrosion of hope is palpable in *We the Living*. At a party, amid guests exchanging tales of conditions abroad, a girl who reports hearing of shopping without ration cards confesses that she does not really believe it (153–54). When their freedom and potential are so completely withdrawn, people gradually lose the ability even to conceive that a better world is possible.

By erasing prospects of a worthwhile future, collectivism punctures the motivation to embrace purposes. It makes no sense to adopt specific personal objectives when any attempts to achieve them may be arbitrarily thwarted at any time. A person is permitted to pursue only those ends that the state approves. Could you start your own business? No. Could you be an engineer? Not if you are not politically correct. Could you simply spend an evening as you like? Not if party meetings call; not if you speak German and the authorities deem it useful to the collective that more of your comrades learn German.

When personal purposes are irrelevant and one's days are dictated by slave masters, it is little wonder that a man would lose his appetite for life. The more clearly a person understands the essential character of collectivist constraints—that the natural course of causal relations will be unpredictably obstructed, that any plans he makes are subject to obstacles imposed by people whose only claim to do so rests in their ability to literally force his compliance, and that reason itself is moot—the more natural it is to concede defeat. If reason is futile, why try to reason? When life is reduced to a crapshoot, playing craps seems a logical response. Leo lives for today, one might say, because today is all that collectivism grants him.

Contrary to this description of Leo as resigned, one might suppose that Leo's defiance of the authorities represents resistance. He does not meekly acquiesce to the government's dictates; he does not dutifully accommodate himself to an approved Soviet job, or study communist homilies, to placate party bosses. Leo has decided to live as *best* he can under the circumstances, seemingly enjoying the finer things he can get his hands on. He thumbs his nose at the authorities, all but daring them to catch and punish him.

Such resistance is more of a surrender than it may superficially appear, however. For, were he a free man, drinking and gambling would not have been Leo's way. He would not have been tempted to become a gigolo. Aimless amusement does not reflect his true identity. What we are seeing, in fact, are simply the tormented squirmings of a defeated soul.

Leo was a smart man. We may be reluctant to acknowledge that. The idea that such a bleak outlook and prodigal waste of talent could in any way be right or even associated with intelligence is anathema to many people's sense of the world. In a free society, where rationality is allowed and rewarded, intelligence is a person's path to success, the tool enabling him to achieve values and attain happiness. Under collectivist clamps, however, Leo's ability to recognize the futility of purpose or rational action only accelerates his decline. It also makes it more wrenching to witness, since we can glimpse what Leo might have been.

Admirable as we find Kira, that admiration is premised on a different kind of society from the one that she inhabits. In the world as it should be, where individuals are free to chart their own course and seek their own happiness, Kira's attitude is exactly right: steadfast adherence to her own judgment of what is possible, what is good, what is worth pursuing.

In the context of collectivism, however, her virtues cannot save her. It is fitting that Kira is killed. For collectivism is opposed—in principle and in practice—to individual life. Thus we observe its smothering of Leo, its cruci-fixion of Andrei, and its physical annihilation of Kira.

The cliché has it that "Where there's life, there's hope." Ayn Rand's portrait of Leo makes plain that where there is no freedom, no future, and no hope, there can be no true life. Under collectivism's vise, all that is possible to an individual is a life that isn't worth having. Thus Andrei commits suicide, Kira risks death in order to escape, and Leo is murdered spiritually, bereft of all desire.

Collectivism kills Leo, just as surely as it kills the others, though he remains breathing at the end. In their penultimate encounter, even Kira accepts this: "His eyes were dead and she turned away, for she felt that those eyes should be closed" (441).

CONCLUSION

The destruction wreaked by collectivism that is portrayed in *We the Living* is not an aberration of a particular regime. The official who tells Kira that a citizen is merely a brick aptly captures the collectivist creed, however varied in details its application might be. The defining ideal of collectivism—the subordination of the individual to the collective—proclaims its hostility to life. For there *is* no collective apart from the particular members of a group. As Ayn Rand wrote in a 1936 letter, "You cannot claim that you have a healthy forest composed of rotting trees. I'm afraid that collectivists cannot see the trees for the forest."[37] Life is inescapably individual. To condemn individuals is to condemn the only kinds of beings that do and can live. Col-lectivism is an antilife philosophy.

If Leo is smart, so is Kira. For she recognizes the spiritual destruction of this doctrine, seeing how collectivism forbids life even to those still living. The irony—and the tragedy—is that collectivism triumphs in *We the Living*.[38] Its enemies are defeated. But *what* is won? For whom? Corpses and broken souls accumulate across its pages—of Andrei and Kira and Leo, of Irina and Sasha, Timoshenko, Maria, Vava, Vasili, Victor, Pavel, Sonia. While collectivism's enemies are defeated, by the nature of collectivism, so are its friends. So is every individual.[39]

NOTES

1. Ayn Rand, "The Psycho-Epistemology of Art," *The Romantic Manifesto: A Philosophy of Literature*, revised edition (New York: Signet, 1975), 15–24, especially 21–22. Also see (in the same collection) "Art and Sense of Life," 34–44, especially 38; and "The Goal of My Writing," 162–72, especially 169–70.

2. In a 1936 letter, Ayn Rand made clear that she considered the novel to be concerned not exclusively with communism but with all forms of collectivism. Michael S. Berliner, ed., *Letters of Ayn Rand* (New York: Dutton, 1995), 33. A film of *We the Living* released in Italy in 1942 was banned when the fascist government realized that its message was antifascist as much as anticommunist. See Leonard Peikoff's introduction to the sixtieth anniversary edition of *We the Living*, ix–x. Hitler, whose Nazis (National Socialists) represented another variant of collectivism, clearly articulated the collectivist attitude: "There will be no license, no free space, in which the individual belongs to himself. This is Socialism— . . . " Hermann Rauschning, *The Voice of Destruction* (New York: Putnam's, 1940), 191–93. A slogan of Cambodian communism ran: "Losing you is not a loss, and keeping you is no specific gain." Stéphane Courtois et al., *The Black Book of Communism: Crimes, Terror, Repression*. Translated by Jonathan Murphy and Mark Kraemer (Cambridge, Mass.: Harvard University Press, 1999), 597.

Ayn Rand critiqued collectivism in many of her nonfiction writings. See, for instance, "The New Fascism: Rule by Consensus," " 'Extremism,' or the Art of Smearing," and "Theory and Practice," in *Capitalism: The Unknown Ideal*, expanded paperback edition (New York: Signet, 1967) and "Racism" and "Collectivized 'Rights,' " in *The Virtue of Selfishness: A New Concept of Egoism* (New York: New American Library, 1964).

3. Courtois, *Black Book*, x. The authors are former Communists or fellow travelers, xii. Many of these examples specifically concern Communism both because that is the species of collectivism encountered in *We the Living* and because the Communist USSR was the powerhouse of collectivist regimes, thus it offers the fairest basis for comparisons.

4. Courtois, *Black Book*, xi. Since that book focuses on Communism, the Nazi deaths are cited as a point of contrast, and are not included in the 85–100 million.

5. Robert Conquest, *Harvest of Sorrow* (New York: Oxford University Press, 1986), 1.

6. Zbigniew Brzezinski, *The Grand Failure—The Birth and Death of Communism in the 20th Century* (New York: Scribner's, 1989), 237.

7. David Horowitz, *The Politics of Bad Faith* (New York: The Free Press, 1998), 98ff. For more on the Soviet economic record, see Stephen Kotkin, *Armageddon Averted—The Soviet Collapse, 1970–2000* (New York: Oxford University Press, 2001).

8. Paul Starobin and Catherine Belton, "What's in it for Putin?" *Business Week*, May 27, 2002, 55.

9. Sheila Fitzpatrick, *Everyday Stalinism—Ordinary Life in Extraordinary Times: Soviet Russia in the 1930's* (New York: Oxford University Press, 1999), 43, 41. *We the Living* is set in the 1920s, when conditions were a bit better, but basically similar.

10. Fitzpatrick, *Everyday Stalinism*, 44.

11. Slavenka Drakulic, *Café Europa—Life After Communism* (New York: Norton, 1996), 72–73.

12. Bryon MacWilliams, "Communism at Uncomfortably Close Quarters," *Chronicle of Higher Education*, April 26, 2002, A56. The book is Ilya Utekhin, *Essays on Communal Life*. Some chapters are available in English at http://utekhin.da.ru.

13. Fitzpatrick, *Everyday Stalinism*, 41. Fitzpatrick quotes a survivor of the Soviet regime, who had expected that in a collectivist society, " 'ideas' would be everything and that 'things' would hardly count" because, as the woman put it in a letter, "everyone would have what they wanted without superfluities." On the contrary, the woman found that things "had never been so important." Things mattered enormously, Fitzpatrick concludes, "for the simple reason that they were so hard to get" (40).

14. Ayn Rand, "The Objectivist Ethics," *Virtue of Selfishness*, 35.

15. Spiritual goods include such things as books, art, friendships, self-respect, and intelligence. For more on spiritual values, see Tara Smith, *Viable Values: A Study of Life as the Root and Reward of Morality* (Lanham, Md.: Rowman & Littlefield, 2000), chapter 5, especially 136–43.

16. Berliner, *Letters*, 18. Also see 12–13.

17. Slavenka Drakulic, *How We Survived Communism and Even Laughed* (New York: Norton, 1991), 179–89.

18. Fitzpatrick, *Everyday Stalinism*, 59–65. Drakulic discusses the criminalization of the populace in *Café Europa*, 112.

19. In various places, people were punished for wearing hats, for instance, or wearing dirty clothes on the streetcar. Fitzpatrick cites several examples. Fitzpatrick, *Everyday Stalinism*, 34. It was a crime to be a "socially dangerous person," a loosely defined catchall category. *Black Book*, 135–36. Ayn Rand offers a perceptive analysis of the reasons for this in *Atlas Shrugged* (New York: Random House, 1957; Signet thirty-fifth anniversary paperback edition, 1992), 406. Dr. Ferris explains that the authorities *want* the laws broken, "since there's no way to rule innocent men."

20. See Courtois, *Black Book*, 420, 483 for some examples of these tactics in practice.

21. For an excellent discussion of the virtue of independence, see Leonard Peikoff, *Objectivism: The Philosophy of Ayn Rand* (New York: Dutton, 1991) 251–59. Fully, the virtue encompasses making one's own way materially as well as intellectually.

22. In the words of Anders Aslund, "the communist system was the most thoroughly politicized system the world has seen." Anders Aslund, *Building Capitalism: The Transformation of the Former Soviet Bloc* (New York: Cambridge University Press, 2002), 23.

23. Ayn Rand describes a second-hander (or social metaphysician) as a person "who regards the consciousness of other men as superior to his own and to the facts of reality." "The Argument from Intimidation," *Virtue of Selfishness*, 165. Also see

"The Nature of the Second-Hander," *For the New Intellectual* (New York: Random House, 1961; Signet paperback edition, 1963), 68–71.

24. For her analysis of the "common good" that this subservience is supposed to advance, I strongly recommend Ayn Rand, "What is Capitalism?" in *Capitalism: The Unknown Ideal*, especially 20–21.

25. Drakulic makes a similar observation, writing that communism breeds masses rather than individuals. *Café Europa*, 104.

26. These attitudes would be applauded by Lenin, who ruthlessly advocated "a bullet in the head" for speculators and who repeatedly employed terror against his own citizens. Courtois, *Black Book*, 59. Lenin's benevolence was equally apparent when he elaborated on the positive results that a domestic famine would bring. Courtois, *Black Book*, 123–24.

27. Fitzpatrick, *Everyday Stalinism*, 47–48.

28. Fitzpatrick, *Everyday Stalinism*, 19, 135, 22.

29. Fitzpatrick reports that people were encouraged to break off relations with a person who was deported and that children of arrested parents were strongly pressured to renounce them. Fitzpatrick, *Everyday Stalinism*, 125, 213.

30. Ayn Rand, "Objectivist Ethics," 35, emphasis hers.

31. Ayn Rand, *The Fountainhead* (New York: Bobbs-Merrill, 1943; Signet fiftieth anniversary paperback edition, 1993), 377.

32. Kira's feelings for Andrei are complex. While she does not value Andrei as she does Leo, she does develop strong feelings for him and in some sense comes to love Andrei.

33. For those familiar with *Atlas Shrugged*: Kira seems to embody the attitude expressed by Dagny, when she asks Galt: "we never had to take any of it seriously, did we?" (702). For Rand's comment on this passage, see Berliner, *Letters*, 583–84.

34. Berliner, *Letters*, 17.

35. Drakulic, *How We Survived*, 7.

36. Drakulic, *Café Europa*, 67. Fitzpatrick writes that Russian collectivism encouraged fatalism and passivity, since a citizen realized that he could not control his own fate. At the same time, because even strictly abiding by the rules afforded no reliable security, Fitzpatrick also found that people took surprising risks. Fitzpatrick, *Everyday Stalinism*, 219, 221.

37. Berliner, *Letters*, 35. For more of Ayn Rand's analysis of this issue, see the entire letter and note 24, above.

38. It does not, of course, triumph over the human spirit, as Kira's attempt to escape and attitude in dying make plain. See Ayn Rand, *The Art of Fiction*, Tore Boeckmann, ed. (New York: Plume, 2000), 174.

39. Thanks to Robert Mayhew for many very helpful comments on an earlier draft of this chapter.

16

The Death Premise in *We the Living* and *Atlas Shrugged*

Onkar Ghate

In her foreword to the revised edition of *We the Living*, written a year after the publication of *Atlas Shrugged*, Ayn Rand explains that the basic theme of *We the Living* is the supreme value of human life (xiii). At the time of writing the novel, she knew that reverence for one's own life is the "fundamental characteristic of the best among men" and that its absence in an individual's soul "represents some enormous evil which had never been identified" (xiv). This evil, she already grasped, is what produces dictatorship, collectivism, and all other forms of human evil. But she did not yet understand the full nature of this evil nor, especially, how an individual could descend to such a subhuman level. She discovered *that* while writing *Atlas Shrugged*.

> In *Atlas Shrugged* I explain the philosophical, psychological and moral meaning of the men who value their own lives and of the men who don't. I show that the first are the Prime Movers of mankind and that the second are metaphysical killers, working for an opportunity to become physical ones. In *Atlas Shrugged*, I show *why* men are motivated either by a life premise or a death premise. In *We the Living*, I show only that they are (xiv).

To be on the life premise is to be motivated by the values life requires. To be on the death premise is to be motivated by the destruction of the values life requires. I will explore some of what *We the Living* already reveals about the death premise and some of what Rand went on to identify about the premise's nature—particularly its root cause—in *Atlas Shrugged*.

In *We the Living*, one might say, Rand is the policeman surveying the criminal and gathering evidence about his habits, patterns, and actions. In *Atlas Shrugged*, she is the detective piecing together all the evidence, explaining the nature of the crime and exposing the criminal's means and motive. It is startling, however, how much Rand already understood about the criminal in writing *We the Living*—and startling how much more she was to discover about his nature by the time she created *Atlas Shrugged*.

To capture in this chapter both of these aspects, I will begin with an overview of Rand's understanding of collectivism as an ideology of death in *We the Living*, and then narrow the focus to the character of Pavel Syerov, one of the principal villains in the novel. I will compare Syerov to the principal villain in *Atlas Shrugged*, James Taggart. The similarities, we will see, are revealing. Both men are on the death premise. But only Rand's characterization of Taggart in *Atlas Shrugged* (a characterization that has greater depth than that of Syerov in *We the Living*) exposes the root cause of the men who are on the death premise.

What *We the Living* does show is that there *is* such a thing as the death premise. The collectivism of communism—the attempt to tie all individuals together and make them "brothers," "comrades," "equals"—*means* destruction and death, particularly the destruction and death of the best individuals, those who strive to grow, to produce, to live. And the novel shows that contrary to the protests of any genuinely idealistic communists, this is what communism (and any other form of collectivism) *must* lead to in practice. Most of communism's leaders, the story makes clear, at some level know this. They pursue collectivism's destructive goal without the excuse of honest error.

Andrei Taganov represents the idealistic communist. You "were the best your Party had to offer the world," the novel's heroine, Kira Argounova, rightly tells him (358). The root of Andrei's idealism is his intellectual honesty: he takes ideas seriously. Kira, for instance, is surprised to find that he is the only one with whom she can discuss ideas (217). Andrei thinks that communism, by removing undesirable, evil elements from society and bringing "equality" to all men, will raise everyone up to the level of the highest individual. Although Andrei dislikes what most people actually make of their lives, he tells Kira that he does not have "the luxury of loathing. I'd rather try to make them worth looking at, to bring them up to my level" (90). In response to Kira's question that his cause therefore is to deny his own life for the sake of millions, Andrei answers "No. To bring millions up to where I want them—for my sake" (89).

Rand, when analyzing the Left years later, commented that the goal of "equal prosperity" for all gave superficial plausibility to the ideology of collectivism.[1] If Andrei's error in being seduced by communism is an honest error, as the novel portrays it to be, then this superficial plausibility is a significant part of the explanation.[2] But the fact remains that the egalitarianism at the heart of collectivism cannot, and is not meant to, lift people up. As Rand wrote more than thirty years after publishing *We the Living*, equality of results (as opposed to equality of individual rights before the law) could be achieved in only two ways: "either by raising all men to the mountain-top—or by razing the mountains."[3] The first method, however, is *metaphysically* impossible, since individuals have different attributes and abilities and make different choices. So the only actual meaning of a crusade for equality of results is a crusade to level society by pulverizing the mountains.[4] Not surprisingly, therefore, this is what is portrayed in page after page of *We the Living*. This massive injustice—this metaphysical inversion, the attempt to exist in defiance of a basic, unalterable fact of reality—is what Kira senses is so evil about the collectivism of communism. "I loathe your ideals," she tells Andrei, "because I know no worse injustice than the giving of the unde-served. Because men are not equal in ability and one can't treat them as if they were" (90).

At this point in the story Andrei does not yet grasp that his quest for equal-ity commits him to razing the mountains. But what *We the Living* makes evi-dent from the start is that even the best of the communists, individuals like Andrei and Stepan Timoshenko, have *no* positive program to offer the world as to how they are going to raise men to the mountaintops. Andrei and Stepan are warriors; force is what they wield. Stepan tells Andrei that they "poured blood" to "wash a clean road for freedom"—but what neither he nor Andrei can describe is the actual road to freedom (321). They think that if they dispose of the Czar and defeat the White Army, that if they put bullets into capitalists and private traders—individuals who dare to scale the moun-tain alone and who in doing so supposedly exploit the rest of the people—then, somehow, all other men will be able to ascend together to the mountaintop. It does not happen.

By chaining men to one another, by preventing any individual from rising alone—an individual who could serve as an example for others to admire, learn from, and emulate—communism reduces men to the lowest common denominator. This is one of the particularly dehumanizing aspects of collec-tivism, something the reader observes throughout the world of *We the Living* and something that more than one character bemoans. "We're all turning into beasts in a beastly struggle," the former owner of a prosperous fur busi-ness tells Kira (257).

The background of Soviet society presented in *We the Living*, an element so crucial to the story, makes it clear that Andrei and Stepan have not simply failed to understand an element of communism. The communist ideology offers *no* reason to think that collectivism can raise people up. All commu-nism appeals to is force, the power of destruction. Like every other version of collectivism, communism can specify no means, just a magical "some-how" of how brute force will produce achievement. A set of posters described early in the novel eloquently captures this aspect of collectivism's nature. "COMRADES! WE ARE THE BUILDERS OF A NEW LIFE!" one of the posters declares. How is this building of a "new life" to be accomplished? By the destruction wrought by egalitarian leveling: the poster depicts "a husky worker whose huge boots crushed tiny palaces." The unavoidable, inhuman consequence of this leveling is announced by the second poster: "LICE SPREAD DISEASE! CITIZENS, UNITE ON THE ANTI-TYPHUS FRONT!" (30–31)

Andrei and Stepan have no, *and could have no*, positive program to offer to the world, to offer to those individuals like Kira, who want to live. Nevertheless, Andrei's and Stepan's error, though massive, is honest. Consequently, they are both horrified by what they have wrought. "We were to raise men to our own level," a disillusioned Andrei tells Kira. "But they don't rise, the men we're ruling, they don't grow, they're shrinking. They're shrinking to a level no human creatures ever reached before" (334).[5] For Andrei, this growing glimpse of the truth (which Kira's example is helping him to understand) leads him to question his ideals.

But the vast majority of Communists, represented by Andrei's foil, Pavel Syerov, already know that there is nothing in communism or collectivism to raise men up. Unlike Andrei or Stepan, they are not deceived into believing that collectivism will create a better world for mankind, yet they embrace collectivism nevertheless. For them, destruction and the breaking of people's lives is not a painful but unavoidable step to a noble goal. For them, destruction and the breaking of people's lives seems to *be* the goal.

The awareness, callous indifference, and even zeal on the part of communism's true practitioners toward the suffering and deaths they cause is made chillingly vivid in the novel. Whereas Stepan is distraught at the suffering he has brought, at seeing a woman starving on the street, coughing blood, Syerov thinks that the individuals waiting three hours in his office, reduced by collectivism to the state of having to beg Syerov for permission to live, should "go to hell" (321, 288).

There is not one genuine achievement on the part of the Communists to speak of in *We the Living*. But observe the energy with which they trample lives. During the Purge, for instance, the Communist leaders gleefully toss students out of the universities—not because of a student's poor grades but because of a student's unchosen relationships (who his parents were, what his father did for a living, etc.). What is to become of these discarded individuals? The Communists know but don't care. How can the country progress when its best and most eager minds have been starved—minds like Leo's and Kira's? The Communists again don't care (209–14). Sonia, to take another example, relishes going after Kira, stripping Kira of the job Andrei obtained for her in the "House of the Peasant," even though that job itself was already mind-destroying (Kira is forced to mouth collectivist dogma). Kira's destruction is not proceeding quickly enough for Sonia's liking (190–225). And for political reasons Victor Dunaev betrays Kira by arranging for a proletarian, Marisha, to take over part of Kira's and Leo's living space; later, to further his party standing, Victor sends his own sister and her future husband to their deaths in Siberia (176–78, 339–54).

Perhaps the best example of the Communists' mentality in *We the Living*, though certainly not the most chilling, is their indifference to and outright contempt for Marisha. It is a compelling example because in this instance their destructive actions cannot be masked by the claim of being done to combat evil "enemies." Marisha is a member of the proletariat, supposedly someone in whose name the Revolution was fought. But at the party to celebrate Victor's and Marisha's marriage, the Communists are unresponsive or hostile to her. She "wandered dejectedly through the crowd of guests. No one looked at her . . ." (301). Sonia admonishes her because "a true proletariat does not marry out of her class" (301). Victor seeks to exploit both her and her family. He does not love her but thinks her proletarian status will help him in the Party: few will dare attack a man with a proletarian wife (300). When she, the devoted wife, tries to take his hand at the party, he jerks it away (301). Victor then makes a toast to "one of the first fighters for the triumph of the Worker-Peasant Soviets," his "beloved father-in-law, Glieb Ilyitch Lavrov!"—though it is clear that Victor knows nothing about the man nor wants to know (304). What motivates the Communists is not love for the proletariat.

As further evidence that the majority of Communists in *We the Living* embrace collectivism despite knowing that it will achieve nothing positive— which means that they embrace the power of destruction for its own sake— consider their contempt for their own, supposedly noble ideas. Victor's speech in which he toasts his father-in-law as "a man who has devoted his life to the cause," one of many such speeches from the Communists in the novel, is clearly fraudulent (304).[6] When Victor's father-in-law names what the Soviets are actually doing to the people—a fact obvious to anyone who chooses to recognize it—the Communists (except Andrei) do not wonder how they could have brought the country to such a state. They do not question their ideology. Instead, Syerov jumps up and shouts "Comrades, there are traitors even in the ranks of the workers!" (304) When Syerov and Sonia are alone and a pregnant Sonia continues to use the ideas of collectivism as a weapon, this time to chain Syerov in marriage, citing his duty "to the future citizen of our republic"—Syerov snaps at her "Cut that out! . . . You're not addressing a Club meeting" (317).

More generally, against the charge that the ideas of collectivism are not achieving the positive goals promised but actually the opposite—that the leaders of the Party are holding on to power for its own sake—the Communist leadership demands that party members abandon ideas and become "flexible." We must not be "over-idealistic," it declares, the "new Communist is of rubber!" (309) And besides, what right does the individual have to his own convictions and the satisfaction of knowing that they are being realized? His duty is not to reach the truth but to obey the collective and its Party "with absolute discipline" (309). A Communist like Andrei, therefore, who takes ideas seriously, is a severe threat to the destroyers populating the party. Andrei will hold the party accountable for its promises. So as the Sonias and Syerovs of the party scheme to consolidate their destructive power, Andrei is actually more of a danger to them than Kira is—which is why, Sonia knows, Andrei too must be destroyed (311).

We the Living exposes the Communists for what subsequent history has revealed them to be: destroyers after destruction. Syerov and the majority of other Communists in the novel are after the power to control and break lives, without even the pretense of honest error. To them, ideas are only tools to further their desire to destroy. *We the Living*, in other words, presents the death premise in action.

But a question remains: How could someone descend to such a depraved state? *We the Living does* present some of the evidence necessary to understand the soul of a man on the death premise; but a reader who lacks Rand's power of philosophical analysis must turn to *Atlas Shrugged* to understand the full meaning of that evidence.[7] To appreciate that both of these points are true, let us compare the character of Pavel Syerov in *We the Living* to that of James Taggart in *Atlas Shrugged*. The similarities between the two, as I previously remarked, are fascinating. But only the more penetrating presentation of Taggart's soul—when seen in contrast to the souls of the heroes of *Atlas Shrugged*—unveils the cause that produces a metaphysical killer.[8]

Let us begin with Syerov's childhood—which is presented in contrast to Andrei's (104–13). Apparent from the outset is Syerov's need to feel superior to other people. He looks down upon Andrei because of Andrei's ragged clothes (Andrei wraps his feet in newspaper to stay warm) (106). When Syerov later clerks in a men's store, he can get his hands on leather shoes and eau-de-cologne; in his mind, this makes him stand above poor workers like Andrei. When Syerov dances with the girls, he likes to tell them "We're not a commoner, dearie. We're a gentleman" (107). Later, he loses his job and has to take work at the factory. At first he is ashamed of his new status. But then he "learns" from communism the nobility of being a poor worker. He can now pass by an old friend "haughtily, as if he had inherited a title" (107). Syerov, however, now resents Andrei's higher (earned) status in the party and resents having to take orders from him (107).[9]

Abstract ideas, it is important to note, are from an early age meaningless to Syerov. They are not means of knowing reality but devices to maintain status. He attends church, immaculately groomed and sneering at Andrei's clothes, in order to study "God's Law"—and steals perfumed soap when he gets the urge. Later, as indicated, Syerov latches on to Marxism, not because he believes its ideas are true and good, as does Andrei (who studies intently), but because Marxism permits Syerov to maintain his image of superiority when he finds himself doing (supposedly) menial work. In the factory, Syerov comes to speak "of the superiority of the proletariat over the paltry petty bourgeoisie, according to Karl Marx" (107).

At both the mental and physical levels, Syerov disdains effort. Intellectually, he does not care to discover whether the ideas he picks up are true or false. Existentially, he expects to obtain things undeserved. In the February Revolution of 1917, Andrei fights for the cause he believes in; Syerov stays home, because "he had a cold" (107). But when the Party seizes power in October of that year, both men are in the streets. In the battle of Melitopol, Andrei risks his life to convince the soldiers he is fighting of the rightness of communism's goal, passionately arguing that they should join his cause. Syerov is nowhere to be seen. But when Andrei's gambit achieves victory, Syerov jumps into the trenches, climbs a pile of sacks, and preaches communist slogans he does not believe, in order to aid his ascent to power (108–9). Notice too that Andrei promises the soldiers of the White Army a better life if they join his cause. Syerov promises them the glee of destroying life (the life of so-called undesirables). "Down with the damn bourgeoisie exploiters!" Syerov shouts. "Loot the looters, comrades!" (109)

James Taggart's childhood is depicted in similar terms, and is presented in contrast to Francisco d'Anconia's.[10] Taggart's early need to feel superior is as striking as Syerov's. He looks down upon the adolescent Francisco for taking supposedly menial jobs, such as a callboy at Taggart Transcontinental and a cabin boy aboard a cargo steamer. "So that's how you spend your winter?" Taggart declares with a smile touched by triumph, "the triumph of finding cause to feel contempt."[11] Francisco, by contrast, is focused on achieving things in the world, not on comparing himself to others.[12] When Taggart has difficulty driving a motorboat, his reaction is not to try to learn how to do it, but to yell at Francisco: "Do you think you can do it any better?"[13] Taggart seems wounded by Francisco's mere presence, often staring at him intensely from a distance. He resents Francisco's ability and loathes the idea of learning from Francisco (just as Syerov loathed the idea of taking orders and learning from Andrei). "It's disgusting," Taggart tells his sister Dagny (another of the heroes of *Atlas Shrugged*), "the way you let that conceited punk order you about."[14]

Abstract ideas are meaningless in Taggart's mind just as they were in Syerov's. Abstract ideas serve merely as a tool to keep people down. Whereas Francisco is devoted to knowledge—one of his childhood mottoes is "Let's find out"—Taggart is uninterested in discovering and exploring the world.[15] When Taggart goes off to college, his studies produce not knowledge but "a manner of odd, quavering belligerence, as if he had found a new weapon."[16] Taggart then proceeds to denounce Francisco for his selfishness and greed, declaring that Francisco has social responsibilities, that the fortune Francisco is going to inherit is just a trust held for those in need. Taggart's newfound ideas have given him the permission and means, in Syerov's words, to "loot the looters."

The young Taggart is also profoundly anti-effort. Intellectually, as we have seen, ideas are simply weapons to him. In the realm of physical matter, he craves the unearned. Francisco thinks he must study and work his way to the top of d'Anconia Copper, but Taggart expects the railroad, Taggart Transcontinental, to be handed to him, undeserved.[17] Francisco is focused on discovering and making things, and laughs because he sees the possibility of something much greater. Taggart stands off at a distance and never partakes in any of the projects or adventures that Francisco and Dagny embark on; he ridicules Francisco for his relentless effort and laughs "as if he wanted to let nothing remain great."[18]

Fast-forwarding to their adult lives, Syerov and Taggart continue to exhibit the same characteristics, but in more developed form. As an adult, Syerov experiences a deeper sense of inferiority and therefore a greater need to feel superior. At his party to celebrate his scheme with the unscrupulous speculator Morozov, Syerov announces to no one in particular, his fist waved menacingly at the room: "Think I'm a piker, don't you? . . . A measly piker . . . We'll, I'll show you . . ." (289). He then whines to his future wife, Sonia, that he is a great man, but depressed because no one appreciates him (291). To alleviate his sense of emptiness, he will ascend to power and keep people down. "I'm going to make the foreign capitalists look like mice," he tells Sonia. "I'm going to give orders to Comrade Lenin himself" (291).

Clearly, ideas are only a tool of domination for the adult Syerov. He gives countless speeches preaching the goals of the party and the ideas of communism, but, as discussed above, he does not believe a word of what he says. Recall that when Sonia brings up collectivist ideas in private, Syerov tells her to "Cut that out!" (317).

The adult Syerov is devoid of positive effort. He has no constructive purpose or goal to achieve in reality. Unlike Andrei, Syerov does not believe in the ideas of communism and is not working to advance them. The few times we witness Syerov by himself, outside of party life, he consequently is aimless and lifeless. For instance, at the party he throws after launching his scheme with Morozov, Syerov invites guests he does not like or want to see and then, at the actual party, stammers around drunk (288–92). Later, when we see him at home, alone with his wife, Sonia, Syerov is laying down, chewing sunflower seeds and spitting the shells into a pile on a discarded newspaper, indifferent to having a child or even to the effort of naming it; in short, "Pavel Syerov looked bored" (409–10).

The only thing that rouses Syerov to action is the opportunity to use Party power to trample lives—which allows him to rise higher in the Party and gain even more power to trample even more lives. He appears purposeful only when his purpose is to destroy. We first meet Syerov when he is converting ideas into daggers, preaching that science is not objective but "a weapon of the class struggle" (71). In the face of student opposition to communist dogma, Syerov intimates that at the front, his gang would simply have put bullets into his opponents' brains (72). He zealously pursues the capture and imprisonment of Leo Kovalensky, even though it is not his job to do so, because such a coup would win him more power from the Party (101–4). He eagerly participates in the purge to kick Kira, Leo, and other promising minds out from the universities (209–11). By the final scene in the novel involving Syerov and Andrei, it is clear that all Syerov cares for is the power to dominate (415–16).

It would be a mistake to think that because Syerov sometimes chases after money, money is a positive value to him. When he sets up the illegal scheme with Morozov, the money Syerov obtains is not a token of any positive achievement on his part nor will it serve as fuel for any subsequent achievement in his life. It represents only the power to control and crush lives. After the scheme is set up and the money is coming in, Syerov drunkenly shouts to the guests at his party that he "can buy you all, guts and souls!" (290). He feels the need to celebrate his scheme with his own kind, but (when sober) does not dare admit to himself what it is that he wants to celebrate. "What'll we celebrate?" his Communist friend asks him when Syerov proposes the party. "Never mind," Syerov answers. "Just celebrate" (288). It is not achievement that moves Syerov or something he wants to celebrate, it is destruction.

The adult James Taggart displays the same characteristics—but in far sharper relief. Like the adult Syerov, a deep sense of inferiority haunts the adult Taggart: he feels an intense need to be a big shot. Late in *Atlas Shrugged*, for instance, he boasts to his wife, Cherryl, that the impending nationalization of d'Anconia Copper that he has helped cook up is a great business deal—bigger than what anyone has dreamed of before. He tells her that she has no idea how big a man she has married. He gloats that Hank Rearden is a great man (Rearden, a great industrialist, is another of the heroes of *Atlas Shrugged*), but that *he*, James Taggart, has beaten both Rearden and Francisco. And Taggart, just like Syerov, whines to his wife—as he senses his own impotence and inner emptiness—that he is misunderstood, that no one loves him for himself.[19]

Abstract ideas have cemented into a weapon for the adult James Taggart, devoid of cognitive meaning. (They play another crucial role for him, mentioned later.) Early in the novel, he uses the logically indefinable notions of the public interest and social responsibility to destroy a competing railroad, the Phoenix-Durango. These moral dogmas, he senses, can sanction any destructive act: "People who are afraid to sacrifice somebody," Taggart drawls, "have no business talking about a common purpose."[20] Late in the novel, he is using the same sort of ideas to seize industrial property south of the border and destroy d'Anconia Copper through nationalization. "It's a deal with a mission—a worthy, public-spirited mission," he tells Cherryl, though he is now having trouble even half-pretending that he believes what he is saying.[21]

The adult James Taggart, like Syerov, is devoid of any positive purpose or ambition. Though he is head of Taggart Transcontinental, he does not value industry or technology; he makes no effort to improve the efficiency or management of the railroad. When we witness Taggart outside of Taggart Transcontinental and outside of his scrambles for political pull, he is even more aimless and lifeless than Syerov is. There is no better illustration of this than the beginning of the brief scene between Taggart and the society girl Betty Pope.[22] At twenty past noon, Taggart stumbles into the living room in his pajamas, in order to find out what time it is, but he cannot be bothered to locate his watch. As he feels a drunken headache coming on, he forgets why he is in the living room. He glances at Betty Pope's clothes strewn across the floor, and wonders why he slept with her; but he cannot be bothered to discover an answer. To him the sexual act has no personal meaning or purpose—he sleeps with women because that is what is done.

What arouses the adult James Taggart (as was the case with the adult Syerov) is only the opportunity to demolish. In this scene with Betty Pope, for instance, the only thing that catches Taggart's interest and makes him act is the opportunity to undermine Dagny. At the Board meeting that afternoon, which he starts getting dressed for, he is "putting the skids" under his sister.[23] *This* is what gives him something to celebrate over dinner. In his role as head of Taggart Transcontinental, he does not advance the railroad, he harms it. He constantly places obstacles in front of Dagny and her business partners. Early in the story, he pours money down the San Sebastian Line despite Dagny's objections; he kills the Phoenix-Durango, Taggart Transcontinental's competitor in Colorado, even though Dagny knows that this will make running their own Colorado line harder, not easier; and he opposes the use of Rearden Metal, which could save the railroad. Unable to conceive that his goal might be destruction, Dagny wonders aloud to Rearden why her brother seems to actively try to harm Rearden's business. Toward the end of the story, Taggart is busy annihilating d'Anconia Copper.[24]

Again, it would be a mistake to think that because Taggart sometimes scurries after money, money represents a value to him. Taggart, like Syerov, concocts schemes to obtain money unearned, such as blindly investing in the San Sebastian Mines of d'Anconia Copper.[25] But money obtained in this way is neither the product of nor the fuel for any positive achievement on Taggart's part. Taggart himself begins to realize this when he is reflecting on his greatest "stunt," the nationalization of d'Anconia Copper.[26] "No—he thought bleakly, in reluctant admission—money meant nothing to him any longer. He had thrown dollars about by the hundreds. . . ."[27] Like Syerov in regard to the scheme with Morozov, Taggart wants to celebrate his greatest stunt. But Taggart also dares not admit what it is that he actually wants to celebrate—because it is not the achievement that earned money represents. "He . . . could not admit that the particular pleasure he wanted was that of celebration, because he could not admit what it was that he wanted to celebrate."[28]

In a more pronounced form than in Syerov's case, what moves James Taggart is not the quest for achievement but for destruction.

To be on the life premise is to be moved by the purpose of achieving the values necessary to sustain and foster life. To be on the death premise is to be moved by the purpose of destroying the values life requires. Clearly, neither Syerov nor Taggart is on the life premise. Neither is concerned with how to reach genuine values, such as how to *make* money—yet life is impossible without value-achievement. Neither formulates positive goals—yet life requires that an individual define and then pursue the personal goals that will bring him success and happiness. Neither is prepared to exert the effort to reach goals—yet the exertion of effort is inherent to the life process. Clearly, from the evidence presented in both *We the Living* and *Atlas Shrugged*, neither Syerov nor Taggart is concerned with the task of living.

But more evil than that, each man relishes the smashing of values and lives, Syerov the smashing of the values and lives of individuals like Kira and Leo, and Taggart the smashing of the values and lives of individuals like Dagny and Rearden and Francisco. The central villain in both *We the Living* and *Atlas Shrugged*, therefore, is on the death premise. But it is only in *Atlas Shrugged* that Rand fully understood and named the fundamental premises and choices that produce so brutalized a human being as a man on the death premise.[29] This newfound knowledge, as we will now see, explains—despite the similarities already noted—the vast difference between the characterization of Pavel Syerov in *We the Living* and that of James Taggart in *Atlas Shrugged*.

It is beyond the scope of this chapter to analyze fully the death premise as presented in *Atlas Shrugged*, or even as presented only through the character of James Taggart. The entire story focuses on the difference between those on the life premise and those on the death premise. Liberation and justice come to the heroes only when they understand fully the meaning of the life premise (which, implicitly, had always been their moving principle) and grasp the nature of the premise that guides their enemies.[30] To delimit the issue, I will restrict my focus to one fundamental aspect: the basic choice that separates a Kira Argounova from a Pavel Syerov, a Dagny Taggart (and the other heroes of *Atlas Shrugged*) from a James Taggart. Note that it will be necessary to understand the root of the life premise in order to understand the root of its opposite.

According to *Atlas Shrugged*, the source of the life and death premises is the primary choice an individual faces, the essence of man's free will: the choice to think or not. The choice to think or not is the choice to focus one's mind or not—the choice to exert the mental effort necessary to be conscious of reality at the abstract, conceptual level of awareness, or not—the choice to activate one's reason or not. The choice to think or not, in Rand's words, is a man's choice to "focus his mind to a full, active, purposefully directed awareness of reality—or . . . [to] unfocus it and let himself drift in a semiconscious daze, merely reacting to any chance stimulus of the immediate moment."[31] John Galt declares to a dying world that this is the fundamental choice it faces:

> [T]o think is an act of choice. The key to what you so recklessly call 'human nature,' the open secret you live with, yet dread to name, is the fact that man is a being of volitional consciousness. Reason does not work automatically; thinking is not a mechanical process; the connections of logic are not made by instinct. The function of your stomach, lungs or heart is automatic; the function of your mind is not. In any hour and issue of your life, you are free to think or to evade that effort.[32]

The protagonists in Rand's novels choose to think consistently and as a way of life. What unites Kira, Leo, and Andrei, for example, is that they are all active thinkers. From age ten, Kira chooses the demanding career of an engineer and then studies passionately in the attempt to achieve her goal (41). More generally, outside of her chosen field of study, she thinks about life and values—about what life is, what things make it possible, and what, things destroy it. She thinks about these issues in a way that few other individuals in her society choose to do. This is what allows her to grasp, for instance, that both collectivism's means and its ends are horrific (88–91). Leo too grasps the evil of collectivism because he thinks about it, and he too is devoted to his studies. A touching scene early in the novel, highlighting the unspoken intimacy between Kira and Leo, is when we witness them at home, not talking much but working and studying, immersed in books and charts and blueprints (136–37). (Contrast this scene of domestic life with the one between Syerov and Sonia, mentioned above.) Andrei too embraces mental effort and the responsibility of reaching the truth; unlike other Communists, as already indicated, Andrei takes ideas seriously. In childhood, he teaches himself to write and studies late into the night, even though it is frowned upon (105–6). He discusses ideas with Kira and does what he does in the service of communism because he is convinced he is right (217, 89). Later, as he learns from Kira's life and example, he questions and judges his party, and when he has gathered sufficient evidence of its evil and his massive error, he changes course.

In *Atlas Shrugged*, more obviously and more emphatically than in *We the Living*, the heroes are thinkers. Dagny, Rearden, Francisco, and Galt spend prodigious amounts of time studying, working on problems, making discoveries, and figuring out new ways of doing things. Against the unthinking, evasive opposition of James Taggart and the other looters, for instance, Dagny keeps the trains running and ensures that the John Galt Line is built. Rearden creates Rearden Metal and discovers a way to combine a truss and an arch to create a new kind of bridge. Francisco designs a new copper smelter. Galt invents a motor.[33]

They exert this same heroic mental effort outside of work. How does Rearden, for instance, trapped as a result of his own errors in a family life that brings him only boredom and pain, manage to free himself? By constantly *thinking* about his life and family, about what they want, about what they are after, about what premises and motives move them.[34] Or how does Galt, when he hears himself sentenced to slavery at the Twentieth Century Motor Company by virtue of his ability, resist? By *thinking* about what philosophy and moral theory, deployed in what manner and counting on what unnamed factor, could produce such monstrous injustice—and then originating a revolutionary new philosophy and moral code.[35]

But in *Atlas Shrugged*, unlike in *We the Living* (when Rand had not yet formulated her theory of free will), the root choice that produces a thinker is essential to the novel's characterization (as well as its theme and plot) and therefore stressed. The heroes are individuals who deliberately choose to place nothing above their awareness of reality. This fact is particularly stressed in Galt's character. When Dagny meets Galt for the first time after crashing in the hidden valley, she sees "a face that had nothing to hide or to escape, a face with no fear of being seen or of seeing, so that the first thing she grasped about him was the intense perceptiveness of his eyes—he looked as if his faculty of sight were his best loved tool. . . ."[36] Later, when Dagny momentarily wishes that she could remain in the valley without hearing about the disintegration of Taggart Transcontinental, Galt (who passionately wants her to stay) tells her in a "ruthless tone, peculiarly his, which sounded implacable by being simple, devoid of any emotional value, save the quality of respect for facts," that she will hear of *every* train wreck, abandoned line and collapsed bridge. "Nobody," he says, "stays in this valley except by a full, conscious choice based on a full, conscious knowledge of every fact involved in his decision. Nobody stays here by faking reality in any manner whatever."[37]

When Galt is captured and a string of enemies beg and threaten him to become economic dictator of the nation, the contrast in mental functioning is striking. Galt chooses to face facts and place no consideration above the facts; to him, abstract knowledge is the indispensable means by which one understands reality and acts within it. Galt knows that nothing can save the looters' system, that they have no value to offer him, and he never pretends otherwise. The moochers and looters, on the other hand, go through various mental contortions to try to twist the facts to fit their desires. Words, to them, are ways of circumventing reality.[38]

Given the plot and narrative structure of *Atlas Shrugged*, however, it is Dagny's and Rearden's inner thoughts and choices that the reader is privy to, not Francisco's or Galt's. Consequently, Dagny and Rearden are the two characters who furnish the best introspective evidence for Rand's view of the root of the life premise.

There is one constant in Dagny's and Rearden's inner life: they *choose* to think. *However* difficult the issue, *however* painful the subject, they choose—across hours, days, and decades—to exert the mental effort required to reach truth. Consider, for instance, the scene when Dagny has quit because of Directive 10-289 (the moratorium on brains) and is staying at a cabin in the mountains in order to think what to do next. She struggles with the issue, trying to understand how she can go on without a purpose, unable to see how she can live without Taggart Transcontinental and yet unable to see how she can serve it under the looters' directives; she struggles, trying to find an answer she cannot find.[39]

Or consider the description of Rearden creating, through countless dead-ends and late nights, spread across the span of ten years, Rearden Metal.[40] That brief passage is a description of a mind that chooses to think.

Or consider Rearden when he is being blackmailed into signing the "Gift Certificate" surrendering Rearden Metal to the looters. He does not wail at the massive injustice. Instead, against enormous pain he *thinks* how his premises and choices could have led him down a road to where his one great achievement—his romance with Dagny—could be used to destroy his other great achievement, Rearden Metal. "It was as if some voice were telling him sternly: This is the time—the scene is lighted—now look. And standing naked in the great light, he was looking quietly, solemnly, stripped of fear, of pain, of hope, with nothing left to him but the desire to know."[41]

The essence of the choice Dagny and Rearden continually make is named when Dagny falls asleep in Rearden's lap, emotionally spent after appearing on Bertram Scudder's radio program to proudly confess her affair with Rearden: Dagny is described as surrendering the responsibility of consciousness.[42] To choose, when awake, the responsibility of consciousness—*that* is what makes Rand's heroes, heroes.

That choice is what puts a man on the life premise. A thinker—*Atlas Shrugged* makes clear—is an individual devoted to life. The choice to think, to focus one's mind, to activate one's reason—is the only way one can come to know reality and successfully act in it. For "a human being," Galt says, "the question 'to be or not to be' is the question 'to think to not to think.'"[43]

A man on the death premise, a man like James Taggart (and by implication

Pavel Syerov), makes the opposite choice. He defaults on the responsibility of consciousness. He consigns his mind to a void. Taggart cannot be bothered with expending the mental effort required to know and deal with reality. "Don't bother me, don't bother me, don't bother me" are Taggart's first words in the novel—and the key to his character.[44] When Eddie Willers, Dagny's assistant, opens Taggart's office door in this scene, Taggart has no idea whether Eddie is bringing good news or bad, but Taggart's response nevertheless is: "Don't bother me." Why? Although Taggart does not know what kind of a messenger Eddie is, at some level Taggart knows that Eddie *is* a messenger—a messenger from reality, presenting facts that may require processing, identification, evaluation, judgment, and/or decision on Taggart's part. *That* effort is what Taggart wishes to escape. He wants to coast mentally—as an unquestionable, unalterable absolute.

Thus whenever some element of reality potentially demands attention, thereby threatening his mental lethargy, Taggart's response is to push it out of his mind by rationalization and evasion. When Eddie in the above-mentioned scene tells Taggart that they have had another train wreck on the Rio Norte Line, Taggart dismisses it by saying that "accidents happen every day"—as though a railroad can do nothing about accidents on its lines.[45] By creating the illusion that corrective action is futile, Taggart can pretend that no thought or effort could fix the problem and so no thought or effort is required of him. When Taggart glimpses a possible solution to the problem—repairing the Rio Norte Line with track from Rearden Steel—he deliberately jettisons it from his consciousness. "Whatever else you say," he tells Eddie, "there's one thing you are not going to mention next—and that's Rearden Steel."[46]

What Galt does for the first time is identify the mental act of evasion that Taggart and his ilk routinely practice: "the act of blanking out, the willful suspension of one's consciousness, the refusal to think—not blindness, but the refusal to see; not ignorance, but the refusal to know . . . the act of unfocusing [one's] mind and inducing an inner fog to escape the responsibility of judgment."[47] Galt knows that understanding the nature and meaning of this act is crucial to understanding the enemies of life, because it is the root of their evil.

The hidden premise behind evasion, Galt explains, is the metaphysical absurdity that the evader's consciousness can control existence. If the evader refuses to name a fact, then the fact does not exist. If Taggart refuses to admit that railroad accidents can be prevented, then they *are not* preventable. If Taggart refuses to admit that obtaining rail from Rearden Steel is the solution to the problems besetting the Rio Norte Line, then it *is not* the solution. In Taggart's mind, any fact and any danger will "remain unreal by the sovereign power of his wish not to see it—like a foghorn within him, blowing, not to sound a warning, but to summon the fog."[48]

In an evader's mind, his wish supercedes reality. Taggart wishes to be able to obtain a fortune without earning it—at the snap of his fingers—and reality should therefore fall in line. Taggart wants to be admired and loved without the responsibility of forming a soul that is admirable—and reality should therefore grant him his wish.[49] Late in the novel, he pleads with Dagny: "I *want* to be president of a railroad. I *want* it. Why can't I have my wish as you always have yours? Why shouldn't I be given fulfillment of my desires as you always fulfill any desire of your own?"[50] To place an "I wish" above an "It is"—that, Galt explains, is the essence of Taggart's mentality.[51]

Notice that this element also forms an aspect of Pavel Syerov's mentality, though it is not stressed in the way that it is in the depiction of James Taggart. Syerov too wants reality to bend to his wishes (a point easier to see with the hindsight made possible by the ideas dramatized in *Atlas Shrugged*). In planning a celebratory party after first cashing in on his illegal scheme with Morozov, Syerov declares that he should not have to worry about expenses when he wants to have a good time (288). Translated into the terms of *Atlas Shrugged*, this means: Syerov should not have to worry about the facts of reality when *he wishes* to have something. Furthermore, when Syerov's unearned money is unexpectedly cut off (Leo and Antonina Pavlovna have spent Syerov's share of the loot), Syerov can no longer effortlessly satisfy his whims. He cannot provide Sonia with a fur coat she does not deserve and he cannot provide a mistress with a bracelet he has not earned. What does this make Syerov feel? Rage, rage toward everything and everyone—he slams the phone down, smashes an inkstand, throws a crumpled letter in his secretary's face and tells a ragged-looking job applicant that he is going to be turned over to the secret police—rage towards existence, because it will no longer bend to his whims (365–66).

What a whim-worshipper like James Taggart or Pavel Syerov wants, fundamentally, is for the universe to be such that thought, purpose, and reason are not required in order to live in it. The whim-worshipper resents and rebels against existence and life: against the basic fact that effort is needed to conform to and remain in reality. This perverse wish, Galt explains, is "the whole of their shabby secret."[52]

But the universe, of course, does demand effort, purpose, thought, reason—if one wants to continue to exist in it. One's only choice is to accept this inexorable fact or die. No amount of wishing or praying, of pretending or faking, of raging against the world or bewailing one's fate in it, can alter the fact that to reap a harvest one must first discover what seeds to plant, in what kind of soil and at what time of year; that to make money one must run a successful business, a business that produces a valuable product like Rearden Metal, not one that produces empty promises like the business of Taggart's friend Orren Boyle; that to be admired and loved one must achieve the virtues of character, such as rationality, honesty, and courage, that lead to admiration and love.

Earlier I observed that both Syerov and Taggart disdain effort. The root of that characteristic, the basic choice that produces it, should now be clear. I also observed that both Syerov and Taggart have a deep sense of inferiority. The root of that characteristic should now be clear as well: it is the same basic choice. Pavel Syerov *is* inferior to Andrei, Leo, and Kira. He lacks what they possess: the thought, the judgment, the mind necessary to understand the world and deal with it. James Taggart *is* inferior to Rearden, Dagny, and Francisco. He lacks what they possess: the thought, the judgment, the mind necessary to understand the world and succeed in it—the kind of mind that creates Rearden Metal, manages Taggart Transcontinental, or runs d'Anconia Copper.[53] What *Atlas Shrugged* makes almost self-evident is the explanation: the inferiority is self-made, self-chosen. In rejecting his mind, Taggart rejects his means of survival and turns himself into a subhuman creature.[54]

To rebel against the effort and thought needed to remain in existence is to *willfully* abandon the only road that leads to life and happiness. It is to embark, instead, on a road whose terminus is one's own death. To resent the requirements of reality is to resent one's *own* existence in it. The inhuman meaning of his basic choice, the antilife meaning of his willful rejection of the responsibility of consciousness, is what a James Taggart dares not face. This is the key to understanding his lust for destruction.

To hide his death wish from himself (and others), a man like Taggart will at first *fake* concern with the values that sustain life. He will *imitate* the thinkers and achievers, the men of purpose, the men whose goal is life. He will try to get money or business success or pleasure or sex—so long as he can maintain the illusion that he can obtain these things without rational thought or real effort. Taggart wants to get money and become head of Taggart Transcontinental without studying or learning, and he wants to sleep with women without forming a soul that is desirable. Such things, he hopes, will prove that his basic choice to reject the responsibility of consciousness is equivalent to Rearden's and Francisco's choice to assume that responsibility, since the results are the same. Indeed, Taggart's basic choice, he feels, is superior to theirs, because it requires no effort while theirs does, yet the results remain the same. His wishing is superior to their thinking. Rearden and Francisco "'spend their lives grubbing for their fortunes penny by penny,'" he tells Cherryl, "'while I can do it like that'—he snapped his fingers—'just like that.'"[55] The unnamed absolute in Taggart's mind is the quest to show that the mindless is superior to the mind, that impotence is superior to ability, that a zero, somehow, is superior to an entity.[56]

But his faking does not work because it *cannot* work. The money he obtains is useless: it does not represent productive ability and he has no positive use for it. The admiration he receives is counterfeit: Cherryl loves him because she thinks he possesses Dagny's soul. The sex he engages in is meaningless: he gets no pleasure from sleeping with Betty Pope or even

Cheryl. The unearned is at most a temporary escape from his self-created emptiness inside—until reality forces Taggart to face, in Galt's terms, the cause of the causeless.[57]

It is the productive effort of the Dagnys, Reardens, and Franciscos of the world that gives meaning to the dollar bills in Taggart's wallet and explains why others will accept the bills from him in exchange for a drink or a bite to eat. It is the virtue achieved by the Dagnys, Reardens, and Franciscos of the world that gives meaning to the concept of admiration. It is the souls created by the Dagnys and Reardens of the world—and the physical desires and responses that their souls create in one another—that gives spiritual meaning to the physical act of sex. The cause of the causeless—that is the inescapable fact which reality keeps forcing Taggart to try to escape.

Like a drug addict who needs greater and greater "fixes" to preserve the illusion that his problems are solved, the seeker of the unearned needs more and more grandiose schemes to pretend that the causeless in fact exists. Observe that at the beginning of the novel, Taggart is simply riding blindly on d'Anconia Copper, hoping to cash in effortlessly on Francisco's judgment in creating the San Sebastian Mines. Toward the end, in order to preserve the illusion of the causeless, Taggart must take over every industrial property south of the border and nationalize all of d'Anconia Copper. But it does not work. It does not get Taggart what he wants.

A fortune is not what Taggart is after; the pursuit of money merely camouflages his real motive. "Money," he thinks to himself late in the novel, as he contemplates the destruction of d'Anconia Copper, "had been his motive . . . nothing worse. Wasn't that a normal motive? A valid one? Wasn't that what they all were after, the Wyatts, the Reardens, the d'Anconias?"[58] But money—as he is realizing in this scene—is really not his motive. If it were, he would have tried, as Francisco did, to discover how to *earn* it. The money in Taggart's wallet is supposed to serve as proof of the causeless, proof of the power of whim. He realizes that he "had thrown dollars about by the hundreds—at that party he had given today—for unfinished drinks, for uneaten delicacies, for unprovoked tips and unexpected whims . . . for the span of any moment, for the clammy stupor of knowing that it is easier to pay than think." Other people struggled against crippling, unjust regulations—railroads went bankrupt, factories went without transportation, young men gave up scientific careers to become dishwashers and bankers committed suicide—so that "he, James Taggart, might sit in a private barroom and pay for the alcohol pouring down Orren Boyle's throat." But unearned money means "nothing to him any longer."[59] The prospect of stealing a fortune now leaves him indifferent. Why? Because whether Taggart is seeking simply to ride on Francisco's coattails, as he tried early in the novel, or to nationalize all of Francisco's property, as he tries late in the novel, what Taggart cannot escape is the fact that Francisco remains the cause of the supposedly causeless. Without Francisco, Taggart's whims are useless.[60]

Taggart cannot escape the metaphysical fact that the (supposedly) causeless *is* caused; his only recourse is to war against this fact. The *cause* of the causeless must be annihilated. In nationalizing d'Anconia Copper, Taggart does not actually want Francisco's fortune, he wants Francisco to lose it.[61]

What drives Taggart from beginning to end, therefore, is his root choice to rebel against the nature of existence. To escape the antilife meaning of his rejection of his rational mind, he must obliterate the *causal* fact that life in reality demands rational thought. And thus a soul like Taggart's, Galt explains, comes to relish "the spectacle of suffering, of poverty, subservience and terror; these give him a feeling of triumph, a proof of the defeat of rational reality. But no other reality exists."[62] To escape his willful default, Taggart must destroy the power of reason—its life-giving power. If he can show reason to be impotent, then he cannot be reproached for willfully abandoning it; no one can say he is evil through and through.

Abstract ideas—anti-reason ones, especially the call for self-sacrifice and the morality of altruism, which Galt describes as the "Morality of Death"[63]—serve both as the principal cover and principal weapon for Taggart's lust to destroy. On the one hand, they tell him that his choice to reject his life is noble: it is evil to live for oneself, good to throw one's life away.[64] On the other hand, such abstract ideas sanction the destruction of rational men. You are greedy and selfish, you should lose your fortune—a young Taggart tells Francisco near the start of the novel. And near the end, Taggart shouts at Galt: "How can you be sure you're right? How can you *know*? Nobody can be sure of his knowledge! Nobody! You're no better than anyone else!"[65]

Taggart *must* destroy the products, the symbols, and the very lives of the rational men, the men who can live and who thus stand as a constant reminder and reproach to a soul that has chosen death. He must smash railroads and steel mills and copper mines, he must torture and torment souls like Cherryl's that are eager to exert the effort necessary to rise, he must see Galt die. The bitter intensity with which the adolescent James Taggart watched Francisco from a distance becomes the hatred with which the adult James Taggart watches Galt being tortured.[66] Taggart must kill, he must kill the good because it is good, he must "kill in order not to learn that the death he desires is his own."[67]

We have now uncovered the root of the death premise. In *We the Living*, Rand showed that there are individuals who embrace life and individuals who war against it. In *Atlas Shrugged* she shows why: a fundamental choice separates the two types of individual.

Ayn Rand already knew in *We the Living* that the life haters did not deserve the excuse that their "noble" end justified their destructive means (89–90). The nature of their souls was much more evil than that. For some unnamed reason, death was their end. In *Atlas Shrugged*, she returns to this issue, but now with full understanding: "The truth about their souls is worse than the obscene excuse you have allowed them, the excuse that the end justifies the means and that the horrors they practice are means to nobler ends. The truth is that those horrors are their ends."[68] In *Atlas Shrugged*, she shows why.

And, thankfully, Ayn Rand does much more than that. *Atlas Shrugged* also reveals the root of Kira Argounova's soul—the intransigent devotion to effort, purpose, thought and reason that *is* the intransigent devotion to life. Only this devotion to one's own life, *Atlas Shrugged* shows, can prevent the metaphysical killers who seized power in 1917 Russia from ever doing so again.

NOTES

1. Ayn Rand, "The Left: Old and New," *Return of the Primitive: The Anti-Industrial Revolution* (New York: Meridian, 1999), 169. She writes: "At a superficial (a *very* superficial) glance, there might have been, for the morally indiscriminating, some plausibility in the notion of enslaving and sacrificing generations of men for the sake of establishing a permanent state of material abundance for all."

2. In his introduction to the sixtieth anniversary edition of *We the Living*, Leonard Peikoff describes Andrei as "totally honest" (vii).

3. Ayn Rand, "The Age of Envy," *Return of the Primitive*, 144.

4. Rand, "The Age of Envy," 144. In *Atlas Shrugged*, one of the whispered stories about the novel's foremost hero, John Galt, is that he discovered the fountain of youth. He "found it on the top of a mountain. It took him ten years to climb that mountain. It broke every bone in his body, it tore the skin off his hands, it made him lose his home, his name, his love. But he climbed it. He found the fountain of youth, which he wanted to bring down to men. Only he never came back." Why? "Because he found that it couldn't be brought down." Ayn Rand, *Atlas Shrugged* (New York: Random House, 1957; Signet thirty-fifth anniversary paperback edition, 1992), 169.

5. For Stepan's disillusionment, see *We the Living*, 318–23.

6. For other examples of such speeches, see, for instance, the speeches made at Andrei's funeral (435–37).

7. I do not mean to imply that there is something deficient about *We the Living*. The story is complete and self-contained. Rand simply went on to discover more about the death premise, knowledge she used to construct the plot of *Atlas Shrugged*.

8. From here on in "Taggart" is used only to refer to James Taggart; "Dagny" or "Dagny Taggart" will be used to refer to his sister, Dagny Taggart.

9. Syerov's resentment of Andrei's status in the Party runs through the novel; for instance, Syerov resents that Andrei intervenes when Syerov is questioning Kira about Leo (103).

10. Francisco d'Anconia, heir to the multinational conglomerate d'Anconia Copper, is one of the heroes of *Atlas Shrugged*.

11. Rand, *Atlas Shrugged*, 91.

12. Rand, *Atlas Shrugged*, 92.

13. Rand, *Atlas Shrugged*, 91.
14. Rand, *Atlas Shrugged*, 93.
15. Rand, *Atlas Shrugged*, 93.
16. Rand, *Atlas Shrugged*, 97.
17. Rand, *Atlas Shrugged*, 98.
18. Rand, *Atlas Shrugged*, 94.
19. Rand, *Atlas Shrugged*, 800–1, 812–14.
20. Rand, *Atlas Shrugged*, 50–51.
21. Rand, *Atlas Shrugged*, 800.
22. Rand, *Atlas Shrugged*, 71–73.
23. Rand, *Atlas Shrugged*, 73.
24. Rand, *Atlas Shrugged*, 56–59, 75–81, 27–28, 85, 796–97.
25. Rand, *Atlas Shrugged*, 52.
26. Rand, *Atlas Shrugged*, 800.
27. Rand, *Atlas Shrugged*, 798.
28. Rand, *Atlas Shrugged*, 796.
29. In her foreword to the revised edition of *We the Living*, Rand describes men on the death premise as brutalized (xiv).
30. Aside from *Atlas Shrugged*, the following nonfiction writings of Rand are very helpful in understanding her analysis of the death premise: "For the New Intellectual," *For the New Intellectual: The Philosophy of Ayn Rand* (New York: Signet 1961), 10–57; "Philosophical Detection," *Philosophy: Who Needs It* (New York: Signet 1984), 12–22; "The Missing Link," *Philosophy: Who Needs It*, 25–45; "Selfishness Without a Self," *Philosophy: Who Needs It*, 46–51; and, especially, "The Age of Envy," 130–58. In this last essay she describes the death premise as hatred of the good for being the good.
31. Ayn Rand, "The Objectivist Ethics," *The Virtue of Selfishness: A New Concept of Egoism* (New York: Signet, 1964), 22.
32. Rand, *Atlas Shrugged*, 930. For more on Rand's theory of free will, see Galt's speech in *Atlas Shrugged*, 927–84 and "The Objectivist Ethics" in *Virtue of Selfishness*, 13–39, especially 19–24. See also Leonard Peikoff, *Objectivism: The Philosophy of Ayn Rand* (New York: Meridian 1993), 55–72.
33. Rand, *Atlas Shrugged*, 173–237; 35–36 and 203; 1073; 674–75.
34. See, for instance, Rand, *Atlas Shrugged*, 150–54.
35. Rand, *Atlas Shrugged*, 927–84.
36. Rand, *Atlas Shrugged*, 647.
37. Rand, *Atlas Shrugged*, 732.
38. Rand, *Atlas Shrugged*, 1008–18, 1022–25.
39. Rand, *Atlas Shrugged*, 562–66.
40. Rand, *Atlas Shrugged*, 35–36.
41. Rand, *Atlas Shrugged*, 518.
42. Rand, *Atlas Shrugged*, 796.
43. Rand, *Atlas Shrugged*, 930.
44. Rand, *Atlas Shrugged*, 15.
45. Rand, *Atlas Shrugged*, 15.
46. Rand, *Atlas Shrugged*, 16.
47. Rand, *Atlas Shrugged*, 935.

48. Rand, *Atlas Shrugged*, 799.

49. Rand, *Atlas Shrugged*, 800, 813–14.

50. Rand, *Atlas Shrugged*, 843. Of course the point is (as the verb tenses of the quoted passage make clear) that Dagny works to earn that which she wants while Taggart expects the unearned.

51. Rand, *Atlas Shrugged*, 952–53.

52. Rand, *Atlas Shrugged*, 952.

53. The issue of course is not whether Taggart possesses the superlative intelligence of a Francisco d'Anconia or only the average intelligence of an Eddie Willers; the issue is whether or not Taggart chooses to use the intelligence that he does possess.

54. See Rand, *Atlas Shrugged*, 972–73.

55. Rand, *Atlas Shrugged*, 800.

56. See Rand, *Atlas Shrugged*, 954.

57. Rand, *Atlas Shrugged*, 954.

58. Rand, *Atlas Shrugged*, 797.

59. Rand, *Atlas Shrugged*, 798.

60. Francisco, following Galt's lead, drives this lesson home to Taggart and the other looters by removing the supposedly nonexistent cause of the causeless. Francisco does not exercise his judgment: the San Sebastian Mines are worthless. Later, Francisco blows up whatever remains of d'Anconia Copper the moment before it is to be nationalized.

61. As Galt says, "They do not want to own your fortune, they want you to lose it" (Rand, *Atlas Shrugged*, 962).

62. Rand, *Atlas Shrugged*, 962.

63. Rand, *Atlas Shrugged*, 942.

64. As but one of many examples, one can see Taggart engaging in such a process of rationalization, now wearing thin, in a conversation with Cherryl toward the end of the story (Rand, *Atlas Shrugged*, 800).

65. Rand, *Atlas Shrugged*, 1022. Rand discusses how irrational philosophical ideas (including altruism) can serve as means of rationalization in "Philosophical Detection," *Philosophy: Who Need It*, 17–22.

66. Rand, *Atlas Shrugged*, 93, 1048–53.

67. Rand, *Atlas Shrugged*, 962.

68. Rand, *Atlas Shrugged*, 962.

Select Bibliography

This bibliography is limited to books and articles by Ayn Rand—and books and articles about Ayn Rand and her philosophy, Objectivism—cited in this collection.

Berliner, Michael S. ed. *Letters of Ayn Rand*. New York: Dutton, 1995; paperback edition, Plume, 1997.

Binswanger, Harry, ed. *The Ayn Rand Lexicon: Objectivism from A to Z*. New York: New American Library, 1986; paperback edition, Meridian, 1988.

Britting, Jeff. *Ayn Rand*. New York: Overlook Press. 2004.

Harriman, David, ed. *Journals of Ayn Rand*. New York: Dutton, 1997; paperback edition, Plume, 1999.

Mayhew, Robert. "Ayn Rand Laughed: Ayn Rand on the Role of Humor in Literature and Life." *The Intellectual Activist* 16, no. 1. January 2002.

———. "Russian Smiles: The Leftist Response to Ayn Rand's HUAC Testimony." *The Intellectual Activist* 16, no. 2. February 2002.

Milgram, Shoshana. "Artist at Work: Ayn Rand's Drafts of *The Fountainhead*." *The Intellectual Activist* 15, nos. 8–9. August–September, 2001.

Paxton, Michael. *Ayn Rand: A Sense of Life*. Layton, Utah: Gibbs Smith, 1998.

Peikoff, Leonard, ed. *The Early Ayn Rand: A Selection from Her Unpublished Fiction*. New York: New American Library, 1984; paperback edition, Signet, 1986.

———. *Objectivism: The Philosophy of Ayn Rand*. New York: Dutton, 1991; paperback edition, New Meridian, 1993.

———. "Philosophy and Psychology in History." *The Objectivist Forum* 6, no. 5. October 1985.

Rand, Ayn. *Anthem*. Fiftieth anniversary paperback edition. New York: Signet, 1995.

———. *The Art of Fiction: A Guide for Writers and Readers*. Edited by Tore Boeckmann. Introduction by Leonard Peikoff. New York: Plume, 2000.

———. *The Art of Nonfiction: A Guide for Writers and Readers*. Edited by Robert Mayhew. Introduction by Peter Schwartz. New York: Plume, 2001.

———. *Atlas Shrugged*. New York: Random House, 1957; thirty-fifth anniversary paperback edition, Signet, 1992.

———. *Capitalism: The Unknown Ideal.* New York: New American Library, 1966; expanded paperback edition, Signet, 1967.

———. *For the New Intellectual.* New York: Random House, 1961; paperback edition, Signet, 1963.

———. *The Fountainhead.* New York: Bobbs-Merrill, 1943; fiftieth anniversary paperback edition, Signet, 1993.

———. "Introductory Note to *The Man Who Laughs.*" *The Objectivist* 6. December 1967.

———. *Night of January 16th.* The final revised edition. New York: Plume, 1987.

———. *Philosophy: Who Needs It.* New York: Bobbs-Merrill, 1982; paperback edition, Signet, 1984.

———. "A Preview." *The Ayn Rand Letter*, 1, nos. 24–26. August–September 1972.

———. *Return of the Primitive: the Anti-Industrial Revolution.* Edited by Peter Schwartz. New York: Meridian, 1999.

———. *The Romantic Manifesto: A Philosophy of Literature.* Revised edition. New York: Signet, 1975.

———. *Russian Writings on Hollywood.* Edited by Michael S. Berliner. Marina del Rey, Calif.: The Ayn Rand Institute Press, 1999.

———. *The Virtue of Selfishness: A New Concept of Egoism.* New York: New American Library, 1964.

———. *The Voice of Reason: Essays in Objectivist Thought.* Leonard Peikoff, ed. New York: New American Library, 1989; paperback edition, Meridian, 1989.

———. *We the Living.* New York: Macmillan, 1936.

———. *We the Living.* London: Cassells, 1937.

———. *We the Living.* Revised edition. New York: Random House, 1959.

———. *We the Living.* Sixtieth anniversary paperback edition. Introduction by Leonard Peikoff. New York: Signet, 1996.

Schwartz, Peter, ed. *The Ayn Rand Column.* New Milford, Conn.: Second Renaissance, 1991.

———. "We The Living—The Movie," *The Intellectual Activist* 4, no. 16 (September 1986).

Smith, Tara. *Viable Values—A Study of Life as the Root and Reward of Morality.* Lanham, Md.: Rowman & Littlefield, 2000.

Index

About the Contributors

Michael S. Berliner holds a Ph.D. in philosophy from Boston University. He was executive director of the Ayn Rand Institute for its first fifteen years and previously taught philosophy of education and philosophy at California State University, Northridge. He created the first two catalogs of the Ayn Rand Papers at the Ayn Rand Archives and is currently compiling a definitive inventory. He is editor of *Letters of Ayn Rand* and Ayn Rand's *Russian Writings on Hollywood*. He has lectured throughout the United States and in Europe, Australia, and Israel on Ayn Rand's life.

Andrew Bernstein holds a Ph.D. in philosophy from the Graduate School of the City University of New York and teaches at Pace University and SUNY Purchase. He is the author of the novel *Heart of a Pagan,* and of the forthcoming *The Capitalist Manifesto: The Historic, Economic and Philosophic Case for Laissez-Faire.* He lectures widely on topics relating to both Ayn Rand's novels and her philosophy of Objectivism. His website is: www.andrewbernstein.net.

Jeff Britting is Archivist of the Ayn Rand Archives, a collection of the Ayn Rand Institute. He is author of the short illustrated biography *Ayn Rand.* He developed and was associate producer of the Academy Award–nominated documentary *Ayn Rand: A Sense of Life* and the feature film *Take Two*, and he coproduced the first stage productions of Ayn Rand's play *Ideal* and her novella *Anthem.* As a composer, he has written incidental music for eleven stage productions and three films, and is currently writing an opera based on an original libretto set in the Middle Ages.

Dina Schein Garmong is Instructor in philosophy at Auburn University. She recently received her Ph.D. in philosophy from the University of Texas,

Austin, having written a dissertation titled "Toward a Truer Understanding of Ethical Egoism." She has translated Ayn Rand's *Russian Writings on Hollywood* and is presently translating the Russian correspondence written to Ayn Rand in the 1920s and 1930s. She regularly lectures on topics in ethics and in literature, and on Ayn Rand's years in Russia.

Onkar Ghate holds a Ph.D. in philosophy from the University of Calgary. A Resident Fellow and Education Programs Manager at the Ayn Rand Institute, he specializes in Ayn Rand's philosophy of Objectivism and teaches philosophy in the Institute's Objectivist Academic Center. He also serves as a writer, editor, and media representative for the Institute. Forthcoming articles include "Postmodernism's Kantian Roots" and (coauthored with Dr. Edwin Locke) "Objectivism: The Proper Alternative to Postmodernism," both to be published in *Post Modernism and Management: Pros, Cons and the Alternative Research in the Sociology of Organizations* (volume 21).

John Lewis holds a Ph.D. in classics from the University of Cambridge. He is Assistant Professor of History at Ashland University, where he is holder of an Anthem Fellowship for the Study of Objectivism. He has published numerous articles on ancient Greek history, law, and political thought. He is presently completing a monograph on the early Greek poet Solon of Athens, as well as a book on the uses of a homeland defense strategy from the Greeks to the modern day.

Robert Mayhew is Associate Professor of Philosophy at Seton Hall University. He is the author of *Aristotle's Criticism of Plato's Republic* and *The Female in Aristotle's Biology: Reason or Rationalization* and of numerous articles on Aristotle. He has translated a play of Aristophanes (*Assembly of Women*) and has edited unpublished material of Ayn Rand's, including *Ayn Rand's Marginalia*, *The Art of Nonfiction: A Guide for Writers and Readers*, and (forthcoming) *Ayn Rand's Q&A*. He has recently completed a book on Ayn Rand's HUAC testimony. His present research interests include Plato's *Laws*.

Scott McConnell is a Researcher in the Ayn Rand Archives, where he manages the Ayn Rand Oral History Program and several Ayn Rand Russian research projects. He has lectured in America, Europe, and Australia on Ayn Rand's life, and is preparing for publication a book titled *100 Voices: An Oral History of Ayn Rand*. He has worked in Hollywood as a script analyst, in Los Angeles as a communications director, and in Australia as a teacher of literature and history. His articles have appeared in a number of publications in Europe, the United States, and Australia.

Shoshana Milgram [Knapp] is Associate Professor of English at Virginia Tech. She has published articles on a variety of nineteenth- and twentieth-century figures in French, Russian, English, and American literature, including Napoleon Bonaparte, Victor Hugo, George Sand, Anton Chekhov, Fyodor Dostoevsky, Leo Tolstoy, Victoria Cross, George Eliot, John Fowles, W. S. Gilbert, Henry James, Ursula K. LeGuin, Vladimir Nabokov, Herbert Spencer, W. T. Stead, E. L. Voynich—and Ayn Rand. She is also the author of introductions to editions of *Toilers of the Sea* and *The Man Who Laughs*, by Victor Hugo, and *The Seafarers*, by Nevil Shute.

Richard E. Ralston received a B.A. in history from the University of Maryland after serving seven years in the U.S. Army. He then completed an M.A. in international relations at the University of Southern California. He has been the Managing Director of the Ayn Rand Institute, and Circulation Director and Publishing Director of *The Christian Science Monitor*. He is the editor of two books, *Communism: Its Rise and Fall in the 20th Century* and *Why Businessmen Need Philosophy*. He is presently the Executive Director of Americans for Free Choice in Medicine.

John Ridpath is former Associate Professor of economics and intellectual history at York University, Toronto. He writes and speaks on the history of ideas and their impact on social change. His present research interests include the ideas influencing the Founding Fathers and early American history, and the philosophy and influence of Friedrich Nietzsche. Shortly before retiring, he was York University's nominee for Canadian professor of the year.

Tara Smith is Associate Professor of philosophy at the University of Texas, Austin. Specializing in moral and political philosophy, she is the author of two books, *Moral Rights and Political Freedom* and *Viable Values: A Study of Life as the Root and Reward of Morality*, as well as articles on such topics as welfare rights, rights conflicts, moral perfection, pride, honesty, love, personal justice, and forgiveness. She is currently writing a book on Ayn Rand's egoistic theory of moral virtues.

Jena Trammell holds a Ph.D. in literature from the University of Tennessee. She is Associate Professor of English at Anderson College, where she teaches world literature and critical theory. Her publications include articles on British medieval poetry and Restoration author John Dryden.